Holocaust Remem

JB

For Elie Wiesel

Holocaust Remembrance

The Shapes of Memory

Edited by
Geoffrey H. Hartman

BLACKWELL
Oxford UK & Cambridge USA

Copyright © Basil Blackwell Ltd 1994

First published 1994

Blackwell Publishers
238 Main Street, Suite 501
Cambridge, Massachusetts 02142
USA

108 Cowley Road
Oxford OX4 1JF
UK

Library of Congress Cataloging-in-Publication Data

Holocaust remembrance: the shapes of memory/edited by Geoffrey Hartman.
      p.   cm.
   Includes bibliographical references (p.) and index.
    ISBN 1-55786-125-0 (alk. paper). — ISBN 1-55786-367-9 (pbk. : alk. paper)
    1. Holocaust, Jewish (1939–1945)—Historiography. 2. Holocaust, Jewish (1939–1945)—Influence. 3. Holocaust memorials.
  I. Hartman, Geoffrey H.
  D804.3.H6494 1994
  940.53'18—dc20   92–41095
                                                 CIP

British Library Cataloguing in Publication Data
A CIP catalogue record for this book is available from the British Library.

Typeset in 10 on 12 pt Sabon
by Photo·graphics, Honiton, Devon
Printed in Great Britain by T. J. Press Ltd, Padstow, Cornwall

This book is printed on acid-free paper

Contents

List of Contributors

Aharon Appelfeld is a well-known Israeli novelist.

Debórah Dwork is the author of *Children with a Star* and Associate Clinical Professor in the Yale Child Study Center.

Sidra DeKoven Ezrahi is a Lecturer in Comparative Jewish Literature at the Hebrew University, Jerusalem.

Shoshana Felman is Professor of French and Comparative Literature at Yale University, and has published (with Dori Laub) *Testimony: crises of witnessing in literature, psychoanalysis and history.*

Mary Felstiner is Professor of History at San Francisco State University.

Nadine Fresco is a French sociologist and researcher at the Centre National de Recherche Scientifique in Paris.

Saul Friedlander is Professor of History at Tel Aviv University, Israel, and the University of California, Los Angeles. He recently edited *Probing the Limits of Representation: Nazism and the "Final Solution".*

Michael Geyer is Professor of History at the University of Chicago.

Haim Gouri, Israeli poet, novelist and filmmaker, was a reporter at the Eichmann trial.

Miriam Hansen is Professor of Film Studies at the University of Chicago.

Geoffrey H. Hartman, the editor of this volume, is Professor of English and Comparative Literature at Yale and Revson Project Director of the Fortunoff Video Archive for Holocaust Testimonies.

Sara Horowitz heads the Jewish Studies program at the University of Delaware.

R. B. Kitaj is the well-known painter, born in Ohio, but now identified with "The School of London".

Lawrence Langer is Professor of English at Simmons College and author of *Holocaust Testimonies: the ruins of memory*, which won a National Book Critics Circle award in 1992.

Giovanni Leoni is an Italian architect.

Alvin Rosenfeld is Professor of English and Director of Jewish Studies at Indiana University.

David G. Roskies teaches at the Jewish Theological Seminary of America. His *Against the Apocalypse: responses to catastrophe in modern Jewish culture* was awarded Phi Beta Kappa's Ralph Waldo Emerson Prize for 1984.

Vera Schwarcz is Professor of Chinese Studies and Director of Wesleyan University's Center for East Asian studies.

Leo Spitzer is Professor of History at Dartmouth College.

Abraham Sutzkever, the Yiddish poet, is a survivor of the Warsaw ghetto living in Israel.

Robert Jan van Pelt is Professor of Humanities at the University of Waterloo in Canada.

David Tracy is Distinguished Service Professor of Catholic Studies at the Divinity School of the University of Chicago.

Annette Wieviorka is a French historian and researcher at the Centre National de Recherche Scientifique in Paris. Her *Déportation et Génocide* was published in 1992.

James E. Young is Professor of English and Jewish Studies at the University of Massachusetts, Amherst. His *The Texture of Memory: Holocaust memorials and meaning in Europe, Israel and America* was published in spring 1993.

List of Plates

Acknowledgments

In assembling this book I have had the advice of many friends and especially of Saul Friedlander, James Young, Aharon Appelfeld, Sidra Ezrahi, and John and Mary Felstiner. John Davey of Blackwell was patient and helpful throughout the long process of its preparation. I also thank Christopher Browning for reading the manuscript and Jeffrey Shoulson and Cliff Spargo for work in its preparation. I dedicate the book to an advocate of memory, and a supporter, from the beginning, of the Fortunoff Video Archive for Holocaust Testimonies.

Geoffrey H. Hartman
New Haven, CT

1

Introduction: Darkness Visible

Geoffrey H. Hartman

No light, but rather darkness visible
Milton, Paradise Lost

Not energy, not messages, not particles, not light.
Light itself falls back down, broken by its own weight
Primo Levi, "The Black Stars"

We think of memory as a residue left in the mind by the ruins of time, and capable of retrieving and even restoring the past. For modernity the great metaphor of such retrieval is furnished by Schliemann's excavations at the end of the last century. Searching for Homer's Troy Schliemann discovered in one of his digs a magnificent gold mask of a face. He boasted: Today I kissed the lips of Agamemnon.

Freud's comparison of psychoanalysis to an archaeological excavation like Schliemann's brought the metaphor directly into contact with memory retrieval as fieldwork both highly emotional and scrupulously scientific. Psychoanalysis cleared away each layer of mental sedimentation in order to find a buried object of desire. There is a beyond to memory in this scenario: myth becomes flesh, becomes history, when Schliemann kisses the mask of Agamemnon. The imagination leaps from fiction to life. That legendary Grecian commander really existed; that magnificent mask must be his persona. The tyranny of Greece over the German mind could not find a better illustration. The tyranny of an imagination that requires emblems of a heroic past could not expose itself more clearly.

The work of recovering "shapes of memory" from the destruction named the Holocaust has so little in common with Schliemann's successful quest that it stands rather as a terrible coda. Can we find a guiding image for that very different, mostly grim, always burdened retrieval? The Jews in Europe were decimated by the Nazi genocide and lost their communal identity. In Germany and Eastern Europe that loss of community has been decisive, irreversible; in other parts of Europe, such as France and Italy, or in Israel and America, new communities have developed, though conscious of a perhaps fatal amputation, and caught between a morbid and a necessary remembrance. The ash that literally covered Jewish lives, and from which we rescue vivid and pathetic snapshots, or cultural and religious artifacts expressive of a civilization at least as old as the Greek, that ash is more contaminating than what may have buried a millennial Troy or a Pompey calcified by natural disaster.

Acting to understand this recent and most disastrous episode in Jewish and German history, the imagination has little occasion to leap. The photographs shown, one after the other, at the end of Gouri's film *Pnei Mered* (literally *Faces of the Revolt*, but publicized as *Fire in the Ashes*), or the different shapes, spiritual and psychological, that the present book assembles, are not heroic, or inevitably heroic; nor are they enlarged, gilded, totemic. They tell of "nothing more than what we are" – rather, of what *they* were who had to face humiliation, persecution and systematic slaughter.

Because the genocide did not occur in the distant past, and because it was unprecedented in its virulent and obsessive focus, there are dangers for the historian greater than those attending other archival quests. The "black sun" of the destruction can produce a melancholy as disabling as any we have known. Dürer's famous picture of a figure sitting dejected, like a fallen angel, in the midst of accumulated instruments of knowledge, the very tools of Enlightenment, points in the present context not only to the role of technology in the genocide but also to the dark (I previously said "contaminating") light shed by the Holocaust on human history.

Even so, and it is one reason for this collection, some creative impulse is felt, perhaps akin to what made Jewish chroniclers and diarists continue to record the destruction to the last moment. David Roskies recalls that many contemporary accounts of pogroms dated from the First World War, and how this kind of narrative began to assume (emotionally, but also for preservation purposes) quasi-sacred status. Dubnov's famous words – even should they be apocryphal – as the *Einsatzgruppen* are eliminating the Jews of Riga, take on symbolic character and darken Schliemann's ecstasy: *Schreib un farschreib!* Keep writing it down!

The same impulse has led to remarkable works of art after the

Holocaust, despite the dangers of trivialization and sensationalism. Among artists who were survivors one thinks of such poets as Celan, Nelly Sachs, Pagis, Cayrol, Kovner and Sutzkever, of Samuel Bak's paintings, of Primo Levi's and Jean Améry's essays, of Charlotte Delbo's fragments and David Rousset's *The Other Kingdom*, of the fiction writers Wiesel, Appelfeld, Semprun, Fink. It was not uncomplicated for them to release that creative energy. Sara Horowitz points out that the hope for collective survival, still inspiring the ghetto writers, was revealed to have been an illusion: after liberation, the total, overriding Nazi commitment to genocide became all too clear. In the dawn of new life, moreover, the liberated were again shunned or disregarded, like the proverbial messenger of bad news. Aharon Appelfeld depicts the survivors as lapsing into a Big Sleep, not unlike the charmed amnesia of national assimilation from which they were so traumatically torn; and Haim Gouri documents the eye-opening impact of the Eichmann trial on an Israeli generation that had encouraged the dormancy of which Appelfeld writes.

"A consuming fever" is how Nietzsche described our era's passion for historical detail. He questioned what use history-writing had for the living. Every day it becomes clearer that facts that must be retrieved are pervaded by error, partiality, myth, and may sink under the weight of our very attempt to correct for distortion. Such terms as stratified, mediated, perspectival, polyphonic, multidimensional enter the critical vocabulary describing both fictional and historical reconstruction. In addition, a post-history (*posthistoire*) trend emerges in contemporary thought, of which Syberberg's *Hitler* film is a chief exhibit. This trend takes a cosmic view of history, distancing it by a montaged and synchronic perspective, mingling German cabaret with a *theatrum mundi* effect, and inducing a frustrated feeling of equivalence as if everything were as spectacularly banal as the Fuehrer's valet.[1] The trend "relativizes," as the expression goes, even the Hitler era, even the Holocaust. It does not deny the experience we have passed through but plays with it in a way that is at once mocking and challenging. This is a further troubling development within historicism, a feverish reaction to the "consuming fever" registered by Nietzsche; and I will return to it later.

For those who do not see the Holocaust as "just another calamity," or who think that even were it comparable to other great massacres we should not allow it to fade from consciousness – because of its magnitude, its blatant criminality, its coordinated exploitation of all modern resources, cultural and technological, and the signal it sends how quickly racist feelings can be mobilized – for those, and I am of their number, post-historical is as unacceptable as historical relativization.

That weak though diplomatic word, "unacceptable," points to a moral dilemma. The issue of history in relation to memory – the issue of what is needful to remember – refuses to disappear. Even considering the exceptional nature of the Holocaust, why reiterate what happened in memoir after memoir, or in fascinated historical tracts outdoing each other in precision? One understands the scribal passion of contemporary witnesses like Dubnov. As family, as friends are killed, each becomes the last Jew, the only survivor: "And I alone have survived to tell thee." One understands, likewise, the need to acquaint relatives and a too silent world immediately after the war. Annette Wieviorka analyzes one such attempt, the *récits* of French survivors, who considered themselves French deportees rather than Jewish victims. But what of the next generation, and now of those growing up fifty years after the Final Solution was launched? What meaning can be extracted from an increasing mass of materials: multiplying films, novels, historical reconstructions, witness accounts, and even, as James Young points out, monuments?

One meaning is to expose and defeat what Primo Levi called the "War on Memory." This war takes many forms. In daily life, and especially in politics, the "blatant beast" of slander and defamation is among the most deadly of these. Extended into the writing of history it relies on ignorant or deliberate and expedient falsification, abetted by prejudicial stereotypes and ethnic or national myths. As Walter Benjamin observed, the dead are not safe from politics. It is well known, for example, that the Jewish identity of the victims was suppressed on monuments and memorial sites built in the Eastern bloc countries. At the same time, the conflict over the convent at Auschwitz might have been avoided had both parties known the history and lay-out of this cluster of camps as clearly as Robert van Pelt and Debórah Dwork explain it. It is never adequate – the essays on monuments by James Young and Giovanni Leoni confirm this point – to allow a memorial to elide its own history, so that it becomes nothing more than sacred and collectivized space. "The very term 'monument' has a treacherous sound," Leoni writes. And Young sees a danger that "once we assign monumental form to memory, we have to some degree divested ourselves of the obligation to remember."[2]

The rise of pedagogical museums helps to overcome this danger. But as the case of the museum at Auschwitz shows, even honorable intentions can lead to a distortive image – to actual physical (topographical) changes. If these cannot be avoided they should not be overlooked: the very process of building and rebuilding such memorial sites must become part of the record. The deeper issue, however, has to do with transmitting "Auschwitz" to the young, to succeeding generations. Recreating a visit to the camp, Eleonora Lev evokes the difficulty of taking one's child there, of accepting and not accepting the sanitized museum atmosphere. "The place we are visiting is only the bottle of formaldehyde where the corpse of memory is kept . . . [Auschwitz] exists not here but is dispersed throughout the world, in fragments, in the survivors' memories . . . day and night, continuing to struggle and gnaw and consume, without refuge."[3]

Some distortion is inherent in every attempt to achieve stability or closure, as history changes into memory and its institutionalization. Otherwise all man-created disasters, as well as some natural ones (the Lisbon earthquake of the eighteenth century comes to mind), would draw us into an endless, emotional vortex. "Curse God and die" may respond to our bitterness of heart, but what we generally do is seek a redemptive perspective to save the good name of humanity or of life itself. Yet the Final Solution's man-made calamity is exceptionally resistant to such a perspective. It threatens to remain an open grave, an open wound in consciousness. In fact, the passage of time has eroded redemptive as well as merely rationalizing meanings faster than they can be replaced. We become, in Maurice Blanchot's words, "guardians of an absent meaning." And in a gesture that is meant to be theoretical rather than religious, we then reflect on the limits of representation, questioning under the impact of this corrosive event our cultural achievements in criticism, literature and historiography.

Lawrence Langer, in his contribution here, and more explicitly in *Holocaust Testimonies: the ruins of memory*, suggests that an older language of moral concern, that of civic humanism, cannot encompass the dilemmas faced by the victims in the camps. What is called for is not a redemptive or heroic vocabulary but, to quote Blanchot again, a "disaster notation," (*écriture du désastre*). Saul Friedlander focusses on the related issue of representational adequacy in the writing of history. For, while no recent event has elicited so much documentation and analysis, knowledge has not become understanding. Moreover, though historicans generally do not let feelings color their research, in this case the topic is approached with a transferential complexity that makes the task of description shakier: there is a mixture of numbness (leading to over-objectification) and emotionalism.[4]

Friedlander offers two hypotheses concerning the deferred or absent meaning of the Holocaust. Each can only be tested by time. The first is that even as bystanders – as non-participant observers, either during the events or in the fifty years since – we suffer something like a trauma, a breach in normal thinking about human and civilized nature; and this breach needs more time to heal. Understanding may have to be deferred to a later generation. The second hypothesis, which parallels Langer's point, is that a new method of representation is necessary, and this too has not come about. But he suggests that historians should heed the individual voice of the victims and introduce it "in a field dominated by political decisions and administrative decrees which neutralize the concreteness of despair and death." Recent attempts to recreate the everyday history (*Alltagsgeschichte*) of Nazi Germany have neglected, if not totally displaced, the everyday history of the victims – which their testimony, as well as Langer's attention to it, so powerfully brings back.

Holocaust testimony as a genre is not one thing, of course, but a complex act whose function may have changed, as Annette Wieviorka suggests, both with the passage of time and the growing use of tape recorder and video camera. In the years immediately after the war, testimony had the status of an archival document whose primary aim was increase of knowledge; today it is rather a means of transmission that keeps the events before our eyes. The volume of testimonies is remarkable; it not only contradicts the notion of the Holocaust as an inexpressible experience (though that retains an emotional truth)[5] but creates an internally complex field of study. Roskies describes the mass of chronicles and memory books – dating back to pogroms earlier in the century – as a library or canon with traditional and specifically Jewish features; and Wieviorka enlarges his description (and the canon) by analyzing differences of structure, literary texture and personal stance between French and Yiddish testimonies that came like a flood between 1945 and 1948.

Shapes of Memory began with the idea that we live in an era of testimony, and that this phenomenon in its very heterogeneity – memory having many shapes, which should not be prematurely unified – deserved to be looked at. Yet testimony does not become, because of its variety, a vague or insubordinate concept. Wieviorka's careful differentiation of testimonial narratives is supplemented by the remarks of Mary Felstiner and Shoshana Felman on the extraordinary layering of historical truth in Lanzmann's *Shoah* and Salomon's *Life or Theater?* What is required is a deeper conceptualization of the act of witnessing (Felman) or an undoing of such simplistic dichotomies as artistic "inner quest" and "historical backdrop" (Felstiner).

Since few events have been documented more thoroughly – though much remains to be sifted and clarified – our focus shifts to memory in its vicissitudes, to the sequelae of a catastrophic experience. The struggle between memory and identity, for example, including national identity, does not let up with time. As Young points out, Polish national memory and Jewish memory haunt many of the same places. And the testimonies already mentioned, recorded years after the event, are often less essential for their historical data than for the way survivors regard themselves now, in their "afterlife." Primo Levi's "The Survivor," a poem written in 1984, depicts a camp prisoner still haunted by his dead companions: "Stand back, leave me alone submerged people. . . . It's not my fault if I live and breathe . . ."

From the beginning, moreover, historical research – still strengthening at the present time its scope and precision – has been accompanied by a "collective memory" transmitted through popular as well as educated circles. This kind of recollection encourages a healing and sometimes politically inspired form of closure. The very events that have jeopardized the community must now reinforce it. As the eyewitnesses pass from the scene and even the most faithful memories fade, the question of what sustains Jewish identity is raised with a new urgency. In this transitional phase the children of the victims play a particular role as transmitters of a difficult, defining legacy. Their situation is special, but it suggests a more than temporary dilemma in that the burden on their emotions, on their capacity to identify, is something we all share to a degree:

> I had lived on the edges of a catastrophe; a distance – impassable, perhaps – separated me from those who had been directly caught up in the tide of events, and despite all my efforts, I remained, in my own eyes, not so much a victim as – a spectator. I was destined, therefore, to wander among several worlds, knowing them, understanding them – better, perhaps, than many others – but nonetheless incapable of feeling an identification without any reticence, incapable of seeing, understanding, and belonging in a single, immediate, total movement.[6]

It could be said that we are all part of that second-generation dilemma: so Alain Finkielkraut defines a new character-type, the "imaginary Jew" who lives after these events yet tries to identify with a vital, now ruined culture.[7] In the diaspora especially, Judaism is marked by this existential and nostalgic quest. *We remain*, facing the attempted murder of an entire people and brutal eradication of its lifeworld. But *we remain* also in a different sense, one that imposes a critical perspective and duty. It is the "generation after" that struggles against as well as for Holocaust remembrance. In Israel (not only in Germany) the idea of overcoming the past has proved to be an illusion. On both the personal level and that of public policy there is enormous tension. For a long time Israel rejected the ethos of the refugees who flooded in, while legitimating itself (as it still does, and increasingly) through Holocaust memory. The essays by Appelfeld and Gouri reflect this contradiction but do not speak fully about the impact of the dead on the living. Or about the way the living appropriate the dead. The generation after, because of its closeness to the survivors, has the essential and ungrateful task of criticizing specific aspects of a Holocaust remembrance that turns into a politics of memory.[8]

"Those who are still alive," Czeslaw Milosz declared in his Nobel Lecture, "receive a mandate from those who are silent forever. They can fulfill their duties only by trying to reconstruct precisely things as they were by wresting the past from fictions and legends." That mandate holds for this volume. Leo Spitzer retrieves a relatively unknown chapter in the transplanting of Austrian Jews, who sought to rebuild their culture exactly as it was, to recreate a memorial community in Bolivia's foreign land. Mary Felstiner introduces the work of a young German painter, Charlotte Salomon, whose cartoon-like explorations of the refugee milieu of the Côte d'Azur reflects its mixture of dream and tragic deracination. Vera Schwarcz, daughter of a survivor, shows how her father's memory tried to break through to itself using her as amanuensis, and how her very choice of a professional field, that of China historian, was influenced by the theme of memory.

Other essayists identify stages in a return of the past after its repression or marginalization. Appelfeld offers a highly stylized collective biography of the inner experience undergone by young survivors restarting life in Israel. Gouri chronicles the impact of the Eichmann trial on Israelis who, like himself, had adopted an anti-diaspora mentality. Michael Geyer and Miriam Hansen, now American academics, but who came of age in post-war Germany, expand Habermas's concern over the public use of history. In particular, they analyze the "explosion into memory" of the genocide, an outpouring from the late 1970s on of memoirs and historical research, further stimulated by the TV serial *Holocaust*. In a country where the crime was planned, the Holocaust suddenly became "popular," thirty years after the liberation of the camps and more than a decade after the 1964 Auschwitz trial in Frankfurt. How should we interpret this shift from scarcity to excess, from the inauthentic silence that officially shielded both Germans and displaced persons to a national obsession?

Even the survivors had fallen silent, especially in West Germany. It took the Auschwitz trial, the first serious accounting demanded by the German state of its citizens, to inspire in Jean Améry the role of what Alvin Rosenfeld calls his moral witness. The rest of Améry's short life was spent driving home the message that the evil that had occurred was "singular and irreducible in its total inner logic and its accursed rationality." It often seemed to Améry as if Hitler had gained a posthumous triumph: so many further crimes against humanity – invasions, tortures, genocidal expulsions, murder squads and gulags – post-dated 1945 and threatened to relativize the Holocaust, to make it no more than a large blip on the screen of history. Yet only a year before his suicide, in the preface to a re-edition (1977) of *At the Mind's Limits*, he continued to insist that "whatever abominations we may have experienced still do not offset the fact that between 1933 and 1945 those things of which I speak in my writings took place among the German people, a people of high intelligence, industrial capacities and unequaled cultural wealth." The issue of authentic witnessing – of remembering the duty to give witness, but also the duty not to falsify one's witness – is David Tracy's concern as well, as he addresses his fellow theologians, and Shoshana Felman's who examines Lanzmann's technique in *Shoah*, a film made of testimonies.

Nadine Fresco fulfills the mandate of which Milosz speaks, with anger but also with cold historical precision. Her essay lays bare the political and sectarian motives of French "negationists" (a more exact term than "revisionists") who deny that the systematic murder of five to six million Jews ever took place. The Jews, according to the negationists, were victims only as a side-effect of a terrible war that also killed millions of others and did not single them out by a genocidal act. In the US, the negationists call for an "open discussion" of the Holocaust, appropriating the language of rights, as if the Book of the Destruction were not open, as if the massive facts and testimonies were not totally available. But the notion that information has been withheld or distorted is so absurd that it must immediately be reinforced by a charge that goes to the heart of the slander. Motivated not by facts but by an all-determining ideology, the negationists resort to defamation and assert the presence of a conspiracy: by capitalist society, the unacknowledged cause of fascism and particularly its industrialization of death (a first "revision," by the extreme left), or by the Jews themselves, who still control the media and impose this hoax on the entire world (a second "revision," by the extreme right).[9]

To Nadine Fresco's decisive and bitter essay I want to add a coda. As Geyer and Hansen point out, the revival of *public* memory in Germany and elsewhere took place only after many years (which is understandable), but, more relevantly, it took place in a changed social and cultural milieu – call it post-modern rather than modern. The exact label does not matter; the significant thing is that now the pressure on memory comes from more than an evaded historical burden, or a post-Holocaust conscience that opens our eyes to "a wretchedness of global extent" (Terrence des Pres). In the democratic part of the world, where the possibilities of recall have vastly increased since 1945, our communication networks no longer allow the plea (if it was ever sincere) that "We could not know" or "We had no idea." Hence the prospect of human guilt becomes limitless again; and new defenses are erected against an intolerable awareness.

These defenses, amounting to outright denial in the case of the negationists, point to the construction of an anti-memory – a representation that takes the colors of memory yet blocks its retrieval. So "Bitburg" was meant to close the books on Germany's guilt, and to foster an unburdened national present. So monuments multiply, not only to redeem but often to profit from a shameful past. (Young's essay on Poland is moving and fairminded on that score.) The signs of such a disburdening of memory are everywhere. Even as public recognition of the Holocaust increases, so do charges about exploiting, profaning, or trivializing the suffering. Many of the more sensitive prefer a respectful silence.[10] Though critical of talkativeness, Elie Wiesel, whose *Night* was called in its earlier, Yiddish version *And the World was Silent*, deserves a special tribute for his insistence that keeping silent only strengthens those who wish to deny or evade knowledge.

The Holocaust should not have happened but it did happen; and so it is a momentous event that draws architects, artists, scholars and intellectuals. Full of action as well as suffering, with episodes of heroism as well as banal failure, presenting evil in its starkest aspect yet also goodness and sacrifice, it remains a mystery that cannot be shrouded in a repressive quiet. Now that public silence has been broken, it will remain broken; and no shame attaches to those who evoke that darkest time to give it meaning, or to dispute the meanings given. No shame, that is, except the one of which Primo Levi spoke, and which tends to corrode our image of the human.

It will require both scholarship and art to defeat an encroaching anti-memory. And the drift toward it can be something commonplace rather than dramatic, something "in the air." Indeed, theorists of the post-modern like Jean Baudrillard, and, as I mentioned previously, movie-makers like Syberberg, contribute to anti-memory in a peculiar way. They seem powerless to overcome by their own spectacular idiom the negative implication of a culture industry that can simulate anything and everything. In the light of media over-exposure the evil of the Holocaust becomes strangely weightless. Both Améry's stubborn refusal to relent as a witness, to allow Germany's present to free itself from its past, and Lanzmann's *Shoah* with its visual and verbal density (scrupulously displayed by Felman), its exhausting quest to record every detail of the Nazi killing machine, do more than save the naked truth from forgetfulness or ideological distortion. They seek to force the return of an older and endangered sense of real presence.[11]

In *The Transparence of Evil*, Jean Baudrillard evokes a reality-loss, a phantomization of both personal and collective identity, and ultimately of the past – of history itself. This reality-loss Baudrillard links to our very capacity, now hugely expanded, for retrieving and disseminating knowledge: we gain a global information technology but it transmits images that could be simulacra. His *"intellectuo-médiatique"* vision of our world (the phrase is actually that of Mme Cresson lashing out at the intellectuals) is so extreme that it runs parallel at certain points to that of the American high-tech fantasist, Philip K. Dick.

There is a new amnesia, according to Baudrillard, produced by an endless process of image-substitution, of representation after represen-tation, of one theory after another. Our "necrospective" too is a symp-tom. "It is because we have disappeared *today* ... that we want to prove we died between 1940 and 1945, at Auschwitz or Hiroshima – that, at least, was real history [*une histoire forte*]." The negationist paradox concerning the supposed impossibility of proving that the Holo-caust occurred is only another expression of this sense of the unreality of the past; we have reached "the impasse of a hallucinatory *fin de siècle*, fascinated by the horror of its origins, for which oblivion is impossible. The only way out is by denial or negation."[12]

Baudrillard combines irony with hyperbole to drive his point home. "One of these days we will ask ourselves if even Heidegger existed." Yet something of this mad, post-history perspective was anticipated by Walter Benjamin. His famous essay of 1936, on the changing status of art in the era of mechanical reproduction, suggests that when techniques like photography transport objects from their original site, from their specific historical locus, they lose the aura of uniqueness. The reprodu-cibility of art – and, by extension, of the newsworthy event – brings us closer to it yet also creates a further distance: a world in which presence is increasingly displaced by representation. A new space for manipulation opens through photomontage: and since the means of reproducing "real" or "authentic" events are generally not in our control but depend on propagandists or the media, hermeneutic suspicion becomes even more necessary than before.

Benjamin's experiment with historical materialism may have been a way to compensate this loss of substance, of historical emplacement. He writes as if the potentially explosive impact of past on present were still possible. He refuses to let memory become remembrance or a mere "inventory" of the past. When I read *A Berlin Childhood* (written circa 1932–3 though not published till 1950), the book's magical realism, a pervasive blend of personal memory and *Kunstmärchen*, strikes me as dated yet also attractively solid: a fetish or talisman. I want to rub it like Aladdin's lamp, or taste it like Proust's madeleine.

Benjamin is a transitional figure who sees the future rather than the past in a ghostly light. The future is dangerously abstract as a motive for progress; the past alone, its very ruins, can be an object of love, of motivating hope. That hope in the past inspires a backward glance like that of the angel of history Benjamin will depict shortly before his death. What the angel sees or remembers turns, however, into something driving and desperate: a Messianism that is not the goal but the end – the abrupt termination of history. It is impossible to think of Benjamin's incursions into the "dark backward and abysm" of time as post-genocidal. Today the interior landscape is marked by ruined or vanished sites or else by a fantastic and facile "virtual reality." The relationship between representation and reality, between mimesis and the object of mimesis seems to have undergone a quasi-geological rift.[13]

I agree with Baudrillard that our sense of reality has been affected; that a media-induced anxiety is promoting a greater or more subtle doubt about simulated evidence than Descartes' famous *malin génie*, his trickster or illusionist demiurge. Yet Baudrillard fails to acknowledge an ordinary and perfectly reasonable suspicion of the world of appearances, or of the way the immediacy of the lived event fades into the past before having been grasped or understood. The pastness of life seems to be a condition for understanding it; as Péguy already remarked, there is an "unbridgeable gulf between the actual and the historical event." Baudrillard also fails to note how the sadness that comes from this feeling of lost time or the unlived life is exploited by groups with a *revanchist* political agenda. This bears directly on denials of the Holocaust: a *civilized* fear of reality-loss is contaminated by a *savage* anti-semitism that preceded the Holocaust and still continues in negationist attacks on the media as "Jewish."

The charge that Jews control the media, and through the media our very image of reality, has a paranoid structure. But already in the nineteenth century a feeling of reality-loss, linked to the weakening of place-bound identity, and redressed by nostalgic evocations of rural homestead, *Heimat* or *vieux pays*, could breed a new and virulent anti-semitism. Jews began to be scapegoats for an imperfect transition of society from a rural economy to industrialization and urbanization. The move from the land to urban centers, the deracination it produced, and the growing role of financial middlemen during this time, led to a politically exploited anti-semitism beyond the anti-Jewish feelings fostered by the church. Identified with capitalism and its "abstract" money, the Jews were soon held responsible for the disintegration of the so-called organic community. Their supposed "semitic" status – however indigenous or settled, they were accused of being without loyalty to the land or the host-nation – imposed on them the image of perpetual aliens. T. S. Eliot's notorious lines from "Gerontion" (1919),

> My house is a decayed house,
> And the jew squats on the window sill, the owner,
> Spawned in some estaminet of Antwerp

express this stereotype: the Jew is a foreign trader, a parasite-usurper of other people's houses, and ultimately of the declining, ancient House of Europe itself, undermined by his arts.

The danger came, supposedly, not only from the traditional Jew of alien or "oriental" aspect. What alarmed even more, from Richard Wagner to Nazi racial science, was the assimilated Jew, Wagner's "plastic [i.e. shape-shifting] demon of decadence," who *seemed* to adapt and fit in. Philip Dick can dream of a machine to distinguish between humans and replicants, but no machine short of extermination could outwit this cold-hearted, dissimulating stranger, using all the cunning at his disposal, all his free-floating, world-wide intelligence and capital, to undermine the national community. It was this anxiety that the Nazi regime cultivated, until extirpation of the "poisonous mushroom," of the entire anti-race of simulacra or subversive look-alikes, became thinkable.[14] At the present time, when non-Jewish waves of immigration are a major concern of European countries, both from an economic and cultural point of view, and when nationalism and xenophobia are reaching another high, one wonders what new violence lies ahead.

Despite the Holocaust, myths of national, ethnic or religious purity continue to persist. While the issue of how to deal with immigrant or resident stranger is never an easy one, the matter cannot be left to explosive popular feelings. Rituals that offer hospitality and laws that protect the foreigner are essential to both Homeric and Biblical times, but episodes like that of the Cyclops and of Sodom and Gomorrah are vivid reminders of a chronic and murderous lawlessness.

In Coleridge's "Ancient Mariner," one of the best-known of modern poems, the mariner transgresses the code of hospitality by killing an albatross that had welcomed the sailors. The albatross turns out to have been the guardian spirit of the polar region into which their ship has strayed. The mariner's punishment for this crime is perpetual exile, a homeless wandering from place to place. Through his powerful tale Coleridge evokes a cosmic and avenging memory that can be triggered even by casual infringements. The lesson seems to be that mankind is itself a trespasser in the universe, dependent on earth's hospitality; to respect other creatures, therefore, both man and beast, is not only a Noachite law prior to special religious revelations but also a symbiotic necessity.

By projecting a cosmic memory as retentive and resentful as our own, Coleridge leads us to understand the consequences. The entanglement of memory and revenge does not cease; persecution does not cease. What his poem presents as fantasy is our daily condition. The question remains what role laws play in this tragedy. Can they, should they, limit revenge by instituting a legalized forgetting (amnesty) or a forgiveness that is its religious counterpart? I regret not providing an essay on this subject. But the issues are quite clear and they center on a perhaps unresolvable conflict. On the one hand, for victims of the Holocaust (and this includes their families, or victims by adoption, or all who have been radically affected) it is not justice alone but also reality – the very sense of reality jeopardized by post-modern amnesia, by anti-memory – that must be recovered through the Eichmann, Barbie, and similar trials. The crimes against humanity disclosed by such legal proceedings are wrested from an increasingly inert historical record and endowed with "judicial presence."[15] On the other hand, to burden later generations with the guilt of parents and grandparents will produce feelings of victimization and damaged identity that increase compensatory assertions such as nationalism and xenophobia. Geyer and Hansen suggest that all of us, and Germans in particular, should fight these assertions by relinquishing the illusory appeal of the unified personality (of a psyche in harmony both with itself, in the classical, Goethean sense, and with the state, in the Fichtean romantic sense); but their prescription may again be utopian. The politics of memory, the acute link of resentful memory with *revanchist* programs, is not likely to disappear.

Amnesty is lawful amnesia; and what takes place at this highly formalized level may also take place in the domain of the social or collective memory. This type of memory has recently intrigued scholars concerned with the impact of catastrophic events on nation or group. Can memory, individual or collective, when besieged by an insomniac stream of both trivial and fearful news – and by the *revenants* Levi depicts – tolerate all this pressure without a sanctioned principle of forgetting? If such a principle is essential, where does it come from and how can we choose critically between alternative modes of amnesia?

Perhaps cultures could be differentiated by describing the degree of their memory-tolerance. But it seems as if the socially constructed memory, no sooner discovered, is already in jeopardy. Following Nietzsche, some contemporary historians fear that it is being eroded by an overload of historical information and the assault of current events.[16] Even epoch-making incidents like the Shoah, swept into that current, are integrated not by distinctive communal forms but by politically motivated analogies. Such false integration is again a form of anti-memory. Rights activists proclaim an "Animal Auschwitz" and the anti-abortion movement a "holocaust of babies." What prompts these analogies is less inadequate knowledge than an overburdened conscience.

Indeed, some thinkers have made a distinction between ancient and modern memory. Mircea Eliade speculates that the ancient world used orgiastic festivals for the purpose of licensed oblivion. He claims that Christianity was less of a cargo-cult kind of religion; that it tolerated more history, more historical consciousness.[17] Given the ecstatic if not orgiastic excesses of fascism, including the anti-semitic phobia of the Romanian Legion of Saint Michael to which Eliade belonged as a young man, one may be allowed to question his assertion of progress.

Moreover, and this is the paradox of a *non-orgiastic* solution, forgetting on a collective scale can itself assume the guise of memory, that is, of a religious or collective type of remembrance ("If I forget thee, O Jerusalem . . ."). It constructs, that is, a highly selective story, focussed on what is basic for the community and turning away from everything else.[18] The collective memory, in the process of making sense of history, shapes a gradually formalized agreement to transmit the meaning of intensely shared events in a way that does not have to be individually struggled for. Canonical interpretation takes over, ceremonies develop, monuments are built. An event is given a memory-place (*lieu de mémoire*)[19] in the form of statue, museum or concentration camp site, and annually repeated day. The repetition involves public rituals that merge individual sorrow or joy with communally prescribed forms of observance.

How are we to distinguish, then, between this collectivized and integrative form of memory and what I have previously called "anti-memory"? The natural scepticism which notes that history is not possible without memory can easily motivate the construction of memorial narratives in the service of an alternative history. The rise of *Pamyat* ("Memory") in Russia, with its blatant anti-semitic nationalism, illustrates the problem. We have no choice, I think, but to accept both the collective memory and the factual burden it reacts to. They cannot substitute for each other. The collective memory uses and produces fictions, yet it must learn from art not to confuse fiction and history, and from history not to succumb to sentimental or mystical ideas about a community's "world–historical" destiny. In this learning process both historian and literary critic play a role.[20]

Today we are certainly more aware of the pathological potential in collective types of thought that claim to unify or heal a community. Yet the appeal of such thought has not seriously diminished, and it can penetrate even historiography. The effort to find an intelligible, comprehensive and objective overview often produces non-trivial but still dubious historical analogies that function just like integrative simplifications in the collective memory. In the historians' debate, as Friedlander has shown,[21] a deep concern for national identity motivates an apologetic rather than objective discourse. In Germany historians who are German and face "a past that will not go away" (Ernst Nolte), are forced into a very particular angle of reflection or subject position. They become actors in a national drama of conscience. For even if Nolte does not *identify* with Hitler's presumed state of mind – Nolte speculates that Auschwitz was Hitler's "Asiatic deed," analogous to and as if compelled by Stalin's eastern (gulag) terror – he backs this empathic insight with enough meretricious detail to make us doubt the claim that he is unbiased. Another historian, Andreas Hillgruber, comes close to identifying explicitly with the point of view of the German soldier fighting on the Eastern front in the final, apocalyptic months of the war. His retrospective (and autobiographical) self-stationing would be more credible in fiction, in a novelistic or dramatic form that could allow a shameful sentiment to emerge as powerful *ressentiment*.

Wound and cure, in this sensitive area, are hard to tell apart. Anthropologists and students of myth, moreover, have shown that death incites superstitious explanations. There exist older societies which do not accept even *natural* death as a possibility but see in it the work of demons. Every death is an act of witchcraft and requires the community to find and convict the guilty party. Once this is done, order is restored. The effort of Nazi propaganda to blame the Jews for Germany's defeat in the First World War and to suggest a Jewish conspiracy to launch a second such war against the *Reich* created a witch-hunt atmosphere. An event like the Shoah, a political mass murder targeting for extinction an entire "race" of defenseless non-combatants, could not have occurred without a terrible superstition motivating it, and cannot now, after the event, be taken into mind without a severe disturbance.

It is not surprising that after the Holocaust so much guilt surfaces in the form of religious types of incrimination as well as reactive and exculpatory schemes of denial. With respect to guilt, there are many that question not only the treatment of immigrants but our entire history of behavior toward the other – the stranger in our gates or the conquered and colonized. Our confidence in the West, in its claim to be civilized, is shaken.[22] Yet, reactively, there are many that blame the victims or count themselves among their number or, seeing victims everywhere, equalize them all, undermining moral distinctions. So the Waffen SS, buried in Bitburg cemetery, are also "victims" of the Third Reich, even though many of them may have committed war crimes and crimes against humanity, especially against the Jews.

The latest threat, however, diagnosed by Baudrillard as post-modern, affects history as well as memory. The influence of the media, the penetration of their simulacra into daily life, prompts a deep anxiety about forgery, or counterfeit evidence. Should historiography be viewed as a self-consuming artifact, and should our basic trust in the reported fact diminish, then conspiracy theories get the upper hand and put everything in doubt except disbelief itself. The world of appearances, the *mediated* world, is felt to have so strong a hold that nothing can disenchant it except a "gnostic" assault that makes of historical research an infinite and so impossible task. That so many regimes and their gods have fallen also contributes to a demystification without bounds, a fanatic incredulity. The result is not only a supercilious and treacherous lucidity but often the return of myth.[23] Because of the conviction that what passes for history is not reality but reconstruction, nostalgia revives for a world elsewhere, for an original sublimity. In his quest for the truth about his birth, Oedipus the King thinks at one point that he may be descended from a god. Those who seek an identity, personal, national or racial, with an intensity that is equivalent to religious passion, seem to have returned to that delusive moment.

Yet there are signs that art has not lost its aura, or history its critical and evidential impact. We should not underestimate the counter-force of literature as it combines with testimony. I don't mean with forms of fiction like docudrama or historical novel. These are, and always have been, problematic if influential constructs. There has emerged, however, a body of works "between history and literature," including witness accounts and remarkable essays that seem to defy the Freudian formula that where trauma is, consciousness is not. So Améry's clarity is not linked to mastering the past. He has not overcome his terror and pain. "No remembering," he writes, "has become a mere memory.... Where is it decreed that enlightenment must be free of emotion?" Primo Levi's *Survival in Auschwitz*, especially its last, Dantesque chapter, is as substantial a work of both testimony and art as we are likely to get. His subject is at the antipodes of Thoreau's *Walden* yet shares with that tranquil book the sense of being a sequence of reflections. He has written essays from hell. And Lanzmann goes so far as to call the searing witness accounts in *Shoah* "resurrections."

The role of art remains mysterious, however, for art is testimony as well as combining with testimony. Levi again is exemplary: his attempt to recall Dante's Canto of Ulysses in the Inferno of Auschwitz, and to communicate his – in that context – ludicrous and solitary cultural faith, moves the remembered text closer to a Scripture. If I limit myself to an art of memory with explicit reference to the Shoah, it is because the historical referent of a more transformative method is difficult to retrieve.

Yet writers born after the Holocaust, or for whom it is an "absent memory" – Alain Finkielkraut of *Le Juif imaginaire*, Henri Raczymow of *Contes d'exil et d'oubli* and *Un Cri sans voix*, David Grossman of *See: under love* – reconstitute the past from stories rather than direct knowledge. This generation creates its own, often exotic world coiled round that absence, and offers the glimpse of a transformative art. The eyewitness generation expressed a return of memory despite trauma; this "second" generation expresses the trauma of memory turning in the void, and is all the more sensitive, therefore, to whatever tries to fill the gap.[24]

The general claim I make is not that the historical memory should be held superior to other cultural virtues, for that could again lead to a simplified or exclusive identity claim. Memory, as the Polish poet and essayist Adam Zagajewski has said, "is an indispensable part of creating culture, agreed; but isn't it true that it records and preserves the creative act rather than expresses itself in it? The elements of creativity have little in common with memory. Innovation, for example, and rebellion: both are rather hostile to memory."

This too, however, simplifies memory's link with creativity. That the relation between them can be unpredictable is shown by Dan Pagis. The poetry of this child survivor from Bukovina moves historical reality offstage, replacing it with an "absent memory" of a deliberate kind, one characterized by a disembodied voice, a discontinuous narrative and ghostly cosmic symbols. But in the last decade of the poet's life, as Sidra Ezrahi points out, his rebellion against memory gives way to a project of retrieval that redeems a portion of the past and provides a historical key. Ezrahi describes this project in detail: moving from a surreal and elliptical poetry to prose-poems and then to short narratives with a documentary valence, Pagis returns from the "exile" of a fictive self-dispersal. On the brink of his own death he dies into life rather than fiction; more precisely, his imagination no longer conspires with the survivor's sense of unreality, of living posthumously. Pagis turns his last writing into a conversation with his dead father – spooky enough, but still a coming to terms with the past. The effort to recall the father who had seemed to abandon him or the town that "forgot" him (Radautz), to reintegrate a deeply effaced reality – including his own first name, changed in Israel to the common "Dan" – produces a minimalism that makes us feel the charge and gravity of every autobiographical allusion.[25]

Art can and does move away from historical reference by a characteristic distancing. Moreover, even so estranging an event as the Shoah may have to be estranged again, through art, insofar as its symbols become trite and ritualistic rather than realizing. Such triteness (or overfamiliarization) overtook Celan's "Deathfugue" and can turn the most telling photo into a cliché. No hostility to memory is implied by attempting to reverse this process, and Anselm Kiefer's paintings, by formally alluding to Celan, create a secondary evocation that acts like the collective memory yet remains individual.

The issue of how memory and history become art is always a complicated one; in the case of the Shoah the question is also whether they *should* become art. Adorno's dictum, "To write poetry after Auschwitz is barbaric" was intended to be, as the context shows, a caution against the media and any aesthetic exploitation. Yet like other prohibitions against representation it heightens the stakes and inscribes itself in the work of those who confront it. For Günther Grass of the Hitler Youth generation, who inherited the evil fame of Nazi Germany, Adorno's caution was translated into "abandoning absolutes, the black and white of ideology; it meant showing belief the door and placing all one's bets on doubt, which turned everything, even the rainbow, to gray. But this imperative yielded wealth of another sort: the heart-rending beauty of all the shades of gray was to be celebrated in damaged language."[26] Life is green, Goethe said, while all knowledge is gray; that, however, was another absolute, just like the abandoned white and black. Perhaps art must now give up its own absolutist pretension and accept some gray matter. It becomes suspicious of itself, of its aestheticizing drive. The reflective and the creative, therefore, often mingle conspicuously.[27]

All these issues (estranging a too-familiar though traumatic history, the "barbaric" effort to wrest beauty or lyricism from it, or the anti-aesthetic mingling of creative and explicitly reflective styles) are seen in the surprising work of Art Spiegelman. His *Maus* and *Maus II* blend the folkloric beast-fable with American popular cartoons in order to retell the story of his survivor-parents, together with its effect on him. Spiegelman's comic-book style is not a simple alienation effect; it mirrors the vision of an adult who becomes a child again as he attempts to absorb extreme knowledge. The cartoons serve as a transitional object helping us toward a difficult truth – though not as innocent an object as it used to be. For they recall the Nazi representation of Jews as rodents as well as our own uneasy conscience about "lower" orders of the creation we slaughter *and* promote to comic strip immortality as Mickey Mouse, Bugs Bunny, Miss Piggy, Elsie, etc.

By his extraordinary adaptation of a popular medium Spiegelman questions whether a fully human knowledge of the Holocaust is possible, or whether as adults, and especially adults in America, we must remain childlike, trapped in a Disneyland sort of truth, a "Mauschwitz." The unreality of this domestication, a consequence also of having to bring the traumatic past into a family context, afflicts the survivors themselves as well as their children. Spiegelman's tag-like inscriptions, not only his pictures, capture the absurdity of attempting to live a normal life after its rupture by Auschwitz. "My parents survived Hell and moved to the suburbs."

Art constructs, in brief, a cultural memory of its own, in which the struggle of the individual with (and often for) experience – including the collective memory itself – never ceases. In a media-mediated age, this struggle may center on the issue of communicability. *Maus* stays on the side of popular culture, which seeks a high degree of direct communication;[28] the transformative method here, the estrangement, is based on a formula that is transgressive yet easily reproduced. Though a shock is given to imaginative habits that assign extreme phenomena to high culture, *Maus* is neither a grotesque nor a gothic exploitation of the horrors of genocide. Its metamorphosis of the human figure recognizes that the Shoah has affected how we think about ourselves as a *species* (the human? race).

Most of the time, however, transmissibility and truth move into opposition. So Paul Celan's untransparent work seeks in the absent community – even among the murdered – a "you" to address. "Speaks true who speaks shadow." The space of conversation, precarious at best, seems fatally injured and a descent to the dead is necessary to restore it. Celan's archaeology is more exemplary for us than Schliemann's.

Even a less opaque artist, Dan Pagis for example, can use dense literary allusions to create something strong and inimitable. A poem entitled "Testimony" compares Nazi guards to their victims. They, the uniformed, booted guards, "were created / in the image," but the writer–victim is said to be merely "a shade. / A different creator made me." The Hebrew word for image used here is *zelem*. The Hebrew word for shade is *zel*. The juxtaposition tells all and deepens the darkness of those root letters and the horror of the fact that Genesis, the act of divine creation, could have led to this. The poet's manichean acknowledgment of evil concludes with an ironic echo of Maimonides' creed, enshrined as a hymn in the prayer book, and thus in Jewish memory:

> And he in his mercy left nothing of me that could die.
> And I fled to him, floated up weightless, blue,
> forgiving – I would even say: apologizing –
> smoke to omnipotent smoke
> that has no face or image.[29]

It is mid-October. In New England the leaves have turned. One or two begin to float in the crisp air. Further north many maples have already shed half their gold, a hectic treasure for the children. I see them in the large frontyard of an old house, running and shouting, five of them, all sizes. A woman is raking the leaves, or trying to. The children, romping around, undo her work; she cuffs them with the rake, as tolerantly as a kitten a perplexing ball or comatose object. The pile of raked leaves grows, and the children invent a new game. They collapse into the pile, spreading out deliciously, while the woman – mother, housekeeper – abets their game, and covers them with the still fragrant, light leaves. At first giggles and squeaks, then, as the tumulus rises to a respectable height, total silence. But only for a minute. For, as if on signal, all emerge simultaneously from the leafy tomb, jumping out, laughing, resurrected, to the mock surprise of the one who is raking and who patiently begins again.

I am on my way to give a lecture on the Holocaust, when I come across the pastoral scene. What am I doing, I ask myself. How can I talk about such matters, here? I cannot reconcile scenes like this with others I know about.

In a fleeting montage, I see or dream I see the green, cursed fields of Auschwitz. A cold calm has settled on them. The blood does not cry from the ground. Yet no place, no wood, meadow, sylvan scene will now be the same. Something more fearful than any gothic horror has entered the landscape. Even in quiet Concord or Unadilla. This moment of contagion does not last, yet it returns unpredictably. I cannot forget any more than I can truly remember. And every morning, punctual as the news, a daily corruptness, page after page, associates with that pang, that pain, and shames the hope I have left.

2

On Testimony

Annette Wieviorka

From the mass of filmed testimonies that emerged in the late 1970s and through the 1980s on the different types of deportation and, specifically, on the extermination of the Jews, Claude Lanzmann's film, *Shoah*, stands out incontestably. Appearing in theaters in 1985, *Shoah* is concerned exclusively with the memory of the extermination of the Jews, and with that alone. First, by the chronological period it covers. Unlike Alain Resnais' *Night and Fog*, which begins in 1933 with Hitler's ascent to power and the opening of the first concentration camp, Dachau, and which focusses on the Nazi concentration system rather than on the extermination of the Jews, the action of *Shoah* "begins in the present at Chelmno, on the Narew River, in Poland. Fifty miles northwest of Lodz, in the heart of a region that once had a large Jewish population, Chelmno was the place in Poland where Jews were first exterminated by gas. Extermination began on December 7, 1941."[1]

It is in the tension between these two reference points, "in the present" and December 7, 1941, that the film's actors — Nazi officials of the extermination, Polish witnesses, Jewish survivors — speak. What they say has nothing to do with the lived experience of the concentration camp, but focusses on the machinery of extermination. The film as a whole gives an impression of radical innovation: that of the work of art.

Yet historians of genocide, even if it might seem to them that the witnesses are speaking for the first time, find themselves on familiar ground. They are aware of the experiences of Mordechai Podchlebnik or Simon Srebnik, the child singer of Chelmno, from their testimonies at the trials of Eichmann or Zuckerman. They have read *I Cannot Forgive*[2] by Rudolph Vbra. They know Richard Glazar from the long interviews that Gitta Sereny conducted with him in writing her admirable book, *Into That Darkness*.[3]

Testimony has changed direction. Print has been replaced by the tape recorder and the video camera. At the same time, the function of testimony has also changed. In the years following the war, the primary aim of testimony was knowledge – knowledge of the modalities of genocide and of the deportation. Testimony had the status of an archival document. Today, despite certain confusions that characterize the French public's understanding of the concentration camp system and the genocide of the Jews (a failure to distinguish between the death camps[4] and the concentration camps, a lack of clarity regarding the location and function of the gas chambers), the purpose of testimony is no longer to obtain knowledge. Time has passed, and the historian does not trust a memory in which the past has begun to blur and which has been enriched by numerous images since the survivor's return to freedom. The mission that has devolved to testimony is no longer to bear witness to inadequately known events, but rather to keep them before our eyes. Testimony is to be a means of transmission to future generations.

Testimony is a novelty only for those who have not encountered it. It is simply astonishing that French historians acquiesced in the same illusion as the general public, and that in order to explain the paucity of the collective memory of the deportation through the 1970s they raised the commonplace that "the deportees did not want or were unable to speak" to the level of a historical truth, without beginning to investigate it or even to reflect on its terms. The deportees? Which group of deportees?[5] The Jewish survivors of the extermination?[6] To speak? About what? Is the totality of the experience of the concentration camp resistant to language? Or only a particular aspect of it?

Reinforcing this commonplace about the supposed silence of the deportees is the notion of the inexpressible. The inexpressible, according to the *Petit Robert* dictionary, is "that which one cannot say, express." At the very heart of the genocide, among those in the ghettos who were able to write, there appeared the idea that the extermination of the Jews implies silence. Thus, to take only one example, Abram Lewin writes in his diary of the Warsaw Ghetto:

> But perhaps because the disaster is so great there is nothing to be gained by expressing in words everything that we feel. Only if we were capable of tearing out by the force of our pent-up anguish the greatest of all mountains, a Mount Everest, and with all our hatred and strength hurling it down on the heads of the German murderers of our young and old – this would be the only fitting reaction on our part. Words are beyond us now.
> Our hearts are empty and made of stone.[7]

But already we face a paradox. The very person who writes in order to testify appeals at the same time to silence. How can we fail to be struck by the fever to testify that gripped the Warsaw ghetto:

> Everyone wrote [...] Journalists and professional writers, of course, but also teachers, social workers, youth, even children. For the most part, they composed journals in which the tragic events of the era were grasped through the prism of personal, lived experience. There were countless such writings, but the majority were destroyed with the extermination of the Jews of Warsaw. Only the contents of the archives of the OS [Oneg Shabbes] were preserved.[8]

These clandestine archives were buried and the bulk of them recovered in 1946 and 1950. One of the unearthed boxes contained the testament, in Yiddish, of three militants who had buried the documents. Among them was David Graber, a 19-year-old worker, who notes on August 3, 1942: "We welcomed each new document with such joy! We were aware of our responsibility. No, we were not afraid of the risk, conscious as we were of perpetuating an entire chapter of history, more precious by far than the life of a partisan."[9]

The victims are certainly beyond words, and yet, dispossessed of everything, words are all they have left. Words which will be the sole trace of an existence conceived not as that of an individual but as that of a people.

After the war, Th. W. Adorno affirmed – and it was much quoted – that "to write poetry after Auschwitz is barbaric," thus posing the problem of the aestheticization of the Catastrophe. Elie Wiesel marked the antinomy at the very heart of the expression "literature of genocide."[10] But Adorno and Wiesel were not referring to the testimony of the deportees, much less to the texts recovered from the ghettoes, which do not fall simply under the rubric of literary creation.

The difficulty arises in transferring the notions of the inexpressible, of necessary silence, into the historian's domain – notions that are perfectly legitimate in the fields of literature, psychoanalysis, or philosophy. What use are such concepts to the historian? The soldiers of the First World War kept saying that their experience was inexpressible, uncommunicable, unthinkable – and it probably was so in part – at the same time that they wrote books by the hundreds. Did this lead historians to abandon the study of the war of the trenches, or to stop using the testimonies? Did we take the soldiers literally, concluding

from their litany — "whoever did not experience the trenches cannot
understand" — that they had disappeared behind a wall of silence?

In the field of history, the notion of the inexpressible is a superficial
one. It has exonerated historians of their task, which is precisely to
read the testimonies of the deportees, to interrogate, even in its silences,
this major source of the history of the deportation. It has shifted
responsibility for the silence of the French historians onto the deportees.

To describe the deportation one must examine, during the brief period
in which a small number of deportees returned,[11] two essential avenues:
radio and the written word. After the liberation the deportees spoke out
in radio programs, and the written press overflowed with testimonies.
Accounts published in the form of books and brochures were especially
numerous: about a hundred for the period between the liberation of
Paris and the end of 1948, when the publication of testimonies dried
up, probably because of a lack of readers and therefore of publishers.
Robert Antelme was right to speak of "a veritable hemorrhage of
expression."[12]

The deportees were the only group exiled from France by Nazism
that produced so rapidly a voluminous testimony. Nothing comparable
occurred among the labor conscripts of the Service du Travail Obliga-
toire (Forced Labor Service), nor among the prisoners of war, whose
numbers were however much greater. The magnitude of this testimony
recalls the literature of the First World War. Jean Norton Cru established
a list of 304 works inspired by the First World War, published between
1915 and 1928.[13] If we consider that the publication of the first testimonies by the deportees took place in only four years, that the number
of deportees, and even more so, of survivors, was incommensurably
smaller than the number of soldiers in the First World War — the first
were in the tens of thousands, the second in the millions — that there
were no major writers among the deportees whereas many eminent men
of letters fought in the Great War, that an entire dimension of the
literature of testimony — private journals and correspondence — was
excluded, with only a few exceptions, by the nature of living conditions
in the concentration camps, then a comparison on the quantitative level
does not work to the disadvantage of the deportees.

The major difference in the production of the two literatures has to
do with their readers. Maurice Rieuneau notes that those who wrote
about the Great War were certain of finding a receptive audience in
the millions of former soldiers.[14] This was not the case for survivors
of the deportation since their number was insufficient to create a true
market. Publishers are not philanthropists; they want their books to
sell. A successful book often leads to the publication of other books on

the same theme. It is the absence of this market of buyers and readers – indicating the indifference of public opinion once the initial shock had passed – which partly explains why the stream of testimonies came to an end.

For deportees who were not writers by profession, the transition from speech to writing may be interpreted as a feeling that they had not been understood. Let us read Primo Levi evoking a recurring dream he had at Auschwitz, a dream which he says was in its essence common to many of the survivors:

> This is my sister here, with some unidentifiable friend and many other people. They are all listening to me and it is this very story that I am telling: the whistle of three notes, the hard bed, my neighbour whom I would like to move, but whom I am afraid to wake as he is stronger than me. I also speak diffusely of our hunger and of the lice-control, and of the Kapo who hit me on the nose and then sent me to wash myself as I was bleeding. It is an intense pleasure, physical, inexpressible, to be at home, among friendly people, and to have so many things to recount: but I cannot help noticing that my listeners do not follow me. In fact, they are completely indifferent: they speak confusedly of other things among themselves, as if I was not there. My sister looks at me, gets up and goes away without a word.

It is, the author continues, a "desolating grief"[15]: an anguish so great that waking up and returning to the reality of Auschwitz are preferable. This suggests that the abundance of testimonies written by the deportees, often during the first months following their return, is symptomatic of a failed communication between the deportees and a society that had not experienced the horrors of the camps. In *The Book of Laughter and Forgetting*, Milan Kundera reports a conversation with a taxi driver suffering from insomnia since the war and who is writing his story: a sailor, his ship had capsized. "He swam three days and three nights. Finally he was saved. For several months he had wavered between life and death, and though he eventually recovered, he had lost the ability to sleep." For whom does he write? asks Kundera. Not for his children. "My kids don't give a damn. [. . .] No, I'm making a book out of it. I think it could do a lot of people a lot of good." And Kundera notes: "The reason we write books is that our kids don't give a damn. We turn to an anonymous world because our wife stops up her ears when we talk to her."[16] Perhaps the survivors wrote because their families stopped up their ears. In this regard, the testimony of Pierre Francès-

Rousseau, *Intact in the Eyes of the World*, written much later, in 1985, is riveting. His sister comes to meet him at the Lutétia hotel, looks him over, questions him, quickly reassures herself. He is intact. She takes his arm: "I'm so glad you're back. Finally I'll be able to talk to someone about my problems."[17]

Did society pay any more attention to the infinite suffering of the survivors than Pierre Francès-Rousseau's sister?

The first testimonies by the survivors of the deportation all share the same structure. They open with the arrest, the stay in prison and the French internment center before deportation. Next is the trip and the shock of arriving at the camp. Then a number of short, usually chronological chapters evoking various aspects of life in the concentration camp: the roll call, food, promiscuity, turf, labor, the camp hierarchy, the different nationalities present. The testimonies generally conclude with the liberation of the camp, sometimes with the survivor's return to France.

This structure is found in the testimonies of all the deportees from France, whether they were deported as part of the Resistance or for a "racial motive," as it was called after the war. However, the itinerary of a "racial deportee" had its special character. Once these deportees were recognized as Jewish, even if they were in the Resistance, they were taken to the camp at Drancy. They then became part of a *Judentransport*, a transport of Jews, in which men, women, and children were mixed together, whereas in the transports to the other camps they were always separated: the women were brought to Ravensbrück, the men to Buchenwald, Dachau, Mauthausen, etc. These racial transports were the only ones to undergo selection upon arrival.[18] In the camps themselves, there were differences. Certain prisoners at Buchenwald or Ravensbrück were able to write. This was the case for Jean Puissant, imprisoned in the invalid block. On wrapping paper, with a pencil forfeited by a Russian in exchange for a piece of bread, he transcribed poems, songs, reflections. Puissant was a teacher who had already published a volume of poetry and written a work on the Yonne dialect; using some discarded German administrative forms he wrote a detective novel, *Antoinette, ou crime à Bois-Avril* (*Antoinette or the Crime at Bois-Avril*), that was published after the war, with a preface by his prison companion, Julien Cain. Thus he wrote two books during his detention: this detective novel and a beautiful book of memories, *La Colline sans oiseaux* (*The Hill without Birds*).[19] Marcel Conversy found himself in a similar situation. In the author's note which prefaces his second work on Buchenwald, the collection of stories *L'Enclos des hommes perdus*[20] (*Enclosure of the Lost*), he writes:

> I had the good fortune of being able to write at the camp itself – which was forbidden on pain of death – since I was lost in the anonymous mass and free of any direct supervision. My first book was finished when I returned from captivity, and I submitted the manuscript to the publisher on May 20, 1945.
>
> This second volume was partially written at Buchenwald.

There is no testimony of this kind on Birkenau. Initially it would seem that the difference lies in the social composition of the prisoners. With the exception of the physicians, the surviving population of Birkenau appears to be on the whole less educated. Among those who wrote testimonies there were no journalists, no writers in the French language. But most importantly, the conditions of life were so terrifying that they left room for nothing outside the struggle for survival. As Simone Veil said to us, reflecting on the differences between her deportation and that of one of her sisters who was arrested for resistance activity and deported to Ravensbrück: "Some women took notes in order to be able to give testimony later. I don't know anyone who was able to do so at Birkenau with the exception of those who worked in the offices. But most of us were assigned to land labor. We were so worn out, trying merely to survive, that we were incapable of procuring the necessary paper and pencil, even less of writing. For several days after my return I had such difficulty reading that I was afraid I would never again be able to take up normal intellectual activity."[21]

Except for a minority of Resistance members who were classified *Nacht und Nebel*,[22] prisoners were allowed to communicate with their families and receive packages. They remained bound to their world, if only by a tenuous thread, and this helped them immensely. As Jean Puissant writes: "I no longer felt alone. As if by a long thread, I felt linked to France."[23] This was never the case for the Jews, who were not allowed to correspond or receive packages. The happiness of receiving letters described by Jean Puissant is echoed by Primo Levi's despair at being deprived of them: "The weekly hour when our 'political' comrades received mail from home was for us the saddest, when we felt the whole burden of being different, estranged, cut off from country, indeed from the human race. It was the hour when we felt the tattoo burn like a wound, and the certainty that none of us would return overwhelmed us like an avalanche of mud. In any case, even if we had been allowed to write a letter – to whom would we have addressed it?

The families of the Jews of Europe had been submerged or dispersed or destroyed."[24]

These differences might appear minute. They are, however, an advance signal of the destruction to come. In forbidding the Jews to write, their annihilation was being prepared.

This will to annihilate a people does not emerge clearly from the testimonies of Jews deported from France.[25] For even during this racial persecution, there persisted a model of civic emancipation that arose out of the French revolution and was transmitted by a Communism which, viewing Nazism as a modality of capitalism, did not admit the specificity of Nazi anti-semitism. The Jewish testimonies are indistinguishable from the testimonies of the French deportees as a whole. They are concerned primarily with the concentration camp system in general – which contained common criminals (prostitutes, black marketeers), political prisoners (Communists, Socialists), Christians, Resistance fighters – rather than with the extermination of a people. Paradoxically, moreover, for a Jew to enter the concentration camp system by way of Auschwitz or Majdanek was to gain a chance of survival, for it meant escaping camps that were purely destruction centers such as Belzec, Sobibor, Chelmno or Treblinka. The tattoo on the left arm thus acquired an ambiguous meaning: a sign of the passage to Auschwitz for everyone (non-Jews were also tattooed) and thus of a confrontation with death, it was also a sign of life. Those who were selected upon arrival for the gas chambers were not tattooed.

All the testimonies of the deportees respond to one imperative: to remember, not to forget. But the imperative of memory never exists for itself, does not suffice unto itself. The majority of those who wrote testimonies justify recording their experience in terms of motives that go beyond the presentation of their own suffering. Sometimes remembering is an obligation towards their dead companions; most often it is motivated by the fear of seeing Germany reborn – an eternal, conquering, warlike Germany, which had initiated war three times. Nazism is only a figure for Germanism. The specificity of Nazi ideology, the anti-semitism at its heart, the extermination of the Jews, are not denied, but rather noted in passing, as if in the margin.

The corpus of works written in Yiddish by the Polish survivors, or by those who had emigrated before the war and maintained ties with Poland, is entirely different from the testimony of the French deportees. For the Polish Jews it is no longer a matter, as it was for the thoroughly assimilated French Jews, of a tragic parenthesis in the life of an individual who could then return to his place in the French community as before.

The French immigrants, in fact, fared better than before: those who enlisted at the beginning of the war acquired real possibilities of becoming naturalized French citizens. As after the First World War, they became French in spilling their blood. For the Polish Jews, the Second World War was not a simple war in which it was natural to suffer and die. Behind the veil of battle the *dritn Hurbn* was unfolding, the third Destruction, as the genocide of the Jews is called in Yiddish. For the Polish survivors the problem was not only to bear witness to Nazi barbarity so that it would never repeat itself (the "never again!"), but also to preserve in memory what had been destroyed. It was a total catastrophe: the disappearance of a people, a culture, and a language – Yiddish.

The "I" of the testimony of the French deportees – non-Jew or assimilated Jew – and the "I" of the Yiddish testimony do not have the same significance. In the former, the "I" expresses the voice of an individual faced with a universe of dehumanization and death. In the latter, it is a polyphonic voice testifying to the destruction of a people and expressing a fear of being effaced from history and from the earth. Ringelblum's *Oneg Shabbes* is emblematic of this will to record and memorialize everything, as is the collective compilation, as soon as the war was over, of memory books[26] – collective memorials, paper monuments to the destroyed communities. Immediately following the liberation, councils that were formed in the camps for displaced persons created committees to gather testimonies and establish the chronicle of the massacre. Very quickly they moved from this chronicling activity to a reconstitution of Jewish life before the genocide. The *yizker-biher* constitute an original literary genre encompassing different types of documents and archival materials, as well as narratives about city or village life between the wars and the destruction of the Jewish community.

Curiously enough, the two corpuses – the mass testimonies about the deportation and the memory books – are rooted in a tradition that began with the First World War. The memory books are part of what David Roskies has called "the modern Library of the Catastrophe,"[27] a library that was inaugurated during the Great War, in which many civilians were killed and deported, and which became a civil war, notably in the Ukraine, where Jews were massacred by the tens, even hundreds of thousands. With the First World War, humanity entered the era of mass murder. The Jewish reaction to this destruction of a number of its communities prefigures its response to the genocide: Jews wrote works that were anchored in the Jewish tradition while simultaneously borrowing from non-Jews the genre of historical narration. For the

Yiddish writers and historians – and this is a major difference from
survivors' testimonies written in French – analyze the extermination in
terms of traditional categories: *Hurbn*, the Yiddish word for the destruction of the two Temples, *Akeda*, the sacrifice of Isaac, and *Kiddush
Hashem* or martyrdom (literally, the "Sanctification of the Name").

The testimonies of the deportees from France, whether Jewish or
non-Jewish, do not generally contain categories of analysis taken from
previous literature. The majority of these testimonies affirm their intention to speak the truth, nothing but the truth, without literature, in a
direct confrontation with the real. There is no universal model. Even
when they refer to an earlier work – Dostoyevsky's *Memories of the
House of the Dead*, for example – it is merely as a popular icon.
Such is the case with Dante, mentioned in many testimonies. With the
exception of Primo Levi, who was well-versed in the work of his
compatriot, the reference to Dante's *Inferno* functions as a stereotype.
It demonstrates, however, an intuitive need for a model, for a precedent,
in the real world as well as in literature:

> The great reservoir of evil in the universe: Dante's *Inferno* plays
> in our culture the role of an absolute yet curiously ambiguous
> reference. Even for those who have never read him, and who see
> in Dante and the *Inferno* hardly more than simple names, this
> "hardly more" has the form of a limit: a negative pole defining
> all others, a limit-experience among all other writings, correspond-
> ing also to a mysterious space in a real topology [. . .]
>
> Somewhat as if the *Inferno* had not really been written as a
> book, but rather visited as a country.[28]

Testimony written in Yiddish or other Jewish languages reflects the
imperative to remember imparted by the Jewish tradition. Today we
must ask ourselves about the function of a testimony that is cut off
from this tradition and addressed to the entire world, Jew and non-Jew
alike. What is forgotten in the imperative to remember when it is
cut off from the Jewish tradition? What do we wish to transmit to
schoolchildren when we expose them to the testimonies? The existence
of evil in man? Sensitivity to the suffering of the generations that were
the victims and witnesses of the genocide? A love of democracy, and a
hatred of systems founded on terror or racial discrimination? The fear
of a new annihilation of the Jewish people?

In a few years, the flesh-and-blood witnesses will be gone. All that
will remain are written or recorded traces, images. It is then that our
ability to respond to these questions will take on its full urgency.

Translated by Kathy Aschheim

3

The Library of Jewish Catastrophe

David G. Roskies

In the Jewish experience of the twentieth century, one cycle of violence rapidly gave way to another: the Kishinev pogrom of 1903 that ushered in the century with more deaths (49) than all the previous pogroms combined; the First World War, where untold numbers of civilians were murdered, robbed and deported along the eastern front; the civil war in the Ukraine which claimed anywhere between 60,000 and 250,000 civilian Jewish lives, and the Holocaust. The immediate problem facing the survivors of these catastrophes was not how to mourn but simply how to preserve a record of the unfolding disaster. For it was now possible for the modern nation state to wipe out entire populations and hide the fact. Something that the rabbis could never have anticipated had been added to the landscape of Jewish catastrophe: that the state would control all lines of communication as well as the lives of all its citizens. Whereas once, in Hadrianic times, the rabbis had coined the phrase *bish'at hashemad* to designate a time of religious persecution, one could now speak of a new category, *bish'at hahashmada*, "in times of mass extermination."[1] Whereas *bish'at hashemad* the rabbis had enjoined the masses to perform Kiddush Hashem, to sanctify God's name in acts of martyrdom, now, in time of mass extermination, the latter-day rabbis enjoined the masses to preserve every scrap of evidence; to consider these documents as if they were *sheymes* – sacred fragments that bore the *shem* or name of God.

I wish to illustrate how painstaking and courageous was the making of a new literature of destruction.[2] The first chapter was written in the wake of the Kishinev pogrom, when Jews in London and New York staged mass rallies in support of the victims and to denounce the tsar, and when members of the ad hoc Hebrew Writers' Union of Odessa called on their fellow Jews (in Hebrew) to mobilize Jewish self-defense units throughout Russia:

> Brothers! The blood of our brethren in Kishinev cries out to us!
> Shake off the dust and become men! Stop weeping and pleading,
> stop lifting your hands for salvation to those who hate and exclude
> you! Look to your own hands for rescue! (p. 158)

This group of Hebrew writers dispatched one of their number, 30-year-old poet Hayyim Nahman Bialik, to collect eyewitness accounts from the survivors. While Bialik returned from Kishinev with several note-books worth of survivor testimony that remained unexploited, his pog-rom poem, "In the City of Slaughter," transformed the way that modern Jews perceived catastrophe. Published under the code name "The Oracle at Nemirov," as if it were recounting the seventeenth-century Cossack revolt, Bialik's epic poem dethroned the Jewish God of History and vilified the survivors for their passivity.[3] Forty years later, in the ghettos of Warsaw, Vilna, and Lodz, Bialik's poem would be constantly cited to measure the distance from pogrom to Final Solution.[4] Thus, on the third day of the Great Deportation, which marked the beginning of the end in the Warsaw ghetto, diarist Abraham Lewin would link Kishinev to Warsaw with this famous line from "In the City of Slaughter": "The sun is shining, the acacia is blooming, and the slaughterer is slaughtering."[5]

   Kishinev became an international *cause célèbre* that gave rise to new forms of political action and poetic response. Then came the first total war in history. The war had barely begun when three leading Jewish intellectuals in Warsaw – I. L. Peretz, Jacob Dinezon and S. Ansky – issued this appeal to their fellow Jews:

> Woe to the people whose history is written by strange hands and
> whose own writers have nothing left but to compose songs of
> lament, prayers and dirges after the fact.
>   Therefore, we turn to our people that is now and evermore
> being dragged into the global maelstrom, to all members of our
> people, men and women, young and old, who live and suffer and
> see and hear, with the following appeal:
> BECOME HISTORIANS YOURSELVES! DON'T DEPEND ON
> THE HANDS OF STRANGERS!
> Record, take it down, and collect! (p. 210)

All relevant documents and photographs were to be mailed – COD, if necessary – to the Jewish Ethnographic Society in Petrograd.
   Though it was early in the war, it was already too late, for in July 1915 the tsarist government closed down the entire Jewish-language

press, imposed strict censorship on all news from the war front and banned the use of the Hebrew alphabet in the mails. It was left to Ansky himself to launch a one-man rescue operation to save the lives, livelihoods, letters and legends of Jews victimized by the war.

Ansky's six-volume chronicle of the war was the second major contribution to the modern Library of Jewish Catastrophe. Titled *Khurbm Galitsye* (*The Destruction of Galicia*), its subtitle defined the geographic, temporal and generic scope of this extraordinary document: *The Jewish Catastrophe in Poland, Galicia and Bukovina, from a Diary, 1914–1917*. In marked contrast to the celebrated European war memoirs and semifictional novels that were to appear, from Henri Barbusse's *Le feu* to Erich Maria Remarque's *All Quiet on the Western Front* to Jaroslav Hašek's *The Good Soldier Schweik*, Ansky used his personal experience to document the fate of an entire collective. Having traveled widely before the war through the backwoods of Volhynia and Podolia on a celebrated ethnographic expedition, he possessed intimate knowledge of Jewish folkways and foibles. As a Russian Socialist-Revolutionary and one-time Narodnik (Populist), he had access to the minds and inner reaches of the Russian military command. As a poet, playwright and journalist, his "diary" would be a literary document in its own right.[6]

Ansky redefined the Literature of Destruction both vertically and horizontally, viz. both in relation to what had come before in Jewish culture and what European gentile survivors and chroniclers of the Great War were doing in their respective languages. No more would Jewish writers be satisfied with composing "songs of lament, prayers and dirges after the fact." Henceforth the Literature of Destruction would draw on eyewitness accounts, would render the concrete and sensual particulars of modern violence, would spare neither victim nor victimizer and would seek the causality of war, revolution and pogrom not in heaven but on earth. In contrast to the European and Anglo-American literature of war, however, the modern Jewish texts would continue to present the catastrophe in terms of the ancient archetypes of Akedah, Hurban, Kiddush Hashem.[7] (New to the repertoire as of 1907 was the crucifixion, now reinterpreted as an icon of Jewish suffering.[8]) Thus, the modern Library of Jewish Catastrophe both grew out of Jewish collective memory and fed back into it. To the ancient and medieval songs of lament, prayers, and dirges were added panoramic chronicles written in the first person but encompassing the fate of the collective.

Ansky represents the new voice of collective memory to emerge from the First World War and a new generation of secular intellectuals with

roots in other cultures as well as their own. In the catastrophe that
followed, his mantle was assumed by Russian–Jewish historian Elias
Tcherikower. Like Ansky, Tcherikower was an active player in the very
events that he would chronicle. Tcherikower, recently returned from
America, moved to Kiev at the end of 1918 to assume a central role
in the Jewish National Secretariat. But no sooner had the Ukraine
proclaimed its independence and no sooner had the Jews been granted
national autonomy than civil war erupted, and the Jews were caught
between all the warring factions: the Whites, the Reds, the Poles, the
Ukrainians. Even as Kiev kept changing hands, Tcherikower organized
an archive to collect and research materials on the Ukrainian pogroms.
The terse Yiddish circular issued in May 1919 began with an invocation
of the *Tokheha*, the Mosaic Curses: "Jews!" it read, "a terrible pogrom-
Tokheha has befallen our cities and towns, and the world does not
know; we ourselves know nothing or very little about it. [Knowledge
of] this must not be suppressed!"[9]

Tcherikower and his staff left several important legacies: three out
of a projected seven-volume series of historical monographs on the
pogroms, as well as Rokhl Feigenberg's *Chronicle of a Dead Town*, a
documentary novel of destruction in which the anatomy of a single
pogrom was recreated in excruciating detail. Their most lasting legacy
of all, however, was the archive itself – as model and metaphor. For
the archive was never safe from the hands of those who wished to see
all evidence of this crime destroyed. Copies of every important document
were therefore made in triplicate and two of them deposited elsewhere
for safekeeping. And a good thing too, for when the Soviets succeeded
in annexing the Ukraine, they made the destruction of the archive a
top priority. Tcherikower managed to smuggle the archive out of the
Soviet Union and reassembled it in Berlin as the Ostjüdisches Histor-
isches Archiv. When Hitler came to power, Tcherikower divided the
archive into two, shipped the lion's share to the YIVO Institute in Vilna
and took the rest with him to Paris. And when the Nazis occupied
northern France, Tcherikower fled to the south, abandoning his archive
in Paris where, at the end of 1940, it was rescued by historian and
former French Foreign Legionnaire Zosa Szajkowski who was dropped
behind enemy lines by the US Air Force to aid the French Resistance.
As for the bulk of the archive in Vilna, the Nazis destroyed it in 1942.

The legacy of this archive on the pogroms, then, is nothing less than
a redefinition of the law of *sheymes*: under extreme conditions every
scrap of paper becomes sacred.

The sheer scope of historical catastrophe had made the old methods
of chronicling obsolete. Besides issuing appeals for all primary sources

to be preserved and collected, East European Jewish historians began to generate their own primary sources using the tools of social science. Foremost among them was the analytic questionnaire, first used by I. L. Peretz back in the 1890s when conducting a statistical expedition through the Tomashow region of Poland, then perfected by S. Ansky's ethnographic expedition on the eve of the First World War. But it was Max Weinreich of the YIVO Institute in Vilna who introduced the latest social scientific methods in order to study the long-range effects of trauma, discrimination and poverty on Jewish adolescents. (Weinreich even coined the Yiddish term for "adolescent.") Under YIVO's auspices, Polish Jewish adolescents began submitting their autobiographies – a new genre for the Jews – for Weinreich and others to examine, while an army of amateur *zamlers*, or collectors, worked the ethnographic and linguistic field on YIVO's behalf.[10] While the Polish government was intent upon eliminating the Jews from all walks of life, the *zamlers*, students and scholars associated with YIVO came to see self-study as the route to emancipation.

Most research projects had barely gotten off the ground by the time the German tanks rolled into Poland, but the ideology and methodology behind a modern Jewish archive were now firmly in place. It should therefore come as no surprise that within a month of the German invasion, an underground archive, nicknamed for clandestine purposes Oneg Shabbes (Enjoyment of the Sabbath), was already being established in Warsaw.[11] By design of its founder and organizational genius, 39-year-old Emanuel Ringelblum, the Oneg Shabbes archive was to be a decidedly modern library that drew upon the cumulative experience of contemporary East European Jewry. Ringelblum, a YIVO-affiliated scholar, began by choosing for his staff young men and women with prior training in the study of Jewish life; with reliable political (read: Labor Zionist) credentials and who were already involved in the life of the collective. Here is how Ringelblum described the hiring process:

Of the several dozen full-time staff, the great majority were self-educated intellectuals, mostly from proletarian parties. We deliberately refrained from drawing professional journalists into our work, because we did not want it to be sensationalized. Our aim was that the sequence of events in each town, the experiences of each Jew – and during the current war each Jew is a world unto himself – should be conveyed as simply and faithfully as possible. Every redundant word, every literary gilding or ornamentation grated upon our ears and provoked our anger. Jewish life in

wartime is so full of tragedy that it is unnecessary to embellish it
with one superfluous line. (p. 389)

Thus Ringelblum also broke with the time-honored practice that favored
archetypal embellishment over temporal details, sacred text over historical context. He wanted to let the facts tell their own story. Finally, in
contrast to the rabbinic stategy of preserving only one, timeless version
of events, Ringelblum went out of his way to gain multiple perspectives
– that of young and old, religious and secular – and to cover the entire
range of Jewish experience in wartime. "We tried to have the same events
described by as many people as possible," he wrote. "By comparing the
different accounts, the historian will not find it difficult to reach the
kernel of historical truth, the actual course of an event." To this end,
the ghetto population was divided up by age, gender, class, religious
persuasion and place of origin; detailed questionnaires were drawn up
to cover every conceivable aspect of Jewish life and death; autobiography
contests were announced, and amateur fieldworkers were co-opted to
work alongside the professionals. The YIVO mandate was being carried
out against all odds.[12]

Yet for all its hard-nosed historical positivism, and for all its desire
to leave nothing out, Oneg Shabbes' work of recording, compiling and
synthesizing the data of Jewish destruction had become, as Chaim
Kaplan put it, *melekhet haqodesh*, a sacred task analogous to the
building of the Tabernacle. The turning point came with the Great
Deportation in the summer of 1942 when 275,000 Jews were shipped
off to Treblinka in cattle cars:

> The work of O[neg] S[habbes], along with the whole of our social
> and economic life, was disrupted. Only a very few comrades kept
> pen in hand during those tragic days and continued to write about
> what was happening in Warsaw. But the work was too sacred
> and too deeply cherished in the hearts of the O[neg] S[habbes]
> co-workers; the social function of O[neg] S[habbes] too important
> for the project to be discontinued. We began to reconstruct the
> period of the Deportation and to collect material on the slaughter-
> house of European Jewry – Treblinka. On the basis of reports
> made by those who returned from various camps in the province,
> we tried to form a picture of the experiences of Jews in the
> provincial cities during the time of the deportation. At the moment
> of writing, the work is proceeding full force. If we only get some
> breathing space, we will be able to ensure that no important fact

about Jewish life in wartime shall remain hidden from the world.
(p. 389)

A life of extremity – there was to be no breathing space – made absolute
demands. What's more, those few who survived the Great Deportation
had to become both historians and threnodists, had to supply the facts
as well as their meaning. Despite their scientific objectives, the chroniclers of the Warsaw ghetto were thrown back to the age-old models
of commemoration – to the liturgy. The most dramatic example was
Rokhl Auerbach, a staff member of Oneg Shabbes almost from its
inception and the one, along with Hirsh Wasser, who dug up part of
the archive in 1946.

Like the best of her generation, Rokhl Auerbach was equally at home
in Yiddish, Hebrew and Polish. She had been a close friend of leading
Jewish intellectuals and writers, such as Dvora Fogel and Bruno Schulz,
and a one-time companion of Yiddish poet Itzik Manger. But both in
the ghetto and on the Aryan side of Warsaw she devoted her energies
to documenting the catastrophe – in Polish. Hers was the first published
account of the Treblinka death camp. While Polish, however, was the
language most accessible for historical documentation, Yiddish remained
the language of collective memory. And so she composed, while in
hiding on the Aryan side, and at great personal risk, a Yiddish prose
epic of the ghetto's destruction, titled "Yizkor, 1943."

What unlocked the memory of those weeks of unsurpassed terror
and what probably enabled her to write in the first place was the liturgy.
From a Jewish woman's perspective, this liturgy began with Hannah's
prayer in 1 Samuel and ended in the recitation of *Yizkor* four times a
year in her grandfather's synagogue back home in Galicia. Here is the
penultimate part of her lament:

> Not long ago, I saw a woman in the streetcar, her head thrown
> back, talking to herself. I thought that she was either drunk or
> out of her mind. It turned out that she was a mother who had
> just received the news that her son, who had been rounded up in
> the street, had been shot.
>
> "My child," she stammered, paying no attention to the other
> people in the streetcar, "my son. My beautiful, beloved son."
>
> I too would like to talk to myself like one mad or drunk, the
> way that woman did in the Book of Judges who poured out her
> heart unto the Lord and whom Eli drove from the Temple.[13]
>
> I may neither groan nor weep. I may not draw attention to
> myself in the street.

And I need to groan; I need to weep. Not four times a year. I feel the need to say *Yizkor* four times a day. (p. 464)

Here was a secular Jew who had to play all roles at once because she might turn out to be the sole survivor. Warsaw was Jerusalem and she its witness-as-threnodist, composing a new Book of Lamentations. She was the last living member of her family who must name the names of all the dead. She was the witness-as-eyewitness who must conjure up before it is too late the face of a murdered people – young and old, rich and poor, noble and corrupt. The memorial prayer served Auerbach as a measure of how much had changed; of the losses that *had* no possible measure. In lieu of the ancient and medieval dirges recited at fixed times and within a sacred space – hers was a private lament with no fixed addressee. Indeed, she chose not to publish it until twenty years after it was written. Inasmuch as Auerbach perceived the Holocaust to be the culmination of all catastrophes that came before, her memorial had to encompass all the bereaved mothers, daughters, wives and lovers who perished along with their men.

That unbelieving Jews would transmit the traditional response to catastrophe – in however dialectical a way – is consistent with the collective ethos of East European Jewry. That the techniques of Jewish collective memory were still viable, even as the whole culture of East European Jewry was being destroyed, testifies to the power of that fusion of sacred and secular. The eyewitness chroniclers of modern Jewish catastrophe – Bialik, Ansky, Tcherikower, Ringelblum, Auerbach and others – found new and even subversive means to merge the events they witnessed into an ongoing saga. Despite their loss, or lack of faith in a God of History, they revived the archetypal reading of that history.

The efforts of these activist–historians demonstrates that the will to bear witness had to be cultivated. It did not arise in mystical fashion out of the Holocaust and its aftermath. Oneg Shabbes and other archives like it drew on forty years of organized and politicized activity to make the chronicling of events a tool of Jewish self-emancipation. Questionnaires, contests and collectors made the act of memorializing a grassroots phenomenon. There is likewise no mystery about the amount of documentation that survived. The greater the perceived destruction, the greater the effort to preserve every documentary scrap. That is precisely why these *sheymes* written *bish'at hahashmada* deserve special status.

They also help to refute the commonly held belief that an adequate response to the Holocaust could only emerge one generation after the event. A careful reading of the Oneg Shabbes archive, itself but one part of the vast Library of Jewish Catastrophe written during the Nazi occupation, shows that a new archetype of catastrophe emerged even as the events were unfolding. Whatever area of post-Holocaust consciousness one mines – whether historiography, theology, social psychology, literature, the graphic arts or music – one discovers the core of that new consciousness in the midst of the Nazi terror.

The encylopedic scope, the way this body of writing combines fact and fiction, or modern and traditional forms of Jewish self-expression, makes it comparable to that other great collective document of the diaspora – the Talmud. Ringelblum is to Oneg Shabbes as Rav Ashi was to the Babylonian Talmud. The ghetto and concentration camp archives, moreover, exist like the Talmud in various recensions. Oneg Shabbes is as distinct from the *Lodz Chronicle* as the diverse holdings of the Zonabend collection from Lodz are distinct from the Sutzkever–Kazcerginski collection from Vilna. And the various ghetto archives compiled over a three- four- and even five-year period of occupation are utterly different from *The Scrolls of Auschwitz* written by members of the *Sonderkommando* in between the gassings of whole "transports" in 1943–4.[14]

Like the Talmud, this literature *of* the Holocaust requires a mental curriculum of languages, history, theology, fiction, folklore, and then some, to master. Many of the relevant documents are still undeciphered, and unpublished even in their original languages. As opposed to the writing *on* the Holocaust that will go on being produced for generations to come, these documents composed during the Holocaust are finite and therefore (like the Talmud) constitute a closed canon. Because of their insistence on the knowability of the destruction – that one could, in Ringelblum's words, convey as simply and faithfully as possible, the sequence of events in each town, the experiences of each Jew – they require a separate hermeneutics.

Perhaps they are sacred, too. Sacred in the way that any torah-related text or *seyfer* is hallowed by the faithful – who obey a strict hierarchy of what *seyfer* may be placed on top of another, and if any page is torn out, that *sheyme* is accorded proper burial. But since they arise out of a secular and revolutionary consciousness that taught Jews to make history by knowing their history, their sanction does not come from God. They derive their authority from the dead whose deeds they chronicle; from those who preserved and buried every scrap of evidence so that the Nazis would not vanquish Jewish memory even as they destroyed the Jews of Europe; and from the living who publish, translate and teach these memorial texts.

4

Voices from the Killing Ground

Sara Horowitz

"What madness is it that drives one to list the various kinds of Jews who were destroyed?" Rachel Auerbach asked herself in "Yizkor, 1943," as the Nazis systematically liquidated the Warsaw ghetto. Written on the "Aryan side" of Warsaw, Auerbach's lament represents one piece of a vast project to document Jewish life and its brutal destruction. Today, though distanced by time and experience from the events she describes, we still struggle to fix the facts, to reckon and mourn losses.

The "madness" that drove Auerbach to document the struggles of the Warsaw ghetto also compelled countless others to write and preserve the memory of Jewish life and death. More than forty years later, in *The Drowned and the Saved*, Primo Levi explains that because the dead cannot tell their own story, survivors like himself must "speak in their stead, by proxy" (p. 984). The stories of those who perished, however, reach us not only "by proxy" through the survivor: they also come directly in the words of some of those who perished. From across the years, diaries, chronicles, even vast archives are unearthed on the killing grounds of the Third Reich. Written privately or cooperatively, thousands of pages survived their authors. This contemporary writing offers us perspectives on the Holocaust quite different from those of memoirs and fictions composed later.

Two of the most extensive sets of records, the *Lodz Ghetto Chronicles* and the Warsaw ghetto *Oneg Shabbes*, reflect a collective effort to record and understand the ongoing events. Against the Nazi attempt to relegate atrocity to a blank page of history – what Himmler referred to as the "unwritten and never-to-be-written page of glory" – Auerbach and others filled the pages of diaries and chronicles, lined the margins of holy books, encoded deceptively innocent letters, charting the progress of annihilation. The "unwritten page" of history appears from the vantage point of its victims.

The *Lodz Ghetto Chronicle* is a comprehensive, day-by-day account of events in the second-largest ghetto of Nazi-controlled Europe. It was produced steadily from January 1941 through July 1944. An official organ of the Archives of the Ghetto Eldest – part of the Jewish Ghetto administration – the *Chronicle* represents the joint efforts of approximately one dozen archive workers with unique access to important classified documents, including the internal records of the Jewish officials and their correspondence with German officials. With the exception of several extensive entries – primarily by Oskar Rosenfeld, Jozef Klementynowski, and Bernard Ostrowski – the personalities of individual contributors disappeared into unsigned contributions. In contrast, *Oneg Shabbes* was the code name for a project conceived and organized by Emanuel Ringelblum, working in secret and independently of officials in the Warsaw ghetto, the largest of Nazi-ruled Europe. The traditional "Oneg Shabbes," a Friday night gathering to celebrate the Sabbath with song and study (literally "enjoyment of the Sabbath"), provided a cover for Ringelblum's group. In addition to Ringelblum's *Notes from the Warsaw Ghetto*, which reflects his background as a social historian, *Oneg Shabbes* includes over a hundred volumes of reports, monographs, diaries, essays, and Nazi and ghetto documents. To give *Oneg Shabbes* a "broad social base," Ringelblum solicited contributions from a diverse group of ghetto inhabitants and incorporated private diaries. Unlike the *Chronicle*, individual contributions to *Oneg Shabbes* often bear the names and recognizable viewpoints of their authors. Other diaries from the Warsaw ghetto that have come to us include the cryptic and abbreviated notes of Adam Czerniakow, Ghetto Eldest, the extensive entries of Chaim Kaplan, and the eclectic and enigmatic jotting of Janusz Korczak.

Even the precarious transmission and accessibility of these works tell us of the conditions under which they were produced and preserved. Ringelblum secreted *Oneg Shabbes* records, along with his own notes, in sealed milk cans which he buried. A considerable portion was recovered after the war, some of it rendered illegible by water damage. The Lodz Ghetto Archives, including multiple copies of the *Chronicle*'s approximately one thousand issues, were hidden in batches in different parts of the ghetto. While the Germans discovered and confiscated one large cache, most of the material was retrieved after the war following the directives of the sole archivist who survived.

As to accessibility, for most readers these narratives come in diminished form: translated, edited, abridged. The distance between the object written and the object read marks the decimation and dissolution of Jewish communities by events which the works document. One may travel to archives housing the actual diaries – in New York, Jerusalem, Warsaw, Vilna – but most readers do not. With the exception of a few professional historians and scholars, readers rarely consult these works in their original languages or search out the original manuscripts. Geographic and linguistic limitations – ours, the readers', not theirs, the writers' – determine which writings contribute to and which are excluded from our sense of the Holocaust.

Who we are as readers also determines which texts become available. The Polish–Jewish culture that informs much of the *Oneg Shabbes* archive feels alien to most Americans and Israelis. When the writing of an assimilated, marginal Jew or else of a Bundist does not match the contemporary political and cultural climate, it rarely finds its way into translation. Indeed, most of the *Oneg Shabbes* documents and much of Ringelblum's own writing have never appeared in English. The present *Notes from the Warsaw Ghetto* represents only half of Ringelblum's original *Ksovim fun ghetto*. We select works that affirm our sense of continuity or at least diminish our sense of discontinuity.

The style, idiom, and format of ghetto narratives, moreover, place special interpretive responsibilities on us. Shimon Huberband's difficult handwriting, his idiosyncratic Yiddish, and the physical erosion of his manuscripts make it impossible for us to read him clearly. The series of slim notebooks which form Adam Czerniakow's diary are often so cryptic and spare that we cannot assuredly recognize the events to which he refers. Jan Korczak's writing is even more impressionistic, personal, enigmatic. That we cannot ask Huberband to clarify, Czerniakow to elaborate, or Korczak to explain is a measure of our loss. Yet, however fragmented, these works must stand in for their authors.

They are remnants that – nevertheless – make our understanding more complex and encompassing, providing a counter-voice to Nazi propaganda. They corroborate and amplify other sources, adding to the body of verifiable facts about the Holocaust. The diaries and chronicles describe how the writers live through, one might also say "die" through, this catastrophic time. What falls inside or outside their boundaries attests to a precarious situation, the difficulty of obtaining reliable information, and the nature of the events themselves.

Yet ghetto writing speaks with a strange confidence as it traces the progressive deprivation of property, livelihood, identity – finally of life itself. "The hand does not waver in writing this down. The hand is guided by a brain that reliably preserves all impressions of the eye and the ear" in the *Lodz Chronicle* (p. 363). By sharp contrast, survivors in later years fear that an insurmountable barrier separates those who have experienced the Holocaust from those who have not. A paradox informs survivor writing, much of which insists that readers *must* understand and *will never* understand what happened. Charlotte Delbo, for example, a French poet who survived Auschwitz, struggles against a language which, in her view, falsifies her experience. Her memoirs complain that ordinary words such as *fear, hunger, evil,* and *fatigue* fall short when used to describe extraordinary circumstances. The problem lies not only in the survivor's inability to speak the unspeakable; it lies also in our inability – as non-participants – to imagine the unimaginable.

Ghetto writings simply plunge the reader into the midst of daily life and death. The *Chronicle* discusses the waning supply of potato peels, a valued and expensive food in Lodz, sometimes available only with a doctor's prescription. Oskar Singer provides the "recipe" for a birthday "babka" his wife prepared for him: "Potato peels ground in the meat grinder, with ersatz coffee and a bit of flour – when done it looks like a deformed briquette" (p. 461). The more mundane ghetto staple, "ersatz food made of ersatz coffee, fried in a pan," was a bitter pancake that "epitomizes the bitterness of ghetto life" (p. 463). The *Chronicle* also reflects the endless rumors about food supplies which radically swing the mood of the ghetto, and notes the build-up of excremental filth, of disease, of the death toll. "One lives in filth, one sleeps in filth, and one eats without observing the basic rules of hygiene" (p. 261). There is a plea for a public laundry to save the ghetto from the ravages of disease.

The reality that unfolds in the diaries and chronicles yields a vision of Jewish existence more varied than the one emerging from retrospective survivor accounts. Even in the shadow of destruction, and distorted by suffering, ghetto writing expresses the vitality and diversity of European Jewish life. There are competing ideologies and social differences. Huberband criticizes the raucous behavior of a distinctive group of young Gerer Hasidim, and laments the "moral decline" of Jewish women. But the *Lodz Chronicle* approves of the "ghetto's latest hit song" lampooning the newly arrived "yekes" or German Jews. "The song treats their ups and downs with good humor and tells of the *yekes*, forever hungry and searching for food, and the 'locals' who make fun of them and quite often take advantage of their naivete and unfamiliarity with local customs" (p. 92). Ringelblum notes the ironic situation of both German and Polish Jews in the Warsaw ghetto. The German Jews keep to themselves, and even await a German victory to take them back home (p. 288). Polish Jews often speak Polish rather than Yiddish, partly as a result of "the powerful linguistic assimilation" that preceded the Nazi invasion, and partly as "a psychological protest against the ghetto – *you* have thrown us into a Jewish Ghetto, but *we'll* show you that it is really a Polish street" (p. 289). Such comments, revealing a complicated and divergent sense of cultural and religious identity, give us a sense not only of the destruction, but of what was destroyed.

Rather than offering a heroic, idealized or nostalgic narrative, ghetto accounts describe critically the policy and behavior of colleagues and leaders. Ringelblum reveals how corruption and opportunism eroded the ghetto from within. The spread of typhus, for example, was abetted rather than contained by the sanitation squad which squandered the disinfection chemicals and blackmailed the more affluent "with the threat of ruining their linen, clothes, and the like" (p. 218). Many ghetto sources condemned the disparity between economic classes – a disparity that often determined who would starve.

However, with rare exceptions, the *Chronicle* refrained from criticizing Rumkowski (the Eldest of the Jews) and his administration. Echoing Rumkowski's insistence on law and obedience, the *Chronicle* condemned smugglers and other dealers who disturbed the ghetto order. (Survivor accounts, by contrast, note that the ability to "organize" – as it came to be called in concentration camps – proved useful for survival.) Unlike the Lodz chroniclers, Ringelblum was highly critical of the ghetto leadership. He termed the Warsaw Ghetto Jewish Council a "den of wickedness and hypocrisy" (p. 245) operating on the "Fuehrer principle" (p. 164); Czerniakow, "a weak man" (p. 316) who was "regarded as an idol" (p. 164); Rumkowski, "extraordinarily ambitious and pretty nutty" (p. 47), a man who "considers himself God's anointed" (p. 48).

The *Lodz Chronicle*'s dispassionate tone carries over to its reports of Nazi brutality. As an official organ of the Ghetto Archives – potentially open to outside scrutiny – it rarely mentions Nazis explicitly. In reports of murders, beatings, and humiliations, the passive voice predominates. Ghetto inhabitants "were shot," "were beaten," or "died" during an arrest. According to one entry,

> Abraham Dab . . . was shot in the shoulder at eleven o'clock this morning on Zaierska Street, near the vehicle gate of the Old Market. . . . Witnesses to the incident claim that the wounded man had been speaking with the sentry beforehand. It was obviously not possible to establish the substance of that conversation. (pp. 38–9)

Presumably – although the *Chronicle* does not say so directly – the sentry shot Dab. Why? The sentry's unavailability for questioning and unaccountability for his action epitomizes the legal powerlessness of the ghetto community. The bland tone reflects the chroniclers' idea of appropriateness in "the dry framework of a chronicle" (p. 150). It also signals the precariousness of their situation. The circumlocution which insures the continuance of the *Chronicle* lends a ghostly quality to what is reported, as though a disembodied menace were hanging over the ghetto. It underscores our own need to read between the lines, to look for the unsaid within the said.

By contrast, Ringelblum's work leaves less to the reader's intuition. He repeatedly identifies the agents of atrocity. Whether part of the German administration, the Jewish Council, the Jewish Police, or the office of the Eldest, people bear explicit moral responsibility for their actions. Yet despite this willingness to render moral judgment and attribute blame, Ringelblum's account contains deliberate omissions. He does not mention Warsaw ghetto resistance, choosing to leave an "incomplete" narrative lest his documents fall into the wrong hands. To protect himself and his diary, he sometimes refers to Nazis by code: "They" or "Others" or the Hebrew *lord and masters*, used ironically, to signify Nazi officials. What these writers omit – as much as what they include – helps us to recall something of the conditions under which their writing took place.

Ghetto accounts bear the mark of the Nazis' deliberate program of disinformation and deception. Though the Lodz chroniclers enjoyed privileged access to documentary material their ghetto was sealed off more hermetically than others: radios and outside newspapers were forbidden. The chroniclers relied on their own reasoning to determine what information to trust. Generally they favored "official" information over the "rumors" that disturbed the ghetto. Yet those rumours often turned out to be more accurate than the information coming through official channels. As the chroniclers eventually learned, many rumors came from illegal radios retained at great peril. Transcripts of radio broadcasts circulated, providing alternative communiqués to those officially sanctioned.

Communication from both Jewish and German sources told wildly conflicting stories. German officials continually assured the ghetto dwellers that they had nothing to fear from "resettlements." However, shipments of baggage arriving in Lodz for sorting contained a suspicious array of personal items, identity papers and other vital documents, which hinted at the fate of their "resettled" owners. At the same time, Lodz Jews received postcards from deported relatives, offering a "reassuring sign that these people are alive and able to work" (p. 349). We now know that the Nazis forced their victims to write postcards which would arrive after they had been murdered. Such trickery left the ghetto writers vulnerable to Nazi disinformation. The *Chronicle* cites a Gestapo report about a spacious and comfortable "labor" camp awaiting the arrival of approximately 100,000 "resettled" ghetto Jews. According to the report, the prior occupants – German nationals – had "left the barracks in perfectly decent order, and even left their furniture for the Jews to use. The food supply at the camp is, apparently, exemplary" (p. 145). This place so glowingly described is the deathcamp Chelmno.

Because chroniclers and diarists at once observe and share the circumstances they describe, their writings combine the studied "objectivity" of the historian with the indignation and despair of the victim. In 1944, for example, the *Chronicle* describes the desperation and degeneration wrought by hunger. Ghetto inhabitants poison themselves with rotten, decomposing potato peels "covered with fetid rubbish, excrement, and sweepings . . . undaunted by the obvious stench, the ghastly pestilence. . . . This is not simple hunger, this is the frenzy of degenerate animals. . . . This must not be, this cannot be" (p. 479). The distance which the narrative asserts between observer and observed masks a more fundamental similarity between the "prosperous, ever so well-nourished bourgeois" who watches and the "degenerate animals" who "grub in this abyss of misery." The same conditions and the same murderous fate rule both. In Leyb Goldin's account of hunger in the Warsaw Ghetto, this distance collapses as he documents his own degeneration: "You feel that today you have fallen a step lower. . . . All these people around you, apparently, began like that. You're on your way . . ."

Such conflation of observer and observed suggests the impossible situation of a corpse delivering its own funeral oration. "Death lurks in every chink, every little crack," Ringelblum wrote (p. 272). The increasing morbidity and mortality rates printed regularly in the *Lodz Chronicle* and the unmanageable accumulation of unburied corpses noted there and in other sources portray the ghettos as cemeteries in the making. By 1942, Ringelblum saw the Jews as "*morituri* – sentenced to death" (p. 320) and waiting out that sentence. Increasing ghetto suicides reveal a mounting despair. As the Lodz and Warsaw archivists write obituaries for their colleagues, the distance between writer and subject narrows. This merging of observer into observed, of mourner into mourned, culminates in the truncation of the narratives themselves. Death or deportation overtakes the diarists and chroniclers, as entire ghettos are liquidated. With few exceptions, the end of narration attests to the writer's death. Unlike survivor memoirs, where the few who live speak on behalf of the many who perished, in the diaries and chronicles the dead speak for themselves.

What prompted this writing in the shadow of death? It could not have been easy to find the stamina and resources in such overwhelming circumstances. In addition to the hunger and grief that sapped their energy, ghetto inmates faced shortages of pen, ink, and paper. Frequent electric power cut-offs at the end of the work day made reading difficult. And yet, Ringelblum asserted, "Everyone wrote" (*OS*, p. 386). By his account, what remains today represents only a small sample of the actual diaristic output in the ghettos. At the same time that writers saw themselves transformed into "90 percent your stomach and a little bit you," as Leyb Goldin describes himself (p. 425), they were documenting that metamorphosis. They would write even at peril. Ringelblum observes, "The drive to write down one's memoirs is powerful: Even young people in labor camps do it. The manuscripts are discovered, torn up, and their authors beaten" (p. 133). What was it that fueled and sustained this documentary urge?

On a personal level, the act of writing often provided a means to persevere without giving way to despair. During an onslaught deliberately designed to dehumanize, writing reminded the diarists that they were thinking, autonomous human beings. It allowed the "little bit you" to prevail over the "90 percent . . . stomach," if only provisionally. Ringelblum proclaimed in his notes, "Let it be said that though we have been sentenced to death and know it, we have not lost our human features; our minds are as active as they were before the war" (p. 299).

Many of the Lodz and Warsaw archivists drew from earlier training – historians, economists, writers, researchers. Working in a professional capacity created a fortifying sense of inner continuity. The *Chronicle* attributes the success of a soup kitchen for the intelligentsia to its "special atmosphere" which made it seem "a sort of club where these people who once were something meet for the midday meal." The kitchen's elegant service and intellectual clientele maintain an illusion that things had not radically changed, meager rations notwithstanding (p. 29). Similarly, by providing status, meaningful work, and a proper office, the Lodz Ghetto Archives reminds its compilers of who they had been. The Archives also provides them with work documents, supplemental food and some distance between themselves and those worse off. The man who spoons spilled soup from a filthy staircase and the boys who grub for rancid potatoes stand in sharp relief to the person describing them. Even when this distance collapses, the act of writing reaffirms one's dignity. As Goldin struggles to distinguish hungry humans from scavenging animals, his very ability to narrate – to assert, "we are not animals" – props his humanity.

On a collective level, the chroniclers and diarists regarded their work as active resistance against the Nazi plan. Ringelblum believed that an explicit account of ghetto atrocity, smuggled out and brought to the attention of ordinary people, would put an end to slaughter. Even Germans, he assumed, would be horrified by the extermination of Jews: "if the German populace knew about it, they [the Nazis] would probably not be able to execute the mass murder" (p. 292). Ghetto writers would preserve a tangible record of their suffering for future readers who would otherwise not know what occurred. Naming games would rescue the memory of the victims from oblivion and call the perpetrators to the judgment of history. In addition they would counter falsified documentation produced by the Nazis. Ringelblum and Czerniakow described staged newsreels filmed by the Nazis in the Warsaw ghetto. "Every scene is directed" (Ringelblum, *Notes*, p. 271). Today, those films survive, but so does the testimony that undermines their authenticity. For Ringelblum,

> one thing is clear to all of us . . . we have fulfilled our duty. . . . Nor will our deaths be meaningless, like the deaths of tens of thousands of Jews. We have struck the enemy a hard blow. We have revealed his Satanic plan to annihilate Polish Jewry, a plan he wished to complete in silence. We have run a line through his calculations and have exposed his cards. (pp. 295–6)

Implicit in the chronicles and diaries is the vision of a posterity resembling the writers'. Huberband evokes an unbroken chain of Jewish tradition linking his contemporaries with their spiritual ancestors and descendants. He sees religious Jews engaged in a holy struggle to maintain an ordained way of life, risking their existence to save sacred books and ritual objects, to obtain kosher meat and poultry, to retain traditional garb and beard. In a report on clandestine visits to the *mikveh* (ritual bathhouse), forcibly shut down, he elaborates:

> We imagined vividly the sight of our forefathers in Spain – how they rescued Torah scrolls, how they prayed with a *minyan* in secret cellars, due to fear of the Inquisition. They certainly never imagined that their descendants would find themselves, four hundred years later, in a much worse situation. (p. 201)

Without access to a *mikveh*, "the problem of the purity . . . became as serious as it was in the days of the ancient Roman edicts against Judaism" (p. 195). By identifying with other historic moments – the

Inquisition, the Roman era – Huberband claims a direct link with the ancestral past, and asserts the continuity of Jewish history in adversity. Through analogy, he offers a source of courage and a rationale for optimism: just as Jews (and Judaism) survived previous crises, so too would they survive the Nazi onslaught. The ghetto Jews compete with and perhaps surpass the merit of their fathers. Moreover, just as Huberband respects and retells the actions of his ancestors, so future generations will find his experiences meaningful. In Huberband's formulation, narrative outlasts death. The religious idiom employed here and throughout his writing anticipates that his readership will resemble the people he describes: torah-literate Jews who will understand both the terminology and its significance without explanation.

Other ghetto writers also envision an audience in their own image. They anticipate the outrage of a future reader – outrage based upon shared values and a common idea of civilization. Generally, they remain untroubled by the suspicions which plague survivor reflections – that these values were killed by the Holocaust, or indeed brought it on. The ghetto writers trust that their words will have the ring of authority, will be believed, will be adequate. They portray Nazism as a form of temporary insanity overtaking a specific and bounded historical moment. As time goes on, they show a dawning sense of their own breach with the past. However, they imagine this breach healed with a German defeat, when sanity will reassert itself.

Survivors, on the other hand, fear the rupture is radical and the madness permanent. Although they have outlasted the Nazi program of extermination and can speak in their own voice on their own behalf, they often do so with less assurance than ghetto writers. In the aftermath, they no longer count on a post-war restoration of "sanity." Posterity has already arrived, and it appears inadequate and unwilling to bear the "legacy" of the Holocaust. The next generation, Primo Levi notes, finds the Holocaust "distant, blurred, historical" (p. 198). In Levi's experience, the audience whose empathy and outrage the ghetto writer counted on, instead "judge with facile hindsight, or ... perhaps feel cruelly repelled" (p. 78) by survivor accounts. Like the ghetto writers, Levi insists, "We must be listened to" (p. 199). Unlike them, he is less certain that his voice will be heard; and if heard, understood; and if understood, effective. *The Drowned and the Saved* attests to his despair that "The experience that we survivors of the Nazi Lagers carry within us are extraneous to the new Western generation and become ever more extraneous as the years pass" (p. 198). While most ghetto writers anticipated judgment and justice when "the world" finds out what has been done to them, survivors acknowledge that little happened when the world found out. In fact, the world may have known more than ghetto writers suspected.

The problem lies not only with posterity ("the world") but with survivors themselves – their ability to remember and portray extreme events that defy belief and expression. Levi blames the "fallacious" nature of memory, too fluid or too rigid to be entrusted with the burden of testimony. He describes memory as, on the one hand, "not carved in stone" (p. 19) and, on the other hand, "fixed in a stereotype . . . crystallized, perfected" (p. 24) by either infrequent or too frequent invocation. The unreliability of memory, the inadequacy of representation, and the indifference of posterity problematize the role of the witness and the nature of testimony. Many survivors wonder whether the sense of mission which fueled ghetto writing has been betrayed. Delbo reflects back on her desire to survive Auschwitz in order to bear witness, "to be the voice which gives the final reckoning. . . . And there I am. . . . My voice is lost. Who hears it? Who knows how to hear it?" Ultimately, survivors know from personal experience and from the retrospective of history what ghetto writers could only suspect: the magnitude of the catastrophe. The world, returned to "normal" after the Holocaust, remains abnormal in the eyes of former victims, profoundly altered by remembered events. The continued impact of the past on the present affects the inner life of survivors; their testimony discredits "civilization" and "culture" – the audience to which ghetto writers once appealed – complicitous with their victimization.

Ironically, then, while ghetto writers could not know whether they would survive – and most did not – their work reflects greater confidence than the testimony of survivors. Because they had not yet experienced the worst of the concentrationary universe, they were more certain of their ability to describe all that occurred. In space and time the distance from Lodz to Chelmno, or from Warsaw to Auschwitz, is short but crucial. Former victims, having survived the death camps, the long marches, having learned the ruthlessness and comprehensiveness of the Nazi genocide, remained silent for years after – silenced by loss, by the experience of atrocity, by a rupture which proves irreparable.

The ghettos, of course, were a prelude to the extreme conditions of the deathcamps. Anonymous, decomposing corpses piled up unburied in the cemeteries; death became an everyday sight in the streets. Coupled with starvation and exhaustion, it numbed the ghetto dwellers emotionally, just as it later numbed the *musselmänner* of the camps, those who had given up all human response, all hope. The *Chronicle* wonders about the "populace's strange reaction" to tragedy:

> Is this some sort of numbing of the nerves, and indifference, or a symptom of an illness that manifests itself in atrophied emotional reactions? After losing those nearest to them, people talk constantly about rations, potatoes, soup, etc.! It is beyond comprehension! Why this lack of warmth toward those they loved? (p. 255)

Ringelblum reports "Extraordinary slackening of kinship ties" where family members betray one another to curry favor and gain privilege.

But in the midst of horror there still remained a semblance of the life the ghetto dwellers once knew: schools, synagogues, jobs, commerce, culture. Although deportations and deaths had begun to fragment families, many remained intact. Oskar Singer celebrated his 1944 birthday with wife, children, and sister. Some people still had adequate shelter, garden plots, window boxes in which to cultivate vegetables, and access to toilets. The excremental filth described in the *Chronicle* does not compare with the filth of the camps. There inmates, often forbidden to use latrines, had to use the same bowl for food, chamber pot, washbasin. Despite suffering and privations, ghetto inhabitants could maintain some measure of dignity. In Lodz, workers mounted hunger strikes to protest inadequate or unequal food distribution, brutal and humiliating treatment by foremen, intolerable working conditions. Although placed in a situation designed to humiliate and dehumanize, the ghetto dwellers have names, not numbers. And the Lodz and Warsaw archivists could work steadily on their projects. Amid disease, starvation, and increasing deportations, they could assert some control over themselves and their bodies.

Ghetto narratives, then, look to history and literature for ways to respond to the Nazi onslaught. Though literary and historical models ultimately do not answer these challenges, they temporarily shore up a sense of connection with the past that promises, by analogy, the continuity of Jewish life. The *Chronicle* asserts, "[A] Jew is a fatalist . . . he consoles himself with the knowledge that he has already suffered greater losses and ordeals and somehow survived them too . . . while we wait for a better tomorrow. Such is our mentality!" (p. 244). Some, like Huberband and Chaim Kaplan, evoked historical precedents which make ghetto suffering meaningful. For them martyrdom functioned as a form of spiritual resistance, maintaining the integrity of the murdered, and inspiring those who remain. Others frequently compared their situation

with the medieval Jewish city. Rumkowski viewed Lodz as an autonomous Jewish city state, and himself as its representative and nego-
tiator. Thus, he wanted Lodz to become indispensable to the economic
well-being of the German body politic, whose leaders he saw as reasonable men who would honor their word. "The plan is work, work, and
more work! . . . I will be able to demonstrate, on the basis of irrefutable
statistics, that the Jews in the ghetto constitute a productive element"
(quoted in *Chronicle*, p. 115). Rumkowski's plan, as well as his rhetoric,
implicitly accepts the Nazi definition of Jew as commodity, as a thing
which will not be disposed of so long as it remains useful. For us
Rumkowski's reiterated equation of "work" with "life" and "peace"
has sinister overtones. It resonates with the slogan above the gate at
Auschwitz I: "Arbeit Macht Frei."

In retrospect, the paradigmatic, autonomous Jewish city state which
informed Rumkowski's decisions was irrelevant to the Nazi plan to
eradicate all traces of Jewish life from Europe. His administration succeeded in delaying, but not commuting, that death sentence. As ghetto
conditions worsened and salvation became increasingly unlikely, some
ghetto writers sense the bankruptcy of such a model, and the unprecedented desperation of their state. Then ghetto writing begins to take
on characteristics of survivor accounts. This evolution is seen in Ringelblum's rejection of historical precedents.

In November, 1940, Ringelblum – like Rumkowski – still sees ghetto
life as "returning to the Middle Ages. . . . The Jews created another
world for themselves in the past, living in it forgot the troubles around
them, allowed no one from the outside to come in" (p. 82). This
formulation casts the Jews as active agents and beneficiaries of ghettoiz-
ation. That Jews neither "created" the ghetto, nor prevented the "outside" from coming in, does not figure in Ringelblum's assessment. By
June, 1942, however, Ringelblum rejects such comparisons. "To my
mind . . . all this search for historical analogy is beside the point.
History does *not* repeat itself. Especially now, now that we stand at
the crossroads, witnessing the death pangs of an old world and the
birth pangs of a new. How can our age be compared with any earlier
one?" (p. 300).

As Ringelblum comes to realize, the Nazis deliberately lulled ghetto
dwellers into outmoded strategies of survival. For example, the rich,
ongoing, and varied cultural life in the ghettos took the edge off despair.
This activity, now described as spiritual and cultural resistance, attests
to the tenacity and resilience of the ghetto dwellers under impossible
conditions. Had the Nazi goal been anything short of total annihilation,
this inner strength would have helped them endure. But the Jews were

death-bound whatever they did. According to a November 1941 report from a high-level official in Warsaw, the German Ghetto Administration deliberately permitted the Jews "maximum freedom . . . in so-called cultural activities." The Jews "have theaters, variety shows, coffee houses, etc. The Jews have opened public schools and to a considerable extent developed the trade school system." The report credits the ghetto's administrative and cultural autonomy with producing "a certain reassurance which is necessary if their economic capacity is to be exploited for our purposes." According to the report, "The Jews are waiting for the end of the war and in the meantime conduct themselves quietly. There has been no sign of any resistance to date" (quoted in Czerniakow, p. 402).

The ghetto writers themselves may have cooperated unwittingly with the German scheme. The *Chronicle* distinguishes between the activities of its Archives and the work of a new research department. On orders from German officials, this department created assemblages of dolls and puppets illustrating Eastern European Jewish types and customs for display outside the ghetto. It was obvious that the Germans intended these exhibits to arouse anti-semitism.

> the figurines and groups depicting the traditional life of Eastern [European] Jews were intended for an exhibit which was to serve as a sort of museum of East European Jewry in Litzmannstadt. We stressed that this department had been formed not at the suggestion of the Chairman but by order of the Ghetto Administration and that the ghetto made a point of remaining aloof from this department, not approving of the direction in which it was moving. (p. 348)

Was the work of the Archives also envisioned by the Nazis (who examined its premises and condoned its activities) as an exhibit documenting an exotic but defunct civilization? In retrospect, every form of resistance short of armed combat may have played into Nazi hands.

Discovery of Nazi duplicity came too late for most ghettos to mount a full-scale armed resistance. As this realization hits the ghetto writers, they denounce their leaders' futile policy of appeasement. According to Ringelblum,

> Whomever you talk to, you hear the same cry: The resettlement should never have been permitted. We should have run out into the street, have set fire to everything in sight, have torn down the walls, and escaped to the Other Side. . . . Now we are ashamed

of ourselves, disgraced in our own eyes, and in the eyes of the
world, where our docility earned us nothing. (p. 326)

As ghetto writing shifts into the mode of survivor memoir – for example,
after the destruction of the Warsaw ghetto when Ringelblum writes
retrospectively about the *Oneg Shabbes* activities – the tone becomes
increasingly bitter and cynical.

A tragic irony informs our reading, an irony born not out of the writer's
artistry but out of our own position in history. For we know how the
story ends even before we begin reading. With rare exceptions the ghetto
writers perished along with their communities. While they continued to
hope for the best, we know the worst: the relentlessness of Nazi atrocity
and the thoroughness of genocide. Because we know more than the
ghetto writers, we read them with conflicting emotions. Their hopeful-
ness both soothes and disturbs us. On the one hand, this writing appeals
because it asserts traditional patterns of meaning we may like to retain
– civilization, martyrology, human dignity. On the other hand, through
the testimony of survivors – those who have come close to "the bottom,"
as Levi says – we see those patterns significantly, perhaps irretrievably,
ruptured.

   In fiction, the survivors can play on this tragic irony. The author,
the audience, and sometimes the narrators, know more than the characters who struggle to survive, blind to what history holds in store. Jurek
Becker's novel, *Jacob the Liar*, describes how when the isolated ghetto
thirsts for reliable news Jacob fabricates information obtained from a
non-existent radio. As Jacob feeds his fellow Jews a series of "broadcasts" predicting an imminent Allied victory and liberation, the ghetto
suicide rate drops. Like the ghetto's cultural and spiritual activities,
Jacob's good news keeps everyone hopeful and cooperative. The novel
ends with the ghetto's liquidation. The narrator – sole survivor of
Jacob's transport – learns what the author, a Lodz ghetto survivor, and
the reader have known all along: that fabricated broadcasts prove no
match for history. Neither the hopes of the ghetto nor the regrets of
the author nor the wishes of the reader could alter the ending. The
narrator feels betrayed – less by the Nazis, than by his own eagerness
for Jacob's false comfort.

   Fictional narrative also dramatizes the difficulties that follow on
liberation. Two days after liberation, the narrator of Jorge Semprun's
novel *The Long Voyage* struggles to explain Buchenwald to two nurses,
showing them ovens, torture implements, half-charred bodies. However
shocking, that sight does not help them understand his experience. The

nurses flee in disgust from the "wasted bodies, with their protruding bones, their sunken chests," while the narrator remembers his "comrades . . . [the] dreadful, fraternal dead" (p. 75). In only two days the bodies have changed from being evidence of a functioning deathcamp to a defunct remnant. What the narrator offers as unmediated reality is already a historical artifact. Even at the dark core of Buchenwald, as yet unsanitized, the Holocaust remains inaccessible to those who have not suffered through it.

Ida Fink's short story "A Scrap of Time" probes the "ruins of memory" to imaginatively reconstruct a death she herself escaped. In order to tell the story of her cousin David – a story she neither saw nor experienced – the narrator must leave the confines of direct witness and enter the realm of imagination and hearsay. Using bits of memory, fragments of narrative, "scraps of time," she traces in her mind the events of David's last day. She must imagine what she can never know – David's last moments, feelings, posture, before he falls victim to mass slaughter. Her willingness to imagine compensates for her lack of direct experience, and the narrator produces a good-enough testimony – one that rescues David's memory from oblivion. By implication, Fink's story addresses our position as readers of Holocaust testimony. The act of reading places us in equivalency to the survivor who narrates. As she is to David, so we are to her: distanced experientially from what we attempt to understand, but willing to engage intellectually, emotionally, imaginatively. Particularly for those who come after, or who were elsewhere, such an engagement constitutes the only means to recover Holocaust experience.

In a private manuscript prepared for his family, a survivor of Mengele's medical "experiments" at Auschwitz warns,

> Be very, very careful, for we are prone to forgetting fast. That which our ancestors suffered in Egypt today has become only a few minutes' hasty reading of the Hagada in anticipation that the matzos dumplings are to appear on the table as soon as possible.

Rather than transmitting meaning, ritual retelling can empty the story of meaning. Many survivors share this fear that the Holocaust will suffer in the retelling, that it will come to future readers as a pre-packaged "event," that the public has grown tired of the Holocaust, and that nothing will change. In the seder ceremony, "remembering" ancestral suffering may turn into a kind of forgetting.

The Haggadah, however, contains not only the story of the Israelites' deliverance from oppression but the story of descendants who transmit the story. So absorbed are they in the telling that they continue until the call for morning prayers. Contemporary participants in the seder also take their place in an unbroken (if diminished) chain of transmission. Can they – as the Haggadah asks – see themselves as though personally liberated from Egypt? What will help them to tell and absorb stories about the Holocaust in a manner that will defeat forgetfulness? The written shards of ghetto life do not fix the Holocaust as an event in some enigmatic and distant past but see it as a series of daily incidents experienced by those whose writing survived the destruction, and those whose writing was destroyed, and those who did not write at all. In combination with survivor testimony, they revive a painful and terrible past in a way that neither domesticates nor falsifies.

5

Jean Améry as Witness

Alvin Rosenfeld

Within the context of Holocaust literature the question "What does it mean to write?" is often synonymous with "What does it mean to bear witness?" I wish to explore that question as it relates to both writers and readers of testimonial literature. Before doing so it is important to note that there is a historical context to these concerns, which needs to be acknowledged.

In the ghettos and death camps of Nazi-occupied Europe, writing in the conventional sense of modern authorial composition was hardly possible, and yet a great deal of writing was done. It served several functions, not the least of which was the felt sense of defying the aggressor by recording the nature and extent of his crimes. As remembrancers the Jewish scribes were as determined as their enemies. "It is difficult to write," noted Chaim Kaplan in the important diary he kept in the Warsaw ghetto, "but I consider it an obligation and am determined to fulfill it with my last ounce of energy. I will write a scroll of agony in order to remember the past in the future."[1] The detailed documentation of the degradation and mass murder of the Jews then in progress was recorded in diaries, journals, and other forms of chronicle and reflection. Most writers knew they probably would not survive the war, but neither would they be merely silent victims. We tend to read their writings today as acts of spiritual resistance, although we are painfully aware that in the end such resistance had no chance against the power of the German forces. The fact that it was destined to be terminal, and a defeated heroism, gives this testimonial literature tragic and elegiac qualities that make for almost unbearable reading. Why, then, do we read these books?

A reasonable answer is that the knowledge gained from the literature of the victims is essential for anyone who wishes to learn about the fate of the Jews under Hitler. But beyond this consideration there is

another, more demanding one, which helps to define the ethical character
of this literature and its particular moral claims on anyone who truly
encounters it *as* a literature of testimony. Books like *The Warsaw Diary
of Chaim A. Kaplan*, Emanuel Ringelblum's *Notes from the Warsaw
Ghetto*, or *The Chronicles of the Lodz Ghetto* are the invaluable but
incomplete eyewitness accounts to a history that had at its defining
center a crime like no other. Apart from its genocidal aims, what
distinguished the Nazi crime against the Jews was the intent of the
criminals to leave behind no witnesses and, hence, no record at all. The
Holocaust was to be a total, silent deed – in the words of one of its key
perpetrators, "an unwritten and never-to-be-written page of glory."[2]
The fact that Himmler's will in this regard has not prevailed is owing
in the first place to the determination of his victims, who found the
courage and the means to persist against him as recording witnesses.
Today, it is owing to the will of readers, who serve as witnesses for
the witnesses. Such readers are aware of the terrifying end of the stories
these writers were unable to finish; and, by being so aware, they have
a crucial role to play in the literature of testimony. They "complete"
the historical and testimonial record by a complementary act that helps
to fulfill Chaim Kaplan's aim to "remember the past in the future."

In addition to the writings of those who perished in the ghettos and
camps, there exists a large body of literature from those who managed
to survive the Nazi terror. For these authors too writing serves as
an act of testimony, although further motives are often felt. Survivor
testimony, oral or written, is a means of retrieval, reflection, description,
and commemoration. It is intended as an act of catharsis, an attempt
to win free from the sufferings of the past, or as an act of protest,
warning, rebellion, and accusation. In all cases, survivor testimony is
offered as a personal contribution to a massive, still accumulating record
of atrocity. At once historical and reflective, it suggests that civilization
is far more tenuous than was heretofore imagined: civilization has
collapsed once, and could collapse again, possibly even in the near future.
Readers are exhorted to take heed, to guard against the possibilities of
a repetition, to learn and apply what are called the "lessons of the
Holocaust" and to do so "now, before it is too late."

There are also books of testimony that speak in other terms – books
that solicit our attention yet acknowledge that the "world" would prefer
to forget rather than remember. They express the fear that it may
already be too late for "lessons" from the past to be learned and applied.
Such testimony is graver and more ominous in what it has to tell us,
for it holds out little consolation for the future; understandably enough,
readers may be inclined to resist its dark and seemingly futile visions.

I wish to argue, however, that it is precisely this more disconsolate literature that conveys some of the most profound truths of those who managed to survive – truths that underline the all-too-common fact that survivors can continue to be victims and that this particular victimization is related, in part, to the sense that their memories carry so little weight with readers. For all the urgency of their testimony, such writers may come to feel that they have failed to find a truly responsive audience and, hence, have failed as agents of memory and moral conscience. Such a realization, when it occurs, can be perilous, as it was in the case of Jean Améry, a survivor–writer of singular importance, to whom I now turn.

Jean Améry is best known for his first book, available since 1980 as *At the Mind's Limits: contemplations by a survivor on Auschwitz and its realities.*[3] The original German edition appeared in 1966 when Améry was already 54. The book was reissued with a new author's preface in 1977, one year before Améry's death. *At the Mind's Limits* stands today as one of the most passionate and crucial works of reflection by a Holocaust survivor.

The author, of mixed Jewish and Catholic parentage, was an Austrian, born as Hans Maier in 1912. The racial laws imposed soon after Hitler assumed power shocked him into full awareness of the threat against the Jews; in 1938 he fled his native country and settled in Belgium. Arrested by the Belgians in 1940 as a German alien, and again by the Gestapo in 1943 as a member of the anti-Nazi resistance, he spent the war years in prisons and concentration camps, including Auschwitz, Buchenwald, and Bergen–Belsen. After liberation from Belsen, he returned to Belgium in 1945, lived in Brussels, and began a career as a journalist and political critic using the name Jean Améry. Although residing in a predominantly French-speaking milieu, Améry chose to remain a German-language writer-in-exile. His favored literary form was the essay; his constant subject, the sufferings of the victims of the Third Reich; his most revealing source of knowledge for the condition of victimization, himself.

At the Mind's Limits, a slim, powerful book of only five essays, describes Améry's experiences in a way that is intensely personal and yet, at the same time, transcends the personal in order to speak about the trauma of Holocaust victims in general. A militant exponent of the value of individual dignity, Améry knew in his flesh the extreme difficulty of maintaining any semblance of dignity in a system such as that of German National Socialism. The title essay, "At the Mind's Limits," reveals how little remained to the prisoner who was deprived of the

effective use of his intellect. Améry's preoccupation here is with the
situation of the intellectual in the camps and specifically with his chances
for survival. He argues that de-intellectualization was an essential part
of the Nazi program, for when the mind proved itself to be incompetent,
individuals disposed to rational behavior were abruptly cut off from
the most vital centers of their self and so rendered helpless. "Beauty:
that was an illusion. Knowledge: that turned out to be a game with
ideas." Spiritually disarmed and intellectually disoriented, the intellectual
faced death defenselessly.

"Torture," the second essay, makes graphically clear the extent of
human loss when one is brutally deprived of the autonomy of one's
body. It is Améry's firm conviction that "torture was not an accidental
quality of the Third Reich, but its essence," indeed, "its apotheosis."
Torture defines the basically depraved and inherently destructive character of Nazism, an ideology "that expressly established . . . the rule of
the antiman . . . as a principle." Other regimes have been contaminated
by the same nihilistic principle, but German National Socialism gave it
a kind of purity. "The Nazis tortured, as did others, because by means
of torture they wanted to obtain information important for national
policy. But in addition, they tortured with the good conscience of
depravity . . .: they tortured because they were torturers." Himself the
victim of torture, Améry offers phenomenological reflections on the
extremity of his own experience that find no parallel in the literature
on this subject.

"How much home does a person need?" changes the focus from
torture to the pain of exile and alienation. The forlorn sense of being
deprived of one's place of origin is accompanied by a concomitant loss
of self-assurance. "I was no longer an I," Améry acknowledges, "and
I did not live within a We." Like the experience of torture, that of exile
is permanently damaging: the wound is not one "that will scar over
with the ticking of time" but is more akin to "an insidious disease that
grows worse with the years."

All three essays are vivid accounts of dispossession and loss of
humanity. The point is made emphatically: such loss is not only radical,
it is irrevocable. Whatever future one might envision for oneself will
not include the restoration of those essential elements of the self that
were taken away years before. Trust in the world, Améry insists, once
removed is never regained.

These are harsh conclusions, yet Améry sets them forth with clarity
and conviction. The question that must come to the fore is, how can
one live with such knowledge? "Resentments," the fourth essay, conveys
the emotional charge behind the author's motivations for writing about

such unbearable experience. He has a strong, understandable grievance against all who collaborated in reducing him to a despised Jew and a deprived, tortured being; and he insists on his right to protest continually. The bold conclusions in the book's final essay, "On the necessity and impossibility of being a Jew," articulate a defiant identity: "a vehemently protesting Jew," Améry reattained the dignity that was denied him as a Nazi victim, when to be Jewish was to be "a dead man on leave, someone to be murdered." By publicly proclaiming himself a Jew, albeit "without positive determinants, [a] Catastrophe Jew," he claims for himself the legitimacy and dignity of one who will not be denied the right to live on his own terms.

In the preface to the first edition of *At the Mind's Limits* Améry noted that he broke twenty years of silence to offer "a phenomenological description of the existence of the victim." He was not writing for his "comrades in fate," for "they know what it is all about," but for "the Germans, who in their overwhelming majority do not, or no longer, feel affected by the darkest and at the same time most characteristic deeds of the Third Reich." He concluded by expressing the idealistic hope that his writings might reach "all those who wish to live together as fellow human beings." But in 1977, when Améry reissued his book, any sign of hope for a better future is gone. His new preface begins on a despondent note and moves toward despair: "Between the time this book was written and today, more than thirteen years have passed. They were not good years. ... Sometimes it seems as though Hitler has gained a posthumous triumph. ... Given this, what is the good of my attempt to reflect on the *conditio inhumana* of the Third Reich? Isn't it all outdated?"

A number of gruesome events had taken place in world politics since his book first appeared; but what troubled Améry most was Germany itself: "When I set about writing, and finished, there was no antisemitism in Germany, or more correctly: where it did exist, it did not dare to show itself. ... The tide has turned. Again an old–new antisemitism impudently raises its disgusting head, without arousing indignation." The danger this time lies on the left and especially within segments of the politically active young. Améry worried that "The young people of the Left," entrapped within "ill-considered ideologies, ... do not slip over unawares to those who are their enemies." The slippage, in fact, was already evident at "anti-Zionist" rallies in German cities, where a familiar street cry was once again being heard: "'Death to the Jewish people.'" These brutal words brought Améry to declare himself in the most unequivocal terms: "The political as well as Jewish Nazi

victim, which I was and am, cannot be silent when under the banner
of anti-Zionism the old, wretched anti-semitism ventures forth. The
impossibility of being a Jew becomes the necessity to be one, and that
means: a vehemently protesting Jew. Let this book, then, . . . be an
appeal to German youth for introspection." Améry, though appalled
that he had to stand up against those whom he had always regarded
as his friends and political allies, was not reluctant to assert himself
forcefully. He had suffered too much to remain quiet in the face of the
possibility of a repetition: "What happened, happened. But *that* it
happened cannot be so easily accepted. I rebel: against my past, against
history, and against a present that places the incomprehensible in the
cold storage of history and thus falsifies it in a revolting way."

This falsification troubled Améry, as did other tendencies in the
political life of Germany just before his death. The 1977 preface to *At
the Mind's Limits* discounts the plausibility of any of the existing
historiographical explanations of Nazism and describes the Nazi regime
as a unique evil, "single and irreducible in its total inner logic and
accursed rationality." He finds that nothing but obfuscation is gained
by relativizing Nazism as part of a general theory of "fascism" or
twentieth-century political barbarism. "It did not happen in a developing
country, nor as the direct continuation of a tyrannical regime, . . . nor
in the bloody struggle of a revolution fearing for its existence. . . . It
happened in Germany." One can try to describe the particular terror
of German National Socialism, but one cannot satisfactorily explain it.
Most of all, Améry argued, one must not attempt to explain it away
through the application of ready-at-hand categories of conventional
enlightenment thinking:

> Clarification would amount to disposal, settlement of the case,
> which can then be placed in the files of history. My book is meant
> to aid in preventing precisely this. For nothing is resolved, no
> conflict is settled, no memory has become a mere memory. . . .
> Nothing has healed, and what was perhaps on the point of healing
> in 1964 is [in 1977] bursting open again as an infected wound.

Acutely aware that the poison seeping from such a wound had the
potential to spread, Améry reissued his book at a time in his life, it is
now clear, when an accumulation of outward events and inner troubles
weighed heavily upon him.[4] Absent from the 1977 preface is any appeal
to "all those who wish to live together as fellow human beings." He
now manifests no particular confidence that he will be heard where his
words most needed to be heard. "I can do no more than give testimony."

He had reached a crucial limit of his own. In October 1978, during a visit to his native Austria, Améry took his own life.

Améry never claimed that his time in Auschwitz and the other camps had made him a better man, but he did believe that his experiences equipped him "to recognize reality." The question therefore arises: What recognition, in the latter years of his life, may have led to his suicide? Such a question is unlikely to yield a definitive answer. Yet a sympathetic reading of his book can reveal the source of the author's bitter feelings as a former victim of the Third Reich. Indeed, "former victim" is almost an oxymoron, for Améry was not able to look upon his victimization as a thing of the past. It was ongoing: he who was tortured remains tortured. Only for the torturers and the nation that produced them was the suffering largely a thing of the past. This radical disjunction between the victim's continuing ordeal and the abnegation of responsibility for it on the part of the victimizer was something that Améry could not abide in silence. It impelled him to write, and shows up with particular force in "Resentments," the essay that most directly illuminates his sense of himself as writer and witness.

The essay begins on a mock-pastoral note, as Améry recounts his summertime journeys through an idyllic, unnamed country. The landscape is attractive, the cities are clean and well run, the citizens tolerant and seemingly urbane. Yet he feels uneasy in this lovely land, and tells us why: "I belong to that fortunately slowly disappearing species of those who . . . are called the victims of Nazism." Although he has still not named the country by name, he admits that he bears a strong retrospective grudge against it that fills him with resentments he does not entirely understand. Thus, he begs the reader's patience (especially that of the German reader, since he is writing in German) as he analyzes his resentments.

The first thing he notes is that some condemn him for continuing to bear his grudge. They resent his resentments, feel victimized by his reminder that he was a victim. In Germany, moreover, now explicitly called by its proper name, he was *their* victim. Apparently this is too much for most of them to face, so they decide they are victims too – "absolute victims" of a cruel war that caused them displacement, hunger, homelessness, and the dismemberment of their country. Yet unlike Améry and others who insist on retaining their status as victims, the Germans manifest a will to "overcome" the misfortunes they suffered as a result of the Third Reich and get on with their lives. As the author is told by a German businessman, "The German people bear no grudge against the Jewish people" and "no longer have any hard feelings toward

the resistance fighters and Jews." Moreover, they have paid the latter
generously through a magnanimous policy of reparations. Why, then,
those grudges and the demand for public atonement? After all, the allied
powers that had fought against Germany in the war had long ago
accepted her back into "the community of nations." As a result, the
country rapidly threw off its pariah status and was busy rebuilding
itself into a modern, democratic state.

But Améry sees himself bound more to the past and its ruins than
to the future and its promises. Whereas the criminals have now entered
a new era, largely free of the taint of their crime, he, its victim, remains
tied to his resentments. Why hang on to these? Because, he answers,
they keep alive the moral truth of the conflict between him and his
torturers, a truth that he insists on retaining even if most of them have
never been moved to acknowledge its existence in the first place: "The
crimes of National Socialism had no moral quality for the doer. . . .
But my resentments are there in order that the crime become a moral
reality for the criminal, in order that he be swept into the truth of his
atrocity."

Nowhere in his writings does Améry idealize suffering, but he does
emphasize that his victimage has an emphatic moral value and that the
only way to understand it was to keep alive its memory in terms that
stress its scandalous character: "The moral person demands annulment
of time – in the particular case under question, by nailing the criminal
to his deed. Thereby, . . . the latter can join his victim as a fellow
human being." Given this view, which originated in a firmly held ethic
of memory, any easy forgiving and forgetting was out of the question.
Release from the iniquities of the past could be had, if at all, only by
recognizing the gross moral trespass against the victims, but since those
who had caused so much suffering were unwilling or unable to acknowledge it on their own, they might be prodded to do so by the surviving
witnesses to their crimes. As Améry understood the continuing conflict
between the German people and those who had suffered so grievously
under them during the Third Reich, a resolution would only be possible
if people like himself, acting on their resentments, continued to protest
the injustices of the past. Aroused by such protest, the German people
might finally awaken to "the fact that they cannot allow a piece of
their national history to be neutralized by time, but must integrate it":

> [Germany] would then, as I sometimes hope, learn to comprehend
> its past acquiescence in the Third Reich as the total negation not
> only of the world that it plagued with war and death but also of
> its own better origins; it would no longer repress or hush up the

twelve years that for us others really were a thousand, but claim them as ... its own negative possession. ... Two groups of people, the overpowered and those who overpowered them, would be joined in the desire that time be turned back and, with it, that history become moral. If this demand were raised by the German people ... it would have tremendous weight.

This passage represents a high point of hope in Améry's book, as it does in the literature of testimony at large. Améry was nothing if not a realist, however, and he recognized that if such an inner German cleansing were ever to take place, it could only be brought about by the Germans themselves: "This writer is not a German, and it is not for him to give advice to this people." But were there figures within the public life of the nation capable of directing a desire for moral reversal on such a scale? Améry knew individual Germans of conscience who suffered inwardly and tried to make amends, but the struggle that he envisioned – a massive, unprecedented "negation of the negation" – had to occur on the national level if it were to be successful. He was calling for a radical turn of heart, nothing less than "the spiritual reduction ... by the German people ... of everything that was carried out in those twelve years." Did he believe the Germans were capable of such a redeeming act?

"Nothing of the sort will happen," he wrote. As he elaborates this negative view, his essay turns from the visionary to the sardonic and reveals in the most painful way that he expected nothing from the Germans in the future:

But what an extravagant daydream I have abandoned myself to! ... All recognizable signs suggest that natural time will reject the moral demands of our resentment and finally extinguish them. The great revolution? Germany will not make it good, and our rancor will have been for nothing.

What Améry feared most but expected to occur eventually was a normalization of Nazism, a process of historical revision that would have the inevitable effect of blurring and ultimately denying the reality of his own experience. Indeed, a self-chosen death spared him from having to witness further signs that the revisionism he foresaw was gathering momentum: the grotesque spectacle at the Bitburg military cemetery in the spring of 1985, some of the arguments that accompanied the German *Historikerstreit*, the popular appeal of the romance of German "everyday" life during the years of the Third Reich, as portrayed in the film

Heimat, the sudden and ominous appearance of neo-Nazis in the streets of German cities, and similar events that continue to punctuate the political culture of Germany. But he already had seen enough in his lifetime to reach some sorrowful conclusions about what was taking place in Germany. "I bear my grudge for reasons of personal salvation," he wrote. As for its effect on the others: "Our resentments . . . have little or no chance at all to make the evil work of the overwhelmers bitter for them." Acknowledging this painful gap between himself and his potential audience in Germany, and finding no way to bridge it, Améry gave up. "Resentments" ends on a grim and mordant note: "We victims must finish with our retroactive rancor, in the sense that the KZ argot once gave to the word 'finish'; it means as much as 'to kill.' Soon we must and will be finished. Until that time has come, we request of those whose peace is disturbed by our grudge that they be patient."

This is writing that seems to testify to the futility of testimony itself. One admires Améry for the clarity and moral stringency of his thinking, and one recognizes, as he did, that his complaint was not widely shared where it most needed to be. That would not keep him from declaring himself, to be sure, for he believed that what he had to say was not only for his own good "but also for the good of the German people." He responded with evident disappointment, moreover, to the way his German readers used his testimony: "What dehumanized me has become a commodity, which I offer for sale." Despite the caustic nature of this remark, Améry continued to write for German audiences.

He kept writing because he wanted to understand the nature of his own extreme experience and because he was convinced others should learn of it. In his lifetime he was more successful with the first aim than the second, but there is no reason to confine his ultimate importance to his own epoch. His mature career as an author was brief – a mere 12 years – but it produced work whose significance should be recognized well into the future.[5] There is, it is true, a price to be paid for reading a book like *At the Mind's Limits*, which projects an order of experience that is distressing. But there is a far higher price to be paid by foregoing an author such as Jean Améry, and that is the diminution of historical and moral consciousness itself. Améry was right in his insistence that we recognize reality for what it is, by which he meant not only that we acknowledge that "what happened, happened" but also that we refuse to assent to the acceptability of what happened. Normalization of the Third Reich, he feared, might be taken as a prelude to its acceptance. Such a development, the early signs of which he already saw, had to be opposed. His rebellion against the past, therefore, was fundamentally a moral rebellion – in his own terms, the requirement that reality include a basic component of justice. Anything short of that he regarded as unreasonable and cause for vigorous protest. Hence, his rancor and resentment were not sustained for their own sake but rather employed in the service of a large and pressing demand: the insistence that "reality is reasonable only so long as it is moral."[6] In Améry's case, indeed, reality was *bearable* only as long as it was moral. It did not finally matter, therefore, whether his protest drew a large number of followers, for protest was for him a necessary means of bearing witness, the form testimony took when most impassioned. And testimony — as he offered it: credible, corrective words about an otherwise incredible, unacceptable order of experience — was not to be denied no matter what its chances of gaining an immediate effect:

> It is certainly true that moral indignation cannot hold its ground against the silently erosive and transformative effects of time. It is hopeless, even if not entirely unjustified, to demand that National Socialism be felt as an outrage with the same emotional intensity as in the years immediately following the Second World War. No doubt there exists something like historical entropy: the historical "heat gradient" disappears; the result is a balance with no order. But in viewing historical processes we should not foster this entropy; on the contrary, we should resist it with all our power.[7]

Améry wrote in opposition to the old evil and in protest against any future attempts to rehabilitate it. The moral stance he took up as a witness against the crimes of the Third Reich was uncompromising. In the aftermath of his death, his success depends entirely on the disposition of his readers toward the important body of testimony and reflection that he left us.

6

Remembering Survival

Lawrence L. Langer

In an essay on "The condition we call exile," Nobel Prize winner Joseph Brodsky speaks of exiled writers as "embodiments of the disheartening idea that a freed man is not a free man, that liberation is just the means of attaining freedom and is not synonymous with it."[1] Unintentionally, he offers us a fresh if disquieting vista for imagining the condition of the Holocaust survivor, who as a "freed man" or woman enters into a different kind of exile that often promises less chance for freedom than the situation Brodsky speaks of. For many Holocaust survivors, liberation meant a new and unexpected (hence unprepared for) form of imprisonment. Survival was synonymous with the recognition of *deprival*. The beckoning future challenging the talent and imagination of the exiled writer was not so readily available to the "freed" victim of the Holocaust.

Words like "survival" and "liberation," with their root meanings of life and freedom, entice us into a kind of verbal enchantment that too easily dispels the miasma of the deathcamp experiences and their residual malodors. As we shall see, in their videotaped testimonies witnesses pay equal homage to what they have "died through," or what has died in and through them, and what they have lived through, though a term like "surmortal" to counter-balance survival would only prove perplexing to the curious reader.

Primo Levi, in his posthumous volume *The Drowned and the Saved*, addresses this issue precisely:

> In the majority of cases, the hour of liberation was neither joyful nor lighthearted. For most it occurred against a tragic background of destruction, slaughter, and suffering. Just as they felt they were again becoming men, that is, responsible, the sorrows of men

returned: the sorrow of the dispersed or lost family; the universal
suffering all around; their own exhaustion, which seemed definitive, past cure; the problems of a life to begin all over again amid
the rubble, often alone. Not "pleasure the son of misery," but
misery the son of misery. Leaving pain behind was delight for
only a few fortunate beings, or only for a few instants, or for very
simple souls; almost always it coincided with a phase of anguish.[2]

That "phase of anguish" appears so often as a continuing concern in
the testimony of witnesses that we would be irresponsible to avoid or
ignore it. Levi exposes part of the problem when he declares that "One
can think that one is suffering at facing the future and instead be
suffering because of one's past."[3] A far more complex variation on this
theme, surfacing repeatedly in the testimonies of witnesses, is the notion
that one can think that one is *rejoicing* at facing the future and instead
be suffering because of one's past. If survivor testimony were modernist
fiction instead of remembered ordeals, we might call the stubborn
determination to find joy at the end of the story a kind of narrative
lure, a subtle attempt to deflect the reader's imagination toward desirable
ends despite the disagreeable content of the narrative itself.

Something of this sort does indeed become part of our experience of
the videotaped survivor testimony, where chronology vies for our attention with what I call frozen moments of anguish. The process roughly
duplicates the movement of the narrative, which tells two stories simultaneously, one of life and one of death. Since the witness has survived,
we can hardly describe his or her testimony as the triumph of despair;
nevertheless, we encounter so often on the screen faces of men and
women who, because of the content of their narratives, remain in despair
of triumphing, that we are left groping for an adequate descriptive
language. One of the most remarkable features of these testimonies is
the bifocal vision they project, as the past invades the present and casts
a long and permanent shadow over the future, obscuring traditional
vocabulary and inviting us to outline a more complex vision of survival.

The paradox is neatly expressed in a pair of couplets from the
Buchenwaldlied or Buchenwald song that prisoners sang each morning
as they marched out to work. Midway through the song appear the
lines: "Ach Buchenwald ich kann dich nicht vergessen / Weil du mein
Schicksal bist" (O Buchenwald, I can't forget you, because you are my
destiny), while the song ends with the lines: "Wir wollen trotzdem 'ja'
zum Leben sagen / Denn einmal kommt der Tag da sind wir frei"
(Nonetheless we wish to say 'yes' to life, because a day will come when
we'll be free). Between the anxieties (die Sorgen) that they bear in their

hearts, and the freedom they yearn for, exists a tension that may be eased by the hopeful sequence of the "lyrics," but not so easily dismissed in the subsequent testimony about it. The witness who actually sings this song during his interview tries to explain what a "destiny" like Buchenwald has meant for him: a loss of continuity with the future. Instead of linking episodes into a unified continuum, his encounter with memory makes him feel like a creature removed from its cocoon too soon. We might call it the enigma of truncated growth, an abortion to time. "So there's no tomorrow, really," observes the interviewer. "No, there isn't any," replies the witness. "If you think there is, you're mistaken."[4]

Memory's encounters with a disintegrating time is one of many seminal themes of these testimonies. Buchenwald as one's destiny implies a loss of control of one's fate. Peter C., another witness, insists that most of his major post-war decisions lead back to his camp experiences. "It seems to me," he says, "that my life was always decided by other people, while I was in railroad cars, and I'm really living on borrowed time." The metaphor is both a cliché and a revelation: looking back, he sees no continuity in his experience from then to now, but a fixed frame that has always existed around his post-war life, though he claims he only became aware of that in later years. No trace of cliché, however, appears in his explanation that "It's very difficult to strike a balance between consciously remembering these things and being possessed by them."[5] Ordinarily, we would expect the process of remembering, through a recovery of images and episodes, to animate the past. But survivors who re-encounter Holocaust reality through testimony often discover, as Peter C. tries to explain, a disjunction between "consciously remembering" in order to reveal to us what they already know, and the sense of "being possessed" by moments or events that have never left them. This forces us to alter our traditional notion of testimony, which presumes a chronology or sequence, the activity of retreating in time and space to a period and place preceding and different from the present.

Two clocks dominate the landscape of Holocaust testimonies, a time clock (ticking from "then" to "now") and a space clock (ticking from "there" to "here"). They seek to sensitize our imaginations to twin currents of remembered experience. One flows persistently from source to mouth, or in more familiar historical terms, from past to present. The other meanders, coils back on itself, contains rocks and rapids, and requires strenuous effort to follow its painful turns, that disturb the mind's expectation of tranquility. To vary the analogy, and translate it into literary terms: the survivor narrative includes a story and a plot.

The "story" is the chronological account of events, beginning with "I was born" and ending with "I was liberated" (though some add epilogues about life after liberation). The "plot" reveals the witness seized by instead of selecting the events, memory's encounter with details embedded in moments of trauma. The role of the interviewer often appears to be to bring the witness back to his or her story: "What happened next?" And witnesses are both willing and reluctant to proceed with the chronology: they frequently hesitate because they know that their most complicated recollections are unrelated to time. "Arrival at Auschwitz" (or other camps) is both a temporal and a psychological experience, tellable and told as story *and* plot: Auschwitz as story enables us to pass through and beyond the event, while Auschwitz as plot stops the chronological clock and fixes the moment permanently in memory and imagination, immune to the vicissitudes of time. The unfolding story brings relief, while the unfolding plot induces pain. Like the witnesses, we struggle to synchronize the two: the most precarious challenges arise when this proves to be impossible.

The ensuing disorientation and reorientation represents a dilemma that witnesses try to share with their audience while constantly feeling frustrated by their effort. Conventionally, liberation meant survival, the end of oppression, the beginning of renewal. The very language we use here is ripe with a spirit of inspiration. But as we listen to the voices in these testimonies, a complex version of existence emerges, which we might call "staying alive" instead of the more consoling and affirmative "survival." Eva K. struggles to verbalize the enigma of a remembering that will not placate but can only disturb. "It's something what is behind in our mind," she says. "Not a philosoph[er], not a nobody who know this answer. How can this be – no connection? I not understand this myself. You still like flowers, I like a nice home, I like to look good. The *Schmerz* [pain] is inside." She is seized by the *illogic* of her situation: "Why I am alive I don't know. Maybe this is a punishment. I don't know." Liberation brings not rejoicing, but a recognition, an epiphany: "at this moment I realize that I am alive and I have nobody and I am living."[6] In Majdanek and Auschwitz, she assures us, the future meant tomorrow, and "tomorrow" meant death. This sense of time as a continuously impending doom stays with her after liberation and becomes part of the inner pain she speaks of, what Primo Levi might have called her phase of anguish.

Memory's inability to orchestrate past discords into present and future harmonies is a burden that haunts these testimonies. "You know," muses Eva K. in dialogue with herself, "I think I'm normal, and still be normal, and still have children, raise families, and talk and walk.

Something *stimmt nicht* (isn't right, doesn't fit together). Something is wrong here. In the chemistry something is wrong." The parallel currents of her being, one turbulent and the other calm, never merge. She experiences both, and can't account for their coexistence within her. Remembering cannot make her nature *then* flow into her nature *now*, cannot dredge a channel between the two to ease the passage. Throughout her testimony, Eva K. has disputed the idea that her strength or her behavior had been instrumental in her survival. Nonetheless, the voice of the interviewer, in the role of a hopeful persona (and incidentally illustrating our difficulty in renouncing conventional expectations), encourages: "you must have been very strong and you must have had a will to survive." But Eva K. merely shrugs and looks away, totally unconvinced by a logic that doesn't correspond to her memory of what she endured and how she behaved. "I'm strong, I'm strong," she concedes, "*aber* [but] when I tell you I never was doing nothing really to live ['to help yourself,' interjects the interviewer, attempting to 'clarify'], my fate push me, you know. I not help myself."[7]

Despite her inability to unify the fragments of her existence, this witness confesses that she wants her children and her grandchildren to "see" what that existence has been. She has imagined an extraordinary device for helping to make this possible. On her tombstone, she says, she intends to have engraved a forearm, with her deathcamp number imprinted on it. An inscription of death on a memorial to the dead? This forearm, from which the fist (symbol of defiance?) has been amputated, this indelible number that cancels the name, what can it signify? Has normal dying been infected by atrocity in this truncated image from a woman who has been twice committed to death? Less an affirmation than a reminder, it challenges us to understand the quality of a life enfolded by two kinds of dying, the rude disruption of the one imposing a permanent sense of "*stimmt nicht*" on the interval leading up to the other.

The interaction of self with destiny has been a hallmark of tragic literature since its inception. Imagine Agamemnon, Othello, or even Faulkner's Sutpen echoing Eva K.'s conclusoin that "My fate push me, you know. I not help myself." What we might call heroic memory died a difficult death in the Holocaust for many of these witnesses, who unlike Eva K. are reluctant to view the "will to survive" as the last gasp of a superseded idea. Self-esteem is crucial to the evolution of heroic memory; the narratives in these testimonies reflect a partially traumatized or maimed self-esteem, lingering like a non-fatal disease without any cure. Uncontaminated heroic memory is virtually unavailable to these witnesses, because for them remembering is invariably associated simultaneously with survival *and* loss. The propulsion of the one, driving the narrative toward life and the future, faces the resistance of the other, tugging the witness and us back toward encounters with atrocity. And this permanently cancels the possibility of meaningful celebration.

Consider the situation of Abraham P. The moment he arrived at Auschwitz on a transport from Hungary with his parents and four brothers remains embedded in memory, separated from time and chronology by an unpreparedness that he still can't explain. "That day so many things happened to us," he declares, "we really couldn't sort them out and I'm still trying to sort them out [nearly forty years later]." His parents and youngest brother are sent to the left, towards death, while he and two older brothers and a younger brother are sent to the right. Abraham P. recalls:

> I told my little kid brother, I said to him, "*Solly, geh tsu Tate un Mame* [go to poppa and momma]." And like a little kid, he followed – he did. Little did I know that I sent him to the crematorium. I am . . . I feel like I killed him. My [older] brother, who lives now in New York . . . every time we see each other he talks about it. He says, "No, I am responsible, because I said the same thing to you. And it's been bothering me too." I've been thinking whether he reached my mother and father, and that he *did* reach my mother and father. He probably told them, he said, "*Avraham hot mir gezogt, ikh zol mit eych gehn* [Abraham said I should go with you.]" I wonder what my mother and father were thinking, especially when they were all . . . when they all went into the crematorium [i.e., the gas chamber]. I can't get it out of my head. It hurts me, it bothers me, I don't know what to do.[8]

The dilemma is almost paradigmatic, so often do similar testimonies recur. The dramas they re-enact are both incomplete and finished. We might call the impelling force in these dramas "energy in pursuit" – but the pursuit is futile. It is futile because the core reality is eternally inaccessible. Consciousness both "knows" and is excluded from the denouement, like the playgoer who leaves the theater early, never experiencing closure, only indirectly learning of the ending. Further complicating the dilemma for survivors is the haunting conviction of responsibility for the catastrophe at which they were not present.

Heroic memory searches for a moral vision, a principle supporting the individual's responsibility for his actions. After all, Abraham P. *did* advise his brother to join his mother and father, thereby "condemning" him to certain death. How can we tell Abraham that both the quest and the principle are *irrelevant* to his narrative? His effort to rescue his brother from oblivion, and to reclaim him for a moral universe founders on the capricious essence of Auschwitz and the Holocaust, where left equaled death and right equaled not life but only death's postponement. Retroactive perception helps us to understand why he is still trying to sort out the moment of arrival at the deathcamp. Bizarre as it may seem, he prefers to accept the possibility of his own responsibility for his little brother's death than to embrace the principle of "systematic caprice" that governed the selection process. As memory seeks to recapture the details of what happened *as* it happened, inappropriate guilt intrudes to obscure the inner chaos implicit in Abraham P.'s confusion. That inner chaos does not reveal itself voluntarily, but needs to be mined by an attentive audience as a corollary to the will to survival that appears to be the climax of these testimonies.

Unlike the witness in video testimonies, the *writer* afflicted with the chaos attending the futile pursuits of memory has available a form of closure that invites order, if not consolation. For example, Buchenwald survivor, novelist (*The Long Voyage, What a Beautiful Sunday!*) and scripwriter (*Z, The Confession, La Guerre est finie*) Jorge Semprun wrestles endlessly in his fiction with the problem of how memory reconstitutes past atrocity in the present. The structure of the narrative in *What a Beautiful Sunday!* allows him to impose a perspective on the camp experience that is unavailable to the oral testifier. The narrator in this novel, himself a Buchenwald survivor, listens to his friends (also camp survivors) talk about their ordeal, and registers dissatisfaction with what we might call their equivalent of video testimony. The narrator assumes the role of audience:

> I listened as he recounted to me, awkwardly, interminably, with the prolixity natural to that sort of narrative, his life in the camp, the life of the camps. Sometimes, when it became too confused, when it went off in all directions, I wanted to chip in. But I could say nothing, of course. I had to preserve my anonymity.

He listens to another friend speaking about Mauthausen, and feels similarly uncomfortable: "Perhaps that isn't the problem for them, recounting convincingly the life of the camps. Perhaps the problem for them is quite simply that they have been there and survived." The fact of having survived thus *interferes* with a convincing portrayal of the experience, and although Semprun does not say so at this point, the palpable reason appears to be the one we have encountered repeatedly in the testimonies we have been examining. Memory can be a palliative as well as an avenue to a darker reality. "The memory is the best recourse," Semprun's narrator later observes, "even if it seems paradoxical at first. The best recourse against the pain of remembering, against the dereliction, against the unspoken, familiar madness. The criminal madness of living the life of a dead man."[9]

Semprun the writer has available an *art* of language that allows verbal formulation to organize and provide a perspective for the paradoxes that assail the "mere" witness. An expression like "living the life of a dead man" raises to the level of consciousness a contradiction that haunts the testifier while remaining only implicit in his or her narrative. What I have called the experiences of survival and deprival achieve the resonance of poetic intensity in Semprun's description of coming back from the camps as a "return from the lethal adventures of life." When Semprun's narrator concludes "There is no such thing as an innocent memory. Not for me anymore,"[10] he unwittingly offers us the words we have been searching for to define the experience of remembering that emerges from so many of these videotaped survivor testimonies: tainted memory.

As audience to these testimonies, we sit in the presence of tainted memory as it dredges up the anguish of loss with a brave face. Examples of such memory abound. One survivor of the Lodz ghetto recalls: "When you're hungry, it gets to the point where you don't mind stealing from your own sister, your own father. . . . I would get up in the middle of the night and slice a piece of bread off my sister's ration. Now I – you would never picture me, and I can't even imagine myself doing that now. But it happened." Although "innocent memory" may appear to be a literary idea, patient listening to testimony allows us to translate it into a practical application and definition: the penalty for survival is the loss not of innocence but of the *memory* of innocence. Liberation brought neither joy nor happiness to Leon W.: "It was an existence, that's all it was. . . . Because too many things happened afterwards. You know, finding out that my family is all gone." The forward momentum that might inspire one to celebrate survival meets a reverse momentum that invites one to mourn loss, and this irreconcilable encounter leads to tainted memory. A painful confusion penetrates Leon W.'s words as he struggles to explain: "I've got something always in the back of my mind which is like a double existence . . . I live life before and a life now [and that life before] is something entirely different from what we have now, and I don't think I can ever forget that."[11] In the years after the war, in a vain attempt to erase the experience from

memory, he refused to talk about it. But the corrosive inroads of tainted
memory are evident in his testimony nearly 35 years later.

Even more explicit is the voice of Martin R., for whom death by
atrocity became an inner reality even though external circumstances
failed to confirm his expectations. Sent to Bergen–Belsen from a Silesian
work camp as Russian troops approached, then to a nearby town to
clean up the rubble from air raids, he remembers bodies everywhere,
"piled up like merchandise." He was convinced that he was doomed
to an identical end: "You know you're going to die. Your brain is
telling you you're through, you're dead. You're just walking, but you're
dead now. I was sure I am dead now." His difficulty with tenses reflects
the problem of narrating today events suspended in time, as if tainted
memory subverted the grammar of chronology too. Another persona
emerges to echo in the present with quivering vitality a voice that
normally would have receded with time: "Now I know I'm gonna die
because inside me, inside me tells me something – 'You're dead.' There's
nothing there. Just to collapse and die. And waiting."[12]

"Arrested development" is a familiar phenomenon, but what are we
to make of its reverse, "arrested destruction"? Martin R. remembers
dragging huge numbers of corpses into mass graves. "And you're scared
to come close," he says, "because you think you're gonna fall in yourself." You push in dead skeletons, "and you see yourself in that skeleton.
That's how you're gonna be dumped too." The murder of his parents
is a source of tainted memory, while his dreams are haunted by Auschwitz and the gas chambers and what he calls "that" death. Ironically,
not having died in a similar manner represents a bizarre failure of
"logic," of the "intended" conclusion to his life. The failure leaves a
hiatus that tainted memory only highlights. Asked by his interviewer
"When did you think it was all over?" he offers a brutally succinct
reply: "It wasn't."[13] The darker side of these testimonies, the one where
memory functions not as a palliative but as an irritant, exposes a
permanently unfulfilled possibility, a disastrous one, to be sure, that
hovers over the imagination of the testifiers. A literary phrase like
returning "from the lethal adventures of life" sounds almost frivolous in
the context of their narration, which "liberates" only further imprisoning
contingencies from the past.

Consider the witness who, after three hours of testimony, suddenly
starts to speak of his fear of marriage and setting up a home after the
war. "A home," he defines, "is something you lose." The dual pattern
of survival–deprival looms through his words:

> I was working hard, and also trying to forget myself, forgetting
> the past. It came back to me like a recording in my head. After

we got married, for the longest time – we were already then in a family way and things were looking up to me. During the day I was working and studying and trying to get ahead, and at night I was fighting the Germans – really fighting. And the SS were after me all the time, and I was striving to save my mother and my sister [both gassed in Auschwitz]. And I was jumping off from building to building and they were shooting at me, and each time the bullet went through my heart.[14]

Thus dreams (or nightmares) nullify the arrested destruction that the accident of survival frustrates, though this proves no consolation to George S., who admits that they didn't know how to handle his waking up screaming every night. Finally, after complaining about pains in his heart, he was hospitalized. Doctors found nothing physically wrong with him.

Life on a pendulum swinging from past to future continues for this witness. The timepiece of his existence ticks in two directions. He devotes the penultimate moment of his testimony to his daughter, a medical student who takes her parents on a tour of the labs at her university. She shows them a jar with a brain in formaldehyde and says: "This is a human brain; treat it with respect." But her father associates the image with the Germans, who brutalized their victims by humiliating their bodies. Trapped between heir and heritage, how is George S. to declare allegiance to this image of dignity without succumbing to the memories of human taint that nothing has purified? His last words identify him as "the sole survivor of the W. and S. families,"[15] not as the progenitor of descendants. The most fitting conclusion after nearly six hours of testimony is a commemoration of his perished relatives.

The pain of recalling deprival modifies if it does not cancel the joy of remembering survival. It would be convenient if we could follow Robert J. Lifton's analysis of the personality of Nazi doctors and speak of a doubling or splitting of the self. But our need to reduce chaos to at least an intellectual order sometimes drives us to find explanations that are more convenient than accurate. I think this is true of Lifton's effort, and I believe it would be equally true were we to try to impose on the complexities of the survival experience a similar kind of psychological order. Unlike much writing about the Holocaust, testimony is prepared, even content, to leave itself unreconciled. Survivor interviews present us with the practice, not the theory of remembering. The efforts of memory in these testimonies liberate a sub-text of loss that punctures the story with fragments of chagrin, a vexation that coexists with whatever relief one feels from the fact of survival. The evidence of these testimonies, illustrated by the operation of what I have called tainted memory, suggests that such relief is less substantial than we have been led to assume. Joseph Brodsky's conclusion that a freed man is not necessarily a free man achieves a special resonance from the repeated spectacle of an imagination *possessed* by the details it believed it was remembering. In this sense, the condition that Brodsky calls exile becomes for us also another form of imprisonment. When a home is defined as something you lose, we recognize how indelible is the stain upon a memory that has lost its innocence. Remembering survival only ratifies the difficulty, not to say the impossibility, of effacing it.

7

Christian Witness and the Shoah

David Tracy

Introduction: On Christian Witness

Christianity is a religion grounded in witness or testimony. The "gospel" genre, unique to Christianity, is a mixed one, uniting witness and narrative. Gospel means proclamatory or testimonial narrative. Within the four canonical gospels, the notion of witness is central for structuring the gospel as a whole, especially in Luke and John. Moreover, the central Christian confession "We believe in Jesus Christ with the apostles" can be translated without loss as "We give witness to Jesus Christ as the true witness of God; we unite our present witness to the memory of the first witnesses, the apostles."[1]

To believe "*in* Jesus Christ" means, for Christians, to find in the ministry, message, fate, death and resurrection of this particular Jew, Jesus of Nazareth, the decisive witness to God, and whom human beings are commanded and empowered to become. To believe "*with* the apostles" means that any Christian tries to hold her/his present witness in continuity with the original witnesses – the "apostles" and the "apostolic writings", i.e. the New Testament. After the list of original witnesses, the apostles, comes the list of later witnesses – the "saints."

Christianity need not be triumphalist in its witnessing. Indeed, the intrinsic anti-triumphalism of Christian self-understanding should begin with the knowledge that all four gospels (despite their crucial differences, even conflicts) are based upon passion narratives. Martin Kahler observed with useful exaggeration that they can be interpreted as passion narratives with extended introductions. The cross, as instrument of both disgrace and death – Paul insisted not on Christ triumphal but on Christ crucified – should deconstruct any Christian temptation to triumphalism from within. At its core Christianity memorializes a narrative of undeserved suffering that Christians cannot forget, even with their belief in resurrection. At the heart of Christianity stands the symbol of the cross as a stark reminder of its origin and destiny.

Christians make the memory of this Jewish Jesus their own by witnessing to his memory in accepting the name "Christian." Correctly viewed, that memory is what Walter Benjamin named it – dangerous and subversive.[2] It should be dangerous, above all, for those who choose to testify to that memory by following in the "way" of Jesus. Such a memory should also subvert all temptations to triumphalism and all desire for the supersession of Judaism. And yet clearly it has not.

Logically, the cross as the central symbol of the religion should undo all temptations of triumphalism. Logically, the Christian tradition of memory would best honor its own witnesses (both the original apostles, and all later witnesses, the saints) by fidelity to the crucified Christ, Himself true witness to God and humankind. But once history intervenes – as it always will – the logic of Christian witness yields something far more complex: a troubling hermeneutics.

For once the specific history of the Jewish people and its traditions enter Christian consciousness, especially after the Shoah, then the logic of the symbols of Christian faith implode into the fragments of a post-Shoah hermeneutics.[3] The first question for a post-Shoah theology based on this hermeneutics is whether Christians can at last face, in repentance and truth, the history of Christian anti-semitism. Part of that first question is facing such pre-Shoah realities as the early "teaching of contempt" tradition in all its violence toward Judaism throughout "Christian" history. It is also facing a new question: if Christians have repented and been transformed, then how was it possible to wish to establish a Carmelite convent at Auschwitz? How does one unite an honest Christian desire to remember, to witness, to pray for all the victims of the Nazis, with the total failure by the Christian community to face the reality of the primary victims at Auschwitz, the slaughtered Jews? Does Christian memory not extend to the most obvious fact of our century: what Auschwitz means to the entire Jewish community and, therefore, one has the right to expect, to the Christian community as well? How were these Christian failures of memory and witness possible? I mean, specifically, the Carmelite failure to consult the Jewish community prior to their decision to build; the failure to reflect on what the symbol of a large cross could mean to the Jewish community as an utterly inappropriate symbol of witness to the Jewish dead.

A facile Christian inclusiveness of witness and memory ("we Christians remember *all* the dead; we witness to *all* suffering") became, through the convent at Auschwitz, one more expression of Christian supersessionism. To assume the Christian desire to pray for all so thoughtlessly, to assume the cross as a symbol for Jewish suffering so carelessly, to misunderstand both Judaism and the history of Catholic anti-semitism as recklessly as Cardinal Glemp did: these actions bear false witness against the Jewish neighbor. Is forgetfulness to become the modern form of contempt?

A second troubling, recent example: How is it possible to declare that splendid philosopher, possible mystic, and truly holy person, Edith Stein, solely a *Christian* "witness" or "martyr" after her murder by the Nazis at Auschwitz? Is it really so difficult for us to face squarely the central fact of the witness of Edith Stein: Edith Stein was murdered because she was a Jew, not because she was a Christian. How can Christians claim that they have faced the Shoah if such actions as the Auschwitz convent continue to occur? How can they really honor Edith Stein and ignore who she was and why she died?

The fact is that Christians, including modern, liberal, dialogical Christians, do not seem to know how to face the Jewish community as "other," much less to know how to join in post-Shoah witness with the Jewish people.[4] Consider this contrast: the Buddhist is so obviously "other" to the contemporary Christian that the Buddhist is rather quickly acknowledged as a genuine other. But the Jew? There, all changes. Christians often tell themselves and their Jewish partners in dialogue how much both share: the covenant, the history of ancient Israel, the Hebrew Bible – above all, the same covenanting God. This easy dialogical sharing is highly suspect. Arthur Cohen insisted that there was no historical reality behind the phrase the "Judaeo-Christian" tradition. That "tradition" is a modern Christian invention designed to cover over "Christian" history and relax the need to repent. The Judaeo-Christian tradition is another false witness and untruthful memory. The hard truth is that the Jewish partner in dialogue has rarely, if ever, been a genuine "other" for the Christian. Rather, Jewish tradition has functioned, in effect, as "projected other" for Christian self-identity.

"The Jew" is the frightening "other" potentially opposing the Christian yearning for an ever more elusive inclusivity and universality: this "other" is overcome by claims of how much Jews and Christians share as two covenantal peoples. Judaism has served to solidify Christianity's fears for its own identity: hence Christian supersessionism and triumphalism from the beginning (the "new covenant") until now. At one end of the spectrum of Christian responses to Judaism is contempt: at the other end, forgetfulness. A logical conclusion of contempt is Auschwitz. A logical conclusion of forgetfulness is a convent at Auschwitz.

Christianity, a religion grounded in witness and remembrance,[5] needs to rethink both of these after the Shoah. Perhaps, as many hope, a post-Shoah Christian theology might one day join in dialogue with a genuine, not projected other, and a post-Shoah Jewish theology. Perhaps Jew and Christian one day might even find it possible to accept Franz Rosenzweig's concept of two covenants as a mutually corroborative witness to Messianic hope. But such a hope is thoroughly vain, on the Christian side, without a rethinking of what a post-Shoah hermeneutics of Christian witness might be. Minimally that Christian hermeneutics must be one that cannot forget the Shoah and therefore can no longer remember anything – even the central Christian confession, even the gospel as confessing narrative, even the grounding passion narrative – in the same way, ever again.

A Hermeneutics of Christian Theology

Hermeneutics teaches us to take a canonical text such as scripture and make it bear upon the present. Not by any subjective wilfullness or distorted application, but – as Gadamer, Ricoeur and others have shown (correcting the Enlightenment's dismissiveness toward religious and symbolic thought)[6] – by a "conversation" that embraces both authoritative text and critical reader. To free understanding from error needs that conversation. It is not enough to identify traditional books as the source of error, or more radically still, to claim that the error lies in the fact of text-dependence itself, in that need of the mind.

Yet to assume that Gadamer's hermeneutic model, a type of careful and caring conversation, is sufficient for our situation is to miss the disclosure forced upon us by the Shoah. The Shoah exposes an unconscious, not conscious error, a systemic, not occasional distortion and illusion, and the fact, moreover, that sin, not mere moral error, is deeply embedded in all the traditions informing our culture.[7] The Shoah demands an acknowledgment that the fundamental model of self-understanding in hermeneutics – of dialogue and reflective argument – may prove adequate only when conscious error rather than systemically distorted unconscious illusion is involved; when only moral fault, not sin is at stake. The Shoah exposes the need for a radical suspicion directed toward every component of our culture: humanist, Enlightenment, or Christian. A Gadamerian hermeneutics of retrieval may be trusted to retrieve (through the model of dialogue) the meaning and truth of the traditions for today, and it may also be trusted to spot confusions and errors as they emerge in the to and fro of a conversation focussed on classic symbols and texts. But only a hermeneutics of suspicion can hope to spot the systemic distortions and illusions, the unconscious or strictly ideological elements in our reception of the classics.

This need for retrieval through suspicion is also applicable to any *religious* community's interpretation of its traditional texts and symbols, including its central texts of witness. What is Christian theology but the self-interpretation by the Christian community of its classics in the light of an ever-changing historical, intellectual, and religious situation?

The rules for interpreting classic texts also apply, then, to Christian texts of witness. Yet some distinctions proper to specifically Christian sources are necessary in order to understand the full force of the Shoah for a Christian self-interpretation. First, it is important to recall that Christianity, like Judaism and unlike Islam, is not strictly a religion of the book. Christianity does affirm, of course, certain texts as authoritative. It approaches its scriptures as the authoritative witness to the religious or revelatory event. But whereas in Islam the Qu'ran is itself the revelation, in Judaism and Christianity the scriptures are not the revelation but rather texts of witness *to* the revelatory event: for Judaism the revelation of Sinai and Exodus; for Christianity, the revelation of the event and person of Jesus Christ.

The hermeneutical structure of Christianity is thereby clear: event of revelation; scriptural texts of witness to the revelation. The scriptures, while they are the religious community's book, cannot determine totally the understanding of either past or present. These texts, which bear witness to the original revelatory event, are canonical through the community's own decision to establish an authoritative witness. Yet ultimately it is the revelatory event that empowers both the scriptural texts (as its original and authoritative witnesses) and all later interpretation. On these hermeneutical grounds – denied only by literalists and fundamentalists among Christian groups – later communities can provide new interpretations of their authoritative texts of witness in the light of succeeding events that bear a religious dimension (as when Christians learn to name the historical event of the Holocaust with the Jewish name, "Shoah").

This hermeneutical position is reinforced by the fact that, in interpreting the New Testament, Christians now know that the original communities were deeply influenced by events contemporary to the gospels.[8] Different New Testament christologies are largely occasioned by the different responses of contemporary communities to the mission to the Gentiles, the persecution (or stability) of a particular Christian group and, above all, the fall of Jerusalem in 70 CE. Indeed, the major representational shift in the New Testament itself was from Mark's

genre of apocalyptic history to Luke's schema of salvation history, with
Christ and Church (in *Luke* and *Acts*) now construed as the mid-points
of secular time. This shift was principally occasioned by the non-arrival
of an expected historical event: the apocalyptic end-time. In sum, the
New Testament itself re-envisions the meaning of the Christ-event in
the light both of what happened in history – the fall of Jerusalem, the
Gentile mission, the persecution (and stability) of the early Christian
communities – and of the great event that did *not* happen, the anticipated
end-time or Second Coming. Historical time, then as now, influences
the diverse and sometimes conflicting interpretations of the Christ-
event.[9]

The interpretation of scriptural texts cannot ignore a critical conversation. For the pre-understanding interpreters bring to the text, as well
as the text's authorized claim, are constantly changing realities. Insofar
as we understand the scriptures at all, we understand them differently
than the original authors did. Insofar as we understand the scriptures
in a post-Shoah situation we understand the revelatory event to which
they witness differently than their original authors did. For to read these
authoritative scriptural texts of witness now is to read them, post-
Shoah, with deep suspicion: suspicion of their effect not only on post-
scriptural witnesses but even (see below) on the scriptural witnesses
themselves. Insofar as Christian theologians understand the Christ-event
now, they understand it differently than the original apostolic witnesses
did. This conclusion, however unsettling to all who believe in a seamless
tradition, is forced upon us by the nature of Christian hermeneutics
and the light – that is, the darkness – of the Shoah. What some of that
specific difference might be for any post-Shoah Christian theology that
seriously witnesses history, we must now try to see more clearly.

The Return to History and the Christian Turn to Witness

Of histories of Christian scriptural interpretation there is no end.
Although many of these histories concentrate so strictly on changes in
interpretive method that they suggest historical events had little or no
influence on the concerns of biblical scholars and theologians, others
show how these events influenced not only the original apostolic communities and the formation of the Christian canon, but also all later
interpretive innovations. The development of typological and allegorical
methods, the "four sense" patristic and medieval mode of reading
scripture, and the innovations of Aquinas and Luther concerning the
primacy of the "literal" sense, were major changes occasioned by the

community's renewed experience of the meaning of the Christ-event within a specific historical context.[10]

In the modern period, the major historical events for new forms of Christian interpretation were the eighteenth-century Enlightenment and the nineteenth-century rise of historical consciousness. These were historical as well as intellectual developments, in the sense of the emergence of new groupings of power and new institutions (even new Foucaultian *epistemes*), and lend themselves – for the moment – more readily than the events of the twentieth century to strictly intellectual inquiry. Hence modern Christian theology often focusses its attention on the crisis of Christian self-understanding occasioned by the Enlightenment and the rise of the historical consciousness. The major shift, during the last two centuries, to revelation as the crux for theology is the clearest illustration of the kind of sea-change which occurred after the onslaught of the Enlightenment on traditional Christian self-understanding.

Indeed, such atypical theologians as Søren Kierkegaard and Reinhold Niebuhr insisted that post-Enlightenment Christianity was in danger of becoming so exclusively a religion of "revelation" that its function as a religion of salvation and praxis could seem in doubt. This Christian retreat from living history was compounded by a pervasive liberal optimism: hence, modern Christian theologies of universalist and inclusivist reconciliation. An irony soon became apparent: the very discovery of the historical consciousness, and the attendant theological obsession with the crisis of Christianity's historical claims, tempted theology to retreat from history. It was Hegel's dialectical optimism, not his observation that history was a slaughter-bench, which largely won the day. The scriptures may have continued to play their authoritative role as narratives producing forms of identity for Christian believers; but for many theologians, newly allied with historico-critical exegetes, the scriptural narratives of witness began to unravel into ever more disparate and singular units. The gains of the historico-critical method and the liberal and modernist theologies which they produced are plain for all to see. But the loss of concrete history under the paradoxical cover of historical consciousness was one whose full impact Christian theology is just beginning to realize.

Neo-orthodox Christian theology did correct the liberals at several crucial points. Above all, Karl Barth's rediscovery of the centrality of the revelatory event can now be seen for what it was: a rediscovery of the fact that the biblical subject matter is the revelatory event to which the scriptures testify. This rediscovery was also occasioned, as is well known, by the shattering impact of the First World War on liberal optimism and self-confidence. Paul Tillich spoke not for himself alone but for all Christian contemporaries of that period when he declared, "My generation learned its theology in the trenches of World War I." And yet even those characteristically neo-orthodox moves did not bring Christian theology into history. Rather, the sheer transcendence and pure verticality of the neo-orthodox understanding of the revelatory event encouraged a theology increasingly privatized, remote from the slaughterhouse of actual history. The frightening lack of concern of the Christian churches towards the Jews of Nazi Germany was the clearest example of that theological defense against history. Even the courageous neo-orthodoxy of the Confessing Church in Germany was not clear on the Jewish question.[11]

In contemporary Christian theology there is one great exception to these observations on the Christian withdrawal from history: feminist and liberation theologies. For behind the communitarian demands of these theologies and behind their suspicious retrieval of half-forgotten, even repressed symbols of witness, lies a single-minded and constant refrain: Christian theology must move past both liberal historical consciousness and neo-orthodox "astonishment," and begin again – as theology – to act for and be a witness to history as a history of suffering. These liberation theologies do not mean by "history" either historiography or the philosophy of history. They do not mean a purely vertical transcendence where history becomes a tangent, a theological accident. They mean history. They mean the concrete struggles of groups, societies, persons, who have been shunted aside by the official story of triumph. They mean that the central theological question is not the modern question of the non-believer but the post-modern question of the non-person – those forgotten ones, living or dead, whose retrieved presence informs the history of renewed Christian witness.

It is the singular achievement of feminist and liberation theologians that they have returned into history, more exactly into the history of those whom official accounts, including the Christian, neglected as non-persons, non-groups, non-history. Through their suspicions, they have recovered repressed elements in the New Testament, such as the profound genre of the apocalyptic, so deeply embarrassing to the liberals and deemed unnecessary by the neo-orthodox.

Central to these post-modern theologies of praxis is a sense of history as rupture, break, discontinuity. Given this new turn toward history, there is even more urgency for Christian thought to face the radical interruption of the Holocaust. Is it possible to insist on the need for a theological return to concrete history and yet not face that event and not witness to the six million? If Christian theologians do face that historical *caesura*,[12] can they, post-Shoah, speak comfortably of the new covenant "fulfillment" themes, always in danger of becoming super-sessionist in tendency? How can Christians not express anger at Mat-thew's portrait of the Jewish people ("His blood be upon us and upon our children") or the use of "the Jews" in John's gospel, or the still uninterrupted use of traditional Pauline law–gospel dichotomies? The witness of the Shoah smashes against and demands new reflection on the original Christian scriptural witnesses of Matthew, John and Paul.

If Christian theology is to enter the reality of history, then surely the Holocaust is a frightening disclosure of the history in which we have lived.[13] Christian theology cannot but face the Holocaust and witness to it as the Shoah – a witness which may demand a methodical suspicion of earlier and traditional teachings. Nor can Christian theology face that rupture without acknowledging as well the long and terrible history of anti-semitism that has been one of the effects of its own tradition. It cannot face that interruption without realizing that the Christian return to history must now be a return through the radical negativity disclosed by the Shoah. Every hermeneutics of retrieval for Christian theology must today include a radical hermeneutics of suspicion on the whole of Christian history, even on the relevant aspects of the original Christian scriptural witness.

For the Holocaust is not merely one more interruptive event added to Hegel's slaughter-bench of history. The Holocaust is a *caesura* within history itself. Today every Christian effort at understanding self, scrip-ture, or tradition – no matter how powerful and believable its her-meneutic retrievals, no matter how fierce and unrelenting its suspicions, – must now endure as not merely unfinished but broken. Any new beginning by Christian theology, any believable hope or witness, must this time be within history – chastened forever by the theological claims upon us of the actual history we have lived. To build a convent at Auschwitz is, for any Christian witnessing to the Shoah, to profane its memory. It is to bear false witness. To call Edith Stein a witness, a martyr, a saint, could become, for Christians, an opportunity for repent-ance and truth. Christians can now witness to Edith Stein, murdered at Auschwitz, as among her people again: the Jewish people.

Perhaps Christian theology can even learn one day a new type of witness, a new theological version of Rosenzweig – a post-Shoah theory of the two covenants where the Christian follows and learns from the Jewish a return to history. Together, Jew and Christian may one day struggle to find a new way to the God to whom the original witnesses at Auschwitz prayed.

8

Film as Witness: Claude
Lanzmann's *Shoah*

Shoshana Felman

I

History and Witness

"If someone else could have written my stories," writes Elie Wiesel, "I would not have written them. I have written them in order to testify. My role is the role of the witness. ... Not to tell, or to tell another story, is ... to commit perjury."[1]

To bear witness is to take responsibility for truth: to speak, implicitly, from within the legal pledge and the juridical imperative of the witness's oath.[2] To testify – before a court of law or before the court of history and of the future; to testify, likewise, before an audience of readers or spectators – is more than to report a fact or an event or to relate what has been lived and remembered. To testify is always, metaphorically, to take the witness's position insofar as the witness is at once engaged in an appeal and bound by an oath. To testify is thus not merely to narrate but to commit oneself, and one's narrative, to others: to *take responsibility* – in speech – for the truth of an occurrence, for something which, by definition, goes beyond the personal.

But if the essence of testimony is impersonal (to enable a decision by a judge or jury – metaphorical or literal – about the true nature of the facts of an occurrence; to enable an objective reconstruction of what history was like, irrespective of the witness), why is it that the witness's speech is so uniquely, literally irreplaceable? "If someone else could have written my stories, I would not have written them." What does it mean that the testimony cannot be simply reported, or narrated by another in its role as testimony? What does it mean that a story – or a history – cannot be told by someone else?

It is this question, I would suggest, that guides the groundbreaking work of Claude Lanzmann in his film *Shoah* (1985), and constitutes at once the profound subject and the shocking originality of the film.

A Vision of Reality

Shoah is a film made exclusively of testimonies: first-hand testimonies by witnesses of the Holocaust, interviewed and filmed by Lanzmann during the eleven years (1974–85) of the film's production. *Shoah* recalls the Holocaust with such a power (a power that no previous film on the subject could attain) that it radically displaces and shakes up not only any common notion we might have entertained about it, but our very vision of reality as such, our very sense of what the world, culture, history, and our life within it, are all about.

But the film is not primarily a historical document on the Holocaust. That is why, in contrast to its cinematic predecessors on the subject, it systematically refuses to use archival footage. It conducts its interviews, and takes its pictures, in the present. Rather than a simple view about the past, the film offers a disorienting vision of the present, a compellingly profound and surprising insight into the complexity of the *relation between history and witnessing*.

It is a film about witnessing: the witnessing of a catastrophe. The limit-experiences, their overwhelming impact, constantly put to the test the witness and witnessing, and at the same time unsettle the very limits of our sense of reality.

Art as Witness

Shoah is also a film about the *relation between art and witnessing*, about film as a medium which expands the capacity for witnessing. To understand *Shoah*, we must explore the question: what are we as spectators made to witness? This expansion of what we in turn can witness comes, however, not only from a rehearsal of the events but from the power of the film as a work of art: from the subtlety of its philosophic and artistic structure and the complexity of the creative process it engages. "The truth kills the possibility of fiction," said Lanzmann in a journalistic interview.[3] But the truth does not kill the possibility of art — on the contrary, it requires it for its transmission, for its realization in our consciousness as witnesses.

Finally, *Shoah* embodies the capacity of art not simply to witness, but to take the witness's stand: the film accepts responsibility for its times by enacting the significance of our era as an *age of testimony*, in which witnessing itself has undergone a major trauma. *Shoah* gives us a historical crisis of witnessing, and displays how, out of this crisis, witnessing becomes, in all senses of the word, a *critical* activity.

On all these levels, Claude Lanzmann asks a varied yet relentless question: what does it mean to be a witness? What does it mean to be a witness to the Holocaust? What does it mean to be a witness to the process of the film? What does testimony mean, if it is not simply (as we commonly perceive it) the observing, recording, and remembering of an event, but a unique and irreplaceable *position* with respect to what is witnessed? What does testimony mean, if it is the *performance of a story* constituted by the fact that, like the oath, it cannot be carried out by anybody else?

The Western Law of Evidence

The specialness of testimony proceeds from the witness's irreplaceable performance of the act of seeing – from the witness's seeing with his/her own eyes. "Mr Vitold," says the Jewish Bund leader to the Polish Courier Jan Karski (who reports it in his cinematic testimony 35 years later, in narrating how the Jewish leader urged him – and persuaded him – to become a crucial visual witness), "I know the Western world. You will be speaking to the English. . . . It will strengthen your report if you will be able to say: '*I saw it myself*'" (p. 171).[4]

In the legal, philosophical and epistemological tradition of the Western world, witnessing is based on, and is formally defined by, first-hand seeing. "Eyewitness testimony" is what constitutes the most decisive law of evidence in courtrooms. "Lawyers have innumerable rules involving hearsay, the character of the defendant or of the witness, opinions given by the witness, and the like, which are in one way or another meant to involve the fact-finding process. But more crucial than any one of these – and possibly more crucial than all put together – is the evidence of eyewitness testimony."[5]

Film, at the same time, is the art par excellence which, like the courtroom (although for different purposes), calls upon *witnessing by seeing*. How does the film use its visual medium to reflect upon eyewitness testimony, both as the law of evidence of its own art and as the law of evidence of history?

II

Victims, Perpetrators and Bystanders: About Seeing

Lanzmann's film is an exploration of the differences between heterogeneous points of view, testimonial stances which can neither be assimilated into, nor subsumed by, one another. There is, first of all, the difference of perspective between groups of witnesses, historical characters who, in response to Lanzmann's inquiry, play their own role as the singularly real actors of the movie, and fall into three basic categories:[6] those who witnessed the disaster as its *victims* (the surviving Jews); those who witnessed the disaster as its *perpetrators* (the ex-Nazis); those who witnessed the disaster as *bystanders* (the Poles). What is at stake in this division is not only a diversity of points of view or of degrees of implication and emotional involvement, but the incommensurability of different topographical and cognitive positions. More concretely, what the categories in the film exhibit is *different performances of the act of seeing.*

Victims, bystanders and perpetrators are here differentiated not so much by what they actually see (what they all see, although discontinuous, does in fact converge strictly), as by what and how they *do not see*, by what and how they *fail to witness*. The Jews see, but do not understand the purpose and the destination of what they see: overwhelmed by their loss and by Nazi deception, they are blind to the full significance of what they witness. Richard Glazar strikingly narrates a moment of perception coupled with incomprehension, an exemplary moment in which the Jews fail to read, or to decipher, what they see with their own eyes:

> Then very slowly, the train turned off the main track and rolled
> . . . through a wood. While he looked out – we'd been able to
> open a window – the old man in our compartment saw a boy
> . . . and he asked the boy in signs, "Where are we?" And the kid
> made a funny gesture. This: (draws a finger across his throat) . . .
>
> *And one of you questioned him?*
>
> Not in words, but in signs, we asked: "what's going on here?"
> And he made that gesture. Like this. We didn't really pay much
> attention to him. We couldn't figure out what he meant. (p. 34)

The Poles, unlike the Jews, *do* see but, as bystanders, they do not quite *look*, they avoid looking directly, and thus they *overlook* at once their responsibility and their complicity as witnesses:

> You couldn't look there. You couldn't talk to a Jew.
> Even going by on the road, you couldn't look there.
>
> *Did they look anyway?*
>
> Yes, vans came and the Jews were moved farther off. You could see them, but on the sly. In sidelong glances. (pp. 97–8)

The Nazis, on the other hand, see to it that both the Jews and the extermination will remain unseen: the death camps are surrounded, for that purpose, with a screen of trees. Franz Suchomel, an ex-guard of Treblinka, testifies:

> Woven into the barbed wire were branches of pine trees. . . . It was known as "camouflage". . . . So everything was screened. People couldn't see anything to the left or right. Nothing. You couldn't see through it. Impossible. (p. 110)

It is not a coincidence that as this testimony is unfolding it is hard for us as viewers of the film to see the witness, who is filmed secretly: as is the case for most of the ex-Nazis, Franz Suchomel agreed to answer Lanzmann's questions, but not to be filmed; he agreed, in other words, to give a testimony, but on the condition that, as witness, *he* should not be seen:

> *Mr Suchomel, we're not discussing you, only Treblinka. You are a very important eyewitness, and you can explain what Treblinka was.*
>
> But don't use my name.
>
> *No, I promised . . .* (p. 54)

In the blurry images of faces taken by a secret camera that has to shoot through a variety of walls and screens, the film makes us see concretely, by the compromise it unavoidably inflicts upon *our* act of seeing (which, of necessity, becomes materially an act of *seeing through*), how the Holocaust was an historical assault on seeing and how, even today, the perpetrators are still by and large invisible: "everything was screened.

You couldn't see anything to the left or right. You couldn't see through it."

Figuren

The essence of the Nazi scheme was to make itself – and to make the Jews – essentially invisible. To make the Jews invisible by confining them to "camouflaged" deathcamps, but also by reducing even the materiality of the dead bodies to smoke and ashes. The opaque *sight* of the dead bodies, as well as the literal reference of the *word* "corpse," is degraded to the transparency of a mere *figure*: a disembodied verbal substitute which signifies abstractly the law – material or linguistic – of indefinite substitutability. The dead bodies are voided of substance and specificity by being treated, in the Nazi jargon, as *figuren*: that which cannot be seen or can be seen through.

> The Germans even forbade us to use the words "corpse" or "victim." The dead were blocks of wood, shit. The Germans made us refer to the bodies as *figuren*, that is, as puppets, as dolls, or as *Schmattes*, which means "rags." (p. 13)

But it is not only the dead bodies of the victims which the Nazis, paradoxically, do not "see." It is also, in some striking cases, the living Jews transported to their death that remain invisible to the chief architects of their final transportation. Walter Stier, head of Reich Railways Department 33 of the Nazi party, chief traffic planner of the death trains ("special trains," in Nazi euphemism), testifies:

> *But you knew that the trains to Treblinka or Auschwitz were –*
>
> Of course we knew. I was the last district. Without me the trains couldn't reach their destination . . .
>
> *Did you know that Treblinka meant extermination?*
>
> Of course not. . . . How could we know? I never went to Treblinka. (p. 135) . . .
>
> *You never saw a train?*
>
> No, never. . . . I never left my desk. We worked day and night. (p. 132)

In the same way, Mrs Michelshon, wife of a Nazi schoolteacher in Chelmno, answers Lanzmann's questions:

Did you see the gas vans?

No. ... Yes, from the outside. They shuttled back and forth. I
never looked inside; I didn't see Jews in them. I only saw things
from outside. (p. 82)

Thus, the diversity of the testimonial stances of victims, bystanders and
perpetrators have in common, paradoxically, a *not seeing.* Through the
testimonies of its witnesses Lanzmann's film makes us see concretely
how the Holocaust unfolds as the unprecedented, inconceivable advent
of *an event without a witness,* an event which consists in planning the
literal erasure of its witnesses.

The incommensurability between different testimonial stances, and
the multiplicity of specific cognitive positions of seeing and not seeing,
are amplified by the many languages in which the testimonies are
delivered (French, German, Sicilian, English, Hebrew, Yiddish, Polish),
a multiplicity which necessitates the presence of a professional translator
as an intermediary. The technique of dubbing is not used, and the
character of the translator is deliberately not edited out of the film –
on the contrary, she is often on the screen, at Lanzmann's side, as
another real actor, because the process of translation is an integral part
of the film. Through the multiplicity of foreign tongues and the delay
incurred by the translation, this incapacity of the act of seeing to
translate itself spontaneously into a meaning, is recapitulated. The film
places us in the position of the witness who sees and hears, but cannot
understand the significance of what is going on until the later intervention of the translator, her delayed rendering of the significance of
the visual/acoustic information. But she also in some ways distorts and
screens it, because (as some witnesses and Lanzmann himself point out),
the translation is not always absolutely accurate.

The palpable foreignness of the film's tongues is emblematic of the
radical foreignness of the experience of the Holocaust, not merely to
us but even to its own participants. Asked whether he has invited the
participants to see the film, Lanzmann answered in the negative: "In
what language would the participants have seen the film?" The original
was a French print: "They don't speak French."[7] The native language
of the filmmaker, the common denominator into which the testimonies
(and original subtitles) are translated and in which the film is thought
out, happens not to be the language of any of the witnesses. It is a
metaphor of the film that its language is a language of translation, as
if the significance of the occurrence could only be articulated in a
language foreign to the language(s) of the occurrence.

Shoah, the Hebrew word which, with the definite article (here missing), designates "The Holocaust," but without the article "catastrophe," also names the very foreignness of languages, the very namelessness of a catastrophe which cannot be possessed by any native tongue and which, within the language of translation, can only be named as the *untranslatable*: that which language cannot witness or that which cannot be articulated in *one* language.

III

The Historian as a Witness

The task of deciphering signs and processing intelligibility – what might be called *the task of the translator*[8] – is, however, carried out within the film not merely by the character of the professional interpreter, but also by two other actors – the historian (Raul Hilberg) and the filmmaker (Claude Lanzmann) – who, like the witnesses, play themselves and who, unlike the witnesses but like the translator, constitute *second-degree witnesses* (witnesses of witnesses). Like the professional interpreter, although in very different ways, the filmmaker in the film and the historian on the screen are catalysts – or agents – of the process of reception. Their reflective witnessing and testimonial stance aid our own reception and assist us in both the effort toward comprehension and in the struggle with the foreignness of signs.

Within the film, then, the historian is not the ultimate authority on history but *one more witness*. The statement of the filmmaker – and the testimony of the film as a whole – are by no means subsumed by the statement or testimony of the historian. Though the filmmaker does embrace the historical insights of Hilberg, which he obviously holds in complete respect and from which he gets both inspiration and instruction, the film also places in perspective the discipline of history as such, in stumbling on (and giving us to see) the very limits of historiography. "*Shoah*" Claude Lanzmann said at Yale,

> is certainly not a historical film. . . . The purpose of *Shoah* is not to transmit knowledge, in spite of the fact that there is knowledge in the film. . . . Hilberg's book, *The Destruction of the European Jews*, was really my Bible for many years. . . . But in spite of this, *Shoah* is not a historical film, it is something else. . . . To condense in one word what the film is for me, I would say that the film is an *incarnation*, a *resurrection*, and that the whole process of the film is a philosophical one.[9]

Hilberg is the spokesman for a vast and impressive knowledge on the Holocaust. Knowledge is shown by the film to be absolutely necessary in the ongoing struggle to resist the blinding impact of the event. But knowledge is not, in and of itself, a sufficiently effective act of seeing. The newness of the film's vision consists precisely in the surprising insight it conveys into the radical ignorance in which all of us are unknowingly plunged with respect to the historical occurrence. This ignorance is not dispelled by a knowledge of history – on the contrary, it *encompasses* it as such. The film shows how historical knowledge can be used for the purpose of a *forgetting* which, ironically enough, includes the gestures of historiography. Historiography can be as much the product of the passion of forgetting as the product of the passion of remembering.

Walter Stier, former head of Reich railways and chief planner for the transports of the Jews to deathcamps, can thus testify:

> *What was Treblinka for you? . . . A destination?*
>
> Yes, that's all.
>
> *But not death.*
>
> No, no . . .
>
> *Extermination came to you as a big surprise?*
>
> Completely . . .
>
> *You had no idea.*
>
> Not the slightest. Like that camp – what was its name? It was in the Oppeln district. . . . I've got it: Auschwitz.
>
> *Yes, Auschwitz was in the Oppeln district. . . . Auschwitz to Krakow is forty miles.*
>
> That's not very far. And we knew nothing. Not a clue.
>
> *But you knew that the Nazis – that Hitler didn't like the Jews?*
>
> That we did. It was well known. . . . But as to their extermination, that was news to us. I mean, even today people deny it. They say there couldn't have been so many Jews. Is it true? I don't know. That's what they say. (pp. 136–8)

To substantiate his own amnesia (of the name of Auschwitz) and his own claim of *not knowing*, Stier implicitly refers here to the *claim of knowledge* – the historical authority – of "revisionist historiographies," works published in a variety of countries by historians who argue that the *number* of the dead cannot be proven and that, since there is according to them no verifiable evidence of the exact extent of the mass murder, the genocide is merely an invention, an exaggeration of the Jews. The Holocaust, in fact, never existed.[10] "But as to their own extermination, that was news to us. I mean, even today, people deny it. They say there could not have been so many Jews. Is it true? I don't know. That's what they say." I am not the one who knows, but there are those who say that what I did not know did not exist. "Is it true? I don't know."

Dr Franz Grassler, on the other hand (formerly Nazi commissioner of the Warsaw Ghetto), comes himself to mimic, in front of the camera, the very gesture of historiography as an alibi to *his* forgetting.

> *You don't remember those days?*
>
> Not much. . . . It's a fact: we tend to forget, thank God, the bad times . . .
>
> *I'll help you to remember. In Warsaw you were Dr Auerswald's deputy.*
>
> Yes . . .
>
> *Dr Grassler, this is Czerniakow's diary. You're mentioned in it.*
>
> It's been printed. It exists?
>
> *He kept a diary that was recently published. He wrote on July 7, 1941 . . .*
>
> July 7, 1941? That's the first time I've relearned a date. May I take notes? After all, it interests me too. So in July I was already there! (pp. 175–6)

In line with the denial of responsibility and memory, the very gesture of such "historiography" comes to embody nothing but the blankness of the page on which the "notes" are taken.

The next section of the film focusses on the historian Hilberg holding, and discussing, Czerniakow's diary. The cinematic editing that follows shifts back and forth, in a sort of shuttle movement, between the face of Grassler (who continues to articulate his own view of the ghetto) and the face of Hilberg (who continues to articulate the content of the diary and the perspective that the author of the diary – Czerniakow –

gives of the ghetto). The Nazi commissioner of the ghetto is thus confronted structurally, not so much with the counter-sentiment of the historian, but with the first-hand witness of the (now dead) author of the diary, the Jewish leader of the ghetto whom the ineluctability of the ghetto's destiny led to end his leadership – and sign his diary – with suicide.

Here, then, the main role of the historian is less to narrate history than to *reverse the suicide*, to take part in a cinematic vision which Lanzmann has defined crucially as an "incarnation" and a "resurrection." "I have taken a historian," Lanzmann enigmatically remarked, "so that he will incarnate a dead man, even though I had someone alive who had been a director of the ghetto."[11] The historian is there to embody, to give flesh and blood to, the dead author of the diary. Unlike the Christian resurrection, though, the vision of the film is to make Czerniakow come alive precisely as a dead man. His "resurrection" does not cancel out his death. The vision of the film is at once to make the dead writer come alive as a historian, and to make, in turn, history and the historian come alive in the uniqueness of the voice of a dead man, and in the silence of his suicide.

The Filmmaker as a Witness

At the side of the historian, *Shoah* finally includes among its list of characters (its list of witnesses) the very presence of the filmmaker in the process of making the film. Travelling between the living and the dead and moving to and fro between the different places and voices in the film, this filmmaker is continuously, though discretely, present in the screen's margin, perhaps as the most silently articulate, the most articulately silent, witness. The creator of the film speaks and testifies, however, in his own voice, in his triple role as the *narrator* of the film (and the signatory – the first person – of the script), as the *interviewer* of the witnesses (the solicitor and the receiver of the testimonies), and as the *inquirer* (the artist as the subject of a quest concerning what the testimonies testify to; the figure of the witness as a questioner, and of the asker not merely as factual investigator but as the bearer of the film's philosophical address and inquiry.)

The three roles of the filmmaker intermix and in effect exist only in their relation to each other. Since the narrator is, as such, also a witness, his story is restricted to the story of the interviewing: the narrative consists of what the interviewer hears. Lanzmann's rigor as narrator is to speak strictly as an interviewer, to abstain, that is, from narrating anything directly in his own person, except for the beginning – the only moment which refers explicitly to the filmmaker as narrator:

> The story begins in the present at Chelmno. . . . Chelmno was the place in Poland where Jews were first exterminated by gas. . . . Of the four hundred thousand men, women and children who went there, only two came out alive. . . . Srebnik, survivor of the last period, was a boy of thirteen when he was sent to Chelmno. . . . I found him in Israel and persuaded that one-time boy singer to return with me to Chelmno. (pp. 3–4)

The opening, narrated in the filmmaker's own voice, at once situates the story in the present and sums up a past which is presented not yet as the story but rather as a pre-history, or a pre-story: the story proper is contemporaneous with the film's speech, which begins, in fact, subsequent to the narrator's written preface, by the actual song of Srebnik re-enacted in the present. The narrator is the "I" who "found" Srebnik and "persuaded" him to "return with me to Chelmno." The narrator opens, or re-opens, the story of the past in the present of the telling. But the "I" of the narrator, of the signatory of the film, has no voice: the opening is projected on the screen as a silent text, as the narrative voice-over of a *writing* with no voice.

On the one hand, then, the narrator has no voice. On the other hand, the continuity of the narrative is insured by Lanzmann's voice, which runs through the film and whose sound constitutes the continuous, connective thread between the different voices and different testimonial episodes. But Lanzmann's voice – the active voice in which we hear the filmmaker speak – is strictly, once again, the voice of the inquirer and interviewer, not of the narrator. As narrator, Lanzmann does not speak but rather vocally recites the words of others, *lends his voice* (on two occasions) to read aloud written documents whose authors cannot speak in their own voice: the letter of the Rabbi of Grabow, warning the Jews of Lodz of the extermination taking place at Chelmno, a letter whose signatory was himself gassed at Chelmno with his entire community ("Do not think" – Lanzmann recites – "that this is written by a madman. Alas, it is the horrible, tragic truth," pp. 83–4), and the Nazi document entitled "Secret Reich Business" concerning technical improvements of the gas vans ("Changes to special vehicles . . . shown by use and experience to be necessary," pp. 103–5), an extraordinary document which might be said to formalize Nazism as such (the way in which the most perverse and most concrete extermination is abstracted into a pure question of technique and function). Lanzmann's voice modulates evenly – with no emotion or comment – the perverse diction of this document punctuated by the coincidental irony embodied by the signatory's name: "signed: Just."

Besides this recitation of the written documents, and a mute reference to his own voice in the written cinematic preface of the silent opening, Lanzmann speaks as interviewer and inquirer, but as narrator he keeps silent. The narrator lets the narrative be carried by others – by the live voices of the witnesses he interviews, whose stories must be able to *speak for themselves*, if they are to testify, that is, to perform their first-hand witness. It is only in this way, by this abstinence of the narrator, that the film can be a narrative of testimony: a narrative of that, precisely, which can neither be reported, nor narrated, by another. The narrative is thus essentially the story of the filmmaker's *listening*: the narrator is the teller of the film only insofar as he is the bearer of that special silence.

In his other roles, however, that of interviewer and of inquirer, the filmmaker, on the contrary, is a transgressor and a breaker of the silence. Of his own transgression the interviewer says to the interviewee whose silence must be broken: "I know it's very hard. I know and I apologize." (p. 117)

Lanzmann as interviewer asks not for explanations of the Holocaust but for concrete descriptions of details and apparently trivial specifics.[12] "Was the weather very cold?" (p. 11) "From the station to the unloading ramp in the camp is how many miles? . . . How long did the trip last?" (p. 33) "Exactly where did the camp begin?" (p. 34) "It was the silence that tipped them off? . . . Can he describe that silence?" (p. 67) "What were the [gas] vans like? . . . What color?" (p. 80). It is not the big generalizations but the minute particulars which translate into a vision and thus help both to dispel the blinding impact of the event and to transgress the silence to which the splintering of eyewitnessing reduced the witness. It is only through the trivia, by small steps – and not by huge strides or leaps – that the barrier of silence can be displaced. The pointed and specific questioning resists, above all, any possible canonization of the experience of the Holocaust. Insofar as the interviewer challenges at once the sacredness (the unspeakability) of death and the sacredness of the deadness (the silence) of the witness, Lanzmann's questions are essentially desacralizing.

> *How did it happen when the women came into the gas chamber?*
> *. . . What did you feel the first time you saw all these naked*
> *women? . . .*

> *But I asked and you didn't answer: What was your impression*
> *the first time you saw these naked women arriving with children?*
> *How did you feel?*
>
> I tell you something. To have a feeling about that . . . it was very
> hard to feel anything, because working there day and night between
> dead people, between bodies, your feeling disappeared, you were
> dead. You had no feeling at all. (pp. 114–16)

Shoah is the story of the liberation of testimony through its desacraliz-
ation. What the interviewer avoids above all is an alliance with the
silence of the witness, the kind of empathic and benevolent alliance
through which interviewer and interviewee often implicitly concur, and
work together, for the mutual comfort of an avoidance of the truth.

It is the silence of the witness's death which Lanzmann must challenge,
in order to revive the Holocaust and to rewrite the *event-without-a-*
witness into witnessing, into history. It is the silence of the witness's
death, and of the witness's deadness, which precisely must be broken,
and transgressed.

> *We have to do it. You know it.*
>
> I won't be able to do it.
>
> *You have to do it. I know it's very hard. I know and I apologize.*
>
> Don't make me go on please.
>
> *Please. We must go on.* (p. 117)

What does *going on* mean? The predicament of having to continue to
bear witness at all costs parallels, for Abraham Bomba, the predicament
faced in the past of having to continue to *live on*, to survive in spite
of the gas chambers, in the face of surrounding death. But to have to
go on *now*, to keep on bearing witness, is more than to relive a past
struggle for survival. Lanzmann calls the witness back as a witness –
into the living present and its pain. If the interviewer's role is to break
the silence, the narrator's role is to insure that the story will go on.[13]

9

Charlotte Salomon's Inward-turning Testimony

Mary Felstiner

What gives artistic testimony a claim to historical truth about the Holocaust? By and large, only artwork or writings that look outward to situation and circumstance have gained the status of documentation on the Jewish catastrophe.[1] When the account of an eyewitness attends more to private than to public matters, it gets valued as a human emblem rather than as historical evidence: consider the critical response to diaries by Anne Frank and Etty Hillesum, and to another eyewitness document with a private perspective – the autobiographical artwork of Charlotte Salomon.[2]

So far, this extraordinary sequence of 1,325 paintings from 1941 to 1942 has worked intimately upon audiences in Europe, Israel, and America, but has seemed too personal, too peculiar, to serve Holocaust historians. When selections from Charlotte Salomon's work were first published in 1963, they were presented as *Charlotte: a diary in pictures* and welcomed as another journal to confirm the lesson of Anne Frank's: humane spirits ultimately outlast monstrous ones. Paul Tillich's moving preface gave readers reason to value an artist only 24 years old when she painted her life: "In these pictures and notes there is something universally human, something that bridges the distance between man and man. . . . The life of a very gifted and sensitive young woman, lived in one of the most terrible periods of European history . . . speaks in the almost primitive simplicity of these pictures."[3]

This approach, largely accountable for the international success of Charlotte Salomon's exhibitions and reproductions, no longer consti- tutes an adequate reading. For the work is not a "diary in pictures" but rather an *autobiographical drama*, as the fuller edition of reproductions, published in 1981, makes clear. What many have perceived as the "primitive simplicity of these pictures" borders on wishful thinking about a complex, theatrical self-scrutiny, created with conscientious craft.

What kind of historical evidence might we expect from eyewitnesses who mainly kept scrupulous track of the self – from I-witnesses, so to speak? Anne Frank's famous diary was "not a warbook," her father insisted; "war is the background." And Judith Doneson, quoting him, agrees: "War ... simply provides the backdrop for Anne's inner quest."[4] Her diary fixes the Holocaust "in a frame, in a thoroughly human setting," according to Alfred Kazin and Ann Birstein.[5] If Anne Frank could barely see the world outside her window, Charlotte Salomon barely bothered with it. "The war raged on, and I sat by the sea and saw deep into the heart of humankind," Charlotte wrote, recalling and recording incidents in the life of her family starting thirty years before.[6] A small proportion of the paintings attempt a documentary account of the persecution of German Jews: these portray the artist's stepmother deprived of a career in music, her father deprived of one in medicine, herself forced out of Germany, away from native land, language, family, everything familiar. But when the paintings treat the time of exile in which they were made – the hazardous years 1939 through 1943 while Charlotte Salomon lived in southern France – they include little else but inner episodes. The conditions of Jewish exile seem unlikely to emerge from a witness who painted as if fleeing into memory not into France. To uncover "that which happened" (as poet Paul Celan referred to the Holocaust), such privately disposed accounts have appeared deficient in range of vision.

And yet: "A painting may be as eloquent about causes as a revolution," historian Peter Gay has written, and a "work of art presents precisely the same causal puzzles as the eruption of a war."[7] To draw out of paintings an eloquence about their causes requires putting aside oppositions like "thoroughly human setting" and "inner quest" vs. historical "background" and wartime "backdrop." These metaphors, separating private expressions from public exigencies, confine "inner" episodes to psychological tokens, while limiting "Holocaust testimony" – a phrase that favors what would work in a judicial setting – to direct reporting of external circumstance. Can these oppositional metaphors be altered?

The dimensions of "that which happened" call for variously calibrated instruments of measure, including what can be gauged from a subjective witness to the self. If we hold up this work of art as a frozen section in the historical process (like tissue taken from a living organism and studied by pathologists), then we can scan it for outside influences that left their traces nowhere else.[8] Where so much was concealed or erased, it makes sense to ask: (1) What conditions, obscured by time and trauma, are clarified by this artist's selection of subject matter? (2) What contexts can be extrapolated from her chosen form? (3) What clues to the impact of events can be extracted from her idiosyncrasies of style? (4) Can Charlotte Salomon's paintings help us toward a new conception, that of *inward-turning testimony*, and so toward a broader usage of personal invention as historical evidence?

Charlotte Salomon, born in 1917, grew up in an assimilated German–Jewish family in Berlin. Unknown to her, almost all her maternal relatives, even her mother, had taken their own lives. The surviving family, principally her grandparents, lied about this legacy all during Charlotte's youth. Her father, a professor at the university hospital, remarried a well-known singer; both lost their professional positions when the Nazis came to power.

But Charlotte, under a strict quota, was admitted as one of two "full-Jewish" students at Berlin's Fine Arts Academy. While she learned conventional techniques there, her eventual mastery of Expressionist color and cropping, her use of radical caricature, un-Volkish folk art and cartoon-like irony, showed her affinity with every style the Nazis were working to suppress. Later, around age 24, certain irreparable breaks impelled her toward a still more radical form of painting.

The first of these breaks followed Kristallnacht in 1938: her parents insisted she leave Berlin for the safety of France's Côte d'Azur, to join her grandparents who had resettled there. When, several years later, she depicts her last hours at home in Berlin, her images follow the flow of memory like a hand-held camera, in and out of her family's rooms, coming to rest in her own. In that room, in that house, in that city, her belongings had their only existence. Yet they seem to dangle in space, nowhere at all.[9] The young woman stares at her vacant suitcase, waiting to know, literally and figuratively, what she can take away with her from Germany (plate 9.1).

Arriving on the Côte d'Azur in 1939, Charlotte found her grandmother deeply depressed, and, shortly after the outbreak of the War, the elderly woman attempted suicide. Suddenly, the grandfather revealed the secret kept from Charlotte for thirteen years since her mother's death: the women in this family, all of them, take their lives. Recognizing this life-threatening legacy as her own, Charlotte determined to save the two women who still survived. She depicts herself, for example, calming or cheering up her suicidal grandmother by singing the chorale of Beethoven's Ninth Symphony, set to Schiller's "Ode to Joy": *Freude schöner Götterfunken Tochter aus Elysium*, "Joy, thou spark from flame immortal, Daughter of Elysium." This all-too-familiar uplift seems incongruously superimposed on a tragic reality. But it was the kind of

Plate 9.1 *Life or Theater?* Charlotte Salomon about to leave Berlin in 1938. Photograph: Charlotte Salomon Foundation/Jewish Historical Museum, Amsterdam.

restorative, from within humanistic German culture, that might have kept a Jewish refugee sane.

In one painting, the grandfather, exhausted from the traumatic family events, fades into the background. The grandmother veers disjointed off the frame. Charlotte herself balances on the edge of a bed and sheds all identity of her own, stripped down to one color and outline, as deprived of features as she had previously been of facts (plate 9.2).[10] In this state of mind she began her autobiographical play, and in this state of heightened receptivity – a blank sheet waiting to be inscribed – she transmitted (even through her private story) something of the life and texture of her surrounding world.

Only occasionally did Charlotte depict, in a direct way, external events on France's Côte d'Azur, the place of her refuge from 1939 on; and so it is the peculiarity of what she chose to record that makes her testimony indispensable.

This notice appears in one of her painting: "*AVIS: Toutes les ressort-*

Plate 9.2 *Life or Theater?* Charlotte, Grandfather and Grandmother. The inscription alludes to Schiller's "Ode to Joy" sung at the climax of Beethoven's Ninth Symphony: "Joy, beautiful divine spark ..."

issantes allemandes sont tenues de quitter sans delai la ville et le département" (plate 9.3).[11] "Notice: All German nationals who are women are ordered to leave the city and the province without delay." In the painting, *ressortissantes allemandes* (those under German jurisdiction) is in the feminine gender, an apparent grammatical mistake in her newly acquired language, corrected (in the 1981 American edition) by changing the phrase to the masculine gender: *"tous les ressortissants allemands ..."* Crediting the feminine form of *"ressortissantes allemandes,"* I searched for an order she might have seen concerning women, and found one that appeared in Nice on 27 May 1940: *"Les femmes ressortissantes allemandes doivent se rendre au centre de Gurs"* ("Women under German Jurisdiction must present themselves at the Gurs center"), on the other side of France (plate 9.4).[12] The feminine usage in Charlotte's text, so unexpected that her version was discounted, opens up an event largely forgotten since then. When German armies forced their way into France in May 1940 – the period Charlotte's painting alludes to – spy-scares and shame drove the French government to evict German exiles, specifying women. As one exile writer quipped bitterly: "It was discovered that refugee women were not less dangerous than men."[13]

Charlotte's autobiography recorded this eviction order that led to her internment with thousands of German (mostly Jewish) women at Gurs in the Pyrenees, the largest concentration camp in France. Portraying an announcement rather than what followed, the painting transmits something overshadowed in post-war accounts: how refugees read (and misread) their situation, what portents first appeared that loosened their faith in France. Up till then, it had seemed almost natural that the

Plate 9.3 *Life or Theater?* "Notice: All German nationals who are women are ordered to leave the city and the province without delay." Photograph: Charlotte Salomon Foundation/Jewish Historical Museum, Amsterdam.

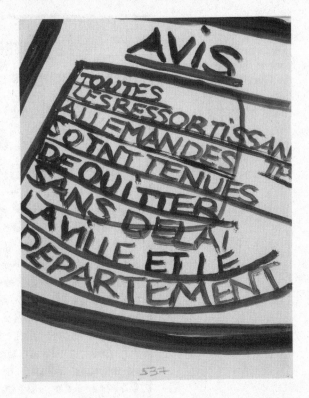

government should require of male foreigners one year's labor service, leaving non-laborers – women, children, the ill, the old – in place.[14] But when the conventional distinction of laborers from non-laborers collapsed, as it did with the internments of German-born women and children in the spring of 1940, trust in rational policy also began to collapse. No wonder this obscure order, alone of all orders at the time, struck Charlotte enough to recreate it: if France does *this*–? Because she took an almost exclusive interest in visual signs impinging on herself, her account testifies to a forgotten sequence: mass internment on the basis of nationality – overriding all accepted distinctions of politics and gender – prefigured imprisonment on the basis of race.

That these paintings generally bypass the daily documentation of collective events, that they deliberately face backward and inward, paradoxically enhances the evidence to be found in them. The very preference for one particular *form* – personal autobiography – bears witness to historical conditions.

Plate 9.4 "Women under German Jurisdiction must present themselves at the Gurs Center."

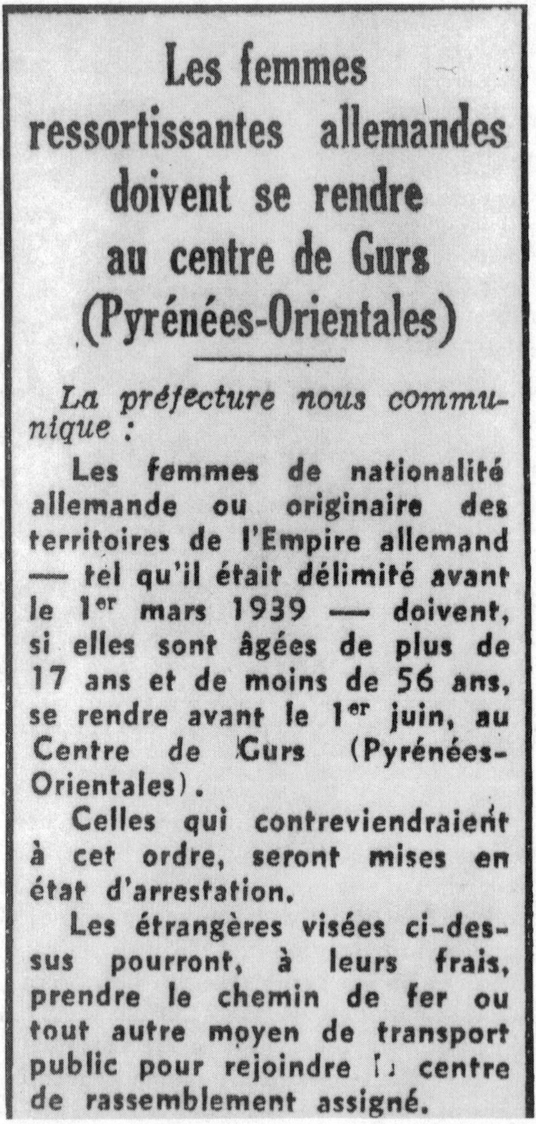

Les femmes ressortissantes allemandes doivent se rendre au centre de Gurs (Pyrénées-Orientales)

La préfecture nous communique :

Les femmes de nationalité allemande ou originaire des territoires de l'Empire allemand — tel qu'il était délimité avant le 1er mars 1939 — doivent, si elles sont âgées de plus de 17 ans et de moins de 56 ans, se rendre avant le 1er juin, au Centre de Gurs (Pyrénées-Orientales).

Celles qui contreviendraient à cet ordre, seront mises en état d'arrestation.

Les étrangères visées ci-dessus pourront, à leurs frais, prendre le chemin de fer ou tout autre moyen de transport public pour rejoindre le centre de rassemblement assigné.

Before Charlotte took to painting her life, all the artwork she created (comforting, decorative scenes, such as rooftops overlooking the sea, a baby asleep, an orchard in bloom) relied on close observation, not on troubled introspection. But something hastened her recourse to autobiography: the paintings turned inward as they absorbed the ambiance of exile. They began to touch on the same themes as self-descriptive writings with titles such as *Exile, Exile in France, Transit, The Inside Story of an Outsider*, which all showed how conditions in France were wearing down the exiles' previous identities.[15] "They were emigrants first of all, and their real selves only in the second place," wrote Lion Feuchtwanger; "the passports of most of them were gradually expiring and were not renewed by the authorities of the Third Reich. So these exiles found it hard to obtain official confirmation that they were who they were."[16] A distinctive number of them probed their pasts for a source of singularity, a confirmation that they were who they were. The shock of being typed as German nationals, though Germany had made them stateless, the dismay at being classed as Hitler's spies, when they would have spied on him, induced numerous writers, and at least one artist, to assert the particularity of each autobiographical past. As bureaucracies flattened the exiles' profiles, some reassembled an identity by straining to find what Charlotte said she "had to find: it is my self, a name for myself."[17]

Estrangement from one's environment, she discovered in exile, permitted the peopling of memory. "What else is there left to us writers in exile but to nourish our memories and write memoirs?" queried Ernst Weiss, a German Jewish writer resettled in Paris.[18] "Take refuge in your innermost self, in your work, flee to where you are no more than your own being, not the citizen of a state, not a plaything of this infernal game," advised Stefan Zweig, an Austrian Jewish exile in Brazil.[19] "I had to go deeper into solitude," Charlotte Salomon wrote from Nice, "then maybe I could find – what I had to find! It is my self: a name for myself. And with that I began Life and Theater."[20] Charlotte's work can symbolize the struggle of uprooted people anywhere, for her self-portrait in a thousand parts magnified a life considered expendable – female, stateless, Jewish. In those years, the making of diaries, autobiographies, and self-portraits manifests just how intently Jews cultivated an individuality the Nazis meant to cut down.

As a form, autobiography bore witness to the outside pressure on the inner identity of exiles. Might a peculiar *style* of self-absorption offer another clue to external surroundings?

For instance, a self-portrait of Charlotte preparing to return from the Pyrenees to Nice in July 1940 invents both an iconography of exile (the repeated packing of suitcases), and something stylistically idiosyncratic – a made-up song whose text dominates the painting: "A little girl, a big bed, after so much suffered, so many dead. . . . A little culture, a few rules, a vacuum at the core. That's all that's left of human beings in these times of ours."[21] By spelling *datums* ("times") as *datuum*, she aligns the times with *vakuum*; and by inscribing the word "vacuum" right on her body, she implicates the artist in the anomie around her. The effect is typical of her style: presenting critical conditions as stagey solos.

Taken at face value, this work falls short as a "testimony," because all-too-real events so often look like scenarios. Even factual references avoid specificity: an impressionistic dabbing of Xs and jots labelled "May 1940" stands for planes and bombs; moreover, the caption "War is declared" seems to confuse the September 1939 declaration of war with the May 1940 invasion of France. Scenes located in southern France do not name the "home on the Côte d'Azur" (Villefranche) where Charlotte first lived, or the "little town in the Pyrenees" (Gurs) where the French government interned her along with thousands of other German-born women.[22] Once when I asked Charlotte's stepmother, Paula Salomon-Lindberg, "Why do you think she never painted Gurs?", she replied: "Ach, my dear, she couldn't make that into theater."[23]

The whole work shows a striking desire to set theatrical grids over historical realities. It abounds in satirical asides, flashback sequences, shifting scenery, fast cuts and slow dissolves – not the way most autobiographies work, not a straight self-description at all. Charlotte introduces the people in her life as "the performers," giving them satiric fictional names. She converts the timespan into stage direction: "This play is set in the period from 1913 to 1940 in Germany, later in Nice" – the play in question being her life.[24] She transforms the "I" of most diaries and autobiographies into a third-person protagonist, directed by a sardonic narrator, scripted by an unnamed artist, who titles the whole ensemble *Leben oder Theater? Ein Singspiel*, "Life or Theater? An Operetta." Arranged in acts and scenes, narrated with dialogues and soliloquies, annotated for musical accompaniment, labelled an operetta, the whole work treats a true story as a script.

How to account for the theatrical style of this autobiography? We could start by looking back to Charlotte's youth in Germany, noting her familiarity (through her stepmother's singing career) with opera, her experience of plays produced by Berlin's Jewish Cultural Guild, her attention to German films as the precise expression of modern life, her training at the Berlin Fine Arts Academy in the illustration of mythical scenes. But even if these cultural holdovers encouraged Charlotte's theatrical bent, the question of an immediate contextual source remains. Did a stage-like ambiance perceptible to her in exile (though no longer to us) leave its trace in her paintings' dramatic form?

Reversals of reality, it turns out, were commonly experienced as theatricality by exiles in southern France. The Mediterranean coast, Franz Schoenberner said wryly, was "the right place to take a long and far view of contemporary history as well as of the ephemeral story of your own life. Germany and the Nazis seemed very distant."[25] That symbolic distance between the Reich and the Riviera made exiles feel the fictionality of their lives: they were obliged to emigrate where they barely used to dream of vacationing, as if they had fallen out of grace into Eden. Topsy-turvy felt like daily life for them, irony seemed another language to be learned. "And here we are [in the south of France]," wrote Alma Mahler-Werfel, "disoriented to the extreme," while Franz Werfel wrote his famous play of reversal, "Jacobowsky and the Colonel," subtitled "Comedy of a Tragedy."[26] Anna Seghers wrote: "You can stay here for any length of time only if you can prove that you intend to leave. Don't you understand that?"[27] And if you intended to leave, you were forced to stay. "Tragic paradoxes happened over and over in this war against the émigrés, managed by the bureaucracy," Alfred Kantorowicz lamented.[28] The paradoxes – anti-Nazis interned as Hitler's spies, unwanted refugees refused exit permits – could at least be grasped if one perceived life as theater: "Elements of comedy were only part of what revealed itself more and more clearly as a tragedy. This famous artistic trick," Franz Schoenberner wrote, "was borrowed from reality."[29]

Among the accounts by exiles in France's southern zone, then, metaphors often linked serious threats with squalid theatrics. Arthur Koestler saw his compatriots as characters in a "penny dreadful," a lowlife melodrama; "only reality was more dreadful." Franz Schoenberner wrote that "it was an agony to watch this bad show as a helpless spectator tucked away somewhere in a corner of the balcony. . . . And while waiting for the end of the world you were counting the last pennies in your pocket and wondering whether you would be able to buy a sandwich in the next intermission."[30] With the same sense of watching history at a cheap show, Charlotte Salomon set the stage and addressed the spectator: "You are hereby informed that you are located in an exclusively Jewish milieu which – for the honor of Germany – was assaulted at that time by one party. . . . Hitler was the name of the founder and creator of this party. In common parlance the party's supporters were simply called Nazis. Their symbol was the swastika."[31] No European needed to be told this: such writing presents an ineluctable fact as the prologue to a show.

It is on this metaphorical level that a work of art encodes its ethos.

As *Life or Theater?* placed a theatrical cast over historical facts, it attested to a quality of the Côte d'Azur that more objective documents fail to express: the place itself seemed staged.

On the one hand, Jews felt safer there than anywhere in France: Jewish worshippers moved about the streets, Jewish artists exhibited their work, Jewish committees aided the influx of refugees from everywhere else. The Côte d'Azur stood at the periphery of persecution, and Jews there faced dangers neither clear nor present. *Life or Theater?* expresses the spirit of a region that stayed long in the seismic outlands, far from the catastrophe's epicenter. "While there were battles everywhere," Charlotte wrote privately, "we stayed fairly tranquil on the Côte d'Azur."[32] It was not occupied by Germans after the 1940 armistice, and unlike other areas of the unoccupied southern zone, it had no regional internment camp, no corral for deportees. When the Germans finally occupied the southern zone in November 1942, the Côte d'Azur was taken over by Italy; and the Italian authorities refused to deport Jews.

But, on the other hand, it was also on the Côte d'Azur that the most virulent French anti-semitic movements tried out their rhetoric and force. This strip of coast, with its intense and open refugee élan and its paramilitary anti-semitism, with its astonishing healthfulness and its nearness to terror, had the air of a melodrama: the natural versus the bestial. When *Life or Theater?* presented historical realities as scenarios and stage sets, it was inscribing an environment whose own theatricality was evident to exiles at the time. An intrinsic equation between life and theater, far from disqualifying this account as testimony, shows its sensitivity to the illusions played out in a place like Nice.

Even subtle shifts of style through the course of *Life or Theater?* can become "eloquent about causes" (to return to Peter Gay's phrase), for they bring to view gradual erosions in the exiles' sense of sanctuary on the Côte d'Azur. Early paintings in *Life or Theater?* are playful cartoon-like scenes crowded with reiterated figures, intensely stippled with color, tagged with musical cues. Such scenes recreate a child's perceptions as well as an artist's exuberance once released from Berlin to the open air of France. In comparison, paintings done a year later, in the winter of 1941–2, look stripped down: musical accompaniments are mostly forgotten, and so are cartoon repetitions; the vibrant palette contracts to a few colors, and words take over the pictorial space until the final tableaux are pure language devoid of imagery. These changes impart a sense of outside pressure on an exile to get her story told. Moreover, when the artist reached the moment, well into the war, of assembling and editing her whole *oeuvre*, she took another significant stylistic shift: she re-made a simple retrospect into a complex spectacle.

The autobiography had apparently begun as a journey so private that the artist admitted, "Even I needed a year to figure out the meaning of this singular work, for many of its texts and melodies, especially in the first sheets, have slipped my mind."[33] On the backs of those first sheets she had often penciled musical and textual comments. But a year or so later, she expanded these notations, transferred them onto transparent sheets, and taped them over the paintings. The transparencies introduce the characters, direct the dialogues, order the action with numbers and arrows, mark out acts and scenes. It would be hard to imagine a more graphic invention for staging a story while keeping its director on the set. In other words, as "the meaning of this singular work" came to the artist, she moved the dramatic signifiers from the back of the paintings right out front. She apparently decided to unwrap a private memoir, to render transparent to others what would otherwise remain opaque.

Figuratively and literally, the artist overlaid her images with the dramatic intentions she discovered toward the end. The last section, set on the Côte d'Azur, opens with a reiterated figure (often repeated in the work) sketching the Mediterranean which turns blue with the sea, then orange with the sun, as if entering the very vista she presents: "Foam; dream. My dreams against a blue background. Why do you build up each time, renewed and clear, out of so much suffering and sorrow? . . . What are you preserving me for?"[34] In the closing scenes the question has its answer: she has been saved for this, for remaking what she remembers, for likening life to theater.

The addition of transparencies and other theatrical devices attests to something beyond Charlotte's own psyche and style: it registers the impact of circumstances that seemed surreal, what one eyewitness called "a hallucinatory spectacle."[35] After a time of illusory calm, while the artist accumulated many unedited scenes, suddenly in the summer of 1942 Nice turned Nazi: the city displayed its first anti-semitic exhibition in the Palais des Fêtes; French officials began the first round-ups in the streets; Jewish leaders witnessed 800 arrests, and the first transport of 500 Jews left for the transit camp of Drancy.[36] As such unexpected pressures threatened each Jew's future existence, Charlotte Salomon revised her story's structure to *require* spectators.

The movement of memoir toward operetta – surely a unique turn – draws our attention to a phenomenon not uncommon in Holocaust diaries and self-portraits: the invention of a captive audience and of rhetorical devices to keep it there. Anne Frank presented herself to the imaginary "Kitty." Felix Nussbaum painted a portrait of himself

presenting his portrait – holding up to the viewers an identity card
which his "real" face replicates.[37] *Life or Theater?* went even further,
conceiving an (inconceivable) audience and fabricating a future in its
very design. As it summoned spectators, it confessed to and contended
against isolation.

This is the paradoxical value of artistic invention as historical evidence: the very constraints on an artwork increase its expressiveness as
an artifact. The annulment of an audience to speak to, the scantiness
of materials to work with, the paucity of caches to put pictures in
– these problems and their creative solutions make vivid the Jewish
catastrophe.[38]

No less than any conventional document, a self-referential and theatrical invention can transcribe conditions it seemed hardly conscious of,
thereby giving historical inquiry a deeper reach. It is not that Charlotte's
play *describes* the Côte d'Azur, for as I have tried to show, it tends in
the opposite direction. Nor does it *reflect* the Côte d'Azur, for it is
never passive enough to serve as mirror. It seems to re-imagine its
environment – not the place itself, but the relation between self and
site, between art and actuality, in any such place.

Life or Theater? suggests an answer to the first question raised: What
gives artistic testimony a claim to historical truth about the Holocaust?
Layering text over picture, explanation over event, drama over document, *Life or Theater?* dissolves subjective and objective truths into
transparency. It even re-imagines chronology – the baseline of evidence
– as a layering of transparent intervals.

The artful times in Charlotte's work do lift her actual times to light.
She made her life story lead up to the moment she chose to paint it:
an autobiographer's chronology. Layered-over self-expressive time is
another kind – "this play is set in the period from 1913 to 1940": a
dramatist's chronology. Over theatrical time she set the artwork's date-
line, "August 1940/41," which she later revised to "August 1941/42,"
after spending "a year to figure out the meaning of this singular work":
a critic's reckoning. Then with bitter irony, she counted "August
1941/42" as the start of a dystopian age, "between heaven and earth
beyond our era in the year 1 of the new salvation":[39] an augurer's
chronology – probably her last touch.

After spending years painting her timely testimony, Charlotte Salomon
was arrested in the month of September 1943, imprisoned two weeks
in France, deported three days and nights eastward, and killed the hour
she arrived at Auschwitz.

10

"Varschreibt!"

R. B. Kitaj

Any Jew who wasn't there in Europe during the events of 1939–45 and who reads deeply enough in those events, may have been afflicted as I was. . . . I entered into a morbid period. The only psychology I know (a little) is the Psychology of Art (pace Malraux), and so I sought, maybe foolishly as some critics say, to paint my way through this morbid period, not knowing if it would have a middle or indeed an end. Every reader who has ploughed through this sinister literature, from the diaries of Ringelblum and Czerniakow and the Stroop Report, through the general histories to the gems – Levi, Celan, Wiesel's *Night*, Appelfeld – will have taken a turn in the road as I did. During this period, after neglecting him most of my life, I discovered the great French painter Georges Rouault with my newly affected eyes, and his lifelong cycle of pictures called *Passion*. It interested me greatly that painters of the Christian Passion had always been so very removed in time from *their* crucial subject. Even the earliest masters (Cimabue, Duccio, Giotto) arrived over a thousand years after the defining moment. I decided I wanted to meet our own Jewish subject, our salient crisis, in the foul breath of its very recent aftermath, feeling all the while as Kafka said in that letter to Brod: "The ensuing despair became their inspiration." The little picture illustrated here was one of my primitive, lame attempts to learn what to paint or not paint. *Varschreibt!* is what the grand old diasporist Simon Dubnov may have uttered as they shot him down in Riga . . . Record it! Write it Down! The stuff of legend. I made a very free transcription after some Picasso sketches of his little boy writing or drawing, enclosing the child's form in a chimney structure. Don't ask me why Picasso; I don't know. I fell upon the chimney as an analogue to the crucifix in European art and used it nervously in several paintings, drawing the objections (some heated, some tepid) I suspected would come from both Christian and Jewish critics. Are we

Plate 10.1 R. B. Kitaj, *Passion (1940–45) Varschreibt!* After Picasso, 1986 (unfinished). Oil on canvas, $16\frac{5}{8} \times 9\frac{1}{2}$ in. Marlborough Fine Art (London) Ltd.

not most profoundly hurt as Primo Levi was when he asked: "Why the Children?" There are some painters who cleave to the Crucifixion and I daresay there will be a few painters who will cleave to the Passion of the one and a half million children who went up in smoke in our time. That is the meaning of this configuration, my dubious small vertical poem in paint (plate 10.1).

When I was growing up in America I didn't know what a Jew was in any intelligent way. No one taught me. I was going to be an artist and that was not connected with recent events in Europe or with refugees in my own family. Being an artist was about Greenwich Village and the Spirit of Romance and European art and all that stuff. I thought you could be almost anything you wanted to be. But, as I grew older and the long post-war silence about the Holocaust (now much remarked upon) started to lift (the Eichmann trial was an early baptism for me), I began to notice a peculiar sense of Jewishness insist upon itself in my painting. In sophisticated modern painting that's not supposed to happen, though it does in sophisticated modern writing. I reckon there have been about eight or ten outstanding Jewish painters since the emancipation. No great painters, no Cezanne or Rembrandt or Matisse, but maybe ten first-rate painters, not one of which has wished to be known as a Jewish artist (Chagall may be an exception). The best of them, Soutine, has a cross on his grave. I don't blame them at all. It's real nice to just be a Very Good Artist and it can be very spiritual, like a nun marrying Christ.

About twenty years ago, Isaiah Berlin told me, speaking of a mutual friend who didn't think of himself as a Jew: "A Jew is a Jew like a table is a table." I always thought Isaiah knew a thing or two about such matters and I was already pondering the Jewish Question as a force in my art in some way I couldn't quite grasp, except that it was a coincident force in my life and our extraordinary times. All art is about oneself in ways we know and ways we don't, and I was drawn to an idea one didn't come across much in modern art: that painting might be about an examined life along with all the other things it can be about. Slowly, and with limited courage and energies I would take up this Jewish Question in the only way I could, at the point in its long history where I found myself.

Artists may disguise themselves in intriguing strategies. They may suppress or neglect deep inner dramas (Degas said making art was like the perpetration of a crime). I have come to believe that the best art is led by the hand of singular passion and obsession into what may be dangerous territory. Even the sublime Matisse confessed he was "frightened sometimes by [his] discoveries." That sort of radicality is what makes great art unusual, rare. And the Jewish Question seems to be a dangerous place, both to me and to those many modernists who have suggested it is not a province where art can thrive. It scares me and obsesses me and draws me to its bosom like a fantastic seductress. And, I confess, I often flee from her and try to forget about Jewishness for a while. That's not easy either. We know enough about Picasso to doubt that he ever left off being a Spaniard, feeling it in his art.

Why are the Jews always in trouble? The catastrophe in Europe and the danger of a second genocide in Israel (whose population centers together are about the size of Greater Indianapolis) began to assume a role in my life in art, like the Christian Passion had played in the lives of so many painters of the past, from Giotto to Matisse. Maybe art is right to gather up its various aesthetics, like seven veils, and dance through our unbeautiful time toward all its Manifest Destinies, from Art for Art's sake to whatever it was Adorno said about poetry after Auschwitz. But my peculiar sense of art was always uneasy with assimilation to these modern dogmas – they still delight, but as modernism gets to be as old as our century, they are showing their age.

I've begun a new painting, inspired by some great lines Kafka wrote to Brod about the predicament of young Jews in their time: "with their hind legs they were still glued to their father's Jewishness and with their waving front legs they found no new ground. The ensuing despair became their inspiration." What an image: those waving front legs seeking after Zionism, America, Socialism, Art, Paris, Assimilation, even the Catholic Church. That was before Kafka's sisters were murdered. The world has changed for the Jews, and I daresay their art, for what it is worth, will have changed too. Our waving front legs may still seek new ground but our hind legs are glued to another sense of Jewishness (post-1945) the fathers never anticipated.

11

Conversation in the Cemetery: Dan Pagis and the Prosaics of Memory

Sidra DeKoven Ezrahi

The town where I was born, Radautz, in the county of Bukovina, threw me out when I was ten. On that day she forgot me, as if I had died, and I forgot her too. We were both satisfied with that.

Forty years later, all at once, she sent me a souvenir. Like an unpleasant aunt whom you're supposed to love just because she is a blood relative. It was a new photograph, her latest winter portrait. A canopied wagon is waiting in the courtyard. The horse, turning its head, gazes affectionately at an elderly man who is busy closing some kind of gate. Ah, it's a funeral. There are just two members left in the Burial Society: the gravedigger and the horse.

But it's a splendid funeral; all around, in the strong wind, thousands of snowflakes are crowding, each one a crystal star with its own particular design. So there is still the same impulse to be special, still the same illusions. Since all snow-stars have just one pattern: six points, a Star of David in fact. In a minute they will all start melting and turn into a mass of plain snow. In their midst my elderly town has prepared a grave for me too.

Dan Pagis, "Souvenir"[1]

What are we to say of the poet of empty spaces and elliptical signs who begins in his last years to build sentences of all the discarded words and conjunctives, the continuities and chronologies, the properties and proprieties, abandoned along the way? How are we to read the poet of undeciphered riddles and uncharted mazes, who in his last writing provides maps and compasses, a whole new syntax to restructure the inscriptions of memory?

With the posthumous publication of Dan Pagis's complete works[2] it becomes evident that this poet (1930–86) – who was born into a German-speaking Jewish home in the Bukovina region of Romania and survived the war years in labor camps in Transnistria to become one of Israel's finest modern writers – was moving at the end of his life through a series of prose forms that signaled new possibilities for engaging the past. The prose-poem "Souvenir" first appeared in Hebrew in 1982 as part of the last book of poetry published during Pagis's lifetime. That short text shows memory not only prodded by a relic of the past but re-incorporated into it, even in a sense, *replaced* by it.

The world of the poet's childhood had been all but effaced in the post-war poetry, the past de-realized, or rather ether-realized as fragments in the outer spaces of the soul.[3] ("On that day she forgot me, as if I had died, and I forgot her too. We were both satisfied with that.") The re-emergence, in the form of a photograph, of the material presence of the past has an impact on the poet's psyche not unlike the rediscovery of the Laocoön statute for the Italian artists of the sixteenth century.[4] Relics are both the metonymies and the authenticating evidence of our foothold in buried worlds – especially when, as in the case of the Laocoön, a person *chances* upon them while ploughing his field or planting his vineyard . . . In the text before us, the physical place evoked by the photograph becomes the repository of memories that, for so many years, had nowhere to land. But the memento takes on the aspect of a *memento mori*; the place of origin, the town that "threw him out" when he was ten, becomes the matrix for the poet's final return, the only possible grave for a life that has been haunted by – as the poetry has been enabled by – weightlessness.

In Nabokov's *Speak, Memory*, as in so many other autobiographies of exiles in the twentieth century, photographs place the self in the context of family and native landscape, reconstructing and rescuing the past; "Souvenir," by contrast, is a verbal rendering of a visual image that contains a generic memory of the *place without the self* – a hollow place to which the Holocaust survivor can return only by surrendering – at last – his mortality. The expulsion and death warrant issued against the poet and his kin in 1939 had pre-empted a post-war return to the sites of childhood through memory's restorative vision, and rendered his survival a kind of computational effort ("I was a mistake . . . forgotten in the sealed boxcar," is a phrase that recurs in poem after poem, like a litany[5]). Having lived vis-à-vis his past "as if [he] had died," that is, having yielded his life unto the fictive, having died *into fiction*, he can now – once the encounter between town and self is re-established in the present – die "for real" or *into* reality. The following is an attempt to explore that shift from the fictive to the real, from the poetic masque to the autobiographical persona, from poetry to prose in the late writings of Dan Pagis.

In a rare interview granted in 1983, three years before his death, Pagis referred to an earlier poem "Akevot" ("Footprints") as the first "crack in the wall of forgetfulness."[6] "Footprints," like many poems in *Gilgul* (1970), was precipitated by an encounter with a physical emblem of his childhood: a room in the New York apartment of distant relatives that "looked exactly like the house of my grandfather in which I had grown up. For years I had tried to ignore the subject of the Holocaust, but the sight of the room, which appalled me, enabled and even forced me to write poems on this subject."[7] The room appears, in the telling, as a kind of nature preserve, a museum-like reconstruction of a lost world. In poems written subsequent to this visit, that room (or its prototype in Bukovina) is refracted into its component parts, which float about without the benefit of narrative or any other gravitational force – with only the taut poetic line to bind the particles together. An ancient chime clock, an Underwood typewriter, a walnut bureau, give way to "the interstellar space" just beyond the door to the library in grandfather's house, and the nine-year old with the "rather thin arms" flies so fast that he's "motionless," leaving behind him the "transparent wake of the past."[8] As if following some metaphysical law of conservation, memory that refuses to die is set loose as a property of the universe, infusing clouds, rain, interplanetary spaces with snippets of human grammar: "As always the trespassing clouds rushed by / and a blind rain went begging and rattled / a can for charity . . ."[9]

Though "Footprints" comes closer than any of Pagis's poems to a sustained memory, it remains a narrative manqué, marking the synapses of future connections until some more compelling relic of the past should surface to force a re-emplotment. Disembodied voices jostle each other in the heavenly spheres and their stories become a patchwork of interrupted conversations, uncompleted journeys. In the end the primary speaker, who "against my will . . . / was continued by this cloud," returns to the earthly stratosphere and hovers above his former home: "Over there, / in that arched blue, on the edge of the air, / I once lived." Just below him "there flickers / this ball of the earth / scarred, covered with footprints."[10]

The footprints are the negative, empty traces of a lived life, memory imprints that survive as the disconnected cameos of lives snuffed out

in mid-motion, as a truncated joke that is a sign of the father's sense
of humor (deprived of referent), as gestures severed from their moorings
in a remembering self:

> Maybe there's a window here — if you don't mind,
> look near that body, maybe you can open up
> a bit. That reminds me
> (pardon me) of the joke about the two Jews
> in the train, they were traveling to
>
> Say something more; talk.
> Can I pass from my body and onwards — [11]

The voice of the de-personed first person is not, then, harnessed to a
sustained, linear act of representation but unleashed in a cosmic echo-
chamber. Fragments of personal and collective memory interact in mutually subversive ways throughout "Footprints," respecting neither the
habit of formulaic or archetypal recall that informs the narrative of
collective biography, nor the minimal laws of physics and biology (the
one-directionality of time and of falling objects) that could secure the
material basis for the *auto*biography.

Yet the very premise of narrative, unresolved as it is in "Footprints,"
opens up possibilities that will be more fully realized toward the end
of Pagis's life. The physical properties that prodded memory in *Gilgul*
will acquire a more consequential and sequential status in the prose-
poems that appear twelve years later. In the 1983 interview (the interview itself is a sign of a new self-regarding), Pagis dwells on the autobiographical reference embedded in "Souvenir." Having heard that there
was a photographic exhibition on "The Last Jews of Radautz" at the
Diaspora Museum in Tel Aviv, the poet went out of his way to avoid
seeing it: "I, of course, did not want to know anything about Radautz,
my hometown, and I denied it [the reflexive term *"hitkahashti"* actually
connotes self-denial], as if I were continuing to forget the place that
had forgotten me . . ."[12]

Yet one photograph seems to have pursued him with the force of
destiny — the town, as it were, seeking out its native son so insistently
that on two other occasions, in entirely unrelated contexts, he found
himself in front of that picture of Radautz (see plate 11.1). These would-
be and actual encounters precipitated a "crisis in [my] relation to place
and time, to reality, to 'realia' that can be given a name, to palpable
things in an actual situation." His "mythical," "distanced," highly "stylized" writing began to give way to an attempt to "take a stand" in the

Plate 11.1 The hearse of the burial society, Radautz, Romania, 1970. Beth Hatefutsoth Exhibition, The Nathan Goldmann Museum of Jewish Diaspora, Tel Aviv. Photograph: Laurence Salzmann.

world through an exploration of the "biographical, the real product of place and time." It is, by Pagis's own admission, a transference of creative weight from "form" to "content," a "linguistic liberation from certain stylized forms," from the "poetics of the 'well-made poem' [in English in the original]" to a more open-ended attempt to enter real time.[13]

The photograph from Radautz seems to have evoked an acknow-ledgment of the presence – or insistence – of the Real no less dramatic than Roland Barthes's affirmation of photography as the place in which "I can never deny that *the thing has been there*."[14] Barthes and Susan Sontag have affirmed the authenticity and ontology of the photograph not only as a mimesis of the experienced world, like writing or painting, but as an artifactual trace of it: "A photograph is not only an image (as a painting is an image), an interpretation of the real; it is also . . . something directly stenciled off the real, like a footprint or a death mask."[15] Disallowing the alienation of the thing from its representation, photography is the medium to which "the referent adheres."[16] Barthes's extraordinary meditation on photography, *Camera Lucida*, triggered by the death of his mother and the discovery of a picture of her as a child (the "Winter Garden Photograph"), provided a reference for his own life that was fast unraveling. It has been argued that *Camera Lucida* is the most referential and conventionally autobiographical of Barthes's writing, coming at the end of his life and reclaiming something like an essentialist self.[17] It was, then, a single photograph that touched off an autobiographical quest for Pagis as for Barthes and a return to a kind of mimetic imperative at the end of a creative life spent circumventing it.

By relinquishing the mimetic project in his poetry, by renouncing the available strategies for structuring experience through the myths or chronologies by which a community remembers, Pagis, more radically perhaps than any other post-Holocaust poet except Paul Celan,[18] had surrendered the "privileged" status of the survivor. His survival seemed to grant him instead the immunity that attends a posthumous voice, its freedom from rather than indebtedness to history. His poetry resisted "sentencing," that is, the logic and compensations of narrative, the comfort of *human* time ("time becomes human time to the extent that it is organized after the manner of a narrative," says Paul Ricoeur[19]). "Autobiography," which appeared in the volume *Moah* (*Brain*) in 1975, begins:

> I died with the first blow and was buried
> among the rocks of the field . . .
>
> If my family is famous,
> not a little of the credit goes to me.
> My brother invented murder,
> my parents invented grief,
> I invented silence.
>
> Afterwards the well-known events took place.
> Our inventions were perfected. One thing led to
>   another,
> orders were given. There were those who murdered
>   in their own way,
> grieved in their own way . . .[20]

The specificity of autobiography and its literary conventions are undermined here by evoking universal myths and by a "metaphysical" violation of human time and telling ("I died with the first blow . . ."). Pagis's poetic voice often emanates from elementary biological particles,

from parts of the body, from pre- or post-historic forms of evolution and
even from inert matter. His "I" becomes so generalized, dehumanized or
unbounded as to preclude any lyric possibility. The self-effacement in
this poetry is not the partial recovery of memory so common to survivor
writing in which the main protagonist is the story itself, struggling –
against amnesia, against repression – to be told.[21]

And yet, having been preserved as a kind of cosmic dust, the fragments
of autobiography that accumulate haphazardly in the (earlier) *poetry*
finally begin to coalesce in the (late) *prose*. At the end of his life, Pagis
begins to fit the pieces into a more conventional tale told by a remembering self. First comes gravity.[22] Next come the words: words "out of
line," no longer contained in sparse, unyielding poetic strophes;[23] words
that are like hungry locusts, covering the books, the face, the mouth
of one who used to choose among them so sparingly;[24] words that
reduce metaphoric ambiguity to simple equations ("since all snow-stars
have just one pattern: six points, *a Star of David in fact*"). The almost
total absence of confessional referents in Pagis's poetry is compensated
in the prose by a wry counter-strategy of intimation, which leads the
reader to believe that the mystery in the poetry is an encoded message
searching for a prosaic resolution:

> You ask me how I write. I'll tell you, but let this be confidential.
> I take a ripe onion, squeeze it, dip the pen into the juice, and
> write. It makes excellent invisible ink: the onion juice is colorless
> (like the tears the onion causes), and after it dries it doesn't leave
> any mark. The page again appears as pure as it was. Only if it's
> brought close to the fire will the writing be revealed, at first
> hesitantly, a letter here, a letter there, and finally, as it should be,
> each and every sentence. There's just one problem. No one knows
> the secret power of the fire, and who would suspect that the pure
> page has anything written on it?[25]

Pagis's most coherent autobiographical statement – a dramatic departure
from the taut, enigmatic poetic line that had become the hallmark of
his writing – appears in the prose sequence "Abba" (Father). This is
the text made visible, the blank page whose writing has materialized
through the secret of the fire. "Abba," though left incomplete at the
poet's death,[26] features what had previously been omitted or denied.
The mise-en-scène, a cemetery, and the temporal frame, the narrator's
yearly visits to his father's grave on the anniversary of his death, seem
to facilitate rather than impede a conversation that was impossible
during the father's lifetime. Pagis's "conversation in the cemetery" is a

genuine dialogue between two definable interlocutors – between a father
and a son whose thirty-five years of estrangement had come from a
radical misunderstanding.

The unlikely setting and timing of these encounters are in inverse
proportion to the matter-of-fact nature of the exchange: the only (?!)
extraordinary aspect is that the father is dead ... creating, granted,
occasional technical problems ("if I were still alive," says the father,
"you could even have done a comparative blood test [to establish
paternity beyond the shadow of a doubt]"[27]). The consciousness that
this conversation is taking place in that narrow period of grace between
the father's death and the son's is not only the prerogative of the reader
with hindsight: there is, at the end, a whimsical projection into the
afterlife, when (what is rare in Pagis's poetic universe) the two interlocutors finally share the same time zone. Yet, despite the metaphysical
premise, what emerges in the main body of this text is so utterly prosaic,
so meticulously and self-consciously accurate in its historical priorities,
so immersed in *conversation* and inimical to the overdetermined nature
of symbolic language,[28] that if it were the writing of an old man, it
might appear that he was, under the aspect of mortality, slyly parodying
or deconstructing the work of a lifetime.

The autobiographical gesture of the survivor generally precedes the
emergence of a fictive self and establishes a baseline of reference and
authenticity; Yiddish novelist Leib Rochman and Italian writer Primo
Levi are two of the many examples that come to mind. Here, however,
autobiography appears at the end of a life of the most elaborate poetic
evasions – and would seem to signify a major conversion rather than
the need to establish a survivor's credibility. Tracing lines of convergence
between the confessions of the saints and modern autobiographical
narrative, John Freccero identifies conversion as the common paradigm:

> What was thematized in Christianity as the conversion of the
> sinner into the saint who tells his story may be thematized in a
> modern narrative in a variety of ways that need have very little
> to do with the Christian experience. The essential paradigm is
> unchanged, for it springs from the formal exigencies of telling
> one's life story rather than from any explicit experience. To state
> the matter hyperbolically, we might say that every narrative of
> the self is the story of a conversion, or to put the matter the other
> way around, a conversion is only a conversion when it is expressed
> in a narrative form that establishes a separation between the self
> as character and the self as author. When he told his life story in

terms of a conversion from paganism to Christianity, Augustine was at the same time establishing a literary genre, the confession, or narrative of the self.[29]

Is Pagis's autobiographical prose creating a "separation between the self as character and the self as author"? Is Pagis not establishing, rather, a "self" to supersede the self-lessness of his poetic voice? Not a separation, then, but a *reintegration* of character and author:

> "You didn't understand your father" [says the deceased father's card partner] . . . "You resemble him but only externally, if you'll forgive me for saying so." I become nervous: "So what then? Does he have to return to life so that I can understand him?" "No, no," says the card-player. "It's you who have to return to life. But if you'll forgive me for saying so, you don't stand much chance of doing that."[30]

Having for some twenty-five years invoked and then refused the solipsism, self-indulgence or self-confirmation that autobiography entails, Pagis now achieves dialogue by constructing a persona ("Dan") who so resembles the author (Dan) as to allow him to re-enter and reappropriate the historical moment. Giving realia a name becomes a major task in the prose writing, a task nearly as consequential as the circumlocutions that characterized the poetry. His native town now materializes as Radautz; his mother as Yuli.[31] But most challenging of all is self-nomination:

> Like the absent-minded professor who
> called home and asked, 'It's me here,
> where should I be?' – so I called and
> asked, 'I'm Dan, who should I be?' and
> in my absent-mindedness I didn't notice
> that the line was busy.
>
> ("A Funny Question")[32]

Only thinly disguised by the wit is the existential shift from *where* to *who* – from tenuous location at the very boundaries of existence to self-defining questions of essence. In explicating Julia Kristeva's theory of the "Borders of Language," Shuli Barzilai represents the collapse of "self-limits" in the psychotic or borderline patient topographically: "Instead of '*Who* am I?' [the borderline] patient asks, '*Where* am I?' . . . The 'borderlander' is always an exile; '"I" is expelled,' or ceases

to be, for, 'How can I be without border?' This absence of identity –
a psychic wandering or loss of place – is congruent with a discourse
produced on the borders of language," and Kristeva locates poetic
language which, "'by its very economy borders on psychosis'" as a kind
of borderline discourse.[33]

Pagis's move away from an altered set of voices echoing at the fragile
borders of language, and toward the recovery of a particular voice with
recognizable limits, remains a gesture which he never lived to complete.
"Dan" the persona, like Dan the writer, is only a marker or signifier
of an original, unrevealed identity:

> "Your name? [asks the father.] Which of them, if you don't
> mind? The name I gave you (okay, it wasn't really me, Aunt Tzili
> suggested it), that resonant Latin name you erased when you came
> to Israel. You chose the most common one: Dan. I never said
> anything. I understood that you wanted to disappear in the coun-
> try, simply to be absorbed into it like water into sand. How does
> it go? If you change your name you change your luck, right? But
> I am grateful that you never changed our family name. Do you
> understand me?" "No, Abba."[34]

"Dan's" interlocutor, the father, appears no less vigorous for being
dead. The diaphanous film between the living and the dead had never
been an impediment to communication in Pagis's poetry – in some sense
it actually facilitated the encounter ("Ready for parting, as if my back
were turned, I see my dead come toward me, transparent and breathing
...."[35]). In "Abba," however, the centrifugal forces that made such
"communication" possible yield to a centripetal thrust that is a genuine
homecoming. The grave provides again (as in the photograph of
Radautz) a compelling center of gravity. As the biblical Moses was
"gathered unto his people," so the poet's father is gathered unto the
son: he is reclaimed as an integral, sentient person; his humor, which
had floated in the outer space of disembodied spirits in "Footprints,"
is reincorporated into a specific center of consciousness. The poetics
of self-transcendence yields to the prosaics of memory: the father's
dematerialization through death suspends, for once, the imperative of
surrealist *poetic* dematerialization, creating its own counter-imperative.
In imagining the father, the author gives him not only a sustained voice
but also a defense, in many ways incriminating to the son ("You think
that you spared me by not speaking to me about the important things.
You had to wait till I died?"[36]). The "important things" revolve around
the son's presumption that his father's immigration to Palestine, in

1934, amounted to an abandonment – an assumption reinforced by his failure to send for the boy after the mother's death a few months later, or, for that matter, any time thereafter. Years of polite estrangement followed the reunion between father and son in Tel Aviv after the war.

The belated reconciliation with the father is buttressed by written evidence: faded letters from mother and grandmother in Bukovina, containing expressions of intense family devotion and confirming the father's intention to bring his wife and son to Palestine. It emerges that after the mother's death the family in Bukovina – who could not imagine that a widower barely able to eke out a living for himself would be able to care properly for a young child in Palestine – prevailed, and the child remained with his grandparents. Marginalia on the pages of the manuscript indicate that, in addition to the letters, the author had intended to incorporate his father's will and a number of photographs into the text of "Abba." Might such photographs have included one of the mother taken a short time before her death, to which the poem "Ein Leben" refers? ("In the month of her death, she is standing by the window frame, / a young woman with a stylish permanent wave / . . .[37]) Or must that photograph remain, like Barthes's Winter Garden photograph, unreproduced precisely because through it the mother has re-engendered the writer for his last, autobiographical act? "(I cannot reproduce the Winter Garden Photograph. It exists only for me. For you, it would be nothing but an indifferent picture, one of the thousand manifestations of the 'ordinary'; . . . in it, for you, no wound.)"[38] Whatever the specific nature of the documentary material, the entire manuscript of "Abba" seems to appeal to some higher court which pronounces the truth to be far more redemptive than fictions generated by the imagination. The use of "evidence" in this narrative is a sign of the extent and the consequences of the "conversion" – the text with its documentary implants reaches through the autobiographical or confessional toward the historical, constituting a further development in the unearthing of objects of the past that come to replace the imaginative compositions of memory. It makes the poet a kind of historian in the sense defined by Ricoeur:

> History as a science removes the explanatory process from the fabric of the narrative and sets it up as a separate problematic. It is not that the narrative is oblivious to the forms "why" and "because," but its connections remain immanent to the emplotment. For historians, the explanatory form is made autonomous; it becomes the distinct object of a process of authentification and justification. In this respect, historians are in the situation of a

judge: placed in the real or potential situation of a dispute, they attempt to prove that one given explanation is better than another. They therefore seek "warrants," the most important of which is documentary proof.[39]

If the move toward narrative in Pagis's late writing is a radical shift toward self-emplotment, the addition of documentary material in the "Abba" text is, then, a further move in the direction of "historiographical" self-authentification and explanation. And the manuscript found in the author's estate tells a tale as revealing as the story contained within it: many of the marginalia annotating the unfinished Hebrew text are written in his mother tongue, *German.*

In the wake of a catastrophe that is contemporaneous with the birth-pangs of a nation, narratives of survival participate in the privileging of history itself as an epic story. Hebrew literature, so saturated with memory and counter-memory, could barely contain Pagis's dismembering poetry which was a radical dis-remembering. But the prosaic "I," newly situated in time and space, relocates the moral center from an imaginary universal space into an historically particularized territory – arguing now not against but within the collective constructs of time and memory. By restoring human time and the voice of a subject clearly located in the present, his remembering prose is at the most fundamental level a re-entry into the epic discourse.[40]

It was the absence not only of a subject in the present but also of any specifically addressed and definable *other* that had made the community of his readers the primary audience in Pagis's poetry and the act of reading so consequential for closure.[41] But in "Abba" the address to a specific other within the text relegates the reader to the more conventional status of voyeur/observer. Any sense of impoverishment in the prose may be a function of such subtle reorientations – leaving its readers deprived, in a sense, of their presence as subjects in the poetry. In addition, our judgment of the scant and unfinished manuscript that was to become Pagis's last will and testament is constrained by the fact that, had he lived, "Abba" would undoubtedly have assumed additional shapes and dimensions. But the text before us is at the very least a signpost of the direction Pagis's last writing was taking into the precincts of a history that denies or defies imagination, that had come unharnessed from the utopian or dystopian thrust into alternative worlds. . . . We seem to have followed the sculptor beyond the "captives" half-imprisoned in their rock, to the unchiseled block of marble lying virginal in his workshop basement. This, the unworked, prosaic matter of his art, becomes its "truest" form.

Even in its incomplete, pristine state, the material under discussion has the spell-binding quality of both a story and a confession. As hermeneutic map, Pagis's late prose is valuable for fixing interpretative strategies: the poems become the text (*peshat*) and the prose its commentary (*drash*). Pagis has drawn closer to the riddle literature that formed the subject of his last research – moving out of an absurd world of inscrutable riddles into an answerable, disenchanted universe. But as full of *presence* as these prose texts are, what is missing (for this reader) is precisely the absences – all the circumlocutions and mysteries that had characterized a Pagis text. A poetry of unfathomable depths poised at the borders of language, of enigmatic signals sent directly to the reader, has yielded to a sane set of surfaces that beckon the reader merely to eavesdrop.

Do we read this prose, then, as an alternative construct of memory, or do we read it as "final words" that provide an ultimate deciphering, a hermeneutic code imposed on that spare poetry of empty spaces? And our uneasiness concerning this shift to a prosaics of memory, is it but that of petulant readers deprived of fictive unlikeliness, of a more obvious type of lyric enchantment?

> Yet not too like, yet not so like to be
> Too near, too clear, saving a little to endow
> Our feigning with the strange unlike, whence
>   springs
> The difference that heavenly pity brings.
> For this, musician, in your girdle fixed
> Bear other perfumes. On your pale head wear
> A band entwining, set with fatal stones.
> Unreal, give back to us what once you gave:
> The imagination that we spurned and crave.
>   Wallace Stevens, "To the One of Fictive Music"

12

Chinese History and Jewish Memory

Vera Schwarcz

Hold with the past, don't lose the past:
If you lose the past, you will easily break;
If you lose the past, even the sword snaps;
If you lose the past, the zither too laments.
And the Master's tears for the loss of the past
In those days fell streaming in torrents.

Meng Jiao, "Autumn Meditations"[1]

Jews need not struggle with the foibles of human memory alone. Before and around them stretch centuries of meditation on the problem of remembrance. We must enter into dialogue with these traditions if we are to hear something more than the music of our personal lamentations. If we listen for the meanings of the Holocaust exclusively in the echo chamber of Jewish history, we will miss reverberations that connect these to a broader human experience. If, on the other hand, we stray too far from the core, from the uniqueness of a particular tradition, we risk the unselfconscious projection of Jewish dilemmas upon histories quite distinct from our own.

Let me offer a personal example. I began the study of Chinese history while trying to distance myself from my parents' experiences of the war in Hungary and Romania. For a full decade (between 1969 and 1979) I researched the problem of modern Chinese intellectuals as if they inhabited a world that had nothing to do with my parents. Then, I went to China as part of the first group of official American exchange scholars. Living in Beijing for a year and half (1979–80) I began to hear something new in the intensity of my conversation with intellectual survivors of the Cultural Revolution: they spoke to me with a candor that was unexpected in those early months of tentative openness with the West. I, in turn, responded with an empathy that went far beyond my language skills and my knowledge of the details of Chinese history.[2]

It took another decade for the common ground between Chinese and Jewish survivors of historical trauma to become fully apparent to me. Longer still, for me to begin to write about the similarities and differences between Chinese intellectuals who were my friends and informants in Beijing, and my parents who were sorting through their memories of the Holocaust in Miami Beach.[3] Now that the process has begun, I have a clearer sense of how the study of Chinese history has enabled me both to stray from and circle back to the most troubling parts of my parents' experiences in Europe. Chinese history has become a tool with which I now probe the intricacies of Jewish remembrance as well as memorial lacunae that still haunt my parents, and me.

The question of how to live with fractured memories haunted the Tang dynasty poet Meng Jiao as well. His "Autumn Meditations," composed in the early ninth century, represent an impassioned warning against the dangers of forgetting.[4] These poems took advantage of a literary tradition that sanctioned the use of one's later maturity for cultural introspection. But they went a step beyond the Confucian sanction for self-reflection in old age. They became a dirge to mourn the loss of commitment to remembrance in a culture seemingly riveted by its own history. Meng Jiao's "Meditations" reveal a man obsessed by the fragility of his contemporaries' attachment to the past. They show us a man unconsoled by the voluminous evidence of China's public memory as recorded in the dynastic annals and their voluminous commentaries.

Meng Jiao wrote about broken swords and mournful zithers to remind his fellow literati about a fact they knew too well: that human minds prefer to wander away from the fragmented, vanishing past to the material rewards of the present. By invoking the torrential tears of the Master – Confucius – Meng Jiao placed himself in a distinctive lineage. This lineage embraces those rememberers who remember others that live by the covenant of "holding with the past." Confucius, the source of this lineage in the fifth century BC, described his mission in the *Analects* as follows: "I am not someone who was born knowing the past. Rather, I am one who quests for it earnestly."[5] By calling himself a "seeker of the past" (*qiu gu zhe*), Confucius became a model for Chinese intellectuals who would reinterpret, dynasty after dynasty, the meanings of inherited history.

This determination to look beyond the codified past and seek historical understanding afresh links Meng Jiao backward to Confucius and forward to our own century in which catastrophic events such as the

Holocaust and the Cultural Revolution (of 1966–9) reopened the wound
of memory. Concern with historical amnesia is, in my view, a shared
obsession among Chinese and Jews who would rehabilitate remembrance
in our time.

This "obsession" shines through Meng Jiao's "Autumn Meditations"
in spite of the melancholy of a man whose sons died in infancy. This
urgent concern overcomes the bitterness of a man who never held a
post above the lowest rank in the provincial hierarchy. It modifies,
even, the obstinacy that led Meng Jiao to write about his losses in a
most difficult, "old style" poetry.

In my ears, Meng Jiao's voice is not sequestered to Tang dynasty
China. It comes through, amplified by my father's voice. My father,
too, spoke endlessly about the need to "hold with the past." He and
his comrades from the labor camp spent their days in Miami worried
about the danger of "losing the past." In fact my father became so
insistent about the past that he wanted to make his memory mine. His
story took hold of me and would not let go until I finished recreating
a world that began before my birth in "liberated," post-war Romania.

I had been born in 1947 in the Transylvanian capital of Cluj. My
father's memories took me back to the shadow-filled avenues of
Kolosvar–Klausenburg – an Austro-Hungarian city I never knew. Yet
this old-world town with its distinguished universities, sophisticated
Jewish merchants – including my maternal grandparents – was it the
same as "my" Cluj? But my city tried to wear the face of a historyless
girl after the war. Only my parents' memories, mostly unvoiced in
Romania, suggested another story.

That story began to be told in America. Only abroad, decades after
the war, did my father become convinced that the present must draw
sustenance from the past. After the move to America he kept telling
me stories that were meant to bridge his losses and adventures during
the Holocaust in Cluj–Kolosvar–Klausenburg back to his parents' home
in the Bucovina of the 1920s and forward to the grandchildren he came
to know after our emigration in 1962. Unlike Meng Jiao, however, my
father was neither a mournful nor an artful rememberer. Although most
of his stories revolved around the years of the war, he told them
with delight and unstructured repetition. Reminiscence was an act of
entertainment he polished daily for family and friends.

In 1982, when my father decided to write down his stories, he asked
me to become the instrument of his remembrance. I refused. For two
years before his death in 1984, I used my involvement with Chinese
history to muffle the call to co-author his memoir. After he died, I faced
the task alone. Over the next three years, I pieced together a manuscript

which he had titled: "Encounters dictated by fate." In the course of this work I had ample time to reflect on the ties that bind me to Chinese rememberers on one hand and to Jewish survivors on the other.

The Rabbi Who Could Not Change My Father's Mind

Meng Jiao, Confucius, and my father share an aversion to stories that simplify history for the sake of morality. This bond was not apparent at first. I uncovered it gradually as I puzzled through the meanings of "Encounters dictated by fate." Over time, it became clear that "fate" was more than a word my father happened upon as he rummaged through his limited English vocabulary (which he nonetheless insisted on using in the memoir project). Fate was a theme he was inserting into all his tales. It was his way of making sense out of senseless circumstances. (This problem also plagued Chinese writers who had to wrestle with the inexplicable forces of their own history. Their word for "fate" was *ming* – a word that connotes both "destiny" and "order/command".) For my father, "fate" was a way to account to himself for survival during a war that proved deadly for his first wife and many of his close friends.

The depth of my father's attachment to his notion of "fate" became apparent in the last year of his life as he lay sick in a Miami hospital. My mother's rabbi, the pious leader of an orthodox congregation, came to visit him. They chatted about this and that, family, illnesses – safe subjects for two men who shared little in common in terms of actual Jewish observance. After a while, my father mentioned that he had been thinking of writing a book of memoirs. He sketched for the rabbi some of his stories about survival during the Holocaust. He spoke of his desire to leave a factual record about "my own particle of experience during the Dark Age of our people."[6]

The rabbi was moved. Interested in the stories as well as the man who told them, he suggested to my father that he change the title. The rabbi argued that the true meaning of these experiences lay in "encounters dictated by faith." My father thought over the proposition. He was touched by the rabbi's interest in the book. He was also not so rash as to argue with a religious leader from his sick bed. But my father did not change his mind. To his dying day, he retained his title and his conviction that "fate" accounted for the strange – both wondrous and terrifying – adventures of his life.

The rabbi had spoken from his special position as a guardian of inspirational stories. He sensed in my father's recollections the possibility of turning Jewish suffering into an occasion for the sanctification of the Name. He knew that my father was not conventionally observant, but he also knew him to be full of religious feeling. "Faith" was a word the rabbi used to appeal to those emotions. But my father was full of other kinds of feelings, too. Passions which he left out of the hospital conversation. Those passions, in the end, guided the selection and coloring of most of my father's Holocaust stories.

Faith certainly could not account for the desire that sent my father out in the middle of the night to make love to a German nurse. This incident, which he locates early in his camp life in 1943, has been called into doubt by his friends who were in the same labor camp at Maros Varashely in Transylvania. Whether true or not, the story is a faithful mirror of desire. It shows my father risking his life after the 9 p.m. curfew just to have sex with the "enemy." War or no war, he found a hole behind the horses' barn through which, my father claimed, it was possible to consummate a pleasurable moment.

A search for pleasure – both in actual experience and in the retelling of it – animated most of my father's survival stories. They reflected a man who saw himself as spared and privileged by fate. "Fate" served to break down conventional notions of "us" and "them," of "good" and "bad." Faith, in the rabbi's sense, could not serve this story-telling purpose. It could not explain, for example, how my father's life was spared by an SS trooper in the woods on the Austrian border. A winter tale that strains the imagination just like the one about the German nurse, this incident is nonetheless as true as my father could recollect it.

He told it often, and always with the following highlights:

> We were fugitives from the forced marches of late 1944. I'm hiding with two friends in the snow-covered forest. Sick with diarrhea, we slow down to relieve ourselves every few steps. The SS finally catch up with us. The leader's face is hooded by a ski hat. His voice does not sound familiar until he asks me: "Aren't you the son of Herman Schwartz, the sculptor?" Then, suddenly, I recognize the German boy who lived in my parents' house as a favorite apprentice. Out of gratitude to my father, the SS officer now sent us toward the Russian lines. He even gave us his supply of sausage and brandy.[7]

Unexpected food, unhoped for good will – these are the details that flesh out my father's notion of "fate." His reminiscences revolved around this fulcrum. It served to balance a tale that would have been unbearably painful otherwise. It let him marvel at how pervasive horror could be turned into ordinary pleasure. My father clearly delighted in the unpredictability of "fate." He felt blessed by it. Not just because he survived, not just because "fate" took care of him somehow. But also because it created a retrospective pattern in a bewildering world.

My father used to talk of "fate" whenever he remembered his first lover, Carla. She was a gentile woman with whom he lived in spite of his parents' objection. When he parted from Carla at a train station in 1938, she expected to see him again shortly. The separation lasted a lifetime, with other marriages and the war in between. "Fate" was also invoked by him during the rare times he spoke about his first wife, Roszi Braun. His last contact with her was in the spring of 1944, during a furlough filled with love-making in Cluj. She was deported soon after his furlough and killed in Auschwitz. Finally, it was to "fate" that my father appealed most often when talking about Kathy, my mother. She had been his girlfriend briefly during his happy-go-lucky bachelor days in Cluj, then she was forbidden to see him by orthodox parents. He met her again at a public beach in 1945, not knowing yet that she had lost her parents, her first husband and one of two daughters.

When he set out to write his memoirs in 1982, my father disclaimed all intention – and ability – for literary construction. He thought he would just "recollect a few true stories in the relaxed atmosphere of sunny Florida."[8] But recollection itself led him to look for literary devices. "Fate" became one such device. As if she were a fickle woman, he wooed and cursed her at once. Sometimes she appeared in his stories like a protective mother, sometimes like an imperious mistress who toyed with his desires. No matter the guise, he always enjoyed her surprises. He never tired of looking for what there was to marvel at next. No one – no rabbi, no God, or even "truth" – dictated my father's adventures. His pleasure in story telling and his attachment to memory did.

A Reluctant Co-Author of Parental Memoirs

Unlike my father, I have little interest in "fate." A thirst for adventure, on the other hand, bound me to my father already in Romania. After our emigration my adventures led me to places that were farther and farther away from my father's stories. The Far East turned out to be the most distant and the most substantive locale for the narrative I sought. Its history became a way of satisfying my curiosity about verifiable facts – a curiosity that was never quenched by my father's tales.

His memoir project challenged and deflected my training as a China historian. So I resisted as long as I could the invitation to co-author his book. This invitation amounted to nothing less than a demand to abandon the country and the discipline that were my intellectual refuge.

My father made this demand clear in the fall of 1982 when he asked me to stop writing about twentieth-century Chinese intellectuals and turn my attention to his more "interesting" and more "lucrative" Holocaust recollections. "Interesting" and "lucrative" were my father's words as he tried to draw me into his memoir project. His determination grew stronger and stronger just as I started to write about my experiences in China. Just when I had a real story of my own – after the year and half in Beijing where I learned Chinese history first hand – my father overwhelmed me with his tales. Some of them I had heard earlier, others seemed irrelevant to the Holocaust, none seemed to me factually reliable.

And yet I could not refuse my father outright. So I suggested that he record his stories in Miami and I would have them transcribed in Connecticut. In the fall of 1983, shortly after he mailed me the first set of tapes, he asked me again to become his collaborator. In a letter that began with praise for my "newly discovered literary talents" (I had just received a contract to publish my China journal), he went on to ask me to enliven his narrative of the past:

> You are at liberty to make any structural changes. Enclosed is $500 for typing expenses, as a deposit on our commercial enterprise. It can turn out to be a success story and will generate an estimated income of $100,000. And being a joint venture, you will have, besides your fame, a little financial income. It cannot hurt you. I don't have to emphasize to you that I have not received literary training. And in order to write a book, it will need a lot of trimming and sprinkling of some 'salt and pepper' to bring alive the characters in my stories. All these details now are in your charge. Please do not hesitate to tell me if the whole thing is worthless. I won't mind at all.[9]

My answer was ambiguous. I did not tell my father his book was worthless. How could I? More importantly, there was something in it that held my attention. I knew we were not going to make a fortune from it. My father, the perennially ill-fated salesman, had misread the market for Holocaust memoirs, just as he had miscalculated the shoe import business with which he had tried to make his fortune in America.

I also knew I did not want to become involved in adding "salt and pepper" to my father's already spicy imagination. I did not want to become drawn into all those stories of his past love affairs. Instead, I gave him advice about how he might make my mother into his collaborator. I gave him suggestions about how to cut and paste the text after the pages were transcribed, how to organize the paragraphs into chapters with subheadings and connecting themes. It was like talking to a distant, younger colleague. Or so I thought.

But, to use my father's expression, "fate" would have it otherwise. He died suddenly of a heart attack before he could do anything more with the text. And so I inherited some one hundred and twenty pages of undigested material. My mother now asked me to do what I had tried to refuse while my father was alive: to create a coherent tale out of his rambling reflections.

I began the project, still reluctantly, during a Paris sabbatical in the winter of 1985. There I unpacked the "Encounters" folder and was inundated by a linguistic jumble. Pages ran together without any break, any theme, any point at all. Half told stories repeated themselves without clarifying either the setting or the characters my father was trying to evoke. At first I approached the pages as a historian faced with a messy archive. Maybe, I thought, these pages will answer some factual questions that had puzzled me for a long time: when did my father's first wife, Rozsi Braun, die? Did she have children before her deportation to Auschwitz? Why did my father join, and then leave the Romanian Communist Party? What led to his arrest on the Romanian border on the eve of our emigration?

But my father's notes left me confused. Rozsi Braun is at one point reported pregnant. In another place she is taken away with two children. At yet another with none. His political involvement with the Communist Party lies masked beneath platitudes about the labor movement of the 1940s and the cruelty of uneducated cadres. The border arrest, too, remains unclear, just like the chronology of the war. The infant my mother lost in 1944 – while trying to save my older sister – is also brought in, but in a way that mystifies rather than explains her short life. She is evoked like a vanishing cloud, devoid of the details I later learned from a yellowed birth certificate and from my mother's laconic information about her first marriage in Budapest.

My father's pages offered me no history. As literature they were even less convincing because of the broken English in which they were written. My despair in the face of these pages went deeper than my father's poor command of the language. It was rooted in the content of these stories – stories that concerned yet did not convince me. I did not want to be drawn into them. I tried to withhold the "salt and pepper" my father had asked for by keeping my own voice as a writer out of the text. For months, I tried to find words that would echo my father's voice. But I was deafened by anger and mourning.

I did not have the benefit of the generational distance and historical perspective that inspired other writers who co-authored family memoirs. My position, for example, was different from Carole Malkin's who retold the journeys of her grandfather, David Toback. Malkin could, and did, shift her grandfather's voice from Yiddish into English. She allowed herself years to study maps of Russia – a country that was comfortably distant from her birthplace in America.[10]

No such literary devices were available to me. I came from the same part of the world as my father. I had grown up with the history that lay buried in his rambling and often distorted tales. Even when I did not know their full content – such as my dead sister's name or way of perishing – they surrounded me like a torn blanket, warm and cold all at once.

In Paris, during the winter following my father's death, I tried to mend the holes in father's stories. The little progress I made in the project was due, in no small measure, to conversations with Nadine Fresco. A member of the "generation after" like myself, she was the author of a very moving article, "La Diaspora des Cendres."[11] In this piece, Nadine had broken the covenant of silence surrounding our anger, jealousy and nostalgia toward parents who went through the Holocaust and toward siblings who never came back. Nadine knew what it was like to grow up with half-told tales, with repetitions that nevery clarify what we need to know the most. She helped me accept some of the rage that swept over me whenever I opened the folder with my father's pages.

But I did not yet understand the particular strategies I used when running from the very history I claimed to want to know. In Paris I pieced together the first part of my father's memoir – the one dealing with his childhood and love affairs in Timisoara. All along I would ask myself: "Why am I wasting time writing about my father's romances, when I could do something more significant on China?" Then, in the middle of the sabbatical, I wrote a paper about the sexual exploits of a Chinese philosopher named Zhang Shenfu. No accident, I now realize.

Zhang Shenfu was an octogenarian whom I had come to know well through a five-year oral history project begun in 1979. He was the shield I used to defend myself against my father's pleas that I co-author his memoir. In time, however, Zhang Shenfu helped me circle back to my father in a more forgiving way. A founder of the Chinese Communist Party, a mathematical logician with inconsistent political commitments, a feminist womanizer – Zhang Shenfu enabled me to make some peace with the contradictions that riddled my father's life and troubled my work on his manuscript. Zhang, like my father, told stories with no apparent moral lessons. He loved and lived in a scattered way that made no sense according to the orthodox, Maoist version of the Chinese revolution. Inadvertently, Zhang opened my ears to my father's tales.

Telling the Tale: New Questions about History and Memory

In the two years after the sabbatical in Paris, I worked simultaneously on my father's memoirs and on a book about Zhang Shenfu.[12] In both projects, I had to overcome an impatience with self-aggrandizing myths before the story-telling voice of my subjects could emerge. My father and Zhang Shenfu together finally led me to try out a story of my own.

In the summer of 1987 I finished piecing together *Encounters Dictated by Fate*. This followed the completion of a chapter of the Zhang book entitled "Time for Telling: the Laughing, Rambling Voice of Zhang Shenfu." In this chapter, I told the story of how I came to work with Zhang and described the various veils his memory wore during our five-year oral history project. From Zhang Shenfu's perspective, our conversations were a continuation of his life-long commitment to "tell the truth." From my point of view, however, we were engaged in something more serious and more playful: the creation of an ironical text that lay beyond the confines of Chinese Communist Party historiography.

The limits of official memory were amply apparent to Zhang Shenfu by the time we met. In our first interview on November 12, 1979, he told me that he was a "rehabilitated rightist," an intellectual whose ideological "crimes" had been recently forgiven by the party. Shortly thereafter, Zhang became a sought-after resource for a revisionist history of the Communist movement. The waiting room of Zhang Shenfu's home became a gathering place for those who wanted to tell a different story than the one authorized by Mao Zedong. This version would give center stage to Zhou Enlai, the man who was introduced into the Communist movement by Zhang Shenfu in Paris in 1921.

The party historians that came to see Zhang before and after my conversations with him were interested primarily in Zhou Enlai, and in a few other bits of politically useful memorabilia. They had neither time for nor interest in Zhang Shenfu's love affairs or his eccentric efforts to combine the philosophies of Russell, Socrates and Confucius. They probably would have been embarrassed by a story Zhang told me repeatedly: "I picked my private penname early, you know. I had it carved on a seal in the 1920s. It read 'thrice lover' (*san hao*). To this day, you see, my weaknesses remain my three loves: books, women and fame."[13]

Zhang's story was kept private because it struck a jarring note in China's public memory. In that realm, the conventions of hagiography ruled supreme. A founder of the Communist Party – such as Zhang Shenfu or Zhou Enlai – had to be free of blemishes. Books, women, and fame could not have been motivating forces in the life of a man who helped introduce Marxism–Leninism into China.

In another context, however, Zhang's story is highly acceptable. That is the tradition of *zizan*, of ironical autobiography. Started by Buddhist monks who inscribed self-mocking eulogies on the margins of their formal portraits, the *zizan* tradition spread out to Confucian intellectuals who sought to break with the conventions of moralistic historiography.[14] For Zhang Shenfu, our conversations provided such a marginal space. They enabled him to keep on inscribing and revising the one-dimensional portrait of his history being painted in Chinese public life.

After Zhang Shenfu's death in June, 1986 (two years after my father's), I listened again to the tapes of our conversations. Then, as I distanced myself from the details of Zhang Shenfu's political career and philosophical development, I heard the connecting theme of our oral history project: self-pleasuring laughter. To my ears, Zhang's voice now sounded a lot like my father's when he let himself ramble away from the well-worn stories of survival during the Holocaust. Once this echo became audible, I was ready to bring my father's *Encounters* manuscript to a close.

I did this in an almost breathless month. During that month – June, 1987 – I worried less about where my father's voice ended and mine began. I entered his messy pages with more ease, shaped their narrative content more readily than I was able to before. I was, in effect, creating a joint text. When it was finished, I offered the text to the "family," that included not only my mother, sister, son, niece and nephew, but also the more extended circle of my father's friends, many of whom had shared the experiences described in the manuscript. When I delivered the draft to Florida in July 1987, I thought I was done.

But my own story had yet to be born. It lay waiting at the edges of the essay that prefaced the manuscript I carried to Miami. In this introduction, I spoke about the process of co-authoring my father's memoir. It was one part of the text that was mine alone. And still it left much unsaid. Most importantly, I knew, it had not laid to rest my anger about the eroticized narrative that my father had created out of the Holocaust. In Florida, my anger met with an unexpected ally: a friend of my father who told me how the Hungarian group used to, by turns, be amused and irritated by father's romantic fantasies of what had happened during the war. They had lived through other stories – truly horrific ones – which my father also knew but had chosen to ignore.

These other rememberers gave me the ammunition I had been looking for. I came back home and wrote a short story called "You Mean There Was No Sex in Auschwitz?"[15] In this autobiographical work I framed the experiences of my father's friends with descriptions of my shame about his love affairs during the war. The story started out as a daughter's *cri de coeur* against a parent's stridently erotic adventures. It ended up calling into question the silence that surrounded the death of my little sister, Agnes.

"The sand was digging into her back, gritty like her father's words," I began.[16] In this story I was determined to call my father's bluff once and for all. But by the third section of the story (after describing the Hungarian comrades over dinner in Miami) the narrative took on a life of its own. It cornered me the moment I gave the name Agnes to the most tragic character: a young woman raped and murdered in Auschwitz.

This was the name of my mother's second child – an unknown and unmentionable sister. Her name had not been spoken in our family until my mother's *Wiedergutmachung* (reparations) case was prepared for the German government in 1971.

Agnes was born on January 10, 1944 and officially notarized into existence on April 29, 1944. These snippets about her come to life for me now as I hold in my hands the frayed birth certificate provided for German lawyers in the 1970s. It tells me that her father was 32 years old at the time of her birth, but is silent about the fact that he was already deported for hard labor. It tells me that our mother was 24, but is mute about the nightmare she faced as she tried to save this infant and another, two-year-old daughter.

Three little letters below the words "gender/female" shout from the page even today: "izr" – "izraelite." This was the explicit, required, religious identification of the infant. Those three letters doomed my baby sister. Eichmann had arrived in Budapest on March 1, 1944. What chance did Agnes have against him? When my mother finally took refuge with a gentile family they refused the risk of a crying infant. My older sister was sent away for a while with a Christian maid.

For Agnes, the only option was a children's home in the Jewish ghetto. There she died. Of starvation or bombings. My mother doesn't know. Nor does she speak about her confusion. Or dwell on, or even mention, the loss unless I ask her. And I don't, because the story frightens me too much. Instead, I let Agnes slip into a story about my father. There, muffled by other angers and fears, she took on another life.

Once Agnes entered the story, I knew it was no longer about my father or even about my distaste for his sexual exploits. It was about secrets withheld from second-generation children – secrets that are more burdensome even than the awful revelations about Stalin whispered to us behind closed doors in Romania. To tell Agnes's tale I had to open a series of doors, the first of which was my father's manuscript. It had started out as a salesman's version of what would be marketable about the Holocaust. It ended up, for me as the co-author, a book about the complexities of self-healing through recollection.

When I finished writing my father's memoir, I found the subject of my next book: the problem of personal and public memory. This time, however, I want to approach the subject explicitly and comparatively through a study of the commitment to remembrance in the Chinese and the Jewish traditions. Now, after years of writing about politically enforced amnesia in the People's Republic on the one hand, and raging against the silences in my parents' recollections on the other, I am taking another look at the connection between history and memory.

"History," to be sure, is no longer the pristine subject it was when I began to quarrel with my father's unverifiable tales. I see it now as a complicated compromise between public and personal mythologies.[17] On both sides what interests me is the way in which memories, however fragmented or fragile, become the bedrock that anchors the disparate details of lived experience. Thus grounded, remembrance wedded to history becomes a narrative that is comprehensible and compelling to future generations.

In both Chinese and Jewish tradition, I am struck by the tenacity of the link between memory and text. In fact memory becomes a text, *the* main text, in both of these cultures. Language provides a key in the two contexts: In Chinese, for example, an expression for "remember" is *ming*. For example, *minggan wunei*, means to "remember with deep gratitude," or more literally, "engraved on my five viscera." As a verb, *ming* means to engrave, to inscribe, to imprint. In the Hebrew Bible, the verb *zachor* – to remember – carries a similar connotation of permanent inscription. Hebrew, however, gives *zachor* the added urgency of a religious commandment, as for example when Rosh Hashana is called Yom Hazikkaron – A Day of Remembrance of the covenant between God and the people of Israel.[18]

The difference between remembrance inscribed in China's naturalistic cosmology and Judaism's monotheism is considerable. It affects, to this day, the various ways in which Jews and Chinese hold their histories in sacred regard. As I trace my way back from Zhang Shenfu and my father, to Confucius and the Bible, these differences become more and more striking. The Chinese literature embroiders the significance of memory in terms that are markedly free of obsession with historical trauma. One of the most common poetical metaphors for remembrance is *menghen* – "dream traces," or more specifically, the traces of a spring dream.

This is not to say that recollections of individual and social losses are absent in Chinese tradition. Rather, they are expressed in a way that is tempered by Daoist and Confucian injunctions against dwelling on the painful parts of the past.[19] These injunctions, in turn, are strengthened by a conscious appreciation of cultural continuity embedded in the Chinese language itself. It provides a direct link between oracle-bone inscriptions to newspaper editorials in the *People's Daily*. The pictograms that were first used for divination in ancient China are recognizable antecedents of the ideographs still used in Chinese writing today. This sense of continuity – both familial and cultural – sets Chinese rememberers apart from more anxious Jewish memorialists.

When I bring together Chinese and Jewish memory metaphors, I am creating a new vocabulary for myself. This purposive lexicon uses the unfamiliarity of Chinese connotations to augment the intimate meanings of Jewish experiences all too close to the bone.

When the knife of unredeemed loss cuts too deeply – as when I woke from a nightmare calling out Agnes's name – I turn to yet another Chinese term for "memory": *Yi*. In this character is embedded a tonal synonym that describes the abundant pleasures of a word that hits its mark. Memory, in this sense, underlies the toil and the joy of writing itself.

With this sense in mind, I see more clearly where my father's book was leading me all along. Although he himself did not have the time or the training to savor the pleasures of writing, my father offered them to me unknowingly.

In the process of creating order out of my father's linguistic morass, I understood for the first time what Saul Friedlander meant in his book *When Memory Comes*: "I must write then. Writing retraces the contours of the past with a possibly less ephemeral stroke than the others, it does at least preserve a presence and it enables one to tell about a child who saw one world founder and another reborn."[20]

I am not the child who saw the world founder. I was born after my parents' rebirth. I was born after they started to forget the war, their lost parents and spouses. Even Agnes. I came along after they forgot to stop forgetting. With my parents' help and that of Chinese history I am beginning to remember times I never knew. More surprisingly still, I am beginning to savor the pleasures of memory by straying into worlds stained by grief, graced by laughter.

13

The Awakening

Aharon Appelfeld

I wish to tell you about a feeling, pervasive and continuous, which has formed the members of my generation and myself. Like all feelings, this one also has a beginning. It was in the spring of 1946, a year after the end of the Second World War, and we arrived with a stream of refugees, children of 12 or 13, short, gaunt, possessing neither proper words nor clothing. Everything that had happened during the long war years was enclosed within us, silent and blind: an oppressive mass of mystery, which had no connection with consciousness. Of course we knew we were free, but that joy was insufficient to still the insulting loss of our childhood. That loss lay dull and quiet, on the bedrock of the soul.

Where are we from? What are we doing here? Sometimes it seemed like a new incarnation. And we . . . leaves drifting on the stream that swept us away. The war years had taught us: a person is not his own master. Will is an illusion. Only blind instinct will sometimes show the way.

In the midst of all this, we found ourselves scattered among farms and kibbutzim. After years of wandering and suffering, the Land of Israel seemed like a broad, soothing domain, drawing us into deep sleep. Indeed, this was our desire: to sleep, to sleep for years, to forget ourselves and be reborn. But some did not allow that desire to sweep us away. They asked – and their questions had a malevolent sound of accusatory metal – What really happened there? How did you come to be spared?

What could we do, young boys of 12 and 13, with so many memories of death? Tell about them? Relive them? Recall them to memory again? Everything looked so dreadful, so unattainable, and so far beyond ourselves. The questions from the outside were useless. They were questions full of endless misunderstanding, questions from this world, having no contact at all with the world from which we came. As though you were catching up with information about the unfathomable abyss or, rather, eternity.

So we learned silence. It was not easy to keep silent. But it was a good way out for all of us. For what, when all is said and done, was there to tell? To us as well it began to sound like something imaginary, which ought not to be believed. Of course there was more in that stillness than merely the inability to translate traumatic sights into normal speech. There was a desire to forget, to bury the bitter memories deep in the bedrock of the soul, in a place where no stranger's eye, not even our own, could get to them. So strong was the desire that we managed to accomplish the impossible. One mustn't talk. One mustn't tell. That was the order of the day, and it did not come just from outside. What didn't we do in order to conceal the dark secret? We forbade ourselves anything which might reveal that we had been there, in that other country. The tiny bit of warmth remaining in the few words we had brought from home was dissipated. We embraced a handful of Hebrew expressions, so that they could provide a cover and a camouflage for us. Let no one find traces of suffering in us. The life instinct, wise and cunning, guided us well along that twisted path. Gradually we shed the miserable marks of suffering. We grew to look like boys from the kibbutz movement. Tanned, sturdy, immersed in the activities of daily life. They stopped asking us, "Where are you from?" and, "How did it happen?" And we grew more confident, now that they no longer pestered us with questions.

But, at night, there were dreams. In that region the terrors still lived, in their full power, sharp and penetrating, as only a naked dream knows how. Yet the drive to forget, if one may call it that, reached even as far as there. So, miraculously, we also stopped dreaming. The prospect of a broad and spacious life, with no more restraints, spread before us now, as though we had been born here, local vegetation, on the tops of these mountains.

Thus the first year went by. In appearance we had forgotten everything. Our bodies grew sturdy, and we throve in the fresh air, which spoke of peace and the earth, of the breadth of the trees, and an abundance of pure blue. Everything we had undergone we grasped – if it was grasped – as a difficult phase about which one doesn't think. With the fragrance of the earth we also absorbed the first Hebrew words written in books. The ancient language, new to us, was folded into our forgetfulness, crisply and cleanly. Without regret, we relinquished the few words we had brought from home, the way one removes a shabby old garment. Never were there better days than those. Now something of the smell of childhood returned in a new form. The timid and flinching movements of our bodies disappeared and in their place emerged graceful motions that no longer feared to touch things.

This was a marvellous oblivion. It nourished us with its beneficence and gave what only profound forgetfulness can impart: liberation, lightness, a feeling of coasting. Perhaps that is how birds feel, soaring between heaven and earth. We did not yet know of the bitter and hostile quality nestled within that marvelous oblivion. Perhaps we did know – but we refused to admit its existence.

I have said "oblivion," but it was actually a latent protest against suffering and fate, and certainly against its immediate cause, our being Jewish. Everything that had happened to us had only happened as a consequence of that. This recognition soon degenerated to its ugliest and most painful phase. At that lowest point the victim took on the malevolence of the evildoer: something wicked lurked within us. The inability to submit a full accounting to oneself and the will to forget fused mysteriously and turned into abysmal loathing. Not loathing for the murderer who had committed the crime but loathing for ourselves. The victim, in his weakness of spirit, took on the wickedness of the evildoer and attributed it to himself. Anything that was Jewish or seemed Jewish appeared feeble, ugly, harmful. Loathing is full of bitterness, but loathing for oneself is the most grievous thing of all.

What didn't we do to uproot everything still linked to the world from which we had come? We built a private penal colony, which, greatly violent, would expunge any memory, so that no sign of the past would still be recognizable in us. And every means was licit in that penal colony. A single slogan hung upon its gate: "Forget and Uproot." Everything was played out in the light of that slogan. No one knew of its existence. It was ours, to our hidden veins.

How many years did that violent self-repression continue? Every year it changed colors, and covered another region of life. The moment a memory or scrap of memory was about to float upwards, we would combat it as one does battle with evil spirits.

The years passed. Life on the outer surface of consciousness continued. This was a life without a dark dimension, life built on a kind of fraud. We knew that something warm and precious in us had been lost on the path to self-forgetfulness. It was something we could not deny. Parents, images from our childhood, tribal incantations, whether in the form of customs or ancestral faith. Without them, what are we? We are hollow, floating on the outermost layer of consciousness. I have said, "We knew." But this was a late knowledge, a belated fright. We were already in that domain from which there is no retreat, and any return seemed like withdrawal from a surrounded front.

So deep was our oblivion that when the day came, and we were roused from slumber, astonishment struck us a stunning blow: how far we had traveled from ourselves! As though we had not been born in Jewish homes, and everything that we had endured was merely twilight, its source no longer attainable. We spoke of the recent past from an alien distance, as if the thing did not concern us.

Just as our oblivion was profound, so our awakening from it was shocking. We woke up dazed, astonished, full of thirst and the desire to restore to ourselves everything we had lost in that dreadful desert of oblivion and self-alienation. Only now did it seem clear for the first time to what vast distances we had exiled ourselves, as though we had been imprisoned all those years by unknown enemies, who had forbidden us any contact with our own secrets.

Ever since that awakening we have clung to the magical course of restoring ourselves to ourselves; and this restoration, this self-adoption, is quite marvelous. Sometimes it seems as if it is summer, and one is returning to one's childhood home, with the eternal tree opposite the patio; but sometimes it seems as though it is autumn, and one is seeing one's parents, and they are young and full of the wonder of their youth; but sometimes it seems that it is not autumn but rather winter, and one is returning to one's grandparents' house, where faith and innocence remain, and the snow is the outward sign of an inner purity.

So the train speeds on. It journeys inward, collecting faces and years on its way. As it penetrates that inner space, the wonder does not cease. Everything is familiar. Familiar to the very depth of the years. And the writer, whose task is introspection, is surprised to discover not only himself on this journey but also the living soul of his people, a soul once despised, scattered and foundering in oblivion. He does not claim he is capable of that which only the greatness of faith can accomplish but he acknowledges that it has been his lot to take part in such wonderworking.

Translated from Hebrew by Jeffrey M. Green

14

Facing the Glass Booth

Haim Gouri

When Prime Minister David Ben-Gurion announced in the Knesset on May 23, 1960 that Adolf Eichmann had been captured, brought to Israel, and was going to stand trial, the announcement was electrifying. As the saying goes, it was "an historic moment." Everyone spoke of the event with awe and pride – the anxiety and the reckoning came later. The radio and the papers kept repeating the news and fueled its cloak-and-dagger aspect: how the *Obersturmbannfuehrer* (lieutenant colonel), head of the Gestapo Section IV B4, who dealt with the "Final Solution," was spirited by agents of the Mossad from Argentina to Israel. But apart from all this drama, the country felt a tremor best described by the poet Natan Alterman:

> The feeling of this event's momentous importance derives from the notion that justice has, for the first time, been grounded in the life of the Jewish people. The placing of Eichmann before a Jewish court was destined to fill a chaotic, inhuman void that was hidden somewhere in the experience of the Jewish people, its trials and tribulations, from the commencement of its exile until today. The verdict was not the essence. Rather, the verdict served to underscore the impotence of justice to achieve retribution.

The year was 1960. Fifteen years had gone by since the end of the Second World War. It seemed that only now had the Jewish people in its homeland taken the time to fully account for the Holocaust. It had passed since 1945 through two and a half stormy years of political and armed struggle against the British mandate, years also of illegal immigration; through a war of independence, the foundation for national rebirth in which many European survivors took an active part while suppressing the Holocaust chapter of their lives; through years of mass immigration in the early 1950s which saw the young nation double within five years, and the Sinai campaign. It was a time of non-stop events, daily hardships, difficulties with immigrant absorption, and skirmishes with terrorists followed by retaliation campaigns.

The Holocaust was nowhere and everywhere in the land. It was buried deep in the hearts and amidst many families. One knew that behind the neighbor's door there was a story. The Holocaust had already appeared in books and in scholarly research. Gradually it penetrated to the younger generation of Israelis. And like a time-bomb it exploded during the notorious Kasztner trial of 1955. This trial probed the fate of Hungarian Jewry and the role of Jewish leadership in Palestine and Europe during the Holocaust. It opened the wounds of Jewish self-reckoning. It underscored the enormity of the issue and the hazards involved when dealing with an emotionally charged subject.

Israel Rudolf Kasztner, a leading figure in Hungarian Jewish life, headed rescue operations in Hungary during the period of deportations to Auschwitz. In 1953 a leaflet appeared, authored by another survivor, Malkiel Gruenwald, accusing Kasztner of collaborating with the Nazis and thereby speeding up the liquidation of Hungarian Jewry. Kasztner became the protagonist of a drama that shall never be resolved. Justice Halevy stated in rendering his judgment that Kasztner "had sold his soul to the devil" by having negotiated with Eichmann and his associates. Others saw him as a Jew who risked his life to save as many lives as possible. In reviewing the case the Supreme Court in 1958 cleared Kasztner's name and found Gruenwald guilty of slander; but Kasztner remained, in the eyes of many, a collaborator and one who hid a terrible truth from his fellow-Jews. By the time Kasztner was cleared, he was dead, having been shot on his doorstep on March 3, 1957. This was not yet the historic trial of the Jewish people against its destroyers.

Only with the capture and trial of Adolf Eichmann was a younger generation of Israelis obliged to confront this terrible chapter in Jewish history. Holocaust survivors were finally given the chance to speak. Overnight, they became the focus of national attention. The Eichmann trial was broadcast daily in its entirety for many months and the printed media reported its proceedings in great detail. While hundreds of thousands listened and read, additional thousands had tickets to the actual proceedings in Jerusalem's municipal auditorium (*Beit HaAm*). I cannot speak on behalf of the survivors. Many had suffered years of alienation and self-suppression. In a harsh land, where human events and fate are intertwined at high temperature, they were, I venture to say, a deprived group of people. Many among them felt that their tragedy and suffering had not been given proper attention.

In many families the true identity of the parents was now unveiled and their life story unearthed. This is a separate issue: the impact of the Holocaust on children born to the survivors. While America pre-empted us with the idea of "one generation after," the Eichmann trial heightened an awareness of the "staircase mystery" – the mystery of who your neighbor was, and where he or she came from. The trial legitimized the disclosure of one's past. What had been silenced and suppressed gushed out and became common knowledge. The Eichmann trial, "historic" in the fullest sense of the term, compelled an entire nation to undergo a process of self-reckoning and overwhelmed it with a painful search for its identity. Who are we? On the one hand Israelis, free in our homeland, speaking our national tongue, served in an army that had not known defeat. On the other hand we belong to the slaughtered Jewish people. This dual identity was not without its complexities, and had to be properly nurtured not to cause further suffering. André Malraux once said about Israel: "The Israelis are not simply a continuation of the Jew, they represent his transformation."

It was the trial, with all its dark implications, that unveiled the duality of our existence – the Jews as a murdered people and the story of Israel as a nation sitting in judgment.

We do not have a geiger counter to gauge the intensity of the trial's radiation on the nation's soul. But one can safely generalize that by the time it ended Israelis knew more, much more, about what had happened to their fellow Jews during the Third Reich. Moreover, the trial provoked harsh, self-directed questions. What had the Jewish community in Palestine (the *Yishuv*), and in the free countries, done during those years, once the systematic annihilation of the Jews became known? How had the leadership, in particular, acted? The leadership was not on trial, of course, but these difficult questions were repeated often enough with regard to the "Judenrat" as well as influential Jews in the free countries. Did the Jews provide, in effect, a handle for the German axe?

I cannot forget a conversation with a close friend, older than myself, who took part in rescue operations in Turkey during the war. I asked him whether the Yishuv had done *all* that was possible in the way of rescue. After a silence he said: "Have you ever seen a city burning? Did you every try to contain its fire with a glass of water?" I asked him whether he thought our lives, at that times, were "*just* another glass of water dousing the burning city." He replied: "That's already a metaphysical question."

The questions that erupted reached the front line of the national agenda: how could a people, so tested by calamity and pain, not react in time to the writing on the wall? Hitler, after all, had publicly declared in his speech to the Reichstag early in January, 1939: "If it were possible for the international Jewish financiers to ignite another world war, the end result would not be the bolshevization of the globe, but rather the destruction of the Jewish race in Europe."

Concerning that period, Zalman Shazar, later the third president of Israel, was said to have remarked: "We did not know the meaning of those words. We thought Nazism meant that Dr Cohen could not be a physician and Dr Levy could not be a lawyer." Why is it that the imagination of the murderers always surpasses the imagination of the victims?

Israelis who grew up with arms in hand could not understand the inherent weakness of diaspora Jewry – without a country of its own, without its own clandestine weapons, surrounded by hostile populations that were, for the most part, apathetic or fearful or Nazi accomplices. The courageous and compassionate were a minority among the nations of Europe. There emerged also the inevitable question, which still has no answer despite so much research and a multitude of monographs: what happened to Germany? How did she become a monster?

Only someone listening day in and day out to the endless succession of testimonies by survivors from all over Europe could begin to comprehend the terrible realities of 1933–45. The situation was best described by a Warsaw rabbi who said that what happened until 1942 had been previously experienced by the Jewish people in its long history. But 1942 and after, the period of the "Final Solution," was without precedent.

The stories finally told by the survivors made others comprehend what could and did happen to communities that were besieged, isolated and destroyed. The stories described the ghetto, the effect of prolonged starvation, the illusion that all would pass, the Nazi deceptions, the close family ties that weakened the wish to resist, and the belief that here it would not happen, together with, finally, the awareness that gripped the victims when it was too late, when the unbelievable had come about.

Permit me to relate a story about the unbelievable. In early 1961 a doctor, Yosef Boshminsky, testified at the trial. "I saw," he said "how the ghetto commandant Schwemberger gave a Jewish youth *eighty* lashes." The witness then testified that "a child's body cannot withstand more than fifty lashes. And the boy remained alive." "Is this boy here in the hall?" asked the attorney-general. "Yes," the witness said in Polish, "Where is he?" "This is he" – and the witness pointed to Captain

Mickey Goldman, a member of the 06 Bureau of the Israel Police, charged with the preparation of documentation for the trial, and sitting a few steps from Eichmann's glass cage.

Yitzhak Zuckerman, commander of Jewish resistance in the Warsaw ghetto after the death of Mordechai Anilevich, asked Captain Goldman: "Why didn't you tell anyone till now?" Goldman replied: "When I reached Palestine after the war I told my aunt and uncle what happened there, and to me. During the night, from behind the wall, I heard my uncle say: they suffered so much they are beginning to imagine things." Zuckerman responded: "Yes, this is the eighty-first blow, which every one of us receives."

For this reason we called the first film in our trilogy on the Holocaust *The Eighty-First Blow*. It is possible to accept disbelief as a normal human reaction, but not when disbelief turns into an excuse or justification for the paralysis that overtakes our humanity and particularly those in leadership positions.

For me, personally, the Eichmann trial was a cruel history lesson. After the war I was sent by the "Haganah"[1] to Europe. It was my first trip out of the country and my first encounter with what remained of the Jewish community in Europe. It included meeting an unknown brother, and this changed my life. The Eichmann trial seemed like an extension of that encounter. As someone who had not been there – in the Holocaust – I felt as though I was going the full distance. Listening to the testimony I often felt what I thought was ultimate pain. But who knows what "ultimate pain" is? Perhaps I shall never know, despite my close attention to the trial. I probably barely reached that region of pain – there is something to the saying "that anyone who was not there will never really understand it."

I learned a new language, that of the witnesses. I also learned the language of Eichmann. He remained opaque even though he looked like everyman. Roger Veilland (author of *Le Drole du Jeu*) said to me after the opening session: "He looks like a good family man, the kind you meet every day going home on the subway". *Un petit bon père de famille.*

Robert Servatius, serving as counsel for the defense, suggested that Eichmann belonged "to the world of Caesars, those who know no tears." A renowned Swiss psychologist, asked for an expert opinion on Eichmann's profile (presented anonymously), said he was willing to travel around the globe to meet "this man." He saw him as the epitome of a schizoid personality, without any capacity for empathy. There were those who pointed out that Eichmann was never caught in a sadistic act of murder. But when testimony was presented that in Budapest he beat a Jewish youth to death, Eichmann reacted as though an honest man had been discovered cheating at cards.

This is not the place to discuss the issue of the "banality of evil,"[2] nor whether other individuals or nations might act in a similar manner. Until now only the Nazis had done so – and in the process had deprived their victims of the right to submit, and even to convert. They made race the sole reason for death.

It was said of Eichmann that he was an efficient and narrow-minded bureaucrat, and if ordered could *triple* within a very short time the Third Reich's potato crop. He drew up the deportation time-schedule for European Jewry. He died without showing remorse. Mickey Goldman was present at the hanging and, in the early morning hours of June 1, 1962, scattered the ashes over the Mediterranean Sea, outside Israel's territorial waters.

After writing my book on the Eichmann trial, *Facing the Glass Booth*, I decided not to return to "that subject," since anyone who gets involved with it "enters a prison from which there is no escape." I stole a ten-year vacation from the topic. But even during that interlude I found myself going back to the experience in a novel, *The Chocolate Deal*, as well as in essays and poems.

I remember the winter of 1947, which I spent among the Jews who had survived in the Rothschild Spital DP camp in devastated Vienna. It was a large building, with murky corridors, redolent of tobacco and ammonia, carbolic soap, naphthalene. One night, in the crowded room, somebody cried out in Yiddish in his sleep. I didn't understand a word. I asked myself: "What happens to a language when most of its speakers have vanished?"

Eventually I did return to "that subject." Between 1972 and 1985 I worked on the trilogy of documentary films comprising *The Eighty-First Blow, Flame in the Ashes* and *The Last Sea*. These dealt, respectively, with the destruction of the Jews, the manifestations of Jewish resistance in Europe, and the Jewish exodus from Europe after the Holocaust. As part of this massive task I collected hundreds of testimonies from persons who were "there" during those dark times. Most of the interviews were recorded in the subjects' homes. Frequently the survivors had their families participate. But there were also those who refused to speak at home and met me in our office.

The experience was extremely painful. My witnesses didn't realize that I was coming to their homes after many similar interviews. At each session I had to conduct myself as with an only child, or as if this were the first time I had heard what had been done to them. More than once I had trouble focussing on relevant questions for the film, because they wanted to tell me their entire story. You cannot conduct conversations like these without an extraordinary amount of attentiveness, empathy, and participation. But precisely these traits were the major source of my agony.

Once I interviewed two women from Hungary who had been among the Mengele twins at Auschwitz. Both had grown up in religious families. While recounting the details of their torture they referred to the "situation" of God vis-à-vis their own. For them God was a real, personal, and incontrovertible being, a protective and comforting force, the "Merciful Father." They had difficulty comprehending the eclipse of God, the disappearance of Providence, the empty Heavens. Their encounter with Dr Mengele compelled them to ask "Why?" During the give-and-take of the interview they regressed to that former time and place as if hypnotized. Then one of them suddenly had trouble breathing. Now I am neither a psychologist nor a hypnotist who assumes a risk because of his profession. I was a writer garnering the voices of survivors for a documentary film. It was a frightening moment. The conversation was too successful.

During those 12 years I reviewed hundreds of hours of testimony, war diaries both printed and in manuscript, documents, certificates and recordings. I even spent a month in Poland. There I came to understand a verse by the poet Uri Zvi Greenberg, in his great dirge for the destroyed Jews of Europe: "As the sea swallows its prey, and no trace remains on the water." In Cracow I was told by a Polish Catholic: "The souls of these tormented Jews will tremble in the void of Poland forever." In Warsaw I went to the Jewish cemetery, the only living spot in those vast spaces of death. In Lublin, on the site of the ghetto, there is a monument with an inscription in Polish and Yiddish: "I seek my brothers in every handful of dust." From there I went to Maidanek. It was a summer's day, but the sky was grey and rain was streaming down. There were flowers and the aroma of the fields. I followed the path all the way to the great mound of ashes covered by a chapel in ancient Slavic style, with a Polish inscription: "May our disaster be a warning to you." There was no mention of the death of the Jews. They were anonymous, citizens of all the countries of Europe, brought to be burned in that place. I stood there for a long while, contemplating what remained of my people. Any inscription in Hebrew letters that remained in the hard stone brought me to the brink of tears. Later, I reached Auschwitz.

But I am an Israeli, born in Tel Aviv, and have borne arms since my youth. I could scarcely comprehend such abysmal weakness. So during those years I investigated the behavior of those from other nations, including prisoners of war, when they found themselves weak and starving, humiliated and dying. There proved to have been no difference between Soviet officers and Jewish grandmothers. The Germans too, tracking through the endless snow, after the fall of Stalingrad displayed apathy and despair, just like the Jews.

It is hard to belong to a murdered people. It is hard to answer the question asked of you: "Where were you, what were you doing, when I was . . .?" I am not a scholar or a historian, but I accept totally the culture of remembrance. It will always be associated with knowing the facts and collecting every scrap of paper, every forgotten voice. When I came back from Poland I knew more. I had even managed to find, in the "Film Polski" archives, original documentary footage.

But as I have noted, I was not "there." We know very well the difference between us and them. Nevertheless, more and more members of the second and third generations enter this memory without exit. People say that time is on the side of the murderers, that the memory of the extermination of the Jews in the German death factories will be obscured and fade away, that only historians will concern themselves with it. I believe this is wrong. I believe that the extermination of the Jewish people in the middle of the twentieth century will affect the course of culture and will be significant for the coming generations.

At times it seems to me that the past is shunted aside by the present. Grave dangers loom over Israel, which continues, as a sovereign state, to live on the edge of a war, and in a seemingly intractable and tragic conflict with its Palestinian and Arab neighbors. Further, the Holocaust continues to follow us in every possible guise, in a film or book that stirs up a tempest, in chance encounters, and in debates characteristic of the younger generation which judges matters in a different light. "The reckoning is not yet complete."

15

Andean Waltz

Leo Spitzer

As a very young child I am told that my grandfather died on the ship when he, my grandmother, and my parents were on the way from Austria to Bolivia. I am shown photos of the Italian liner "Virgilio," and of my parents with other passengers. The ship, I eventually find out, is transporting over a thousand refugees from Nazi Germany, Austria, Czechoslovakia, and the civil war in Spain. Mother has a big belly in the photographs, and she explains jokingly that I am "in there" – a stowaway on the voyage. I am also told that the Virgilio's captain wanted to bury my grandfather at sea. This would have been a violation of orthodox Jewish law mandating the interment of a body in the ground. My grandmother and father objected – less, my mother tells me, from religious conviction than from some elemental unwillingness to have his final resting place be an unmarked spot in the ocean. Their protestations and pleas were to no avail until a Jewish fellow passenger, with personal financial resources, made an arrangement for the ship to make an unscheduled landing in La Guaira. There the body was dressed in a shroud and buried in earth, in the Jewish cemetery of Caracas.

When I am born in La Paz some months later I am named Leopoldo, after my grandfather, given his Hebrew name Gershon, and nicknamed Poldi: the same diminutive that had been his. While I am still a young child, my parents tell me that they have given me my grandfather's names to honor the departed and to maintain a continuity between the past and the present. Only many years later, in hindsight, do I realize that their effort to maintain continuities – to perpetuate something of the lost in the new – was manifested in many different ways during their years in Bolivia. Indeed, I realize that this effort was a central characteristic of the Jewish refugee experience in that Andean land . . .

Before the rise of Nazism in Central Europe, very few Jews, perhaps

less than a hundred from Alsace, Poland, and Russia, had settled in
Bolivia. In the early 1930s, this relatively isolated republic of some three
million persons – the site of great pre-Hispanic Indian civilizations –
was inhabited by a ruling minority claiming Spanish descent, a larger
mestizo population, and a subordinated Aymara and Quechua Indian
majority. European travelers visiting Bolivia in the early decades of the
twentieth century considered it as among the least "Europeanized" of
the South American nations.[1]

But in the mid-1930s, and until the end of the first year of the
Second World War, thousands of refugees from Nazi-dominated Central
Europe, the majority of them Jews, fled to Bolivia to escape an increasingly vehement persecution. Wealthier or "better connected" refugees,
who emigrated soon after the Nazis came to power, had acquired visas
and found a haven in "countries of choice" – Great Britain, the United
States, Australia, Palestine, Argentina, Brazil. The tightening of immigration to these countries, however, virtually closed off entry for the
large number of persons desperate to leave in the late 1930s.[2] By the
end of the decade Bolivia was one of very few places to accept Jewish
immigrants. Some 20,000 refugees, from Germany, Austria, Czechoslovakia, and Hungary, arrived between 1938 and 1940 – a number
which, when calculated as a percentage of Bolivia's total "non-Indian"
population at the time, gives some sense of how substantial the demo-
graphic impact of this Central European immigrant influx must have
been. The new arrivals settled primarily in La Paz, 12,500 feet above
sea level, as well as in Cochabamba, Oruro, Sucre, and in small mining
and agricultural communities throughout the land.

*It is July 1941 in Cochabamba. Dr Heinrich Stern, born in Nordhausen
am Harz and a recent immigrant to Bolivia, reflects in a note written
to himself:*

> "The path was rocky and rough, steep and lonely. Now I sit on
> a rock and look about me. Thorny shrubbery, thicket, tall cactus,
> stones and stones. In the distance, two, no three wretched huts;
> mountains all around, giant, furrowed mountains. The sun sinks
> lower; its rays bring a magic glow to the peaks. Loneliness, frightful
> loneliness; and strangeness. In the far distance two women,
> wrapped in red ochre shawls, climb uphill. Their appearance
> increases my sense of loneliness, of abandonment. *Indianerland-
> schaft!* Indian landscape! My new homeland! Is this my new
> homeland?
>   Dark thoughts waltz through my brain. They torment me, they

repeatedly knock and sting against my forehead. They circle about the horizon and want to penetrate the distant mountain wall; and they search and inquire: The sky above me, is it not the sky of the old homeland? No, it seems to be – or am I only imagining it – more glaring, more poisonous. Only the clouds cast a smile of friendliness on me, reminders of other environs. But the land remains hostile. A landscape of the uncivilized – *Indianerland-schaft*, Indian landscape. Gigantic, strange, melancholy and lonely . . ."[3]

Bewilderment. Nostalgia. Yearning. Difference. An alien world – a world of others. *Indianerlandschaft*. These impressions were widely shared by immigrants after arriving in Bolivia. Could one have expected anything else? Before leaving Europe, Bolivia had been little more than a place on a map of South America. Many of the refugees knew virtually nothing about it. In their eagerness to find a country that would accept them, they were ready to go anywhere that would permit them to live in safety. "Bolivia – quick, where is it?" was Egon Schwarz's response on receiving his visa through the Hilfsverein (Refugee Aid Society) from the Paris consulate. "We would have gone to the moon," Andres Simon recalled. "Bolivia was a closer possibility, but the moon we saw every night. It was more real to us." "I knew about Bolivia what you know about the North Pole," Renata Schwarz said to me. "Maybe you know more about the North Pole."[4]

If the refugees knew anything at all about the country to which they were emigrating, it was either extremely limited or stereotypical. Some of them, having lived in the larger European cities or traveled to them in their search for visas, had briefly encountered consular officials – the first Bolivian nationals they had ever met. Many, perhaps most, had only a remote sense of the cultural and ethnic milieu into which they were entering. Spanish-speaking, Catholic, Indian: these were the terms they vaguely associated with the Bolivians. But these were broad, generic identifiers which hardly prepared the refugees for the immense cultural and social differences they would have to face. Their preconceptions of the land and its people were shaped by information which varied greatly in reliability and perspective. Some of it came from old, half-forgotten, world geography and world culture lectures they had received back in school. More up-to-date, but not necessarily more trustworthy information came in letters from those who had preceded them to Bolivia, or from the second- and third-hand retelling of the contents of such letters. Some was acquired "post visa," by reading the entry "Bolivia" in encyclopedias and geographical atlases. And a certain, surely not insignificant amount, was derived from accounts in popular literature – a literature that routinely represented the landscape and people of South America as mysterious, exotic, if not forbidding, and that simplified or blurred the particularity and diversity of both.

Werner Guttentag, for example, emigrated from Germany to Bolivia via Holland 1939. Before leaving Europe, he decided he would move to Cochabamba (where he still resides) simply on the basis of its relatively central location on the map of Bolivia – which, he maintains, he examined closely for the first time only after learning that he and his parents had received visas to go there. His pre-departure image of Bolivia's indigenous populations, he recalls, came from reading "the Inca novels" of the immensely popular German author of adventure books, Karl May – a writer who had never set foot in South America, and whose colorful and seemingly authentic ethnographic representation of its people was largely invented, the imaginary creations of a fertile mind.[5]

> We absolutely didn't know what was awaiting us. We didn't know about the people, or their customs, or traditions. We did not expect the altitude to be so oppressive. On the train from Arica to La Paz, people's noses and ears were bleeding. Some were hemorrhaging . . .[6]

> The Indios. We never had seen anything like them. Already on the train, at stops, a real novelty: we looked at them; they looked at us . . .[7]

> What immediately impressed me about La Paz was the smell – a terrible impression. The streets smelled horrible. The Indians urinated and defecated in the streets. The women squatted right down in the street, lifted up their skirts, and did their thing. There were no public sanitary facilities. And they brought their llama herds through the streets. And the llamas spat and left their little traces . . .[8]

> The Indian women wore multiple skirts and colorful *mantas*. They were sometimes beautifully, richly dressed, with gold and silver pins and gold earrings. But they had no culture. They had no civilization . . .[9]

> I noticed that I was in a black land. Not that the people were Negroes, but so many men and women were dressed in black or dark clothing. Only sometime afterwards did I learn that they were still in mourning clothes – mourning their dead, casualties

in the disastrous Chaco war that Bolivia had fought with Paraguay . . .[10]

Music . . . the noise of a never-before-heard, never-ending, melancholy Indian music, whose monotone initially grates the nerves, but which one never again forgets after hearing it played night after night for months on end . . .[11]

. . . [Here] practically nothing is as one knows it, either in society or in nature. The person who applies middle-European standards to what is seen and experienced will never understand . . .[12]

". . . [N]othing is as one knows it, either in society or nature" – that was said by Egon Schwarz soon after his arrival. There was little in the cultural background or experience of the refugees that would echo sympathetically and provide a familiar referent to ease their integration. Neither the cities nor the countryside reminded those who had left Germany, Austria, or any of the Central European countries of the Austro-German *Kulturkreis*, of places they had known before.

For the refugees, a harsh physical environment was the first impediment to adjustment. When they arrived in La Paz or in the Andean highland (some 12 to 14,000 feet above sea-level) many came down with altitude-sickness – *soroche* – and suffered shortness of breath, sleeplessness, and aches in head and body. Those with lung or heart problems found the altitude unbearable. If they moved to the subtropical or tropical lowlands, they encountered high temperature and humidity, and faced the danger of contracting illnesses for which their native European environment had provided no immunity or tolerance. But it was mainly the immense *foreignness* of the culture that incited feelings of alienation – they were truly outsiders, strangers in a strange land. The various indigenous people looked different, they dressed differently, their customs, practices, festivals, and foods were unfamiliar, they communicated in languages that none of the immigrants had ever heard, their psychology and world view seemed unfathomable.[13]

Photographs from the earliest years of the immigration are quite illuminating in this regard.[14] In family albums especially – where a sense of period and place is reflected through the principle of selection and arrangement – three types of pictures predominate.[15] The first, of individual refugees and their families, is no doubt meant both as a private record and as a way of telling about the past. But many of the albums also contain numerous photos of nature: of the immense snow-capped peaks of the Cordillera Real, of the rugged starkness of the Altiplano and the precipitous roads and pathways down from the *cumbres* to the lowlands, and of the lush beauty of the tropical forests with their jungle-like vegetation. And they often feature photographs of indigenous peoples, busy in the marketplace, with llama herds, or dressed up in elaborate costumes, wearing exquisite masks, playing instruments, dancing and performing in *fiestas*. These photos attest to an intense fascination with the strangeness of the environment in which the refugees found themselves. Yet they also seem to represent a desire to capture a trace of the unknown, to frame it, to order it, and, by making it visually accessible if not familiar, to exert some measure of control over it.

The refugees, of course, were themselves not a homogeneous group. Their origins and social status had been diverse in Central Europe, ranging across generational, educational, political and class lines. There were engineers, doctors, lawyers, musicians, actors and artists, as well as a large number of both skilled and unskilled workers whose living had been interrupted by Nazi exclusionary decrees. The majority were Jews or married to Jews. Some, however, were non-Jewish *political* refugees: Communists, Socialists and others persecuted by the Nazi regime. The Jews themselves differed greatly in the degree of their identification with their religion and its traditions. There were Zionists among them, atheists, orthodox believers, "High Holiday" Jews, and non-practitioners. They shared a common identity as Jews only in the sense, perhaps, that they had all been defined as "Jews" from the outside – that the Nazis had "othered" them as Jews.

No matter what their background differences had been, the vast majority of refugees arrived in dire straits, with few personal possessions and very little money. This had a leveling effect, cutting across previous class distinctions. There were other factors too that helped to create a sense of collective identity, aiding the refugees' adjustment and survival. Despite differences of detail, their common history of persecution was certainly one of these. Each and every one of the refugees had been identified as undesirable, stripped of citizenship and possessions. They were all "in the same boat." The war back in Europe, and the fact that so many had relatives and friends from whom they had been separated, was also an ever-present reality of which they were collectively conscious and which bonded them together. They kept themselves – each other – informed about the war from accounts in the press and radio, and they shared efforts to discover the fate of those left behind. In this regard, the German language (which they still spoke at home and among themselves), served as a vehicle of inquiry, information and unity. It allowed them to communicate intimately and to express themselves with a degree of familiarity that most could never attain in Spanish. German permitted them to maintain a wider connection with refugees and immigrants in other countries and throughout Bolivia – by means of their own newspaper, the *Rundschau vom Illimani* which Ernst Schumacher established in La Paz in 1939, or the important *Aufbau* of New York, or *Jüdische Wochenschau* in Buenos Aires.[16]

But it was memory – its employment to connect their present to a particular version of the past – that served as the creative tool of adjustment, helping to ease cultural uprootedness and alienation. No sooner had they arrived in Bolivia when a process began by which the immigrants recalled, negotiated, and reshaped their memories of Europe. They re-created institutions, symbolic practices, and a style of life which they had previously shared. Their collective memory became the basis on which a communal "culture" was built to serve changed needs.

It was no doubt from their recollections of the *Israelitische Kultusgemeinden* of Berlin and Vienna that one of the first centers of immigrant activity, the *Comunidad Israelita*, was founded at La Paz in 1939, by refugees from Germany and Austria. This communal organization established a Jewish temple in which religious services were held, an old people's home, a *Kinderheim* serving as kindergarten and day-care center, and a school, *La Escuela Boliviana-Israelita*. But, from its inception, the *Comunidad* also fulfilled a less utilitarian social function. Its quarters became a clubhouse where people could gather, eat meals, read newspapers, play cards, chess, or ping-pong – where they could gossip, socialize, exchange information, and reminisce about their lives, loves, and the past.[17] The *Comunidad* was turned into a version of an institution that many of the immigrants would have remembered with nostalgia: the *Klublokal* or coffee house of Central Europe.

Moreover, within a relatively short period, extending from 1939 to the early 1940s, the refugees founded other organizations, established shops and restaurants, and developed familiar cultural activities. A glance through the pages of the *Rundschau vom Illimani* and *Jüdische Wochenschau* provides illustrative examples. The "Hogar Austriaco" ("Austrian Home," as the Austrian Club was called), the associations "Das Andere Deutschland" and "Freies Deutschland" (the "Other Germany" and "Free Germany"), the League of Women of the *Comunidad* and the Macabi Sports Club; the Cafe Viena, Club Metropol, Cafe-Restaurant Weiner; the Pension Neumann, Pension Europa; the Haberdashery Berlin, Casa Paris-Viena, Peleteria Viena; the "Buchhandlung La America" advertising German editions of Franz Werfel, Paul Zech, Bruno Weil; the *Kleinkunstbühne* (Cabaret theater) presenting scenes from Schnitzler, von Hoffmanstahl, Beer-Hoffmann, as well as readings of German classics; the Colegium Musicum with its chamber-music

concerts and recitals featuring Mozart, Beethoven, and Schubert played
by musicians trained at conservatories in Vienna, Prague and Berlin:
these and many others, attest to the range of the immigrants' economic
and institutional adjustment in Bolivia, and confirm the character of
their symbolic reconnection with Central Europe.[18]

Children of the refugees – especially during the early years of the
immigration – received both formal and informal tuition strongly influenced by cultural memories of Europe. The purpose behind the establishment of the Escuela Boliviana-Israelita, for example, was twofold: the
school offered courses in Spanish, so that recently arrived children might
learn the language of the land, and it taught them the three Rs as well
as Jewish religion and history. From its inception Bolivian officials also
required the school to hire a Bolivian teacher to instruct its pupils in
local and national history – what the Bolivians called *educación cívica*.[19]
Apart from the Spanish language classes and *educación cívica*, however,
the pedagogical methods and general curriculum of the Escuela Boliviana-Israelita differed little from those employed in elementary schools in
Germany and Austria before the rise of Nazism. The referent examples
the immigrant teachers used in their subjects of instruction derived, as
one might have expected, from their Central European background.

*Sifting through memorabilia of which I became the keeper when my
mother died:*

*I look at my report cards for grades one through four from the
Escuela Boliviana-Israelita. Seeing my grades in geography and music,
I try to recall if I was in my first or second school year when Dr Asher
first taught us to locate the Danube, Rhein, and the Alps on a map of
Europe, and when it was that Mr Aaron, who played a portable piano
and the accordion, taught us to sing the* Hatikvah *as well as German
folk songs. . . .*

I find five of my childhood books. Two of them, Max und Moritz:
eine Bubengeschichte in sieben Streichen *(Max and Moritz: a Boys' Tale
in Seven Episodes) by Wilhelm Busch (my copy published in Santiago
de Chile), and H. Hoffman's* Der Struwwelpeter, *are cautionary tales
which my parents and grandmother read aloud to me dozens of times.
They contain my scribblings and, probably, the earliest existent sample
of my nickname, Poldi, printed in pencil in my own handwriting. It is,
I am quite certain, because of the horrible penalty paid by Konrad, in
"Die Geschichte vom Daumen-Lutscher," ("The Story of the Thumb-
Sucker") and Paulinchen, in "Die gar traurige Geschichte mit dem
Feuerzeug," ("The Truly Sad Story With the Lighter") that I never
sucked my thumb and was fearful about playing with matches. Two*

other books – an illustrated German children's edition of Grimm's Fairy
Tales *and Frida Schanz's* Schulkindergeschichten *– were also read to
me by my grandmother Lina. The fifth, a children's book in Spanish
and printed on wartime paper now yellowed by time, is* Beethoven, El
Sacrificio de Un Niño. *Beethoven and Johann Strauss were my father's
favorite composers. . . .*

*I discover an undated Hogar Austriaco cabaret-program. It introduces
a show,* "Radio Wien Sendet: Ein Wunschkabarett" ("Radio Vienna
Broadcasts: a Cabaret on Demand") *and lists, among its entertainment
numbers,* "In einem Wiener Vorstadtvarieté" ("In a Viennese Suburban
Music Hall"), "Ein Maederl aus Moedling," ("A Lass from Moedling"),
"Frauen sind zum Kuessen da" ("Women are Made to be Kissed"), *and
various other skits in Viennese dialect. . . .*

In spite of the persecution they had endured, therefore, and Nazi efforts
to depict them as "the other," it was Austro/German culture – and, in
particular, Jewish bourgeois culture as it had existed in the capital cities
– which provided the refugees with a model for emulation and a common
locus for identification. This held true even for persons, like my parents,
who had come from a working-class background and whose political
sympathies lay with Marxism. Commenting on the character of this
identification with some irony, Egon Schwarz noted how often the
immigrants began their sentences with the phrase "Back home in Germany . . ." or "Back home in our country . . .", and how one man, in
a conversation with him, had actually exclaimed: "Back home in our
concentration camp . . ."[20] At the very time when European Jewish
bourgeois culture was being ruthlessly and systematically destroyed by
the Nazis, these refugees attempted to revive aspects of it in an alien
land thousands of miles away: in a country that offered them a haven,
but in which many – perhaps most – felt they were mere sojourners.

> "I never thought our family would stay in Bolivia. I really believed
> that the Nazis would be destroyed, and that we would return to
> Vienna to help rebuild a Social Democratic Austria." . . .[21]

> "For me, Bolivia was temporary, a sort of bridge to somewhere
> else. I didn't want to return to Germany. I thought of Argentina,
> maybe. Or the US." . . .[22]

> "I think back: Even when my father began to make a reasonably
> good living, we never acquired anything – furniture, apartment,
> auto – which would appear as if we were putting down permanent

roots in the land. My parents were always waiting for their quota number to come up so they could go to the United States." ...[23]

"We didn't know where we could end up. Maybe permanently in Bolivia. But we needed to maintain what we prized." ...[24]

As many of them phrased it in their recollections, "their need" to re-establish a Central European identity had discernible consequences even within the immigrant community. It maintained an old rift imported to Bolivia from Europe between the then numerically much larger German-speaking group from the Austro/German *Kulturkreis*, and the smaller, predominantly Yiddish-speaking, Jewish group from Poland, Russia, and other parts of Eastern Europe.[25] The German-speakers, who were considered "highly assimilated" and referred to as *Yekkes* by the East Europeans, tended to fraternize with each other, keeping their social distance from the *Polacos* (as the East Europeans were called) whom they often viewed as "more primitive," "less cultured." This division – effectively bridged in the realm of economic interaction, and on occasions when the immigrants, as *Jews*, rallied together in celebration or against some "outside" threat – was maintained institutionally, in the establishment, for example, of the *Circulo Israelita* of the *Polacos* as an organization with distinct cultural offerings separate from the Austro/German *Comunidad Israelita*.[26]

But the communal identity constructed by the refugees had an especially profound and enduring influence on relationships between them and the native Bolivians. Refugees, recalling their emigration to Bolivia in writing or oral testimony, have been universally grateful to Bolivians for saving their lives.[27] From the earliest days of their arrival, moreover, they began to develop business relationships with them, based on mutual trust and good will. Bolivians, in this respect, "made space" for the immigrants, allowing them to participate in every imaginable entrepren-eurial – but not professional – activity. Bolivians also "made space" physically and culturally, so the immigrants could establish their own institutions. Paradoxically, however, the very institutions the refugees created, and the symbols and memories on which they relied for their collective identity, were also instrumental in maintaining barriers between the refugees and the Bolivians. Culturally and, in many respects, socially, Bolivians and refugees remained each other's "other".

The cultural distance seemed most unbridgeable between refugees and "Indians" – the Aymara and Quechua in the highlands, as well as the people belonging to smaller indigenous groups in the tropical lowlands of the country. Although the contact between Europeans and individual Indios could be quite intimate, their relationship was always a hierarchical one: master–servant, employer–laborer. Aymara and Quechua women worked as domestic servants and took care of the children of even the poorest immigrants; while the men were hired for various menial tasks on an hourly basis, as carriers of heavy loads, as day laborers, or, on rarer occasions, as shop assistants and unskilled workers. Many refugees did show admiration for the cultural achievements of the pre-Columbian Tiahuanaco and Inca ancestors of the Aymara and Quechua; they did value indigenous craft skills, particularly weaving and gold and silver jewelry, and they purchased items for personal use. But it was unusual for any refugee to learn more than a few words of an indigenous language, or to engage in any informal intercourse with people who made up the vast majority of Bolivia's population.

One might have expected some greater interchange between the refugees and those Bolivians closer to them in social background: with the Spanish-speaking white and *mestizo* middle classes, and with members of the professional and ruling elites. But here the immigrants' reconstituted culture – based on Central European–Jewish bourgeois values, on the German language, on a certain conception of "modernity," on literature, music and hygiene, and on their liberal and materialistic world view – proved irreconcilable with what was perceived to be a deeply rooted Catholicism, intensely private family lifestyle, social conservatism, and industrial "backwardness" of middle- and upper-class Bolivians.

Those middle- and upper-class Bolivians, of course, also maintained largely impermeable barriers between themselves and the immigrants. Flirtations and sexual encounters did occasionally occur. But marriages between Bolivians and refugees were rare, and, in the few instances where they took place, viewed by members of both groups as eccentric.[28] Despite business and professional dealings with the immigrants, moreover, it was highly uncommon for Bolivians to invite them to their house.

Indeed, expressions of anti-semitic prejudice by Bolivians were not unusual. Rooted in religious biases derived from the Spanish–Catholic popular tradition blaming Jews for the killing of Christ, and in stereotypes depicting Jews as unscrupulous money-grubbers in league with the Devil, the epithet "*Judio*" ("Jew") was sometimes hurled contemptuously at immigrants, or scrawled as graffiti on their doors and walls. More ominously, virulent anti-semitism, inspired by Nazi propaganda, found its way into Bolivia as well. In a Bolivian Chamber of Deputies' debate of 1942 over an immigration bill seeking the exclusion of Jews, Deputy Zuazo Cuenca read aloud portions from *The Protocols of the*

Elders of Zion, that scurrilous forgery implicating Jews in acts of ritual murder – a copy of which, it was revealed later, Zuazo Cuenca had received from the German Office of Propaganda. The newspaper *La Calle*, in one of its many editorials on the bill, lamented the "inundation" of the country by immigrants "with very beaked noses": by members of the "Jewish race" who were waiting "to fall like a ravenous invading horde upon the cities of Bolivia," and who were planning to gain control of the government. Jews, as "a race," some Bolivians in influential positions argued, posed a danger to Bolivia's "nationality" and should be expelled.[29]

It is of course important to put Bolivian anti-semitism in perspective. Throughout the war years, many Bolivians forcefully attacked anti-semitism and came to the defense of the immigrants. Their voices and opinions, expressed in forums and in print, provided a strong counterpoint to hatemongering, and presented the immigrants with a more positive image.[30] But the open expression of anti-semitism in Bolivia certainly contributed to the fears and insecurities which inspired the refugees to maintain close-knit institutional bonds and a collective identity. It also helped to convince many of them that Bolivia could never be their permanent home – that their future lay elsewhere.

In view of the immigrants' awareness of the potential threat that Bolivian anti-semitism posed for their safety, it is remarkable that, in *the present-day memory* of the refugees, it does not play an important role. This is a clear illustration of the constructed nature of memory – of the ways in which individuals and groups recall, reorganize, and distort their present memory to represent the past. Quite possibly, for present-day survivors of the immigration still living in Bolivia, the memory of that virulent anti-semitism might awaken old insecurities and stir up unpleasant communal tensions, better left dormant. Having settled in Bolivia, found acceptance, and prospered economically, they recall their past selectively, reconstructing it to safeguard their current well-being. And for those who left Bolivia to settle elsewhere, Bolivian anti-semitism is usually remembered as a relatively minor episode within a sojourn fraught with challenges and difficulties, but also characterized by relative tolerance. No matter how short their residence in Bolivia had been, this Andean land inserted itself into the memory of the emigres as the place which gave them refuge when all others had rejected them. "For better or for worse," Ilse Hertz observed in her recollection of the emigration, "Bolivians permitted us to live."[31] It was in Bolivia that the refugees escaped the horrors of the Nazi Holocaust. Consciousness of that overwhelming fact is the background against which their present-day memories have been constructed.

But the refugees' downplaying of Bolivian anti-semitism also illuminates another characteristic of memory. It demonstrates that memories are *historically situated* in a particular place and time, and recalled from the perspective of *that present*. It indicates that they are constructed narratives whose prime function, as David Lowenthal has recognized, "is not to preserve the past but to adapt it so as to enrich and manipulate the present."[32] And being situated in the present means that memory – what is "recalled" of the past – operates within a temporal realm in which alternative versions are conceivable. Memory may thus change over time: what is recalled at one particular moment can differ considerably, both qualitatively and in content, from what one remembered at an earlier time, or would remember in the future. Each occasion of remembering can alter a memory, and "riveting" a memory in writing – anchoring it to a specific historical moment – does not insure it from challenge by other, different representations.

Moreover, by interrogating refugee recollections over time – also my own childhood memories of Bolivia and my present role as historian who uses recollections as historical sources – the intimate connection between memory and identity is highlighted as well. The person we feel we are, or have become, is linked through the recollection of past experiences to our earlier selves. Like the memories which sanction it, identity is synthesized differently at different times in our lives. And that synthesis occurs not only through the connection one constructs between the present and the past but also by one's idea *in the present* of the nature and promise of a *future*. What ultimately determines for ourselves how we respond to the world around us is that dynamic relationship between our individual, subjective notion of *self-in-the-present* with our notion of *self-in-the-future* – an interpretive and changing relationship.[33]

In this respect, the refugees' construction of a collective identity, based on their memories of European bourgeois life, seems reasonable at a time, during the war years, when their sense of future was equivocal, if not uncertain. A question, nonetheless, remains. Might the refugees' adjustment in Bolivia have been different, had they been more willing to modify their cultural memories and integrate more completely into Bolivian society? Would their cultural memories of the European world into which Jews had assimilated – with which they had tried to identify so fully before the rise of exclusionary anti-semitism and persecution – have been less likely to inspire imitation if news of the death camps and the extent of Austrian/German involvement in them had been confirmed earlier?

Two recollections:

In my most vivid early memory I return home from the Kinderheim one day in 1945 and meet my father hurrying up the stairs with a letter in his hand. He gathers us together in the kitchen – my mother, grandparents, Uncle Ferri, Uncle Julius – and tells us that Frieda – Ferri's sister, my father's niece – is alive; that she survived a series of concentration camps; that she is free, and has re-established contact. But the letter he reads from Frieda is frightening as well. It describes how her mother, father, and younger sister were shot before her eyes by the Germans, and how she was selected to work while others were marched off to die. I recall the scene in the room while he read; I still hear, as though it occurred yesterday, the crying, everyone in the room weeping, embracing, shouting. Included with the letter is a photograph: Frieda as lonely and lone survivor, smiling at the photographer, reconnecting with us who are together, comforting each other. . . .

Looking through family pictures, I find photos taken at the Austrian Club in La Paz, two years after the war. Some show my mother and other women at a Dirndl ball, dressed in Austrian folk costumes, and my father, my uncle Ferri and other men wearing lederhosen, Alpine knee-socks, and Tyrolean hats. Similar pictures of the same vintage from an Hogar Austriaco banquet. In their background one can clearly see the Club's wallhangings: two Austrian flags, a lithograph of Old Vienna, and lampshades emblazoned with the Austrian republican coat of arms. . . .

16

German–Jewish Memory and National Consciousness

Michael Geyer and Miriam Hansen

[A] bizarre design: a jagged edifice with slanting walls that resembles a lightning bolt, slashed by a central axis mainly consisting of empty spaces the architect refers to as "voids". . . . [T]heir purpose was to draw attention to the vacuum in Berlin left by the disappearance of tens of thousands of Jews. . . . The idea was not to create a monument to Berlin's lost Jews but to reconnect the German and Jewish experience as it had met in the city's past, so no visitors could pass through the museum without being aware of the Jewish presence, nor could a Jewish visitor withdraw to a separate wing and sink into the past of Jews alone. At issue, too, was the overwhelming void created by the sudden absence of Jews in a pulsing City in which the great Jewish personalities like the physicist Albert Einstein and the painter Max Liebermann left their mark.

Auschwitz as "sign of history" (*Geschichtszeichen*)[1] exemplified by the design for the extension of the Berlin City Museum by Daniel Liebeskind.[2]

How to reflect upon a genocidal past? How to sustain a present that is flooded with the pain of past destruction? How to redeem the German–Jewish catastrophe? These questions have lost none of their urgency, though time is passing.

Throughout the first post-war decades in Germany, answers were sought by challenging the inability of perpetrators and bystanders to acknowledge the genocide and mourn its victims.[3] A whole generation stood accused. Powerful indictments were launched as belated acts of conscience and resistance by some members of that same generation. Their message of moral and spiritual renewal, often combined with a critique of consumer society, was eagerly picked up by the post-war generation and became the driving force behind the German youth rebellion during the 1960s.

However, as the post-war era drew to an end, the certainty and self-righteousness of this rebellion dwindled fast, notwithstanding holdovers from that period such as *The Nasty Girl*. At present, what has replaced it – like a return of the repressed – is a near-obsessive emphasis on both the Holocaust and the Nazi era. Memory in Germany, like history too, has become, since the mid-1970s or so, an uncanny thing for wartime, post-war, and post-post-war generations alike. They discover not only that there is memory and that there is history, but also that having both in excess is where the problem of reflecting upon a genocidal past begins anew. Today, we can no longer say that the Germans have no memory of the Holocaust or that memory is denied.

Yet a concern about forgetfulness is as warranted as ever. Germany's unification is too commonly seen as a means of leaving behind an "unpleasant" or "unfortunate" chapter of German history so as to return to "normalcy." The well-known formulas raise apprehension about the revival of a "Jewish problem."[4] At the same time it is evident that even those who want to forget no longer "repress" the past. Occasions like Bitburg make it clear that just about everyone documents/historicizes/remembers/recollects/commemorates/memorializes. The critical commentary on "working-through" the German past[5] has become one of a general "working-over" that past, involving governments, popes, journalists and professional historians. They remember *in order to forget*. And these rituals of remembering are the benevolent versions. Others, including Hans Juergen Syberberg, have begun to remember so as to prepare revenge.[6] No, the problem is no longer "never to forget": it is how to remember.

What enables us, and Germans in particular, to give presence to the Holocaust – the act, the victims, and the perpetrators? How does one mourn what Edith Wyschogrod calls "man-made mass death?"[7] How would *you* remember and mourn *your* genocide – coming from the land of murderers? This question, not meant to solicit sympathy but to acknowledge the problem, has tied Jews and Germans together. Jewish memory cannot be considered separate from the German one. One memory will be implicated in the other's story, as long as there is a German and a Jewish identity, and as long as both sides are able to tell their stories, and there are, again, Jews living in Germany *as Jews*.

Most Germans living today cannot proceed in quite the same manner that was suggested to their/our parents. The large majority are no longer contemporaries of the Third Reich. Therefore, their desire or need to mourn will be different from those who brought Hitler to power, who identified with or tolerated the Nazi regime, or who refused to take responsibility for what happened. It will also be different from those who were exiled and persecuted by the Nazi regime. Remembering and mourning will be different because the Third Reich is no longer part of a lived experience: it has become an imaginative construct. To be sure, even as that construct, the Third Reich is more of a presence than the post-war generation is likely to acknowledge. It enters their life as an uneasy knowledge about the range of choices and possible moral failure in their grandparents' and parents' lives. (Helmut Kohl's statement on the "blessing of late birth" is a peculiar repression of that fact.) Since the Third Reich is handed down as imagination rather than as actual experience, remembering the Holocaust has shifted from being an issue of motivation (the willingness to remember) to an issue of representation (how to construct the presence of the past). This corresponds to a simultaneous shift from a question of guilt to one of responsibility.[8]

The transition from lived experience to representation has already occurred. It was anything but mute and subterraneous. On the contrary, it set loose an avalanche of public expressions: in the mid-1970s an intense, embattled search for remembrance rocked German intellectual, cultural and, repeatedly, political life. The repressions of the past seemed to be swept away. The moment of catharsis had arrived.

Yet this outpouring of memory hardly fulfilled the expectations of those who had demanded it. Why, for example, should this wave of remembrance drive a German Jew like Henryk Broder from his country of birth?[9] It was commonly assumed that the acknowledgment of the Holocaust as a German deed would facilitate, if not a new German–Jewish symbiosis, then a rapprochement and possibly a reconciliation. Something like this happened, but also the opposite. Germans have become more conscious of the Nazi past and its crimes, but, at the same time, have invoked the power of imagination to insist on the authenticity of their national character. More aware of the German–Jewish past *and* of the presence of Jews in their midst, this very recognition has led to resentment as much as to reconciliation.

The Holocaust and the Nazi regime, moreover, did not return as personal memory. The individual labor of remembering was overlaid by the mass-production of memory. The film *Hitler: a Career* (1977), television broadcasts of *Holocaust* (1979), and then *Heimat* (1984) were stages in this development, each production moving Germans very deeply – and each leading them in very different directions. The more these representations of the Holocaust captured the German mind, the more Holocaust memory became mass produced, mass mediated, and did not turn into what the intellectuals of the post-war years had hoped for. The open remembrance of the Nazi past inspired a culture industry aiming at mass consumption. It began to capture the imagination of all those who listen to radio, watch TV and go to the movies.[10]

That is, German memory-work became less and less private and individual. Intended to release individuals from their ties to a collective shaped by the Nazi past and, by implication, to reconstruct the "integral personality,"[11] it succeeded only half way in this. While freeing the individual from the taint of Nazi *Volksgemeinschaft*, it launched the search for a new language of collective identity which resulted, paradoxically, in a recovery of older and more universalist, but no less troubled, expressions of Germanness. It cut the link to the past but initiated historicizing narratives of the present as, for example, in the paintings of Anselm Kiefer.[12] What we have witnessed over the past two decades is the creation of a public *through* these collective rituals and representations of remembering.

How to enable remembrance in order to keep the memory of the Holocaust alive in the midst of these transformations remains the question. This task is all the more urgent, since the Holocaust is becoming exclusively dependent on the representational intellect. For our transition beyond the post-war years entails the recognition of the passing away of our parents as living witnesses of the Holocaust.

Two Recollections

I still wonder about my parents who, ever since I can recall, talked about their Jewish neighbors, where they were during *Kristallnacht* and the 1940 deportation of Jews in Freiburg, and commented on how various family members had sympathized with the Nazis while others had not. During local outings they remembered towns as having been Jewish or with a substantial Jewish population. They mentioned individual Jews who had lived in the neighborhood. It is not as if they had an urge or a desire to speak out. The subject remained awkward, not least because the memory of (Jewish) difference before the 1930s had a different language in the post-war, post-Holocaust present. What was once casually asserted or talked about – the specific features of German and Jewish culture – was now sensitized by the knowledge that this difference had been used to motivate annihilation.

When such recollections came to my parents, they spoke. But about mass annihilation they would talk only when I asked. I was a history student, then, in the early 1970s; and they said they had seen nothing, although they did recall terrible rumors. That the rumors could be true, they deduced from the euthanasia programs, which they knew about (although they had not seen anything specific). They said that they chose not to think about the fate of the Jews because it was too frightful to imagine. I sensed that they had experienced more than they told me, and dropped the topic. But they did not accept lightly having been passive, although no one could figure out what might have been done. (We talked about that in the context of my mother's choice between munitions factory or Luftwaffe, and her desire to be a florist). While father seemed to be more resigned, mother despaired more passionately. It was their (post-war?) character. However, they did consider non-thinking a sin, a lack of compassion or *caritas*.

The presence of the past was symbolized for them by the parting words of the wife of their parents' neighbor, deported in 1940. There were always two versions of those words: that her fate (she being an upper-middle-class lady) would come upon my grandparents' head (on the working class, Catholic renters) or that what the Nazis were doing to the Jews, they would do next to most Germans.

I cannot say that I grew up in a family that forgot, beause the two versions of this prediction had much to do with the one catastrophe for which there was virtually no story at all. Around the time of All Souls we always put candles on a mass grave, dug for the victims of the allied bombing of November 27, 1944, who included my half-sister and my aunt (my father's first wife). We did it silently, and Hildegund's and Bertel's names were inscribed on the commemorative stone.

There were other bits and pieces of recollection, and I believe that this is true of many more of us than post-war literature would have it. There was never any doubt that the past was with us. The silence about it had less to do with fathers and mothers than with sons and daughters. The silence was my own. And this is strange in view of what the books say, because at that point I am supposed to have rebelled in order to find out what I already knew. Instead, my family was swept up in the Vatican II liturgical movement. Of Jews and their Holocaust I knew little more than those who had not heard or did not care to listen.

I did listen. I was aware of the synagogue in Freiburg and of the erased inscription above the entrance of the university. I knew about the Jews in Randen (up a steep hill), about the Jewish community of Gailingen and the smaller one in Wangen (a bit further away at the Swiss border), or of Ihringen near where my father's grandparents came from. I learnt about German Jews and the Holocaust in school – not sufficiently, but enough that I could have known or could have shown interest. But my lack of imagination was quite extraordinary. The knowledge I gained simply deepened and reinforced the absence of Jews from Germany, because it located them securely in the past – or in Israel.

Throughout adolescence I knew Jews only as Holocaust images from history books, or from newspapers as Israelis who fought battles in the air or the desert. My own moment of awkwardness came in Oxford when I met a couple from Israel, and in Ann Arbor when, for the first time, I consciously saw a synagogue. I recognized then that there was a living Jewish culture and, by inference, that there had been one in Germany. The experience of my friends who had remained in Germany was different: they discovered a culture that had been destroyed and, by inference, Jews who had survived. Needless to say these inferences were not automatic, self-evident, or stable: they touched some people very deeply while they left others cold. My friends in Germany began to reconstruct the traces of Jewish culture, which often involved nasty skirmishes with local officials. Haltingly, I began to read our Jewish thinkers, and with increasing rage as I recognized their absence in my German life.

As far back as I can remember, the Holocaust was an acknowledged fact in my parents' house. Neighbors, friends, the whole town seemed to know what I had been told early on: that my mother was Jewish and that my grandparents had been killed in Auschwitz. What that knowledge meant and how and when it came to mean anything is another matter. My mother lit candles before a photo of her parents every year on their birthdays, but she might have done so had they died a different kind of death. She did not identify as Jewish, at least not in a religious or even cultural sense. She rarely talked about her parents, let alone about the way they might have spent their last years, months, days.

The Holocaust was present in my family as a powerful abstraction, a moral imperative that provided the political justification for their return (or, in my mother's case, move) to Germany after the war. As a concrete and personal experience, however, it was clearly taboo, in ways that the circumstances of my father's persecution by the Nazis, his narrow escape via Belgium to England, the afflictions of his friends in the resistance, like Wilhelm Leuschner and Carlo Mierendorff, including the particular mode of their deaths, were not.

The silence began to lift in the 1960s. I was given Anne Frank's diary and told of family friends who had survived in hiding; but I still recall vividly the almost physical shock when I discovered, in my parents' library, an American book of photographs documenting the liberation of Dachau. I watched my mother run the gauntlet of the restitution process, having to find evidence for the length of her parents' captivity, since compensation depended on how long they survived rather than on the fact of their having been murdered. I accompanied her to the Frankfurt Auschwitz trial (she volunteered to help the witnesses), where survivors attempted to talk of the experience of mass annihilation, often for the first time in public. Like many at the trial, we displaced the pain and anger over what the victims tried to say onto the obstacles that prevented them from doing so, whether the legalistic violence of the court procedure or so-called "personality problems." Then came the Six-Day War and my mother's rediscovery of Jewishness via an identification with Israel. But, if I remember right, it made me, in turn, quietly abandon any active concern with the Holocaust and the vicissitudes of German–Jewish identity.

My experience in learning about the Holocaust in high school was not different from my classmates'. Whatever identification there might have been was moral and political, rather than personal; a matter of the past rather than the present. I chose to write my senior essay on a chapter of my father's biography: the resistance movement in Darmstadt and southern Hesse. Similarly, when I enrolled at Frankfurt University in 1967, being Jewish did not mean anything, in a social and cultural sense. Adorno and Horkheimer were beacons of critical theory, not German Jews returned from exile; anti-semitism epitomized the general negativity of fascism, rather than an experienced threat to Jewish lives and careers. During the heyday of the student movement one did not know who was Jewish and who was not, nor did it matter. It was not a category of identification, as class or dialect were: no German–Jewish culture existed to identify with or study.

It was not until the late 1970s and early 1980s, after I had emigrated to the United States, that I found a living example of what was absent in Germany. By that time, however, the discourse on the Holocaust and on German–Jewish identity had changed in Germany, too; friends turned out to have been Jewish all along, intellectual activities and journals crystallized around Jewish questions (e.g. *Babylon*), and synagogues began to flourish. I had a (German–) Jewish existence to contend with. It reminded me of what I had missed when I was growing up. At the same time, I could not say that I now was part of it.

If German–Jewish culture had been an absent presence, so was anti-semitism. Having grown up under the glass bell of my parents' semi-public status as victims of Nazi persecution, I did not believe that, after Auschwitz, anti-semitism could still be possible. There was the exception: a salesman in the neighborhood foodstore warned my mother against eggs imported from Israel, referring to them as "Jew-eggs." He was more or less coerced by the store owner to send a bouquet of flowers with apologies. But my own first-hand encounter with the anti-semitic vernacular did not come until I was 17, working a summer job in the mail room of a local publishing house. I had a minor nervous breakdown – not so much because of what the man said (I can't even recall his remarks exactly), but rather because I had been listening to his stories about fighting at Stalingrad when he was barely out of school, and his Russian captivity, and had become fascinated with his anger. I had never experienced this kind of subterranean emotion before; I had thought I knew Germans because I was one of them.

Today, living as a German Jew in America, I begin to understand that growing up Jewish in post-war Germany did not necessarily grant me better access to memory than my non-Jewish contemporaries had. On the contrary, the fact that I was at once marginal and privileged may have blocked even the awareness of not remembering. Ironically, the privilege conferred upon my family because of their status as histori-cal victims prevented me, for a long time, from recognizing my cultural and psychosocial marginality, and understanding it in terms of the very absence the privilege was supposed to mask.

Returning to Germany today, we both enter a new and different world. We have witnessed the German struggles with the Nazi past and how they have changed the national consciousness. We now confront, from afar, a unified nation state. Germans have come together in what is our name as well. We do not share that German experience of the last 15 years, and observe with impatience competing efforts to reauthenticate Germany's name. As long as Germans can tolerate the lack of national-ism (as well as our own inadvertent negation of authenticity, and disbelief in any and all millennial dreams) we are happy to be part of them. As long as Germany can include that difference, we do not lose our identity. We do not feel that we have to be liberated:[13] our identities have always been fragments that we put together kaleidoscopically, thus giving meaning to a German name beyond "authenticity."

The Rise of Historical Consciousness

Recollections change; they differ now from what they were only a short while ago. In the following, we will attempt to make sense of the changing shape of memory during the 1970s and 1980s. In particular, we will argue: (1) that remembering the past in (West) Germany emerged as a collective and public movement that was linked to the rise of a new national consciousness; (2) that this wave of remembrances had less to do with the past than with a historical transformation of the present; (3) that the "memory movement" along with other new social movements of the 1970s testifies to the breakdown of older lifeworlds and the emergence of new, possibly post-modern, forms of subjectivity and sociability; and (4) that these new forms of remembrance are ineluctably tied to the electronic media and thus to a spectacularization of the past, in particular of the Holocaust. During the last two decades in Germany, remembering has become nothing less than a social movement that began to formulate a renascent language of national identity.

The abundance of written, scripted, painted, filmed recollections from the 1970s on seem to be highly personal narratives. However, when Prousts and Benjamins multiply, it is hard to believe in spontaneity. And as much as these memoirs want to differ from one another, their triggers are not Madeleines, not private occasions, but an immensely public and specifically German concern. They use the power of personal memory to develop a public narrative.

This explosion into memory is but one aspect of what has been called a turn to history.[14] Superficially, it is seen in the popular and vastly increased interest in exhibitions and documentaries. It is often accompanied by an active concern for historical sites, among which those of the Third Reich figure prominently. Thanks to the efforts of a history workshop movement the emplacements of forced labor camps in virtually every town are now known, and guidebooks to even small towns and villages are available. At concentration camp sites like Dachau the shift from the initial activities of victims to the concern of conscious young Germans is particularly noteworthy. Often these activities are linked to the exploration of new forms of representation, from discussion groups to the revival of historical plays and the staging of historical parades. The social movement of remembrance invests objects of the past and particularly the sites of the Third Reich with a pathos that is crucial for the recovery of a historical consciousness.

This pathos is most clearly expressed in the wave of autobiographical writings that have become a prominent feature in Germany. What began in the 1960s as a literature in the manner of *J'accuse* turned, in the 1980s, into public self-reflection and mourning about the past. A new genre of "confessionals" emerged, peculiarly German and quite unlike anything in neighboring countries.[15] Christa Wolf in particular shaped this kind of literary reminiscence.[16] However, Wolf did not trust the nascent collectivism of such recollections. Like so many intellectuals of the post-war era, she acted out her defiance of a forgetful nation, emphasizing private and individual experience at the very moment things began to change. Her act of defiance was both duplicated and submerged in a broad and swelling stream of confessional literature. The autobiographic boom in Germany, despite its painfully private aspect, hides the fact that the past has become a public matter.

So public acts of remembering become a historical force. However, we cannot conclude that the cause of remembrance is the Holocaust. The latter is, to be sure, the object of memory. But it is *the German present* that brings the Nazi past, literally and figuratively, "into play." The most common interpretation of the social movement of remembrance is summed up in the famous dictum about a "past that does not pass away."[17] It is said that the burden of that past continues to weigh heavily on Germany, due to the unspeakable nature of the crimes committed in Germany's name. Hence, it becomes an "unmasterable past" that imposes itself on the present. But this argument is as true as it is self-serving and misleading. It is true inasmuch as the Nazi past has lost none of its significance for the living. It is utterly false in that it presumes that *the past* imposes itself upon the Germans, as if it were a natural or a metaphysical force. This presumption is self-serving for those who act as agents of that past in the present. It creates the figure of the omniscient historian who speaks for the past – all of it. More importantly, this presumption effaces the mediated and increasingly nationalized quality of the past. Ever since the late 1960s Germans have begun to forsake the history of the allies and the victims in order to view the past on their own terms – a process that climaxed in the national recovery of historical pathos we have described.

Again Christa Wolf is a good witness for reading and misreading this process. After all, she was the one author who had pointedly asserted the present in her recovery of the past – a visit to her childhood town in today's Poland, mixed with reflections on her life in the German Democratic Republic and global political issues. But the present she describes is so far away and so alienated from her own person; her remarks on it seem wooden. Her past, on the other hand, is so vivid and her insights into her experience so prescient! No doubt, this is one kind of experience, but not the one that ultimately shaped the recovery of the past in the 1970s and 1980s. That experience knows no such distance from the present but is motivated by the rise of a German national consciousness in a process of historicizing the present. This is the key to the puzzling and contradictory memory movement of the last twenty years. What had been the *pièce de résistance* of the German

subconscious in the 1950s has become working material for the formation of the German consciousness in the 1980s.

Everyone is aware of the phenomenally successful TV mini-series
Holocaust, and the just as successful German counter-production of
Heimat. Yet these films are hardly ever seen in the context of the
hundreds of melodramas, docudramas, documentaries, and talk shows
about the Nazi past. The problem with existing studies is that they
present the mediated rituals of public remembering as if they were
private, basically passive acts of consumption. They neglect the politicized quality of collective, "popular" memory. Politically staged events
like Bitburg, or ongoing controversies about a national memorial for
victims of the Third Reich, or the museum projects of the Kohl government, are notorious. They make sense only within the context of myriad
local events pervaded by and, in turn, reshaping national politics. The
German politics of remembering the past has been remarkably undemo-
cratic.

It is impossible to make sense of a past that does not go away
unless we acknowledge that *the present desires and needs it*. Academic
fragmentation of this moment of recollection into an "objective" past
and a pure present masks this urgency, effaces its inherent tensions and,
as a result, misunderstands the crisis. In turning memories into a series
of objects (films, paintings, books), academic debates observe only that
every aspect of life in Germany has, for some time, been inundated
with recollections of the past. They do not see that a national *imaginaire*
is being formed in which the present summons and commands the past.
And so, finally, we tend to miss what is new about the last twenty
years: that remembering has become a national discourse as much as
a discourse about the nation.

The fact of this difference between an emerging national discourse
and a discourse on the nation is an unsettling and indeed a shocking
phenomenon.[18] This is not what one expected to happen all over again
in the land of poets and philosophers. But popular memory has slipped
out of the institutional control of high culture, the universities and the
state. The rise of a historicizing, national consciousness comes in the
midst of a breakdown of the institution of history.

From this vantage point, the process of forgetting and remembering
the Holocaust begins to look different. The common idea that there
was a repression of the past during the post-war years now points first
and foremost to a near total usurpation of memory – every kind of
memory – by the post-war state and its institutions. It is difficult to say

if the Germans liked this state of affairs (and indicated their preference by voting for Adenauer). For, at that time, even if they had wanted to remember, there was no public space or collective language for memory experience. Memory remained private or marginal (i.e. what our parents said at home), or it was state sponsored and institutional (i.e. official commemorations and academic histories). In short, there was an institution of history, but no national, and certainly no historicizing, popular consciousness.

In contrast, the national discourse on memory which emerged in the 1970s was fashioned from many private memories. Individual testimonies opened up public spaces for remembering. They formed a national consciousness and a collective idiom. We should not be disturbed by the observation that private and personal memories beame a public force. But we must spell out the consequences to indicate the far-reaching effects of this turn of events. It means that the rise of this historical self-consciousness in Germany may end in a reconstitution of bourgeois society. That is, working through the past has become the ground for the rearticulation of a (post-modern) German *Kulturnation*.

Why should there be a lingering anxiety about this recovery of bourgeois sensibilities, which we could embrace eagerly enough? Well – German history is not just any history. One is troubled by the recovery of German *Buergerlichkeit* because many historians, and such intellectuals as Thomas Mann, have seen in it one source of the Nazi regime. Another consideration may be more disturbing still. If a German national consciousness has indeed emerged from collective processes of remembrance, this means that Germans have forged it on the basis of *their* memory of the Holocaust, from the very destruction they meted out only a generation ago! Even if this act redeems the past and its victims, it entails an appropriation and transfer of the memory of the Holocaust. We begin to recognize how problematic German memory is.

Explanations for the social and political transformations of the 1970s and 1980s have pointed to the emergence of a post-materialist society, but this assessment makes little sense of the startling changes. These were years of heightened terrorism and repression, when the trust in a benevolent, patriarchal state broke down; of rising economic insecurity, when German Keynesianism, hailed only ten years before, failed; of a growing security dilemma, when the credibility of nuclear deterrence collapsed and drew the Schmidt government with it; and of a festering legitimacy gap as a result of the deep split over *Ostpolitik*. Political observers spoke of a crisis of governance – a crisis which came to a head in the hot autumn of terrorism and counter-terrorism of 1977. The political consensus that had held German society together collapsed.

Perhaps it would be more appropriate to speak of a crisis of the liberal state. In that crisis the state's previous control over the public representation of the Holocaust also broke down.

The explosive growth of the so-called new social movements did more than challenge the established party system and its narrow politics. These movements were a vociferous element in a more general revitalization of communal forms of association and sociability. The Germans themselves have named this reconfiguration of private lives and their social networks "leisure culture" (*Freizeitkultur*), which sounds innocent but is not. For it was the insistence on an often luxurious privacy that destroyed the cultural and material remnants of the old *Volksgemeinschaft*. It was the insistence on consumption as a lifestyle and on a newly ethnicized cosmopolitanism that finally broke the control of the state over the private sphere. If the new social movements attacked state control directly, leisure culture eroded it. There was nothing heroic about this, but it was extraordinarily effective. In quick succession we find, in the late 1970s, the resurgence of a private sphere and its articulation in a series of competing (and consuming) publics.

At this very moment memories pour forth. There is a belated triumph of private emotions. This triumph comes not as psychotherapy but as a media-mediated event with its own way of working-through the past. Nothing expresses the surge of memories better than the paradoxical success of both Fest's *Hitler* and of *Holocaust*. The two spectacles are commonly juxtaposed, because *Hitler* elides what *Holocaust* puts at its center: annihilation. But they are, in fact, intimately linked. The audiences of both spectacles appropriated it all: the rise of Hitler the magician, and the tragedy of the victims. They were moved by both films, because each was about re-imaging the past as the ground for a compact between the generations. A post-war youth, separated from the one that had directly experienced war and annihilation, received the Nazi period as image and narrative. Thus distanced and yet present, the Third Reich became accessible.

This recovery of the past, though a moment of genuine contrition and moral politics, was also an exorcism in which dammed-up emotions were released into purgative images. Neither simply the force of the past nor the rendition of the Holocaust as melodrama, but the market-driven interplay between representation and receptive audience led to confessional memories that were the exact opposite of *Erinnerungen* or internalizations. They were *external memories*, expressive acts of a "spectacular" imagination combining with technology to organize everyday experience. A civil society arose based on an image-filled collective consciousness that relieved individuals of their internal worlds.

The appeal of this "society of the spectacle"[19] is commonly over-looked, despite a history of indictments going back to Hegel. It is a society in which old realities, old perceptions, old habits lose their meaning and people begin to retrace – *Spurensuche* – what they call experience (*Erfahrung*).[20] This recovery, not of an authentic individual or *Volk* but of a media-inspired imagery of solidarity, and a consumer-oriented person ready to consume even the past, placed the Holocaust at the center of the public debate over the Third Reich in the late 1970s.

Reliving the Holocaust as spectacle flowed into other manifest changes. Memory came forth as part of a general process of reordering everyday life. It was part of the discovery that one could be a Jew in Germany (and that one could convert to Judaism), but also that one could do Yoga as a woman in her fifties, or live as a widow with a good Turkish man. It meant that the next vacation would be spent in Israel or in the Mark Brandenburg; that grandfathers could undertake a belated self-therapy for their hateful violence and stupid pride; that one could publicly grieve for unknown and unrelated people – incom-mensurate activities, yet tremors that reformed the body politic.

One might call this recovery of the past a simulation – but contrary to Baudrillard's insinuations it had profound consequences.[21] It climaxed in the image-driven activation of memory and in the externalized replay of what was left of the Nazi mentality. Only this process clarified how much of that lifeworld was left and how deeply it had shaped the second and third generations. It also became evident how quickly Ger-man society was moving away from that past. In fact, the main problem with the 1980s was that the history of the Holocaust was now literally consumed. The unimaginable catastrophe fed into an ultimately ordi-nary, if astounding and far-reaching, readjustment or reconstruction of experience, and the source of an emerging national consciousness.

Fears about a return of the past are common among Germany's neighbors and in the United States. But the past is not what is to be feared. Rather, it is the present and the future; for the Germans have begun to remember on their own terms. They have begun to create their own destiny in turning their past, the lived experience of only a short while ago, into history. This is the source of an extraordinary empowerment, and it is to be seen whether this newly gained power is used for redemptive ends.

Presence and Absence

"Angels have no memory."

Barbarella

Neither Adorno nor Mitscherlich could conceive of a situation in which death – man-made mass death – could become spectacle, and the inner worlds of memory would be commodified. Nor could they have imagined that an active culture of remembrance would emerge in which the recollection of the past would flow, at one and the same time, into a compassionate moral politics and into a politics of outrage about the loss of historical innocence and the victimization of the Germans. Least of all could Adorno and Mitscherlich have imagined that the redemptive memory of the past, as national therapy, would challenge the ideal that citizens be "integral personalities."

American academics, in particular, still expect the Germans to come to terms with their past without seeing that it has already happened. As residents of the United States we observed the transformation in Germany and the way American approaches have become dated, like an early 1970s road map still in use in the United States, which gets you hopelessly lost in contemporary Germany. In our own biography, parents have moved ahead of their children. Germans and German Jews have reconstructed their lives, while émigres like us are caught in a time and space warp.

The new mode of German remembrance has its incongruities. The most difficult and perplexing is its new awareness of the Holocaust in the midst of a reconstitution of post-Nazi, post-post-war lifeworlds. This rediscovery entails a strong element of shock and even terror, especially the terror of a subject-position being restored rather than overcome. The murder of the Jews is being recognized as an integral yet non-integratable part of German history. *Heimat*, for example, the TV series that followed *Holocaust*, at last "sees" what happened, yet places the annihilation of the Jews at the margins of the Germany narrative. It happened; it was a catastrophe; it was done by Germans; it is mourned; but it succumbs to the assertion of a renovated national consciousness. Thus one German spelling of "survival" is "continuity," or in the words of Helmut Kohl: "Each of us knows that, after the Second World War, we in the Federal Republic set out to learn from history. But learning from history does not mean that we drop out of history. Obviously, to history belongs the affirmation of the continuity of history."[22] In this interpretation of the present, to remember entails an affirmation of continuity in the face of its extreme rupture. This way of remembering runs the danger of accepting the absence of the Jews, even of cannibalizing the memory of victims for the purpose of reconstructing German history.[23]

There are contrary developments as well. The very presence and renewed self-articulation of a Jewish diaspora in Germany is one of them. But the most hopeful indication of a German working-through of the past is the possibility of keeping alive the memory of the victims. For some, particularly in the United States, this proves difficult, because such cross-over recollections unsettle identities. For others, particularly in Germany, it harms the process of recovery, because it prevents the healing reintegration of a unified personality. Both views rely on a return to certain *buergerlich* sensibilities of Germans and German Jews, even when they have begun to leave this heritage behind – recognizing its implication in the Holocaust.

The ability to sustain – rather than usurp – the memory of Jewish victims depends on a concept of the subject as a divided subjectivity, one that could bear a recognition of the violence of the past. The "integral personality" is challenged by a portion of history that cannot be integrated. Such memory-work, therefore, recovers not a single history but several histories; not the negation of death through the rhetorical assertion of continuity, but the remembrance of absence. This kind of complex identity rather than some facile multiculturalism is the chance for a redeeming future. The remembrance of the absent Jews requires a concrete knowledge both of their religious and their secular culture and an obligation to the residual Jewish communities; above all, it means recollecting the loss to German life of that once closely identified community.

The Holocaust is now written into the act of representation itself. It is inscribed there as the remembrance of past lives and their mass death: as the re-imagining of an unimaginable "violence of linkage" (*Gewalt des Zusammenhangs*)[24] that holds Germans and Jews together ever since the moment of genocide. To understand Auschwitz in this way as a "sign of history" is the task of the post-war generation.

17

Negating the Dead

Nadine Fresco*

The Nazis put their imagination and zeal in the service of a vast
undertaking: the elimination of the largest possible number of Jews.
But as "the final solution of the Jewish question" was being carried
out, the promoters of the undertaking were confronted with two huge
problems: how to dispose of the millions of corpses produced and how
to carry out that double liquidation – first of the living, then of the
dead – as discreetly as an operation of such scope allowed. Ever since
the end of the war, but in a much more organized and public way
during the 1980s, self-styled "revisionists" have engaged a variant of
the problem that had so concerned the Nazis: how to dispose of those
millions of dead Jews who continue to burden the Western conscience
and how, unlike the Nazis, to do it in such a way that the publicity
created around it would make up for the small number of people
involved in the enterprise.[1]

Thus a peculiar representation of this genocide, a representation that
began its life during the first few years after the war, gradually developed
in different countries, prompted by contradictory ideological and political commitments. It attained its most radical and public form in the
late 1970s, and it merged these opposing ideologies in the late 1980s.
The representation consists quite simply in denying that the genocide
took place. By fabricating and propagating such a denial, "revisionist"
groups have actually provided proof of the weight and imprint left by
the genocide: their relentless rejection of the specificity of this event has
finally led them, in just as relentless a way, to declare that it never took
place at all. Indeed, their radical denial forces them, paradoxically, to
return constantly to the fact of genocide as an intolerable but inevitable
reference point. They live totally, obsessively, dedicated to their cause,
determined to prove that the crime did not take place and that the dead
were not killed.

The name of "revisionists" they themselves adopted for some years is intended to make them the glorious heirs of a long history of struggles coming from within the working-class movement.[2] At the same time, they have declared themselves the "revisionist school" in opposition to the "exterminationist school" (*sic*), which they identify with "official history." In doing so, they hope to benefit from that combination of seriousness and intellectual respectability that attaches to the notion of a historical school, while at the same time demonstrating a supposed freedom of thought resolutely hostile to any form of orthodoxy or "official history." Their principal thesis is that the genocide is a swindle, a lie fabricated after the war by the Jews in order to extort, by way of reparations, millions of marks from the unfortunate Germans. And that the Germans, together with the Palestinians, are the main victims of this monumental fraud.

The precursor, in France, of this "revision" of the Second World War was a leading theoretician of neo-Fascism, Maurice Bardèche, the author of two books bearing the eloquent titles *Nüremberg ou la Terre promise* and *Nüremberg II ou les Faux-Monnayeurs*.[3] Bardèche entered politics after his brother-in-law, Robert Brasillach, was condemned to death in 1945. Brasillach had been the notorious editorial director of a leading collaborationist paper, the virulently anti-semitic, extreme-right weekly, *Je suis partout*.

As early as 1948, Bardèche wrote that "for three years we have been living through a falsification of history." But at that time neither he nor anyone else dared to claim that the genocide had not taken place. The time was not yet ripe for conceiving and diffusing a strictly negationist literature. We had to wait thirty more years to discover, in 1978, Robert Faurisson, a literature professor at the University of Lyons, who explained how, after years of painstaking work, he had come to the conclusion that "the non-existence of the 'gas chambers' was good news for poor humanity – good news that it would be wrong to keep hidden any longer."[4]

The time had finally come to deny the genocide. It was no longer 1945, when the extermination was being revealed in its full extent. Since the Six Day War of June 1967 between Israel and the Arab countries, the attitude of French society to the Jews had undergone a change. When General de Gaulle, then president of France, and speaking of that war, referred to the Jews as "that élite people, self-confident and domineering," Raymond Aron wrote: "General de Gaulle has knowingly, intentionally, opened up a new period in Jewish history and perhaps a new period of anti-semitism. Anything is now possible. It is all starting again. There is no question, of course, of persecution: just

'ill-will.' It is not the time of contempt, but the time of suspicion."[5]
And since everything was becoming possible once more, one could now
make public the supposedly scientific declaration that the Jews had not
been exterminated by the Nazis and that the Zionists were at the origin
of this hoax of the twentieth century.[6]

Other Faurissons, belonging to the extreme right, and often overtly
nostalgic about the Third Reich, had already made public appearances
in Europe and in the United States. The originality of the situation in
France during the 1980s stems from a political fact. Those who immediately put at the service of Faurisson's theses their time, their energy,
the funds they could raise, and a wide range of publications, and who,
ever since, have devoted themselves unstintingly to getting rid of the
millions of Jewish corpses that seemed to burden them so much, have
sprung from a political tradition radically opposed to the right. This
handful of negationist activists were, for the most part, ultra-left militants, who regrouped in the early 1980s around what had originally
been a Paris bookstore, La Vieille Taupe (The Old Mole). This Latin
Quarter bookshop was well-known to students of the May 1968 movement, who could find there revolutionary texts and leftist pamphlets.
In the disillusion that followed the exaltation of 1968, a group around
La Vieille Taupe had assumed a particularly pure and uncompromising
orientation, declaring that if the revolution had failed, it was only
because it had lacked revolutionary leadership, and that we were entering
one of those phases in the history of the working class when the
consciousness of the proletariat was concentrated in but a few individuals, who happened to be the thinkers of this new Vieille Taupe.

Those happy few, potential saviours of the communist movement,
were reviving a central theme of Bordiguism, named after Amadeo
Bordiga, one of the founders in 1921 of the Italian Communist Party.
This ultra-leftist trend in Marxism, characterized by a constant inflation
of abstract and rigid rhetorics, claimed the invariance of capitalism and
the lack of any real difference between Fascism and democracy. Fifteen
years after the end of the war, *Programme communiste*, the French
review of what remained of Bordiguism, published an article entitled
"Auschwitz or the Great Alibi." At a time (1960) when the future
negationists around La Vieille Taupe were scarcely twenty, and still had
a few illusions to lose before finally turning into guardians of the truth,
the genocide was still too recent not to have taken place. The analysis
of their Bordiguist elders did not in any way question the reality of the
event. What those who regarded themselves as the sole heirs of Marx's
thought and of the unchanging nature of his theory denounced, was
the use of the genocide by the imperialist conquerors of the Nazis

(whether bourgeois or supposed Marxists) to set up a fictitious opposition between the democracies and the Fascist regimes in order to dupe the proletarian masses with a false enemy.

True theoreticians of the revolution will not have their constancy disturbed by historical events. The ultimate explanation of any phenomenon, including anti-semitism, being necessarily of an economic order, they found a construction of reality that would take account of these theoretical imperatives. The article "Auschwitz or the Great Alibi" is a perfect illustration of this. "By virtue of their previous history, the Jews now find themselves essentially in the middle and petty bourgeoisie. Now this class is condemned by the irresistible advance of the concentration of capital." Anti-semitism results "directly from the economic constraint" that led the German petty bourgeoisie to sacrifice

one of its parts [the Jews], thus hoping to save and guarantee the existence of others. . . . In "normal" times, and when only a small number is involved, those whom capitalism rejects from the process of production can simply be left to starve by themselves. But it was impossible to do this in wartime, when millions of men were involved: such a "disorder" would have paralysed everything. Capitalism, therefore, had to organize their death. . . . Indeed German capitalism had found it difficult to resign itself to murder pure and simple. Not, of course, out of humane feelings, but because there was nothing to be gained by it. . . . [The Jews were destroyed] not because they were Jews, but because they were ejected from the production process, were useless to production.

Such, then, was the thesis defended in 1960 by the champions of economico-logical materialism. They declared once more "the fundamental identity of fascist and anti-fascist ideologies." The worst consequence of Fascism was precisely this anti-Fascist ideology produced by capitalism in order to dupe and immobilize the working class. A false, supposedly diabolical enemy concealed the exploitation to which the workers were being subjected. "The horrors of capitalist death must make the proletariat forget the horrors of capitalist life and the fact that the two are indissolubly linked."[7]

In 1970, ten years after the original appearance (unnoticed at the time) of this article, La Vieille Taupe republished in the form of a separate pamphlet this denunciation of the great alibi.[8] In 1970, the ultra-leftist militants of La Vieille Taupe still believed in the reality and horror of genocide as capitalist death. But time was working on the side of negationism. In yet another ten years the members of the Vieille

Taupe group, politically idle, and reduced to ruminating on revolutionary theory, learnt in the press about a literature professor who was
denying the gas chambers. For revolutionary theory to be reborn, the
previous ideological edifice of anti-Fascism had first to be dismantled.
Hence some members of the Vieille Taupe group welcomed a specialist
in the hypercriticism of literary texts, far removed from Bordiguism or
revolutionary ideology, who publicly attacked what constituted the very
basis of the lying edifice of democracy's anti-Fascism: the extermination
of the Jews in the gas chambers. What the Bordiguists had hitherto
dared to conceive and denounce only as an alibi was presented by this
audacious professor as quite simply an invention, fabricated by the
Zionists and disseminated by the propaganda of the victors of the
Second World War. Offering its services to Faurisson, who had hitherto
been more inclined to frequent people of the right,[9] this new Vieille
Taupe was turned into a publishing house in the interests of the cause.
It rapidly became the focus of those happy few who still regarded
themselves as the true revolutionaries. Suddenly converted to
negationism, they were saved by this exalting task of demolishing the
gas chambers from the political unemployment in which they had veg-
etated since the disillusioning days following May 1968.

Thus we have passed, in the twenty years from 1960 to 1980, from
the as yet hesitant characterization of Auschwitz as alibi, to the radical
construction of Auschwitz as myth. The times – and people's viewpoints
– had certainly changed. The vision of Jewish survivors, liberated from
the camps and learning to live in the new state of Israel, had given way
to that of Israeli soldiers occupying Palestinian territory and bombarding
other camps. This image of the victim transformed into conqueror or
executioner, which exerted a profound effect on both Jews and non-
Jews, had a very special impact on future negationists. They freed
themselves at last of a "transference Zionism"[10] that, according to
them, imbued a public opinion incapable of understanding that "the
creation of the State of Israel has obviously nothing to do with what
took place between the Nazis and the Jewish communities of Europe."[11]
    The revolutionaries of La Vieille Taupe took the plunge and aban-
doned the scheme of the alibi in favour of the imposture thesis. Something had jammed the cogs of Bordiguist reasoning: for the upholders
of an economic interpretation of the world, it was neither logical nor
rational that capital, by perpetuating a genocide, should have sacrificed
the labour power of millions of deported Jews. The Bordiguists had
previously asserted that capital had found it difficult to resign itself to
a genocide that was unprofitable. The negationists who took up the

story twisted and distorted reality to make it, in the end, conform to the theory entrusted with the task of accounting for it: the genocide simply had not taken place.

Some of the moles, born during the very years in which the mass murder of the Jews occurred, had taken an active part in the anti-colonial struggles of their generation, especially about Algeria and Vietnam. Aware of the self-betrayal of so many liberation movements once they had attained power, these freethinkers became, at least in their own eyes, the last guarantors of the principles of world revolution and sole guardians of its theoretical virtue. Full-time destroyers of taboos of all kinds, as so many shackles on revolutionary truth, they were all the more determined to unmask the lies of "official" history in that they themselves had been the dupes of those lies in their youth. Only the intransigence of their present crusade could atone for past short-sightedness.

One is not born a "revisionist." One has to undergo, rather, a radical conversion to the demanding truth offered by an elite of clear-sighted individuals, practitioners of a suspicious and systematic cynicism that serves as a theoretical apparatus. Those non-dupes rigorously practice the most implacable conformism, that of anti-conformism, which they have raised to an ultimate virtue. Having decreed once and for all that a commonly accepted truth was a lie, they see themselves as breakers of idols and demystifiers of the lies of a corrupt bourgeois world. Unlike the general run of mankind, they will be "advocates of no enslaved thought."[12] They risk "tearing away the veil of ideology," a risk that "intellectuals are almost always reluctant to take because their essential social function, and usually their living, consists of being the weavers of this ideological veil." Some of them now support the Palestinian cause all the more fervently because, at an age when they still possessed some regrettable flexibility of judgement, they were weak enough to share the dominant climate of opinion, favorable to Zionism. Fully conscious of the importance of their contribution to "the work of exposing and criticizing the dominant ideology" at work in "the Judaeo–Israelo–Zionist world," they also know, made wiser by age, though unblunted in their combatant ardor, that an enormous amount of work remains to be done in "digging galleries through the layers of ideological sediment and reaching the hard rock of theoretical and practical truth."[13]

History teaches us that events and individuals who have made their mark on the world are a special temptation to negative lucubrations of all kinds. In 1827, a few years after the Emperor's death, a certain

Jean-Baptiste Pérès published a curious little book entitled *Comme quoi Napoléon n'a jamais existé ou Grand erratum source d'un nombre infini d'errata à noter dans l'histoire du XIXe siècle* (*How Napoleon Never Existed or Grand Erratum, Source of an Infinite Number of Errata to be Noted in the History of the Nineteenth Century*). It began with these words: "Napoleon Bonaparte, of whom so many things have been said and written, did not even exist. He is no more than an allegorical figure."[14] But such lucubrations aside, the permanent revision of knowledge that characterizes the discipline we call history does not deny or systematically invalidate everything that attests to the reality of a fact – does not confuse the exercise of doubt with the practice of suspicion. The negationists, however, set themselves up as judges in a trial in which what is at stake is not "knowing the precise sequence of events that occurred at Auschwitz, but checking whether the evidence produced in support of the exterminationist thesis is convincing,"[15] a trial that takes place only because they deny the existence of the subject of the action and will therefore necessarily be led, when the verdict arrives, to declare as unproven any evidence that contradicts their a priori. They controvert any fact that does not conform to their theory. Instead of adapting their ideas to reality, they adapt reality to their ideas. Attached to a single historical theme – the extermination of the Jews, which witnesses found unspeakable, survivors incommunicable, and everybody else unthinkable, and which, with time, had become unimaginable – they have lost sight of the frontier between reality and fiction, and declared as reality the fiction that *they* have produced. These unfettered thinkers, who have already given more than ten years of their lives to demolishing the gas chambers, seem to have no other prospect but that of gradually locking themselves into a rigid, paranoid view of the world that corresponds to the enormous and pathetic resentment they carry inside them.

A founder had to be chosen for this movement, and it was of course easier for ultra-left negationists to fix on Paul Rassinier rather than on Maurice Bardèche. Even if the latter had at one point become the former's publisher. Born in 1906, Rassinier joined the Communist Party at the age of 18 and was expelled in 1932, before joining the ranks of the French Socialist Party (SFIO). While a school teacher in a small town in eastern France, he was resolutely and actively pacifist, and he supported the Munich Pact, by which Chamberlain and Daladier believed or pretended to believe that they had staved off war, but he joined the Resistance in 1943. Arrested in October 1943, he was deported, first to Buchenwald, then to Dora, where he remained until the liberation of the camp in April 1945.

In his first book *Passage de la ligne* (*Crossing the Meridian*),[16] Rassinier describes the everyday life of deportees, at the mercy of the kapos, especially the Communist kapos, whose abusive violence he denounces, because "much more than the SS they were obstacles to the humanization of the camp". "It is better to deal with God," he adds, "than with his saints". Two years later, in *Le Mensonge d'Ulysse* (*The Lie of Ulysses*), he attacks the "fantastic accounts" of former deportees, "in which they usually pass themselves off as saints, heroes, or martyrs". But already, while criticizing various witnesses for their exaggeration and invention, he interweaves, without any comment, an account of the "war crimes" practiced by the other side on German prisoners, and a story of acts committed in a French prison against a printer found guilty in 1946. (This latter account was communicated by A. Paraz, an anti-semitic pamphlet writer, who authored the preface to the second edition of *Le Mensonge d'Ulysse*.) We see here the beginnings of negationist logic: criticism of what the Germans did has been too harsh, exaggerated – *others* were no better. It is worth remarking in passing that the evidence of what those *others* did is not put in doubt.

Rassinier explains how "taking the concentration camps to be a means of putting opponents out of action, one can easily turn them into instruments of extermination in principle and elaborate endlessly on the purpose of this extermination". He adds that "if one has decided that the purpose of the camps was to exterminate, it is obvious that labor becomes just a negligible element in the theory of the exterminatory mystique" (p. 158). These heavy-handed comments express Rassinier's feeling that testimonies or analyses that insist on the extermination of the "racial" deportees minimize his own experience of forced labor.

A "revisionist" before the term was coined, but still a prudent one, he writes: "My opinion on the gas chambers. They did exist: not as many as people think. Exterminations by this means there were: not as many as has been said". He adds that his ambition has been "only to open up the way for a critical examination". As for the Communists, they "had a personal interest in this affair: in taking the witness box by storm and shouting at the top of their voices, they avoided standing in the dock as the accused." They also had "a political interest, on a world scale: by concentrating public opinion on the Nazi camps, they make it forget the Russian camps". What we see at work here is the next stage in negationist reasoning: the others did not only do *as much*, but it is possible – the rhetorical use of the words "political interest" suggests, at first, no more than a strong suspicion – that in fact they did *more*. This might well be why they have so much "interest" in accusing the Nazis. One can also see how suspicion falls at this stage more on the Communists than on the Jews.

Rassinier's tone becomes markedly harsher and more vindictive in his preface to later reprints of these first two books. He had meanwhile been the object of several court cases, instigated by those whom he had attacked. His preface admits that "it may be that those in charge of some of the camps [a footnote adds: "and this does not refer only to the SS!"] used gas chambers, intended for some other purpose, to asphyxiate people". But the question that now arises, he alleges, is the following:

> Why did the authors of eyewitness accounts [i.e. the Communist kapos] accredit with such remarkable unanimity the current version? Having shamelessly stolen our food and clothing, manhandled, brutalized, beaten us to an indescribable degree, having killed off – according to the statistics – 82 percent of us, the survivors of the concentration camp bureaucracy saw in the gas chambers a providential means – the only one – of explaining all those corpses and exculpating themselves.

It was enough, according to this reasoning, to see who profited. In a few years, Rassinier had moved from resentment to accusation.

Condemned by the Communists whom he had attacked and by the Socialists for Paraz's preface to his book, he was, quite naturally, welcomed with open arms by the extreme right, which could not but rejoice at the godsend of those statements by a man of the left with a service record as a deportee and member of the Resistance. Published by extreme-right publishers, Rassinier then began to attack the Jews directly, no longer content just "to smell out imposture." His next book launches, for the first time, into the obsessive calculations that were to allow him, when confronted by the "advocates of the six million," to use "the most terrible argument against the statistics put out by the Center for Jewish Documentation: the emigration of the European Jewish population between 1933 and 1945." He reduces, in a single paragraph, the number of "dead and vanished" to "500,000 or about 1 million."[17]

In his next book, *Le véritable procès Eichmann ou les vainqueurs incorrigibles* (*The True Eichmann Trial or the Incorrigible Conquerors*),[18] Rassinier expresses his feelings more overtly:

> Massed at the foot of a sort of Wailing Wall extended to the scale of the entire Earth, day and night for the last fifteen years, the Zionists throughout the world . . . have never ceased to utter, in an ever more macabre way, cries of pain that are more and more

heart-rending, with the purpose of publicly raising to its true proportions, which they regard as apocalyptic to say the least, the horror of the cruel treatment meted out to the Jewish world by Nazism, and to increase accordingly the extent of the reparations that the State of Israel is receiving from Germany.

In a further book, *Le Drame des juifs européens* (*The Drama of the European Jews*), Rassinier no longer even pretends to distinguish between Zionists and Jews.[19] The drama does not lie in the fact that "six million of them were exterminated, as they claim, but only in the fact that they have claimed it." Denouncing the "Rabbinate, a convenient screen in the shadow of which the most ambitious, the most widespread and the most solidly based commercial enterprise of all time has continued to prosper," he adds that:

> one shudders at the thought of what the Jewish type of the future might be if, with Judaism proliferating among the blacks and yellows as it has proliferated in Europe, and the international Zionist movement seducing them in turn, those black and yellow Jews also take it into their heads to participate in this enterprise of crossbreeding all through a land that, after all, has been "promised" to them too.

It is hardly surprising, then, that the part of his book devoted to this major obsession is called "The Jewish migration or the 'Wandering Jew.'" "In order to understand fully the movement of the European Jewish population between 1933 and 1945, a rapid historical overview of the Jewish migration on the world scale seems indispensable: in short, the history of the 'Wandering Jew.'" To calculate the number of Jews who died during the Second World War, we must first go back to the Jewish migration of the . . . eighteenth century BC (!), which took place "at a time when the other human migrations had long since settled". In his last book, *Les Responsables de la seconde guerre mondiale* (*Those Responsible for the Second World War*),[20] the supposed victims are actually the guilty parties, since:

> taking note of the [Nazi] doctrine that removed a people of seventy-million inhabitants from their financial market, all the Jews in the world, instead of looking for a compromise, which would have been all the easier to find since Hitler was also looking for one, raised the heat of the debate by declaring themselves at once, and by their own admission, to be on a war footing, not only with

the Nazi ideology – which was their perfectly legitimate right and would, at most, have resulted in an academic dispute – but also with Germany itself, which suggested a military intervention.

It is of this same Rassinier that the French far-left negationists of today say that he died "convinced that his work would come into its own and that mankind would finally produce a generation capable of understanding it."[21] Of the hate-filled, insane obsessions into which Rassinier gradually sank, the old moles, self-proclaimed revolutionaries for eternity, concede that "one finds in his writings linguistic excesses and sometimes debatable statements." They nevertheless prophesy that "one day, Rassinier will have to be rehabilitated" and that "he wrote in advance of his time."[22]

The Talmudic story of the cauldron, which Freud takes up in his analysis of the witticism, is well known. When A gives back a cauldron he has borrowed, B complains that it has a hole in it. A defends himself by replying that: (1) he gave the cauldron back in good condition; (2) the cauldron already had a hole in it when he borrowed it; and (3) he had never borrowed the cauldron from B. The negationists have finally arrived at this kind of reasoning: (1) the Jews are responsible for what they accuse the Nazis of, since it was they who declared war on Germany; (2) the crime of which they accuse the Nazis, genocide, did not take place; (3) the supposed victims are in fact the conquerors, since they have organized a swindle that has brought them millions of marks by way of reparation. The cauldron-type thought constituted by negationism reveals a logic that is truly unanswerable, since its conclusion has not the slightest connection with its premise.

In these times of obscurantism, the old moles argue, stifled under capitalist lies and Zionist swindles, the truth that alone is revolutionary has not yet touched the proletarian masses. Such a situation makes indispensable the tactical mobilization of all available forces in the struggle against this imposture of the twentieth century. Wearing a rhetorical coat of mail, which defends their theoretico-practical compromises past, present and to come, and protects their moral and intellectual integrity from all taint, the ultra-left negationists have gradually allied themselves with the only fellow-travelers that adversity allows them at the moment: with born demystifiers on the edge of mental pathology, textual obsessives, and anti-semitic shock troops recruited from within the extreme right. A few years after the revolutionary entry of La Vieille Taupe into the negationist struggle, the latest recruit, Henri Roques, tried to pass off as a university thesis an eminently "revisionist" reading of Nazi documents. In the late 1950s this man, then under the name of Henri Jalin, had come into relative prominence as a leader of a Fascist organization, the French Phalange.[23] The pure guardians of the revolution now appear to be collaborating with the extreme right in their plan to demolish the gas chambers and turn the Nazi genocide into a Jewish lie.

"The terrible thing about looking for the truth is that one finds it," declares the epigraph inscribed on publications emanating from La Vieille Taupe. "We merit all our encounters," François Mauriac wrote. The similarity between some of the itineraries of these negationists of yesterday and today suggests rather than the terrible thing about finding the truth is that one has looked for it. It is difficult to believe, reading Rassinier, that his resentment, his paranoia, his obsession with a Jewish plot were only the consequences of his repeated contacts with anti-semitic publishers. So virulent and all-encompassing a passion must have pre-existed his collaboration with those who were previously his political enemies. That holds for Rassinier yesterday, and today for the watchmen of revolutionary consciousness who have become Rassinier's rehabilitators or Faurisson's promoters or Rocques' associates – everybody merits his encounters.

The active negationists, those who write and distribute this fiction in France, are very few in number. Their devotion body and soul to the cause that animates them, their determination to exploit and manipulate to the full everything that can serve it, are not enough to explain what has been clear for some time: that their ideas are finding an echo in late twentieth-century French society. But it is also true that time has not stood still since the end of the Second World War. By the late 1970s, Faurisson had not yet managed to emerge from obscurity, despite constantly sending off texts to the press that he desperately wanted to have published: La Vieille Taupe knew nothing of that textual critic, and probably still believed in the gas chambers; and Henri Rocques would not have found a university jury, as obliging as the one of 1985, to back such a thesis, or would not even have embarked on the adventure of academic recognition.

Yet it must also be said that during the same period, Jean-Marie Le Pen, president of the National Front, the first extreme-right party in France with a sizeable membership since the end of the war, would not have called the gas chambers "a mere detail" in the history of that war, as he did in a broadcast of 1987. The growth of racism in France, in a time of economic crisis, allowed Le Pen to be a candidate in the presidential elections of spring 1988 on an overtly xenophobic pro-gramme. We were assured at the time that such statements about the gas chambers would discredit the candidate and that he would receive fewer votes in the presidential elections than in the earlier, European elections, where 10 percent of French voters had supported the National Front. The reality was different: eight months after his comments on the "point of detail," Le Pen received 14.41 percent of the votes cast in the first round of the presidential elections in April 1988.

What the negationists are laboring for with such determination is the final solution of the Final Solution. Such a program unfortunately does not upset everybody in a country in which many had for so long been accustomed to an anti-semitism that *knew* that Dreyfus was guilty, and others had denounced their next-door neighbor to the Gestapo. But after what is still called, in an immutable cliché, "the blackest hours in our history," this age-old anti-semitism, so legitimized, so acceptable in certain milieux before the war, found itself silenced, gagged behind the high walls then being erected to the glory of the Resistance and against the infamy of collaboration. Since then, this anti-semitism has been forced to live squeezed between censorship and repression. The virtues of censorship are still to be proved; repression does not last forever; and the dead themselves have a limited lifespan. The number of those who deported or killed Jews during the war, but also the number of those who were brutally deprived of people they loved and whose disappearance still makes them suffer today, that number is constantly diminishing. The memory of that horror could have found some assuagement by the natural action of the passage of time. But the perverse exploits of those negationists who have given so many years of their lives, so much resentment disguised as the search for truth, trying to exterminate that memory just before it subsides into history, paradoxically extends both the horror and the pain.

Translated by Alan Sheridan

*It is essential to specify that this chapter was written in 1988, and has been only slightly revised for publication.

18

"The First Blow": Projects for the Camp at Fossoli

Giovanni Leoni

Fossoli is a hamlet in the Commune of Carpi, a small town situated in the central Po Plain in North Italy. In June 1942 work was started there by the Italian Ministry of War for the building of an internment camp for prisoners of war. The camp, initially composed of tents which were then replaced by huts, became operative halfway through July of the same year. During the night of September 8–9, 1943, the camp was placed under military occupation by German troops. Following the armistice of September 8, Italy itself was included in the territories where the "Final Solution," proposed by Himmler at the Gross Wannsee conference of 1942, was to be applied. Thus the former Prisoner of War Camp no. 73 at Fossoli was earmarked as one of the places to be converted into a special concentration camp; and from February 1944 to August of the same year it acted as a *Durchgangslager*, a transit camp for sorting the racial and political prisoners destined for Auschwitz, Bergen–Belsen, Ravensbrück, Buchenwald and Mauthausen. Because of the special characteristics of the Fossoli camp, intended as a transit point, and the disappearance of the registers and all other lists of names, it is hard to estimate how many prisoners passed through, but the most recent assessments put the figure at between four and five thousand. Unlike the camp at San Sabba (converted from a rice mill on the outskirts of Trieste), Fossoli was never a labor or extermination camp. But it was undoubtedly the most important Italian concentration camp, above all for the Jewish victims of persecution who would be sent to extermination centers in the Greater German Reich. Once its function as southern terminus in the European camp system had lapsed, Fossoli was put to uses that considerably altered its physical features. First and foremost of these was as housing for the Nomadelfia community: in 1947, with the aim of gathering children whom the war had orphaned, it was turned into a kind of "happy village" in intentional contrast to its former function. Today the buildings of Fossoli are abandoned ruins,[1] but their original purpose is still plain to see.

The town of Carpi has more than once addressed the problem of how to preserve the memory of Italy's racial (and political) deportations. The first concrete result was a "Monument-Museum" devoted to those deported by the Nazis. It was installed in Pio Castle, the town's main building located in its central square. The competition for plans was initiated in 1963, and the winning group, consisting of Ludovico B. Belgiojoso, Enrico Peresutti, Ernesto N. Rogers and Renato Guttuso (BBPR), was also entrusted with carrying out the work. Opened on October 14, 1973, the museum occupies the entire south wing of the castle's ground floor.

Inside the museum the walls are carved with passages selected by Nelo Risi from *Letters of European Resistance Fighters Condemned to Death*.[2] These alternate with graffiti designed by artists such as Guttuso, Cagli, Levi, Longoni. One room is called the "Sala dei Nomi" ("Hall of Names") because the entire wall surface is engraved with the names of Italian deportees murdered in the death camps (plate 18.1). The museum features a historical introduction by Primo Levi and exhibits documentary materials and mementos collected by Lica and Albe Steiner. In the adjacent courtyard the exhibition continues with a series of concrete slabs bearing the names of the most notorious extermination camps.

Most striking in all this is the massive emphasis on writing. One has the impression that the team assembled by architect Belgiojoso (who had been interned at Fossoli) has deliberately foregone the expressive potential proper to architecture, feeling it incumbent to entrust the remembrance of such tremendous historical events to a means of communication which is more immediate, or at any rate more explicatory. Since a "Monument-Museum" implies a form of historical narrative, the need was to find, so to speak, a rhetorical solution, one employing discourse. The designers opted to keep the architecture as far as possible in the background, as a simple framework on which to hang a tale told in words.

Belgiojoso himself has said:

> We chose the letters of persons condemned to death because the mementos were so few. We felt it necessary to recreate, above all at such a distance in time, a testimony to the period that should speak more eloquently than these few objects could by themselves. We sought to use three elements: writings, paintings and graffiti, and lastly, of course, mementos. Since the latter were unimpressive

Plate 18.1 BBPR "Monument Museum" devoted to political and racial deportees, "Sala dei Nomi" ("Hall of Names"), Pio Castle, Carpi. Photograph: Aleardo Menozzi.

in themselves, we felt it out of place to devise inscriptions for them, and therefore chose other texts, written by deportees, which had greater significance. Ours is not a retelling of history, rather a documentation. In Italy we have a high tradition of memorial architecture, so that the possibility of recording an event architecturally is certainly not lacking. However, it is much easier to commemorate victory than suffering like that of deportation.[3]

Of course, the construction of a Monument-Museum, in the center of the city could only be preliminary to the more necessary work, a prelude to direct intervention on the remains of the old prison structure. To this end, the Commune of Carpi set up in 1989 an international architecture competition with the aim of building a museum, enclosed in a large park, on the site of the Fossoli camp, as a center for the study of deportation.

To understand the real nature of the task confronting those who took part in the competition, an inquiry is necessary into the specific feature of Fossoli as part of the European concentration-camp system. As a base for sorting prisoners and as the first stage of a journey towards camps in the Third Reich, Fossoli was of special significance. Primo Levi, who was held there in January 1944, offers us the impression of a place where astonishment rather than horror reigned, where the sheer surprise of finding oneself there had yet to give place to suffering. But at the station at Carpi, alongside the train bound for Poland, the first experience of beatings occurred, the first entirely unexpected violence, and face-to-face encounters with what was perhaps the most complex aspect of deportation under the Nazis, from a human and psychological point of view: an excessive and gratuitous brutality, inexplicable suffering inflicted over and above the logic of war. "How," Levi inquires, "can you beat a person except in anger?"[4] Jean Améry has written that the first blow is already tantamount to torture, and torture is the essence of National Socialism.[5]

Fossoli can indeed be seen as the first blow, and for this very reason the place is deeply associated with the essential experience of the concentration camp, the *Lager*. It can legitimately be considered a symbol of that experience, regardless of its other, direct associations with the subsequent stages of extermination. And this is inherent in all the projects put forward in the competition and provides a consistent key to interpreting those that may differ greatly from one another.

The immediate link between the Fossoli camp and the significance of deportation taken as a whole enables us to perceive how, over and above ethical and human problems far more complex than normally arise in an architectural competition, the participants had also to face a very serious difficulty, perhaps almost impossible to overcome entirely, and which we shall try to analyze.

We begin by asking what makes the experience of the concentration camp unique. Accounts by those who underwent that experience tell of fear, pain, cruelty, courage, solidarity and many other such emotions and relationships. But these may be common to other episodes of captivity and war. What seems, however, to distinguish the experiences suffered in the concentration camp from any other is that their pain is unable to find expression. To give some precision to this hypothesis let us invoke two authors already mentioned, Primo Levi and Jean Améry.

From their personal experience of the concentration camp, they have analyzed its procedures and characteristics most lucidly and honestly, in a way that eschews rhetorical complacency.

Primo Levi recalls a nightmare that recurred during his captivity and duly became reality after he was freed: "Something of this kind I had dreamed, we had all dreamed, during the nights at Auschwitz. We spoke but were not listened to, we regained liberty yet remained alone."[6] What makes the loneliness all the more anguished, the fear "of telling a story and not being listened to" all the more boundless, is an awareness that the difficulty of the story passes all possibility of understanding. The accounts of deportees are at once "simple and incomprehensible." They may give innumerable details about life in the camp, but a totally negative experience remains unspoken, it can only be suggested. "We realised," writes Levi, "that our language lacks words to express this offence: the demolition of the person."[7] The non-existence of an internee unfolds in a realm of its own, void of all context; witness the harsh episode of the chemistry exam described in *Survival in Auschwitz*, where a camp official and Levi, humanly akin and called on to speak on a subject common to them, exchange glances "as though through the glass wall of an aquarium between two beings living in different media."[8]

Entering the camp is similarly marked by a radical break:

> We retained memories of our previous lives, but veiled and remote, and thus profoundly sweet and sad, like the recollections everyone cherishes of early childhood and all things that have come to an end; whereas for each one of us the moment of entry into the camp acted as the wellspring of a different sequence of memories, closer and sharper, constantly confirmed by present experience, like wounds daily reopened.[9]

Here was a new sort of time, devoid of qualities, or rather suspended, time flattened out into a purely present dimension. "Today, even this today, which this morning appeared insuperable and eternal, we have punctured, through every one of its moments. There it lies, finished and at once forgotten; already it is no longer a day, it has left no trace in anyone's memory."[10]

The impossibility of conferring new qualities, if only negative, on "camp time," of lending it characteristics of its own through an act of memory, becomes clear with liberation. Levi's account presents liberation not as a *moment*, or a clean break in a continuum of events, but as the onset (confused and indistinct) of a challenge to survival, in many respects not unlike the previous one. The real breaking point would rather seem to coincide with the arrival of the "liberating joy of telling," when at long last a barrier of memories can begin to be erected against the sensation of annihilation given by the camp. The story of this battle fought on behalf of memory is, as we know, the story of Levi's own literary and intellectual adventure. But, as he himself has written with commendable toughness, the battle is essentially a losing one. In one of his last books, *The Drowned and the Saved*, he writes:

> I repeat, we, the survivors, are not the real witnesses. This is an awkward notion that I have grasped only gradually, while reading the accounts of others and, years later, rereading my own. We survivors are a minority, as tiny as it is anomalous: the only ones who by transgression or cunning or sheer luck managed to avoid going under. Those who did, who stared at the Gorgon, did not return to tell the tale, or remained dumb. But it is they, the "moslems," the drowned, the full witnesses, whose statements would have had a general significance. . . . The demolition carried to its bitter end, the job completed, these things nobody has recounted, as nobody has ever returned to tell of his own death. Even if the drowned had had pen and paper, they would not have borne witness because they began to die before their bodily death. Weeks and months before their extinction they already lost the gift of observing, recording, comparing and expressing themselves. We speak in their stead, by proxy. I cannot tell whether we have done so, whether we do so, out of a kind of moral obligation towards those who have been silenced, or whether it is not rather in order to purge ourselves of their memory; but undoubtedly there is a strong and lasting impulse behind what we do.[11]

Améry disagrees with Levi on certain points, but he concurs on the impossibility of giving a full account of the "total surrender" that represented the achieved aim of the concentration camp. As we already noted, Améry holds that torture is the very essence of National Socialism as well as the modality governing relations within the camp. He describes it as pure suffering that cannot be mitigated by ascribing any sense to it. All prior imagination of it pales before the sheer physical quality of the pain. "The pain was what it was. There is nothing further to add. The qualities of the sensations cannot be compared or described. They set the bounds beyond which verbal communication is impossible."[12]

Thus it is out of the question to reconstruct an adequate picture of that pain for posterity. Yet there remains, *forever present*, the encounter with it. But that is not all. The experience of this pain devoid of all meaning marks the direct contact of consciousness with one's own physicality, and since this emerges at the very moment in which body and mind are subjected to an agonizing restriction, the experience is absolute: of death undergone in life. The experience of pain described by Améry thus far can still be compared to other experiences: for example, to a physical injury which causes an irreversible handicap, and which is felt to be a partial death of the body. The essential difference is that in the camp one man deliberately inflicts that pain on another, and the pain becomes for that other a *permanent* condition of his existence. This pain, moreover, is inflicted not on one person alone, but on many; and on persons not chosen at random but individuals belonging to well-defined racial or social groups.

The conscious will of the aggressor brings about the slow destruction of the bodily susbtance of the victim, imposing a lingering death of a very different kind from that which may characterize other extreme situations. Hence there arises that serious consequence Améry has described. An overpowering pain that is unable to find expression becomes the mute suffering of one who has lost not merely the faculty but even the will to give it expression. But to renounce all expression means also to renounce the ability to possess reality, to produce a consciousness of one's own relationship with what exists outside oneself.

So we approach the specific point of our theme. Just as an inexpressible experience underlies life in the concentration camp, so the bodies of the inmates, deprived of all ability or will to give expression to themselves, move within the camp as if already invisible. The prisoner has been stripped of home, belongings, clothes – but not only that: he is forbidden to create new habits for himself or to seek a new role. The continual head-shaving, the order to hand over one's clothes, needlessly and continually repeated, the checks to make sure beds are tidy – these are the aspects of camp life dwelt on in the literature, and they show how the internee is obstructed in every way from creating a space of his own, from lending even the simplest character to personal appearance or the place where he is condemned to exist. Nor is the interior realm of sleep untouched, as is witnessed by one of the most moving passages in Levi's book. "I fell into a sour, restless sleep. This is not repose: for I feel threatened, ambushed; at any moment I am ready to shrink into a posture of defence. I dream that I am lying asleep on a road, on a bridge, across a doorway through which a host of people come and go."[13]

The crude architecture of the camp also expresses the will of the executioner, whereas of the victim no trace remains of what the executioner has willed him to be. All construction of meaning, like all construction of reality, is left to the SS, for whom the reduction of prisoners to total silence has been erected into a program. As Levi notes, the entire history of the Third Reich can be read as a "war against memory," whether directly through a destruction of documents and witnesses, or in a more subtle and systematic sense: the victim is deprived of all autonomy, even while still alive he has no visibility as an individual.

The inexpressibility of the concentration camp experience constitutes one of the most insidious traps connected with this historical phenomenon, when we consider that the very existence of the camps has been denied. One need hardly add that however hard it may be to recount the agony of human reduction and negation, this is a task that must be attempted. Levi confesses to failure; Améry founders on the brink of the unsayable; but this does not diminish their attempts, does not preclude fresh efforts to make the victims speak in a language more vivid, more their own.

Legion are the difficulties in telling a story that a survivor like Levi has once more succeeded in grasping. The task becomes even more complicated when one seeks to restore to the victims not so much a voice as an image, to "embody" them in the midst of an architecture that expresses the oppressor's will. As we have already suggested (in connection with the work carried out in Pio Castle) the simple erection of a monument is not enough. The very term "monument" has a treacherous sound, for it is associated with the idea of celebration and assumes the existence of some solid collective memory which will appeal to the majority of people. But intellectuals like Levi and Améry have cast grave doubt on the possibility of commemorating an event like deportation.[14] Above all, we must ask ourselves seriously if that absolute vacuum lodged within the spirit of many of the victims could ever be expressed in the form of a collective memory, the common heritage of future generations and the object of real empathy.

This negative recognition is one the survivors have had to come to terms with. And for those without direct knowledge of the events, solidarity and, above all, the will to understand appear as the only possible attitudes. For this reason the decision to create a study-center on the very site where a camp arose is surely a fruitful one. It may be the right way to offer continual opportunities for inquiry about the place and the historical events associated with it.

Searching for some trends among the projects put forward in the competition for Fossoli, we can single out three main tendencies, well represented by the trio of winners: Lodovico B. Belgiojoso, Roberto Maestro, Gian Luca Tura.[15] The first, Belgiojoso's, could be described as denunciatory realism. It consists of a faithful reconstruction, if not of the camp as a whole, at least of the original spatial relationships and the atmosphere. The major pitfall in a project of this kind is plain enough. Strictly from the point of view of the project, to recreate the atmosphere of the camp obviously involves temporarily identifying with the mind set of those who built it. Victims of the camp, and those whose sympathy with them is awakened, are necessarily revolted by the sight of a preserved or reconstructed site.

The reconstruction must therefore be followed by an act of denunciation, and this is precisely what Belgiojoso achieves in his "Linear Labyrinth." This is an exhibition route that runs through the park, alongside the concentration camp, traced out by wings of differing sizes and orientation, made of rough concrete and sometimes covered with plaster. On their surface a sequence of inscriptions, graffiti, and ceramic and mosaic inlays, illustrates the history of deportation not only from an Italian but also a European perspective.

Since the act of denunciation cannot be expressed in architectural terms, it requires the more explicit medium of language. As in the Monument-Museum in Pio Castle and for the same reasons, Belgiojoso has recourse to other forms of expression, above all narrating a story – this in order to distance himself from the negative values of a place he has deliberately chosen to recreate as a warning. One understands why this is the solution most often put forward by those, like Belgiojoso, who have had personal experience of deportation.

The second architectural proposal, Maestro's, involves an attempt to express the significance of the place and its historical context in a poetic and symbolic way by transmuting a verbal into a formal architectural idiom. Maestro, having composed a lyrical scenario that assembles allusions to Fossoli and its historical fate, converts this prose poem into architectural inventions pregnant with older meanings. The corner-stone of the project is a large building on a square plan, sited between the concentration camp and the park. This building contains a labyrinth, screened on the camp side by a high wall, beyond which is Ariadne's Hall, a terraced chamber in semi-darkness with a flooded area. Both the wall and the labyrinth are pierced by a fissure symbolizing Ariadne's thread. From this labyrinth a path leads to the large circular garden which occupies much of the park, and which alludes formally to a Renaissance ideal of city planning (plate 18.2). At the center of the circle are four oak trees; beneath them stone benches form a ring "to serve as a meeting-place for discussion, as in the democracies of old." The original barrack-blocks of the camp would mostly be used for the cultivation of flowers of various hues, commemorating the colored triangles by which the prisoners were once classified. Four of the bar-

Plate 18.2 A lyrical scenario for the camp at Fossoli. By Robert Maestro.

rack-blocks, however, are intended to be a "memory sequence," reproducing the effects of time – from almost total obliteration to partial restoration.

The problem inherent in this project is the mistrust (noted by Améry) in the possibility of giving a metaphorical formulation to the suffering undergone in the camps. Maestro confesses he is apprehensive that the imagined forms are inadequate to convey the experience to which they refer.

The third solution could roughly be called "minimalist." It involves limiting the architect's intervention, his transformation of already existing materials. The focus is on ways to facilitate the deciphering and interpretation of the site and its ruins. In Tura's proposal the remains of the camp are meticulously preserved, without restoration or reconstruction. The main object of his plan is to create a path which leads the visitor on an evocative route through the ruins. This is realized by constructing intentionally unobtrusive elements, such as raised earth levels or small wooden or iron structures integrated with the existing barrack-blocks. In this, as in all the projects presented, the visitors' attention is focused on the routes that will guide them around the site. An especially interesting feature of this third solution is the way buildings are placed on the boundary of the camp. This intends to pose a question about the boundary as a demarcation point between the camp and the world beyond it.

Though the three solutions use different means of expression, they are at one in their effort to represent a pain that cannot be recreated, to give a sort of visibility to it. In the first case, by reconstructing the trauma through an architectural setting that is used as a supportive frame for the narrative. In the second case, by venturing into the realm of the indescribable by allusion and poetic means. And in the third, by walking among the ruins, seeking the traces and voices of those who suffered there.

Translated by R. W. Timothy Keates and Anthony Collinssplatt

19

Jewish Memory in Poland

James E. Young

> Sandstone is good
> for honing scythes
> so all that is left
> is a rib of stone
> here a foot of stone
> a tibia
> there a shinbone
> a bone of sto
> a shank of st

Of Jewish life and death in Poland, only the fragments remain. Forty-five years after the Shoah, a new generation comes to know a millennium of Jewish civilization in Poland by its absence and the rubble of its destruction: dilapidated synagogues, uprooted and plowed-under cemeteries, warehouses piled high with religious artifacts. Whether suggested in the glimpse of a doorjamb's missing mezuzah or synagogue turned into granary, or in the growing number of tombstone-fragment monuments in otherwise abandoned Jewish cemeteries, absence and brokenness emerge as twin memorial motifs indigenous to a landscape of shattered *matzevoth*. In an architectural impulse akin to the poet's broken epitaph,[1] fragments of shattered Jewish tombstones have become the predominant iconographic figure by which public memory of the Shoah is being constructed in Poland today.

Unlike the suspended sounds and broken lines in Ficowski's poem, however, which we mend by completing the unfinished rhyme, memorial-makers here suggest that neither past worlds nor memory of them can be made whole again. For even as these remnants are gathered up and pieced together in the Polish villages like Węgrów, Kazimierz,

Przasnysz and Zamosc, the fragments are not recuperated so much as reorganized around the theme of their own destruction. They represent a newly collected Jewish memory, retrieved piece by jagged piece in a form that emblematizes both the destruction and the impossibility of recovery. Rather than mending the words in a fissured epitaph, they preserve the break: in this way, broken-tombstone monuments commemorate their own fragility, gather and exhibit the fragments *as* fragments, never as restored wholeness.

Broken tombstones and similar remnants of Jewish life in Poland have now become the loci around which contemporary memory assembles. In dark storerooms, or scattered over the countryside, such remnants remain inert and amnesiac. But gathered and consecrated, they project a specific public image of both the Jewish past in Poland and its destruction. The fragments may still be broken, but finally they are pieced together into some order, if only that which signifies disorder. I would like to explore both the construction of Poland's "tombstone monuments" and the ways they embody Holocaust memory in a land nearly bereft of Jewish rememberers.

Emblems of brokenness have their own history in Jewish tradition. Tombstone reliefs of broken candlesticks, or a splintered tree, or a bridge half torn away, are among several repeating images recalling life interrupted by death. In a gesture to this tradition, Polish architects not only incorporate stylized versions of the Jewish cemetery as a memorial motif, but often rend the monuments themselves.

The expansive memorial at Treblinka sets 17,000 granite shards in concrete to resemble a great, craggy graveyard. At the center of this landscape of fragments, an obelisk of granite blocks stands cleaved from top to bottom (plate 19.1). The former site of the Płaszów concentration camp near Kraków displays a gargantuan stone sculpture of five sharply etched figures in mourning, cut front to back, edge to edge, by a great horizontal gash at about lapel lavel. This contemporary memorial motif appears to descend directly from ancient Jewish funerary images.

Immediately after the war, some 250,000 Polish Jews returned to find themselves aliens in communities that may have been 50 percent Jewish before the war. With the synagogues destroyed or gutted, survivors coming home to Sandomierz, Łuków, and Siedlce, among other small towns, walked out to their cemeteries to mourn their murdered families. But many returnees found only ruins: even the mourning places had been demolished. In wiping out a people, the Nazis not only destroyed those who would have preserved the memory of past generations; they also took pains to obliterate the spaces where the murdered

Plate 19.1 Treblinka. Photograph: James E. Young.

might be remembered. Some of the oldest cemeteries, like that of Warsaw's Praga neighborhood, where tens of thousands lay buried, were literally scraped off the face of the earth. In other instances – recalling the treatment of Jews themselves at the hands of Germans – the tombstones were machine-gunned, clubbed into pieces by sledgehammers, ground into dust. Or the *matzevoth* were put to work: uprooted, carted off, and used to pave roadways, sidewalks, and courtyards. Those left in place often bore scars inflicted by other vandals, their graves robbed by local Poles searching for buried gold. Without a Jewish community to maintain them the cemeteries crumbled, and many were eventually buried beneath the earth's own cover of trees and tall grass. Still others were paved over for highways and playgrounds.[2]

The returning survivors set to work, therefore, reconsecrating these sites, a memorial work before memory could begin. Occasionally this meant gathering up pieces of *matzevoth* and piling them into great, loose heaps, as in Siedlce and Łódź. Other survivors in Łuków, Sandomierz, and Myślenice built pyramids and pastiche obelisks out of the scattered tombstone fragments. In Łódź, they began but never finished such a monument. Near the center of this, the largest, Jewish graveyard in Europe, hundreds of tombstones still lie stacked today in immovable piles. They had been gathered shortly after the war by survivors who hoped to build a tombstone pyramid like that at Sandomierz or Łuków. Not being able to agree on the final conception, the Jews who eventually left Łódź once more had also to abandon their memorial project. When I came across these layered sheaves of *matzevoth* 45 years later, I couldn't help but see them still as a memorial: not to the destruction itself, but to vacated memory (plates 19.2 and 19.3). The unerected monument reminded me of one consequence of so vast a destruction: with no one left to preserve the memory of those who came before, memorial activity ceases altogether, except in the eyes of visitors.

By turning to the only materials available – broken bits of *matzevoth* and mortar – survivors and community volunteers in Kraków and Warsaw did not restore the sites of remembrance so much as they created new ones, formalizing the destruction. The collage retaining-walls here are made of wedges of black syenite cutting into shards of white marble. Epitaphs are preserved in pieces, with chunks of the aleph-bet splintered in all directions: Polish script breaks into Hebrew, sentences are cut off mid-word, mid-letter (plate 19.4). When legible, the epitaphs read stammeringly, like this one from the wall in Kraków:

Plate 19.2 Stacked tombstones in Łódź Jewish Cemetery. Photograph: James E. Young.

Plate 19.3 Łódź
Jewish Cemetery.
Photograph: James
E. Young.

Plate 19.4 Retaining
wall built of broken
tombstones at
Warsaw Jewish
Cemetery.
Photograph: James
E. Young.

> Here lies our teach rab
> Benjamin Zeev Wolf the son of Ga
> of blessed mem

Mind pours itself into the gaps between fragments, like so much mortar, to bind the remnants together. We are reminded that memory is never seamless, but always a montage of collected fragments, recomposed by each person and generation.

Where the Germans could destroy synagogues they always did: every last one of Poland's old and distinctive wooden synagogues was burned to the ground. Once in awhile they also exerted themselves in razing the sturdier masonry synagogues. The caretaker of the Jewish cemetery in Międzyrzecz Podlaski relates that it took a German demolition unit more than one month to level the eighteenth-century synagogue there.[3]

But in most cases, these stone structures were so well built – and useful to the Germans – that nearly all of Poland's masonry synagogues remain standing to this day. Without Jewish congregations to inhabit them most have been converted to some other use: a hotel in Biecz, a bakery in Gorlice, a factory in Radymno, a garage in Ostroleka.[4]

The synagogue in Kazimierz on the Vistula, one of the oldest examples of masonry architecture in Poland, still stands just off the market square in the center of town: it is now the Vistula Cinema. Though less than half of its 5,000 inhabitants before the war were Jewish, this picturesque village is remembered by many Poles as essentially a Jewish town. Merchants today still speak a smattering of Yiddish learned from their Jewish neighbors. Scholem Asch once said that in Kazimierz even the Vistula River spoke to him in Yiddish. But as is the case for every former Jewish village in Poland, only a few cultural traces remain: some Yiddish idioms, a handful of buildings, the cemetery, and now a memorial to the town's murdered Jews.

On a Sunday afternoon two summers ago, the market square in Kazimierz was alive with the colors of women's flowered skirts, farmers' fruits and vegetables, and dozens of children at play. My Polish friend asked a young girl selling ice cream where the synagogue was. She pointed directly across the open square and replied matter-of-factly, "the cinema is there." No, not the cinema, my friend repeated, the synagogue is what we're looking for. "Yes, I know," the young girl looked up, "but the synagogue is the cinema." We walked across the square to number seven and passed through a narrow alley where we found an old stone building set just behind the marketplace, its façade covered by scaffolding (plate 19.5). Next to the open wooden door, teenagers crowded around a small window box with a sign announcing movie times for the Vistula Cinema. Inside the lobby, at the door into the sanctuary, a ticket taker stood instead of a shammes, and moviegoers streamed in like congregants on the high holidays.

Entering, we found girls still sitting upstairs in the women's gallery, but now with their sweethearts. The windows were boarded up on the outside and plastered over on the inside to keep light from coming in. The walls were whitewashed and clean, and the original wooden floor was polished to a shine. No one seemed to mind when I pulled the screen slightly away from the wall to peek behind it: the frame for the holy ark was intact. As an architectural edifice the former synagogue now housed its current inhabitants in specific ways. The graceful arches, cool limestone walls, and masonry all combine to frame the film in progress. The ark may be covered by the moviescreen and its images, but devoted viewers still face in its direction. Later we overheard teen-

Plate 19.5 Former
synagogue, now
Vistula Cinema in
Kazimierz.
Photograph: James
E. Young.

agers asking each other about the film they had seen the night before
at "the synagogue." What the villagers may have forgotten their language still remembers, if only as a dead metaphor.

The friendly manager insisted that the decision to put a cinema in
the synagogue was made with the Jews in mind. "After all," he said,
"this could not be just a restaurant or work space, but a monument to
culture. Only a museum or music hall would have been more appropriate." In fact, he continued, the initial aim of the city planners in 1953
had been to restore the synagogue to its pre-war condition and turn it
into a Jewish museum. But because there were no Jews left to visit the
synagogue even as a museum, and no film-house in Kazimierz, the
planning committee decided to turn it into a cinema and all-purpose
auditorium. Just recently, he told us proudly, UNESCO had held an

international symposium here on the world's dwindling supply of drinking water. He couldn't recall whether the speakers knew of the auditorium's origin. A plaque on the back of the building, dedicated in 1985 to the Jews of Kazimierz murdered by the Germans, does not mention that this had been the community's house of prayer.

With nothing but this tablet to remind visitors of the town's Jewish past, the imposing tombstone-wall monument just outside town, on the road to Szreniawy, is all the more startling. On one of their photo expeditions, Monika and Stanisław Krajewski, two members of the Citizens' Committee for the Preservation of Jewish Monuments in Poland, met with Kazimierz architect Tadeusz Augustynek, who had been commissioned by the town to build a monument at the Jewish cemetery. He showed them his design for a great pastiche wall, 3 meters high and 25 meters long, composed of salvagable tombstones from the cemetery, and torn vertically by a jagged crack. Anxious to see this conception realized, the Krajewskis spent most of the summer of 1983 sorting and cleaning tombstones and helping to construct the monument.[5]

According to Monika Krajewska, the first step involved a literal digging up of the past, a memorial archaeology that reminded all involved of what was lost. It had been nearly forty years since the Jewish cemetery tombstones were uprooted by the Germans and laid as paving in the town's Franciscan Monastery, converted into Gestapo headquarters. People in Kazimierz now recall with satisfaction that the Polish laborers had taken pains to lay the inscribed sides of the stones face-down in a graded layer of soft dirt, which saved the epitaphs from being erased beneath the feet of pedestrians and wheels of carts. But one man remarked that with the blank side up villagers were not reminded of the source of these paving stones every time they walked on them.

Dug out of the streets by a few of the same laborers who had laid them forty years earlier, the stones were first gathered into great, leaning heaps in the town square. They were then transported back to the nearly empty Jewish graveyard. The Krajewskis spent most of that August marking tops and bottoms of gravestones and separating those of the men from those of the women. Since men and women had been buried separately here, the architect and his helpers chose to preserve this separation in the monument itself: not to affirm an archaic custom, they said, but to respect this particular community's tradition.

In Poland a careful balance is constantly being struck between building new structures and preserving the remains of old ones. With the country chronically plagued by shortages of building materials, no one was

Plate 19.6 Tombstone-
wall monument in
Kazimierz, designed
by Tadeusz
Augustynek, 1984.
Photograph: James
E. Young.

surprised to learn that there would not be enough mortar to finish the
monument during that summer. The following winter, snow and rain
washed off the marks distinguishing women's from men's tombstones.
It wasn't until a year later, in August 1984, that more materials were
forthcoming. The Krajewskis returned to mark the stones again, and
by that autumn the monument was complete.

Today, while rounding a curve on the road out of town, a freestanding
wall comes strikingly into view: the tombstones in it catch the western
light well into the late afternoon, and glow almost incandescently against
the lush forest behind it. Perched atop a steep green knoll, the fragment-
wall dominates the clearing, and a great crack dominates the monument
(plates 19.6 and 19.7). Drivers always slow down, and many leave their
cars to study the monument and its Polish inscription to the murdered
Jews of Kazimierz. Men's tombstones are on the right, women's on the
left. Monika Krajewska says that the designer has placed all the rounded

Plate 19.7 Detail of
tombstone-wall
monument,
Kazimierz.
Photograph: James
E. Young.

stones with candlesticks and candelabra at the top, as if to allow their flames to burn into the sky. A small cluster of unbroken tombstones is arranged in front of the wall – a visual echo of the newly restored headstones standing out of sight behind the wall. Unlike the polished marble surfaces of the fractured tombstone walls in Warsaw and Kraków, these limestone *matzevoth* are porous and rough to the touch. Their faces are weathered and textured by time that wears down all inscriptions. The wall commemorates the painstaking piecing together of lost Jewish memory, but its jagged breach also suggests the devastation that remains.

These monuments lead a curious double life in Poland: one in the consciousness of the local community and another in that of Jewish visitors. On the one hand, they continue to serve as essential commemorative sites for the visitors. But in a country with only 5,000 Jews left, it was inevitable that Jewish memory would also be collected and expressed in particularly Polish ways. It could not be otherwise. For once the state reassembles the fragments, it necessarily recalls even the most disparate events in ways that unify them nationally. The state's "recollection" of Polish Jewry has been accomplished – to some extent – in Warsaw's new "Memorial Route of Jewish Martyrdom and Struggle," dedicated in 1988 on the forty-fifth anniversary of the Warsaw ghetto uprising.

Unveiled along with the new Umschlagplatz[6] memorial, this tour is a walking narrative that unites several monuments in the area of the former ghetto – now a great burial mound of rubble 16 feet high, covered by trees, parks, and apartments. According to the Umschlagplatz Memorial Commission, the existing flagstone dedicated to the Jewish Fighting Organization headquarters on Miła Street, Nathan Rapoport's Ghetto Monument on Zamenhof Street, and a small plaque on nearby Stawki Street incribed to the Umschlagplatz, "were not linked together, did not form a legible whole." That is, they could not be "read" in such a way as to make them cohere in narrative sequence. The new route proposes to "link these monuments together, confer on them their rightful status and incorporate them into Warsaw's symbolic space." Thus, the state integrates Jewish memory into its own national constellation of meaning. Whether or not the Jewish fighters of the ghetto uprising were regarded as Polish national heroes at the time, they are now recast as such whenever the state commemorates the uprising.[7]

The result is a prescribed trail winding through several city blocks, its nineteen stations marked by black, *matzevah*-shaped syenite tablets, each inscribed in both Polish and Hebrew. To bind together Polish and

Jewish memory from the outset, the route begins with a "tree of common remembrance," suggesting that the experiences of Jews and Poles cleave to one another. The tablet at the first station is inscribed to "the common [*meshutaf*] memory of Polish Jews murdered at the hands of the Germans between the years 1939 and 1945 and to the Poles who died extending aid to the Jews." But as my friend and I – Pole and Jew – stood side by side before this tree, I wondered whether each of us actually shared the other's memory of events. Was ours a "common remembrance?" Or was it only the site of remembrance we shared, a common *place* of memory, where each was invited to remember in his own way?

From here, we followed the memorial trail with stops at the foundation of the Ghetto in 1940, Rapoport's Monument, and the Jewish Fighting Organization's bunker. Having commenced our walk in common memory, we now continued along the trail of heroism. The path leads to tablets recalling the archivist Emanuel Ringelblum, Polish Workers' Party activist Jezef Lewartowski, and fighters Arie Wilner, Meir Majerowicz, and Frumka Plotnick. In addition, inspirational figures like Schmuel Zygelboim, Janusz Korczak, Rabbi Yitzhak Nyssenbaum, and poet Yitzhak Katzenelson are remembered just before the path ends at the Umschlagplatz – the last Warsaw stop for 350,000 Jews on their way to Treblinka.

For years both visitors and local survivors complained that the small plaque on a freestanding brick wall next to a gas station was inadequate to mark the Umschlagplatz. But the new memorial, which replaces the old one at the corner of Stawki and Karmelicka Streets, is clearly visible at this busy intersection. Now it is the Polish taxi driver who complains. "Forty-five years later," one driver confided to me, "the Jews have taken their revenge on us. Look, no more gas pumps." Warsaw's favorite filling station has indeed been closed down, its empty driveway now adorned by flower planters. The Umschlagplatz memorial, adjacent to it, is an outdoor enclosure, open overhead. On this morning, an old woman carrying groceries has entered the marble space, apparently to rest on her way home. She is joined by two young men strolling by. All pause to examine the four white marble walls, about 10 feet high, as was the ghetto wall.

A horizontal band of black marble rings the outside walls about two-thirds of the way up, reminiscent of a tallit (Jewish prayer shawl). When I asked what they saw, the two young Poles replied that it looked like a black mourning band. They weren't so sure what to make of the black round-topped slab balancing over the entrance off Stawki Street, which turns the entrance itself into a kind of absent *matzevah*. Directly opposite the entry inside, a section of the wall extends upward into another tablet shape, broken by a narrow vertical portal just wide enough to view a tree growing outside the wall – a symbol of hope, according to the designers (plate 19.8).

Standing in the center of this space, we were gently nudged off balance by the skewed angles of the walls: the corners are disjoined, leaving narrow gaps between walls, and the area itself is trapezoidal. Instead of being consoled through reassuring closure, square angles, and predictable forms, our senses were jarred by disquieting and oblique shapes. Architecture, normally a comfort in the strength of its regular forms, here uses broken geometry to recall disjunction and skewed realities.

The white marble walls were so bright when the sun shone that their inscriptions became difficult to read: "On this path of suffering and death in the years 1942–43, over 300,000 Jews from the Warsaw Ghetto were driven to the gas chambers of the Nazi extermination camps." According to committee members, debate during the design sessions centered not on the content of the inscriptions so much as on the languages to be used. Would this memorial be inscribed in the language of the community, or its visitors, or victims, or all of these? The

Plate 19.8 Umschlagplatz Monument in Warsaw, designed by Hanna Szmalenberg and Wladyslaw Klamerins. Photograph: James E. Young.

committee recognized that the choice of languages could not be innocent but would project the kinds of audience and, by extension, the kinds of remembrance. Some committee members argued for Polish and Yiddish only, since it was, after all, a Polish monument to Jewish victims. Others insisted that both languages of the victims – Yiddish and Hebrew – be included. One hardliner complained that Hebrew was also the language of the Zionists and shouldn't be used (as it was not used in the Jewish pavilion at Auschwitz, for example, where for many years inscriptions came in Polish and Yiddish only). But these are the living Jews now, rejoined another committee member, so we must incorporate both the Yiddish of the victims and the Hebrew of the survivors, many of whom live in Israel. Besides, he pointed out, the Jewish Fighting Organization in the ghetto was composed almost entirely of Zionist fighters from both left- and right-wing parties. Other committee members insisted that since so many of the survivors are now in America – the main source of potential visitors – English must also be included as the tourist's lingua franca. It was finally agreed that victims, survivors, community, and tourists all be invited to remember here: the monument is dedicated in Yiddish, Hebrew, Polish, and English.

At first, the committee had also hoped to inscribe every one of the 300,000 names belonging to Jews who passed through the "transfer place" on their way to Treblinka. But this idea was quickly abandoned as the difficulties of such a task – tracking down every victim – became apparent. Instead, the committee decided to list the different first names of as many of the victims as could be accounted for. Listed alphabetically and mixing men and women, every Batia, Chaim, Dina, and Mordechai inscribed here would thus remember all so named. By referring to first names of the dead this way, the wall recalls the memorial function implicit in the European Jewish naming tradition, wherein every newborn is a "yad vashem" – a figurative hand and name, that is, memorial to a deceased family member.

The Polish government has several compelling reasons for preserving Jewish memorials to the Holocaust period and even building new ones like the Umschlagplatz Monument and the Memorial Route. First, by reincorporating Polish Jewry – even in absentia – into the national heritage, the state creates the possibility for representing the Polish experience of World War II through the figure of its murdered Jewish part; the Jews' destruction in Poland comes increasingly to represent (and thereby magnify) the devastation of the entire country and points toward the averted genocide of the Polish nation as a whole.[8] Next, by nationalizing the memory of the Holocaust, the former government prevented it from being marshaled against the state's interests by dissident groups. State commemorations at the Warsaw Ghetto Memorial, for example, used to make it more difficult for the Solidarity Trade Union to adopt this space as its own place of resistance. The essential question here is less whether Poles remember themselves or their former Jewish compatriots in these monuments, than what the consequences are for one people's understanding of its past when remembered in the figure of another people.

On a recent trip to the Jewish cemetry in Łódź, I was reminded of yet another impulse underlying the renaissance of Jewish memory in Poland today. So many years after survivors left Łódź, their memorial project abandoned, the cemetery is beginning to stir with new activity. Workers hired by the Nissenbaum Family Foundation have begun to restore the chapel and to cut new paths into the cemetery's forested grounds: great swaths that allow visitors to survey the massive scale of this graveyard. On the day I was there in July 1988, the workers were idle, though still happy to show me around. According to their foreman, they had not been paid since April and were worried that the restoration project – and hence their jobs – had been terminated. "The workers are resentful," the foreman told me, "because they were promised long-term jobs restoring the cemetery, constructing monuments out of the tombstones, and they are supposed to be paid well by Jews from the West." He then asked me why the Jews wouldn't take better care of their cemetery here in Łódź, why with all their western money, they wouldn't want to repair their former "home." In turn, I asked why the local community was so interested in such a project. "It is good work," the foreman replied, "and it will bring good tourists."

He was right. Hundreds of Jewish tourist groups from America, western Europe, and Israel visit Poland every year on so-called "Holocaust tours." Led by scholars and survivors, groups from the United Jewish Appeal, the American Jewish Congress, and even various survivor and ghetto fighters associations, spend anywhere from three days to three weeks taking in the sights of the Polish memorial landscape: deathcamps, cemeteries, former synagogues, Jewish museums, and monuments. In fact, there is a burgeoning memorial industry in Poland today: first, a memorial is proposed to a lost Jewish community; next, funds are solicited from abroad to pay for materials and labor; then, local craftsmen, architects, and builders are paid to build the memorial. When finished, these memorials become great tourist attractions, drawing hundreds of Western (mostly Jewish) tourists to villages with little else to offer but this memory of an absence. In lieu of waiting families and communities, monuments built for and often founded by Western visitors now invite survivors to return as tourists.

Though it is by no means clear that the Polish government is quite so calculating, new Jewish memorial projects find increasing sympathy at both state and local levels. With more Jewish memorials than any other country in Europe (nearly 2,100 by the state's count), Poland has plans for hundreds more. Before we pass judgment on such memorial intentions, however, we need to recognize similar impulses underlying any nation's landmarks: most are built simultaneously to remember and to attract rememberers. In America as in Poland, tourists are invited primarily for their contribution to local economies. The touristic consumption of monuments may not be as lofty, or as praiseworthy, as other aspects of the memorial process. But it is a dimension that cannot be ignored in coming to understand the combination of thought, work, and motives now sustaining Holocaust memory in any land.

The final tragedy in Poland may be that images of death and rituals of mourning have all but displaced traditional tenets of life and learning as central figures of Jewish faith. In the aftermath of the Holocaust, much of Jewish life in Poland has become one long commemoration of the dead, transforming young Polish Jews and non-Jews alike into perennial caretakers and archivists. Instead of communities, we have community records; instead of a people, their gravestones. In a country without rabbis or a Hebrew press, young Jews are as likely to learn their Hebrew from the inscriptions of tombstones as from torah scrolls – a violation of the Talmudic warning not to study the texts of *matzevoth*. Instead of being versed in mishnah and gemara, a generation of Polish Jews that is painfully renewing itself will know the psalms, if at all, only from conventional citations on tombstone epitaphs. Theirs will be a Hebrew of lamentation only, whose narrative describes lost lives, whose sole prayer will be the Kaddish.

Stunted as it is, this conception of Jewish life does suggest a qualified return to another tenet of Judaism: the memory-work by which Jews have traditionally defined themselves in relationship to past events. In this sense, the memorial activity retains distinctly traditional proportions. The constant repair of Jewish graveyards, the gathering of fragments to save them from further deterioration, the maintenance of archives at Auschwitz and the Jewish Historical Institute in Warsaw: these also keep the ancient obligation to remember. Perhaps the only lasting memorials to the era of the Shoah will come not in finished monuments at all, but in the perpetual activity of memory: in the debate over which kinds of memory should be preserved, in whose interest, for which audience. Instead of allowing the past to rigidify in its monumental forms, we would vivify memory through the memory-work itself

– whereby events, their recollection, and the role monuments play in our lives remain animate, never completed.

For neither time nor its markers ever really stand still. Even as I write, chunks of mortar holding these monuments together crumble and fall away, lichens cover their surfaces, and grass grows high around their bases. All the while, hundreds of miles away, a political regime is toppled, and a whole generation of monuments suddenly becomes obsolete, their past meanings irrelevant to the new order. Of course, a monument's meanings were always changing, along with the changing face of the monument itself. But every regime, even the new, hopes that the meanings in its monuments will remain as eternal as it imagines itself to be.

Indeed, since writing these last words, the fall of old regimes and the rise of new throughout Eastern Europe have made the fragile and transient nature of monuments all the more apparent. The stones marking four million victims at Birkenau, for example, have been uprooted and scattered in piles, while historians revise downward their politically inflated number. Likewise, the museum narratives at Auschwitz are being carefully rewritten to excise their formerly Marxist cast. As official understanding of the period changes to reflect that of the new, noncommunist regime, alternative forms and sites are found to accommodate new memory. Any record of the memorials in Poland must therefore be as provisional as the memorials themselves. In fact, perhaps the "everlasting memorial" exists only in the mind of the visitor, who recalls a single journey to the memory-site, unmodified by later visits never made.

With such changes in mind, the study of Holocaust monuments should encompass every aspect of their being: from conception through construction, then from their reception in the local community to their place in the national commemorative cycle. Finally, the lives of these memorials should include our own responses to them, as well as the retelling of their histories. Taken together, these stages comprise a genuine *activity* of memory, by which artifacts of ages past are invigorated by the present moment, even as they condition our understanding of the world around us.

It is not enough to ask whether or not our memorials remember the Holocaust, or even how they remember it. We should also ask to what ends we have remembered. That is, how do we respond to the current moment in light of our remembered past? This is to recognize that the shape of memory cannot be divorced from the actions taken in its behalf, and that memory without consequences contains the seeds of its own destruction. For were we passively to remark only the contours of these memorials, were we to leave unexplored their genesis, and remain unchanged by the recollective act, it could be said that we have not remembered at all.

20

Reclaiming Auschwitz

Debórah Dwork and Robert Jan van Pelt

Auschwitz, or as the Poles know it, Oswiecim, is the most significant memorial site of the Shoah. It is also the most complex: neither its shape nor location are fixed. There are many component parts to what we call "Auschwitz," and while a number are still to be seen, some are no longer discernible. Auschwitz I, the *Stammlager* (or main camp), remains at the edge of the town of Oswiecim; Auschwitz II, or Birkenau, borders the village of Brzezinka, a few miles to the west (see plate 20.1). It is these sites which are visited. Auschwitz III, east of Oswiecim near the village of Monowice, was a labor camp. Its inmates constructed an enormous industrial plant for the IG Farben company intended to manufacture synthetic rubber, or buna, but nothing was produced. The factory remains, but the camp has disappeared. No one visits it now. And then there were the peripheral camps, those at Rajsko, Brzeszce, Trzebinia, and other places. Only stones mark them; occasionally a building survives, like the greenhouses and laboratory in Rajsko, but there is no indication that they were part of the Auschwitz complex.

Auschwitz I alone appears to be intact. The presentation of the buildings does not convey a sense of abstract history, but of tangible actuality. Former inmates take sightseers through the site, instilling them with lived memory – or so we are to believe. In *Writing and Rewriting the Holocaust*, James Young has noted such claims to authenticity. He observed that in memorial camps such as Auschwitz and Majdanek, "the icons of destruction seem to appropriate the very authority of original events themselves." According to Young, this authority derived from the fact that these camps had been preserved "almost exactly as the Russians found them forty years ago."

> Guard towers, barbed wire, barracks and crematoria – abstracted elsewhere, even mythologized – here stand palpably intact. Nothing

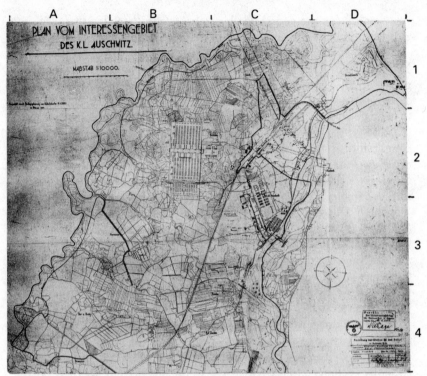

Plate 20.1 Detail from a map showing the 40-square-kilometer "Field of Interest" (*Interessengebiet*) of Auschwitz. This area included the main camp Auschwitz I (C.2/3) and, at the edge of the village of Birkenau, Auschwitz II (B.2). Between the two camps was the station of Auschwitz (C.2). Civilians who lived in the city of Auschwitz still used the station, and therefore the station was not included in the Field of Interest. The map shows Auschwitz I with the projected "Extension of the Protective Custody Camp" (*Schutzhaftlagererweiterung*) that connected the old part of the camp to the area of the station. The plan of Auschwitz II depicts the projected size of the camp. Roughly 3/5 of that plan was actually realized. Drawing by SS-lieutenant Dejaco. National Museum, Auschwitz.

but airy time seems to mediate between the visitor and past realities, which are not merely *re*-presented by these artifacts but present in them. As literal fragments and remnants of events, these artifacts of catastrophe collapse the distinction between themselves and what they invoke. Claiming the authority of *un*reconstructed realities, the memorial camps invite us not only to mistake their reality for the actual death camps' reality but also to confuse an implicit, monumentalized vision for unmediated history.[1]

Yet Auschwitz I, though apparently unchanged, is quite different from the camp the Soviets liberated in 1945 (see plate 20.2). In its present aspect it is essentially as it was after the initial German 1940–2 program to transform the Polish military barracks into a concentration camp (A).[2] In 1942, however, Auschwitz I was changed further with the completion of the first stages of a plan to quadruple the size of the camp (B); another project (1941–4) created a separate industrial area three times the camp's original size (C). The expansion of the concentration camp proper was designed to include 45 brick two-story barracks (of which 15 were completed) to increase the capacity of Auschwitz I (see plate 20.3) from 10,000 to 30,000 inmates (a), five work halls (b) which also were built, and a number of buildings which remained on the drawing board: a large prison (c), a hospital (d), new reception buildings (e) (of which one, the present visitor reception center (f), was built), a *Kommandantur* or administration building (g) with a large hall for festive occasions (h), an exhibition gallery (j) and so on.

Those buildings of the *Schutzhaftlagererweiterung* ("extension of the protective custody camp") which were completed today remain intact. Thus, though there is no indication that the pleasant, yellow stucco structures belonged to the Auschwitz of the Shoah, they are there, visible to the visitor who arrives at the parking lot of the memorial camp. Partly hidden by a grove of trees and a concrete wall, these erstwhile work halls and barracks are now used as military quarters for the Polish army and as low-income housing. They are off limits to the tourists. Yet they belonged to the camp when it was liberated. A misconstruction of history begins right in the parking lot: visitors think they have arrived at the periphery of Auschwitz I; in fact they are already in the middle of the camp as it existed in 1945.

Plate 20.2 Plan showing the existing, projected and destroyed parts of Auschwitz I. A: the original camp; B: the *Schutzhaftlagererweiterung*; C: the industrial area; a: two-storey barracks; b: work halls; c: camp prison; d: hospital; e: reception building; f: reception center; g: *Kommandantur*, h: great hall; j: exhibition gallery; k: gate with inscription "Arbeit Macht Frei"; l: projected gate; m: delousing unit; n: crematory; o: Block 4; p: Block 5; q: Block 11; r: convent. Drawing by Rakel Stephanian and Robert Jan van Pelt.

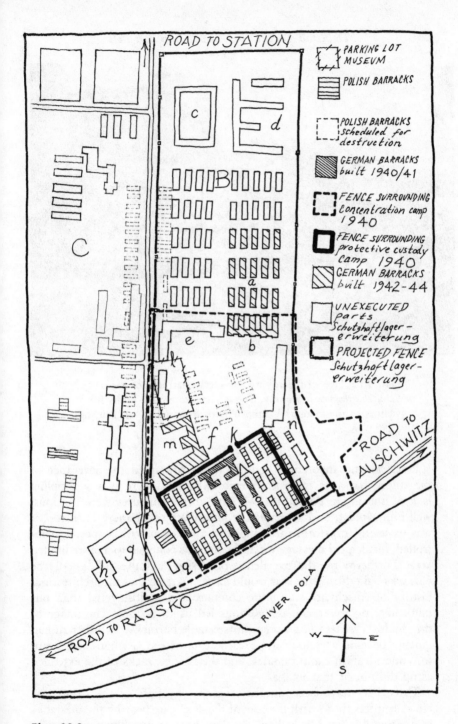

ROAD TO STATION

PARKING LOT MUSEUM

POLISH BARRACKS

POLISH BARRACKS scheduled for destruction

GERMAN BARRACKS built 1940/41

FENCE SURROUNDING Concentration camp 1940

FENCE SURROUNDING protective custody Camp 1940

GERMAN BARRACKS built 1942-44

UNEXECUTED parts Schutzhaftlager-erweiterung

PROJECTED FENCE Schutzhaftlager-erweiterung

ROAD TO AUSCHWITZ

ROAD TO RAJSKO

RIVER SOLA

N
W   E
S

Plate 20.2

Plate 20.3 Five of the twenty completed barracks of the
Schutzhaftlagererweiterung. These barracks are off limits for
visitors to the memorial camp. Photo: Robert Jan van Pelt, fall
1990.

Practical and theoretical considerations prompted the severance of
the stucco barracks from the memorial camp. There was a crippling
lack of housing in Poland in 1945, and these structures were spacious,
well built, intact, and available for immediate occupancy. Then too, it
was easier to transform the camp into a museum with a specific, con-
trolled, ideological message when the site was confined to a more limited
area. Furthermore, the excellence of design and the solidity of the
barracks built during the war would have suggested that the architectural
history of Auschwitz was more complex and multi-layered than our
immediate post-war era assumptions led us to believe. The image of
the shoddy *Pferdestallbaracken* (horse stable barracks) in Birkenau had
quickly become a canonical representation of the Germans' contempt
for concentration camp inmates, and the new barracks of the extended
camp did not fit that image.

There may have been another reason why part of the camp was
effaced; it has to do with the role of the steel gate bearing the infamous
inscription "Arbeit Macht Frei" (k). For the post-Auschwitz generation,

that gate symbolizes the threshold that separates the *oikomene* (the human community) from the planet Auschwitz. It is a fixed point in our collective memory, and therefore the canonical beginning of the tour through the camp. In fact, however, the inscribed arch did not have a central position in the history of Auschwitz. First, it played no role in the Judaeocide. Indeed, very few of the Jews deported to Auschwitz ever saw that gate. Arriving at the Auschwitz train station, the Jews were marched or taken by truck to Birkenau; later a spur rail line was laid and the transports went there directly. Furthermore, although the arch was the main gate to Auschwitz I in 1941, in the expansion program the following year it became an internal structure separating the original camp from the extended domain. From 1942 to 1945, the main entrance to the camp was exactly at the point where one now enters the parking lot – a passage presently marked by a kiosk for the parking attendant. If more building materials had been allocated to the camp in 1942, visitors now would pass through a monumental, two-story gate complex worthy of the importance of the camp within the Germans' plans for the New Order (l).

Yet our memory clings to the inscription above the gate as the modern version of Dante's *Lasciate ogni Speranza* ("Abandon all hope") at the entrance of his Inferno. Nothing is labeled or inscribed before that point, and therefore visitors to Auschwitz I are denied what may be the most interesting exhibit: the reception center adjacent to the parking lot (f). Today it is a multi-use building to meet tourists' needs, with a restaurant, cafeteria, post office, money exchange, cinema, book shop, conference room and hotel. Most visitors assume that the structure was built some time after 1945, even though the quality of both the workmanship and the materials far exceeds anything built in post-war Oswiecim. Designated by the Auschwitz Central Architectural Office as building number KL/BW160,[3] it was conceived in 1941 and constructed in 1942 (see plate 20.4). It served as the prisoners' reception center, and included a delousing installation with 19 gas chambers for *clothing* (m), a bath house for the prisoners, a laundry, and so on. Visitors who now enter the building to the left of the restaurant do so at precisely the point where the civilians were inducted into the camp. The little vestibule is still largely the same, but current visitors are herded through a new corridor along the north-east side of the building which was created after the war. During the war the prisoners passed through a series of large rooms, each designated for a specific function. First, they were registered and tattooed, then they surrendered their valuables, and finally they were forced to undress. Their garments were taken to the delousing unit while they went in a different direction to be shaved.

Plate 20.4 Elevation of KL/BW 160 as seen from the parking lot
of the memorial camp. To the right is the wing that housed the
prisoners' bath. It is now used as a cafeteria. To the left is the
three-arched entry to the former prisoners' reception center.
These arches do not appear in the original plans of the building,
yet were added in a later phase of the design to complement the
arched portico that gave access to the furnace room that
connected the prisoners' laundry to the prisoners' reception
center. Photograph: Robert Jan van Pelt, fall 1990.

The gas chambers for the clothing were parallel to the shower room
for the inmates – a juxtaposition that was to merge into a single lethal
construct in Birkenau. The prisoners dried in the next room and then
were pushed into another where striped pyjamas were thrown at them.
Entering this labyrinth as a captured civilian, the regulation prisoner
left through the porch facing the gate with the inscription "Arbeit Macht
Frei." The oral testimonies and memoirs of survivors attest to the
shattering impact of this ritual of humiliating baptism into the kingdom
of death. The building where it occurred ought to have been marked
by an inscription, but it was not, and now stands incognito.

The architecture designed to enact the metamorphosis from *Mensch*
to *Untermensch* was intact when the Soviets liberated the camp in 1945.

All traces of that purpose were subsequently removed. The guidebook for sale in the bookstore does not mention the building at all. Perhaps those who created the museum could not reconcile the implications of that labyrinth with their ideology of resistance; an ideology that denied the reality of total victimization. Perhaps it was simply a question of resources and the need for tourist services. Whether for doctrinal or practical reasons, the destruction of the original arrangement within the present visitor reception center is a post-war obfuscation and a loss.

There have been additions to the camp the Russians found in 1945 as well as deletions, and the suppression of the prisoner reception site is matched by the reconstruction of Crematory I just outside the north-east perimeter of the present museum camp (n). With its chimney and gas chamber, the crematory (KL/BW11 and KL/BW14) functions as the solemn conclusion for tours through the camp. Visitors are not told that what they see is a post-war reconstruction;[4] its homicidal gas chamber had been abandoned in 1942, and at the end of 1943 the three furnaces were dismantled. Modified further in the fall of 1944, the building became an air-raid shelter with an emergency operating room.

When Auschwitz was transformed into a museum after the war, the decision was taken to concentrate the history of the whole complex in one of its component parts. The infamous crematories where the mass murders had taken place were ruins in Birkenau, a few kilometers distant. The committee felt that a crematory was required at the end of the memorial journey, and Crematory I was reconstructed to speak for the history of the four crematoria at Birkenau. This program of usurpation was rather detailed. A chimney, the ultimate symbol of Birkenau, was recreated; four hatched openings in the roof, as if for pouring Zyklon-B into the gas chamber below, were installed, and two of the three furnaces were remodeled. There are no signs to explain these restitutions, they were not marked at the time, and the guides remain silent about it when they take visitors through this "palpably intact" building that is presumed by the tourist to be the place where *it happened.*[5]

The reconstruction of Crematory I encapsulates the pervasive problem of conflicting memories that troubles the memorial site. In its present form, the *Panstwowe Muzeum Oswiecim Brzezinka* offers only the main camp at Auschwitz. Birkenau is not developed for visits; one can enter, but on one's own. The standard guided tour does not include an excursion to the principal site of the Judaeocide although it was *there* that the countless transports arrived and the four chimneys smoked (plate

20.5). Auschwitz I alone was designated to be the permanent exhibit. There were, as always, practical reasons (Birkenau had been largely dismantled when most of the portable stables used as barracks were taken away after the war to shelter the homeless in Warsaw), but there were also deeper, more compelling motivations for the decision. First, the fate of the Jews did not have an important place on the national agenda of post-war Poland. And second, Auschwitz I had been established as the Nazis' instrument to subjugate the *Poles* into serfdom – an enslavement the Poles rightly interpreted as the initial steps to a "Final Solution" to a Polish problem. Auschwitz I was a tremendously significant site in Polish history, and it made sense that a *Panstwowe Muzeum* would concentrate the nation's meager resources on it.

Plate 20.5 An overview of a part of Building Section 2 of Birkenau showing the infamous horse stable barracks. The barracks with chimneys were dwelling units; the barracks without chimneys provided latrines. The concentration of 400 latrines in these barracks and the long distance between a significant part of the dwelling barracks to the latrine barracks created catastrophic hygiene conditions. Photograph made by SS-sergeant Kamann, winter 1943. National Museum, Auschwitz.

The result of this combination of expediency and historical experience is an exhibition that relies on a few paltry exhibits in Blocks 4 (o) and 5 (p) of Auschwitz I. These alone relate the mass murder of Jews perpetrated in Birkenau. In Block 4, two rooms are dedicated to a description of the process of extermination to which Jews – and not Poles – were subjected in the death camp. In one of these rooms the history of Birkenau is presented through a large model of Crematory II which depicts people entering, undressing, and dying. This graphic, almost pornographic, exhibit is not, and was not meant to be, informative. Its intention is, literally, to "re-present," to make the fate of the Jews symbolically present within the context of Auschwitz I. That goal is also achieved through the transposition of rooms with hair, eye glasses, crutches, suitcases, and so on from Birkenau to Block 5 in Auschwitz I. These endow the commemorative camp with the history of the nearby murder machinery.

The main camp first and foremost preserved Polish – not Jewish – history, however, and the decision to relegate Birkenau to a position of secondary importance reflects a specific ideology of remembrance recently described by the Canadian sociologist Iwona Irwin-Zarecka:

> Auschwitz . . . is *not*, for Poles, a symbol of Jewish suffering. Rather, it is a general symbol of "man's inhumanity to man" and a symbol of the Polish tragedy at the hands of the Nazis. It is a powerful reminder of the evil of *racism*, and not a singular reminder of the deadliness of anti-Semitism. In the most literal sense of memories evoked on site, it is an "Auschwitz without Jews."[6]

This ideology elucidates the extraordinary significance of "The Block of Death" to the Poles (q). They rightly claim the infamous camp prison located in Block 11 as a martyrium, and recently it has been recognized as such by the Roman Catholic church. Father Kolbe, the central protagonist in the story of Block 11, volunteered to die in the place of a Jewish father. Kolbe's moral choice fits the traditional notion of martyrdom and his example is one of the few moments of grace in this abyss of misery. But it is also almost irrelevant. Father Kolbe's death was exceptional because he died voluntarily while nearly all the other millions of victims never had a choice at all. In a fundamental way his memorial in Block 11 fits the conventional, chivalric ideology of a hero who fights and dies on behalf of someone else. Pervasive and dominant, this concept of heroism is reflected in the official symbol of the memorial camp (a shield with two drawn swords) and the official banner which flies over

Block 11 in Auschwitz I and the monument in Birkenau (the red triangle of the gentile political prisoners superimposed on the uniform motif of vertical blue and white stripes). There is no room in this ideology for women like Mrs Zuckner who, during the selection in Birkenau on 22 August 1944, held fast to the hand of a little girl she knew. As her then 15-year old daughter Esther recalled, "This was the last time I saw my mother. She went with that neighbor's child. So when we talk about heroes, mind you, this was a hero: a woman who would not let a four-year-old child go by herself."[7]

A visit to Auschwitz I takes time, and visitors from abroad who spend the preceding night in the relative comfort of the Holiday Inn in the somewhat distant city of Cracow have little time left after their late arrival in Auschwitz, their lunch and guided tour, to undertake more than a cursory trip to the enormous site at Birkenau (plate 20.6). Late in the afternoon the buses drop them off before the gate, and most

Plate 20.6 Partial view of the landscape of Building Section 2 of Birkenau. The chimneys remained after the horse stable barracks were removed in the immediate post-war years to be used as emergency shelters in Warsaw. Photo: Robert Jan van Pelt, fall 1990.

groups limit their visit to a stroll along the ramp towards the monument at its end. For Jewish visitors there is a sense of relief as the absence of interpretation at Birkenau at least spares them the pain engendered by the official interpretation provided at the main camp. The bleakness of Birkenau fits the Jewish need to remember the genocide as Shoah. The site has not been appropriated, its space falsified by real but transposed objects, as in Auschwitz I. Certainly the bronze medallion nailed to the monument and depicting drawn swords, the red-triangle banner hanging from a flagpole, and the large cross in front of the *Kommandantur* of Birkenau (which was recently transformed into a Roman Catholic chapel) are inappropriate in the place where a million Jews died. But they are physically so insignificant in relation to the overwhelming desolation of the site that most people fail to notice them.

Nevertheless, time and again, Birkenau too is annexed, albeit insidiously. As the vast expanse of the camp can easily accommodate large crowds, the monument has become the focus of public ceremonies. Inexact allusions, snatches of misinformation, and inappropriate metaphors uttered at such gatherings generate histories that corrode the history of the Judaeocide. The most stunning of these revisions occurred on the occasion of the Pope's visit on June 7, 1979. At that time the church represented one of the two pillars of Polish resistance against communism (the other was Solidarnosc), and it seemed opportune to the church leadership for the Pope to visit Auschwitz, a martyrium of the Polish nation. Many in those heady days hoped that the church would provide spiritual leadership for a reconciliation of Polish and Jewish history. It did not, and in hindsight that is not surprising. As Iwona Irwin-Zarecka has explained, the remembrance of common victimization does not offer a moral challenge. Jews are remembered only as one group of victims among many, and Polish responsibility, especially towards the three million Polish Jews, is resolutely ignored. Standing amidst the ruins of the crematories where three generations of Jews burned and in front of a memorial that remembered the "Six Million," the Pope interpreted the Polish inscription to mean that "six million Poles lost their lives during the Second World War: a fifth of the nation."[8] The Pope made a true historical statement, yet the place where he chose to do so, between the ruins of Crematory II and Crematory III, gave it a new and infelicitous significance. Speaking as a Pole to a Polish audience, the Pope gave a further twist to the scandal of "Auschwitz without Jews." As Iwona Irwin-Zarecka has observed, "the persistent commemoration of six million Polish victims of genocide – a figure which includes the three million Polish Jews – testifies to the ease of appropriating the Jewish dead as one's own." But, she continued,

The figure of "six million Poles" does more than that. It also grants the dead Jew the status of a Pole, in a post-mortem acceptance of the Jews' membership in the Polish family. And this renders a reading of the past which makes that past unrecognizable. The Jew not only appears to be mourned on a par with others – which he was not – he also appears to have always belonged, which he did not. The destruction of the Jewish community, when reclaimed as the loss of Polish lives, acquires a sense of trauma which it did not have, at least for the majority. And the sharing in suffering, together with assigning all the blame to the Nazis, helps eliminate questions about the Poles' action and inaction towards the Jews.[9]

The issue of usurpation is not a simple one. When the Pope took the decision to go to Birkenau, the process of appropriation began, no matter what he would say. The choice to go to that site was the first step. But there is a hierarchy of arrogation, and a concomitant hierarchy of responsibility . Falsifying the boundaries of a site, or the purpose of certain structures (as in Auschwitz I) constitutes one level of appropriation; the Pope's visit to Birkenau is another; and the words he spoke yet a third. The onus for each varies. We are less responsible for a site we inherit than for words deliberately uttered there.

In direct response to the Pope's call for a beacon of (Catholic) piety amidst the evil of Auschwitz–Birkenau, a few Carmelite nuns sought and obtained permission to found a convent in a building just outside the camp's perimeter but close to Block 11. The structure they chose had been a theater before the war (r). During the occupation it functioned as a storehouse; plans to transform it into an SS casino and a centerpiece in the new *Kommandantur* were never carried out. The nuns moved in unobtrusively and conducted their business quietly. Other buildings around the camp are used for various purposes, and the establishment of the convent was not particularly remarkable until Belgian Catholics exploited the situation. In an appeal to raise money for the sisters, the Catholic charity *Aide à l'Eglise en détresse* presented the convent as a "spiritual fortress and a guarantee of the conversion of strayed brothers from our countries as well as proof of our desire to erase the outrages so often done to the Vicar of Christ."[10] Triumphalist in its premise, militant in tone, and offensive to Jews, this statement of purpose triggered a five-year battle of quarrelsome assertions, self-righteous statements, sanctimonious professions, frivolous pronouncements, irreverent protests and even physical tussles that must prove, as far as the history of the memorial site at Auschwitz is concerned, of only passing significance: by 1992 the nuns will have vacated the building at the fence, and will have moved to a new center of prayer built at the respectful distance of 550 yards from the perimeter of the camp.

This painful episode has left an unresolved issue: the legacy of Edith Stein and its role in the memorial camp. A convert to Roman Catholicism, Stein had entered a Carmelite convent under the name of Sister Benedicta of the Cross. For the Germans, however, Sister Benedicta was still a Jew. She was arrested and transported to Birkenau where she was killed a few hundred yards north-west from the present monument. She was one of the thousands of victims in the first mass murders of Jews in Birkenau in the summer of 1942, when eight hundred people at a time were exterminated in "Bunker II," a peasant cottage with crude gas chambers. (With the installation of the large gas chambers of Crematory II and III in early 1943, Bunker II was temporarily abandoned only to be reopened in the summer of 1944 when it was known as Bunker V. In the late fall of that year Bunker II/V was destroyed and the site abandoned.)

Stein's death was nothing more than a tragic footnote in the history of Birkenau until John Paul II announced his intention to initiate the beatification process for "the Carmelite Sister Benedicta of the Cross ... who was a descendant of a Jewish family living in Wroclow."[11] Stein had died because she had been born a Jew, yet on his 1979 visit the Pope claimed her for the church. According to him she had died the death of a Christian martyr *and* a daughter of the Jewish people. As a prominent Catholic theologian, Cardinal Joseph Ratzinger, has explained:

> It is important to note that Edith Stein, agnostic, atheistic, once she became a Catholic was saying: "Now I feel myself back to true Judaism." Because not only did she regain the faith in God, but finding the faith in Christ, she entered in the full heritage of Abraham. ... Entering the union with Christ, she entered in the heart of Judaism. Following the thought of St. Paul we can say that becoming a Christian, I became a true Jew.[12]

In short, Auschwitz was a new Golgotha, and the Jews had died there, as John Paul II declared in a speech of May 1, 1987, with Christ's Cross placed over their shoulders.[13]

This Christian, triumphalist appropriation of Jewish suffering is clearly manifested around the remains of Bunker II. Pious visitors placed a cross in the ruins of the gas chambers where Jews, including Stein, were killed. Upset by this, Jews erected a Star of David affixed to a post. A battle of symbols and a proliferation of crosses and stars ensued.

One star was even nailed to the top of a 10-meter-high utility pole. This star-and-cross war ended when a group of Warsaw schoolchildren erected a large cross with a Star of David nailed to it. To the children it seemed a fitting compromise. Unfortunately, however, the union of the two symbols reflects very precisely one of the Church's triumphalist doctrines: the significance of the death of the Six Million (Jews) as witnesses to the truth of His Cross.

The memorial site of Auschwitz is a very troubled place, both because of what happened there and because of the way people remember and commemorate it. The commission established in the autumn of 1989 by Prime Minister Tadeusz Mazowiecki, to transform the memorial camp into a site acceptable to all concerned, faces a difficult task. There is no simple solution, but a basic understanding of the phenomenology of architectonic space may be helpful. To recognize the falsifications and confusions in Auschwitz is important. But in the end, what remains after a visit to Birkenau is the sheer scale of the place. Physically it is enormous, and what transpired there was enormous. Serious visitors begin to walk, and continue walking for days on end to cover the huge terrain. In the end the pain in one's legs testifies *not* to the anguish of the victims, but to the universal significance of Birkenau. It is a black hole that can encompass within its perimeters the whole of the Vatican City with most of the great Basilicas of Christendom in addition.

A phenomenology of Auschwitz I and II in which Jews, Poles, Catholics, and others discover the site for themselves and with each other must recognize the two most important aspects of the relationship between space and the body. The fundamental characteristic distinguishing people and animals from the rest of nature is their ability to move freely over the surface of the earth; a special attribute of human beings is their upright position which allows them to gaze beyond the known. People "stand out" from nature. Erect, upright, they look neither up nor down, but out to the horizon. The space they inhabit is a horizontal plane, which we shall call the space of the living. Neither the ground below that plane nor the sky above it is readily accessible to or permanently habitable by human beings. Traditionally, the ground below us was perceived to be the realm of the dead, while the heavens belonged to the gods.

The space of nature or, as we shall call it, the space of the dead, is a vertical plane. Unlike human beings, an erect and healthy tree (for example) does not move in a horizontal plane; its roots burrow into the earth and its branches grow to the sun. Thus the tree grows vertically. In this "vertical" space objects fall down (like water from a mountain, leaves from a tree in autumn, or the ruins of a building) and things move up (grass grows, smoke spirals). Human beings do not inhabit this vertical plane. It is the dead buried below or, as the faithful of some religions believe, dwelling on high, who belong to this space.

When architects design and build for the living, they can ignore the potential conflict between these two genres of space. The space of nature enters their thoughts only with regard to problems of structural stability. When, however, they are asked to design a site where many people are buried or have died, they are forced to confront the clash between the vertical space of nature and the horizontal space of the living. Is the ground below our feet hallowed or cursed? Do the dead rest in peace or are they troubled?

When designing cemeteries or memorializing killing grounds, architects have two choices: either they try to obfuscate the collision of vertical and horizontal, or they accentuate it. If they choose the former, they will attempt, architectonically, to bridge the horizontal space of the living and the vertical space of the dead. A traditional way to do so is with large stones which mark, and are part of, the horizontal space of the living. Yet the living cannot enter these objects; they sit heavily on the earth as if in surrender to the force of gravity that rules the space of nature. In these stones or cenotaphs, the clash between the opposites of horizontal and vertical, life and death appears dulled. Their message is: "and yet the dead are somehow still with us."

Architects can also choose to emphasize the difference between the space of the living and the space of the dead. They can erect statues of the dead. Like the massive stone cenotaphs, these statues punctuate the space of the living – often at places of great political importance. But, unlike the stones, these monuments do not appear heavy, or pulled towards the earth. Artistically imbued with a sense of life, they claim a place among people and refuse to surrender to the space of the dead.[14] Used especially to honor heroes, these statues proclaim triumphantly in front of parliament houses and in the middle of market places that "their sacrifice was not in vain."[15]

Finally, architects can opt to embody the full force of abandonment, of perdition, of Shoah. A horizontal slab that in no way intrudes into the space of the living refuses to be a mark. Old churches in Europe sometimes have floors composed of slabs of stone that, on closer inspection, turn out to cover graves. Having inadvertently walked over them while enjoying the rhythm of the arches, the color of the windows, or the geometry of the vaults, visitors recognize, with some dismay, that they either committed sacrilege, or that the dead are truly lost to us.[16]

The monument in Treblinka (1964), designed by Adam Haupt and

Franciszek Duszenko, is an example of an attempt to create a bridge between the space of the dead and the space of the living. Thousands of stones scattered over the abandoned site of the camp are simultaneously tombstones in that they point to the dead below (or above), and markers on a map, representations of the places where the Jews who died there once lived. The smallest stones stand for the shtetls, the larger ones for the towns. The central monument, a towering rock that resembles the trilithons of Stonehenge, symbolizes the 300,000 Jews of Warsaw. Konnilyn Feig, a thoughtful scholar of the camps, grasped the monument's powerful unification of the vertical space which remained and the horizontal space that was obliterated, but which each living generation re-establishes for itself. "The memorial – the sensitive, *strong*, unique memorial – brings it all back through the shape and the thrusting of thousands of stones pointing to the sky like a vast field of arms reaching upward, imploring." This vertical space is counterbalanced by the arrangement of the stones around the central Warsaw marker. "The majesty, the awesome dignity of the silent stone field encircling the central monument. The stones, everywhere, go on forever, creating an eerie but beautiful aura around the ash field."[17] Eerie, because all attempts to mix the space of the dead and that of the living, must be unsettling.

Few designers dare to surrender to the space of nature, the space of the dead. To design a monument that fully obeys the demands of the space of the dead implies the ultimate acknowledgment that the dead are gone forever. Only once did a team of designers attempt to give form to the chasm that has opened between the six million dead and the living, an abyss the latter cannot traverse. In the late 1950s, a group of Polish architects and sculptors led by Oskar and Zofia Hansen submitted a radical proposal to the international competition for a monument in Auschwitz–Birkenau. (Theirs was one of the 426 projects from architects of 30 countries, and it won the first prize.)[18] Their design refused to allow the ruins of the camps to become objects for others to arrogate. There was no suggestion in their design that there is some way in which the living could trace the steps of the victims, understand their experiences, or share their memory.

The architects proposed to close the infamous gate of Birkenau through which the trains transporting the victims had rolled to the platform and the selections. No one was ever to pass through that gate again. But they knew that it would be unacceptable, indeed reprehensible simply to close the camp as if it were a place of lethal contamination. If no one were to enter it, the site and the event would slip into oblivion, and this the architects did not want at all. It was their goal to *confront* the living with oblivion, to bring them face to face with the essential truth of the site: the fact that, ultimately, no memory could connect them to Birkenau's past. Their plan forced the visitor to the desolate realization that one merely passes along the event one had hoped to grasp.

The designers proposed to remove a few meters of the barbed wire fence north of the main gate to the camp, thus creating the illusion that the visitors had to sneak through an accidental opening. But they were not to walk on its soil. A special path of granite, 60 meters wide and 1,000 meters long, was to slash diagonally across the grid of the camp, towards the ruins of the crematoria. Slightly elevated, it would float effortlessly over the camp, along the remains of the barracks. The path would not touch them, and would provide no devotional stations. The only interruptions of the granite strip were to be identical open rectangles, like graves cut out of the floor, to frame the few remaining fragments of the barracks. Slightly larger than the perimeter of the barracks, these holes in the granite walkway (around which one had to walk) were to set the foundations and chimneys as if they were precious relics. The architects did not plan to stabilize the ruins framed by the openings in the granite path: with time they would change. When they designed it, almost all of the barracks had already been removed, and only their chimneys remained standing, uneasily. They appeared to be (as the poet Wolfgang Borchert described the chimneys amidst the ruins of Hamburg) "like the bones of a giant skeleton. Like tombstones. Like fingers of corpses, clutching at God, threatening heaven. The bare, bony, burnt, bent fingers of corpses."[19] Only a temporary concession to our need for symbols, it was anticipated that the chimneys would fall into pieces, and grass would cover the rubble. For some time even this ruin-grass would be imbued with memory. But eventually nature would regain possession of the site, leaving the layers of history below to be excavated by archaeologists in the distant future. In the end there would be only that strange granite path traversing the former railroad tracks and ending at the foundations of Crematory II. The walkway did not pass over the scenes of greatest evil: while the undressing room was to jot forwards into the path, the gas chamber was to remain outside it. The visitor would leave by another opening in the barbed-wire fence. There was to be no monument, no inscription, nothing (see plate 20.7).

For the designers, the suffering of the victims and the life that had been within the camp had become a history not to be excavated: *that* history could never be memory. The design did not provide for a place of rest, a spot where a visitor could remain. Only one part of the camp

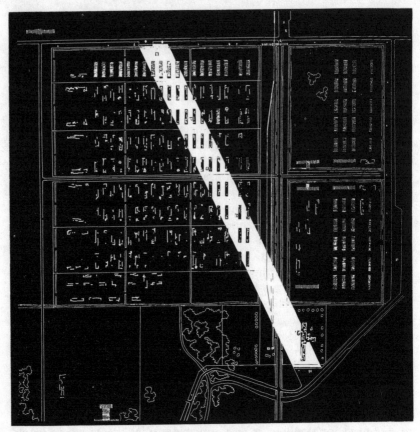

Plate 20.7 Plan of the design for a monument at Birkenau
created by the group of architects and sculptors headed by Oskar
Hansen. As published in the Dutch architectural journal *Forum* 9
(1959), p. 287. The granite walkway is indicated by the white
band.

could be memory, and it was the world of the perpetrators. Much easier
to represent, that world did not belong to the deep recesses of history,
but still aggressively framed the horizon of the living. The architects
proposed to preserve and maintain the guard towers and the other
structures surrounding the perimeter of the camp. Powerful objects in
the geography of our world, they were to remain intact.

The proposal was relentless. It prohibited encounter and refused to
surrender to the illusion of memory. There were no stones to touch,
no center to stand strongly against the ravages of time, no majesty or

dignity, no eerie but beautiful aura. There was to be no inscription commemorating the six million. Only silence and the bizarre granite walkway to pose the question for future generations: What happened here?

The proposal received the highest award but was not built. Brilliant in its conception, it had failed to take into account that there were survivors. And they had been omitted from the design. The survivors protested that there was no place for them, and they were right. They would have been locked out from their own experience, or locked in forever.

These objections were articulated 15 years after liberation and at that time they were correct. It would have been unfitting, inappropriate, and above all inaccurate to have constructed a memorial, a transformation of history into a granite-shaped memory, without acknowledging the survivors. The situation in the near future, however, will not be the same as that of the 1950s. When there are no survivors, there will be no memory to connect the living with Birkenau's past. Soon, perhaps, it will be fitting, appropriate, and accurate to construct the Hansens' vision of a memorial with its message of desolation and separation. Future generations may walk through Birkenau but, not being of it, they will be constrained to walk over it. It will be their lot to pass over that terrain, unable to grasp the events of the killing fields.

21

Trauma, Memory, and Transference

Saul Friedlander

It has been observed by psychologists that survivors of traumatic events are divided into two well-defined groups: those who repress their past *en bloc*, and those whose memory of the offense persists, as though carved in stone, prevailing over all previous or subsequent experiences. Now, not by choice but by nature, I belong to the second group. Of my two years of life outside the law I have not forgotten a single thing. Without any deliberate effort, memory continues to restore to me events, faces, words, sensations, as if at that time my mind had gone through a period of exalted receptivity, during which not a detail was lost.

Primo Levi, *Moments of Reprieve*

German historians and students of history have the obligation to understand that victims of Nazi persecution and their bereaved relatives can even regard it as a forfeiture of the right to their form of memory if historical research on contemporary history, operating only in scientific terms, makes claims in its academic arrogance to a monopoly when it comes to questions and concepts pertaining to the Nazi period. . . . Respect for the victims of Nazi crimes demands that this mythical memory be granted a place. . . . Among the problems faced by a younger generation of German historians more focused on rational understanding is certainly also the fact that they must deal with just such a contrary form of memory among those who were persecuted and harmed by the Nazi regime, and among their descendants – a form of memory which functions to coarsen historical recollection.

Martin Broszat, in Martin Broszat and Saul Friedlander, "A controversy about the Historicisation of National Socialism" (Peter Baldwin, ed., *Reworking the Past*, p. 106)

The mythical quality that he (Broszat) attributed to the memory of the victims is inherent in the event itself . . . and no historical analysis will be able to solve this. All historical work on the events of this period will have to be pursued or considered in its relation to the events of Auschwitz (*Zum Grossen Ganzen von Auschwitz*). . . . Here, all historicization reaches its limits (*Hier stoesst alle Historisierung an ihre Grenze*).

Christian Meier, obituary of Martin Broszat, *Vierteljahrshefte für Zeitgeschichte*, Vol. 38 (1990)

In a short autobiographical text, "The Awakening," written a few years ago, Aharon Appelfeld speaks of his generation. He describes how Jewish children who survived the war, entirely losing touch with their past after their arrival in Israel, came to loathe their prior identity. Whenever a fragment of memory resurfaced, they did everything in their power to obliterate it. Years later, however, "the awakening" came.

This rediscovery of the past was, in Appelfeld's words, a miraculous rebirth, an experience of some sort of personal and collective redemption.[1] Such redemptive feeling is rather unusual: today, says Appelfeld, he would have written his text somewhat differently.

Quite another picture is presented by the hundreds of videotaped interviews with surviving victims of the Holocaust, discussed by Lawrence Langer in *Holocaust Testimony: the ruins of memory*.[2] (Various synonyms for the extermination of the Jews of Europe will be used here: Holocaust, Shoah, "Auschwitz," the "Final Solution." All of them are currently utilized, but none seems adequate.) For these witnesses, memory and survival do not seem to entail any cathartic rediscovery of a harmonious self, of a heroic memory, of a unifying moral principle. "The efforts of memory in these testimonies," writes Langer, "liberate a subtext of loss that punctures the story with fragments of chagrin, a vexation that coexists with whatever relief one feels from the fact of survival. The evidence of these testimonies . . . suggests that such a relief is less substantial than we have been led to assume."[3]

Langer distinguishes between various categories of memory, each corresponding to a specific relationship between the remembered self and the surrounding world of destruction, as well as between the perceptions the present self has of the contemporary world and of the past. The gist of Langer's argument is that a fundamental difference remains between a deep memory totally centered on the years of the Shoah and a common memory that "restores the self to the normal pre- and post-camp routines, but also offers detached portraits, from the vantage point of today, of what it must have been like then." Deep memory and common memory are ultimately irreducible to each other. Any

attempt at building a coherent self founders on the intractable return
of the repressed and recurring deep memory. "It is enough stories for
today, Richieu," says Art Spiegelman's survivor father, in the very last
line of the second book of *Maus*: the dying father is addressing his son
Artie with the name of the younger brother, Richieu, who died in the
Holocaust some 45 years before. Deep memory.

Individual *common* memory, as well as collective memory, tends to
restore or establish coherence, closure, and possibly a redemptive stance,
notwithstanding the resistance of deep memory at the individual level.
The question remains whether at the collective level as well an event
such as the Shoah may, after all the survivors have disappeared, leave
traces of a deep memory beyond individual recall, which will defy any
attempt to give it meaning.

This text, which deals mainly, but not exclusively, with the vantage
point of the victims, focusses on patterns of historical representation in
their global sense – on professional history as well as on major trends
of historical consciousness. I shall first summarize some interpretations
of Jewish historical consciousness and catastrophe, both in general terms
and in relation to the Shoah, then examine certain defenses that appear
in the historical rendition of the Nazi epoch and the Shoah. Finally, I
shall address what "working through" means in regard to these historical
narratives and also to global trends of historical consciousness.

Historical Consciousness and Catastrophe

Appelfeld's narrative of a redemptive recovery of the past is undoubtedly
the expression of a genuine individual experience, although somewhat
atypical. Moreover, it is consonant with the structure of previous
attempts at public integration of the Shoah in early Israeli consciousness
and its national rituals. A catastrophe like no other in the history of
the Jewish people led to a quintessential historical redemption, the
birth of a sovereign Jewish state. This sequence of "Catastrophe and
Redemption," deeply rooted in visionary religious tradition, found its
expression in the official equalizing of *Shoah* and *Gvurah*, of martyrdom
and heroism.

Yet this officially supported ideological interpretation was *not*
reinforced as time went by; on the contrary, it suffered a progressive
erosion from the late 1960s on among a growing segment of the Israeli
public. While over the last few years the Shoah seems more present than
before in Israel and wider Jewish consciousness, its interpretation

is increasingly multifaceted and lacking in consensual interpretation. Thus a long-term trend seems to subvert the early ideological stances.[4]

In fact, this non-integration of the Shoah at the level of collective consciousness appears as a *new* phenomenon within Jewish tradition. It has been argued that Judaism, over the course of its history, developed a collective memory working with fixed patterns to integrate catastrophic events.[5] Such patterns, rooted in a paradigm linked to Judaism's archetypal catastrophe, the destruction of the Temple, yet carrying the seed of messianic redemption, are said to have contributed to its "creative survival." Throughout the ages Jews have responded to history in ritualized forms grounded both in biblical tradition (The Book of Lamentations) and in medieval and early modern reworkings of the basic redemptive paradigm. What is striking, however, is that these "responses to apocalypse" become less convincing – and their authors seem less certain of their validity – when they confront the Shoah both during the war and after it.

Whereas some scholars dealt with patterns of memory expressed in Jewish traditions and secular literature, and others explored Yiddish literature and Jewish popular culture in Eastern Europe, Columbia historian Yosef Yerushalmi addressed historical writing as a genre. The thesis he presented in *Zakhor* is well-known: the world of Jewish tradition integrated catastrophic or disruptive historical events through a set pattern of archetypal responses. The contemporary Jewish historian cannot but question such an immobile structure and invokes the rules of scientific investigation against the redeeming power of myth. Yerushalmi addressed the Shoah in a few lines only. The gist of his argument is that notwithstanding the unparalleled amount of historical investigation engendered by this catastrophe, the Jewish world is awaiting a redeeming myth, as in the wake of the expulsion from Spain, when it embraced the mystical symbolism of the Kabbalah. In the meantime, literary fiction serves as a surrogate.[6]

Yet today, some fifty years after the events, no mythical framework seems to be taking hold of the Jewish imagination, nor does the best of literature and art dealing with the Shoah offer any redemptive stance. In fact, the opposite appears to be true.

In no recent work of art is this lack of closure as obvious as in Claude Lanzmann's film *Shoah*. Each individual testimony remains a story unresolved. The overall narration is neither linear nor circular; it is a spiral recoiling unto itself, then moving into new territory through a succession of forays. As the film unfolds, and particularly in the last sequence, the mythical redemptive moment, elevated by early Israeli memory to the same metahistorical meaning as the catastrophe itself, becomes just another episode in the story of total extermination. The Warsaw ghetto uprising principally conveys the bitterness of its survivors: "If you could lick my heart," say Antek Zuckerman, second in command of the ghetto uprising, "it would poison you." In Primo Levi's *The Drowned and the Saved*, in Ida Fink's muted echoes of the past, in any number of works published over the last years, no redemptive theme or sign of resolution is evident.

Defenses

If one accepts the suggestion that for the community of the victims, and for others as well, the Nazi epoch and the Holocaust remain an unmastered past – a "past that refuses to go away," as a notorious saying has it – then both the extreme character of the events and the indeterminacy surrounding their historical significance create even for the professional historian a field of projections, of unconscious shapings and reshapings, of an authentic transferential situation. As Dominick LaCapra writes:

> The Holocaust presents the historian with transference in the most traumatic form conceivable – but in a form that will vary with the difference in subject position of the analyst. Whether the historian or analyst is a survivor, a relative of survivors, a former Nazi, a former collaborator, a relative of former Nazis or collaborators, a younger Jew or German distanced from more immediate contact with survival, participation, or collaboration, or a relative "outsider" to these problems will make a difference even in the meaning of statements that may be formally identical.[7]

No doubt, any generalizing statement in such matters can have only the barest indicative value. There are any number of possible psychological aspects linked to each of the subject positions previously mentioned by LaCapra. It suffices to recall shame, guilt, self-hatred, and all the shades of ambivalence among the surviving victims in order to perceive the difference in narratives produced from an apparently well-defined single vantage point. For German contemporaries of the Nazi epoch, particularly those who were adolescents or young adults at the end of the war, the whole range of internal conflicts may be as daunting in the variety of its results as it is for the victims. Moreover, complex personal circumstances must often be taken into account. Consider, for instance, the notorious and controversial book of Andreas Hillgruber: *Two Kinds of Ruin.*[8] Having been a youngster in the Wehrmacht fighting the Russians in Eastern Prussia, and having had to flee his hometown of Koenigsberg, must have a bearing on Hillgruber's peculiar identification with the German populations of the East and the retreating units of the Wehrmacht during the last year of the war – notwithstanding the fact that the resistance of the Wehrmacht meant continuation of Nazi extermination policies behind the Eastern front. Thus, an identification with previous personal experience is repressed for a long time, but unexpected acting out can hardly be avoided.

If, for the sake of simplicity, we consider both German and Jewish contemporaries of the Nazi period – contemporary adults, adolescents, or children, even the children of these groups – what was traumatic for the one group was obviously not traumatic for the other. For Jews of whatever age, the fundamental traumatic situation was and is the Shoah and its sequels; for Germans, it was national defeat (including flight from the Russians and loss of sovereignty) following upon national exhilaration. To that, however, a sequel must be added, regardless of its psychological definition: the information, growing over time, about Nazi crimes, especially the genocide. The victims of Nazism cope with a fundamentally traumatic situation, whereas many Germans have to cope with a widening stain, with potential shame or guilt.

Studies abound concerning the repression of the Nazi epoch in the German public sphere, including the early phases of history writing. Massive denial was blatant in the historical work of the late 1940s and 1950s. In the 1960s, signs of a transformation appeared, and that new approach dominated the late 1960s and 1970s. From then on various forms of denial and defensive reactions surfaced in a new guise. The "Historians' Controversy" of the late 1980s became an unusual case of "acting out."[9] But how could one not mention the German student movement of the late 1960s? In clashing with their parents' generation, they were fighting Nazism itself. "Fascism" as an overall tag, along with the new awareness it created, shielded many of them from the *specificity* of the Nazi past and such ideological generalizations became deeply embedded in subsequent historical discourse about Nazism. In short, the burden of the past, both at the individual and the generational level, continues to afflict the historians as well as the survivor community.

Straight denial has not disappeared, although it is not massive. Until the late 1970s, for instance, the accepted mythology established a clear distinction between the behavior of the Wehrmacht and that of the SS units on the eastern front. To this day, the topic remains an area of repression, even within the most painstaking historiography.[10]

It has recently been noted that "this collective amnesia is so powerful that it infects even those very scholars who have done so much to cure it." A historian, for instance, who had written the most substantial study of Nazi indoctrination in the Wehrmacht concludes by doubting its effect on the troops, and notes that he personally cannot recall ever having been exposed to political education during his own service in the Wehrmacht. Another who had done much to show the involvement of the lower ranks in the realization of the "Final Solution" states unequivocally that "the mentality of the average *Landser* was charac- terized by soberness and the rejection of the far-from-reality propaganda tirades" and that the troops "had little influence" on and "could hardly find a way of avoiding the escalation of the violence," which was in any case part of "the conduct of war by both sides."[11]

Far more widespread is a defense that could be termed "splitting off." It recently found expression in the debate about "the historicization of National Socialism." Early discussions of this issue left the place of "Auschwitz" unmentioned. In the polemic that ensued, the *centrality* of Auschwitz was first relegated to the domain of the victims' specific memory (see my epigraph); then it was suggested that the quasi-mythical dimension of Auschwitz in the victims' memory had to be taken into account *alongside* a more nuanced approach to the history of the epoch. In short, facts perfectly well known – too well known in a sense – were split off from the main argument, as they were bound to create problems for the new approach to the history of Germany under Nazism. No clear way of integrating them was suggested.[12]

Various forms of avoidance, including the splitting off mechanism, have led to a growing fragmentation in the representation of the Nazi epoch.[13] The study of Nazism disintegrates into discrete, specialized and unrelated domains, and so understates the "already well-known" facts of mass extermination and atrocity. There is ever-more minute research into various aspects of everyday life and social change[14] during the Nazi era, without any compelling overall interpretive framework.[15] Film has expressed many of these shifts, one way or the other. The producer and director Edgar Reitz complained that NBC's *Holocaust* had stolen German memory. In response, he produced *Heimat* which may well have stolen the victims' memory. Then came Lanzmann's *Shoah*. *Heimat* may eventually push away *Shoah*; *Shoah* may be too unbearable to neutralize *Heimat*. Almost of necessity, the aesthetic enticement to remember the "Heimat" will prevail over the ethical imperative of remembering the "Shoah."

Turning to the historical or testimonial discourse of the victims, one encounters defenses that are not always *outwardly* different from what is perceptible on the German historical scene. Such similarity covers, however, totally different positions.

The 15 or 20 years of "latency" that followed the war in regard to talking or writing about the Shoah, particularly in the United States, should not be equated with massive repression exclusively, in contradistinction to the German scene. The silence did not exist *within* the survivor community. It was maintained in relation to the outside world, and was often imposed by shame, the shame of telling a story that must appear unbelievable, and was, in any case, entirely out of tune with surrounding society. The silence was breached, especially in Israel, by the debates from 1951 on concerning the reparations agreement with Germany, the Kastner trial, and finally Eichmann's capture and trial. These provided intense moments of emotional upheaval in a context dominated by the contrary currents of vulnerable awareness and steadfast avoidance, both in the national and the private domain.

Against this background, the more sustained silence of the intellectuals, and particularly the historians, must be mentioned. The most renowned Jewish historians of the post-war period did not allude to the Shoah during the 1940s and 1950s, or for that matter at any time later on. Like their German counterparts, Felix Gilbert and Lewis Namier became temporarily experts on Nazi diplomacy and strategy. Hans Rosenberg kept to nineteenth-century German social and economic history, and at Columbia, Franz Neumann, the celebrated author of *Behemoth*, tried to dissuade Raul Hilberg from writing his dissertation on the extermination of the Jews of Europe.[16] "Auschwitz" as such – not other facets of Nazism – seemed out of bounds. In their references to the Shoah, Theodor Adorno, Hannah Arendt, and, obviously, Salo Baron were exceptions within the wider Jewish intellectual landscape, as were the specialists at YIVO in New York, those working in Israel, or self-taught historians such as Leon Poliakov in France and Gerald Reitlinger in England. As for some of the best interpreters of modern German history, their silence or casual reference to the Holocaust is a chapter in itself.

The fragmentation of the historical field that characterizes current German historical writing on the Nazi epoch also appears, though somewhat differently, in Jewish historiography. Jewish historians too seem to be at a loss to produce an overall history of the extermination of the Jews of Europe that is not a mere textbook presentation, or an analysis of the internal cogs and wheels of the destruction machinery, or a compendium of separate monographs. The "Final Solution" in its epoch has not yet found its historian; and the problem cannot be reduced to a mere technical issue.

A closer look indicates that after the initial period of silence, and with the exclusion of ideologically dominated historiography, most historians approaching the subject have dealt either with descriptions of the background or with narrations of the Shoah, but never, to my knowledge, with an *integrated* approach to both. There may be several unconscious motivations for this division of historical labor, chiefly among historians who were contemporaries of the Nazi epoch. Their emotional and intellectual life was marked by largely unbridged ruptures, whether in terms of direct experience or of sudden awareness: these ruptures (we could use the concept of deep memory in an attenuated sense) reappear in various facets of their work, in more ways than can be dealt with here. As for the following generation, its work seems to stay close to the patterns set by its predecessors. In short, notwithstanding the immense effort of documentary and monographic research and straightforward textbook presentation, historical interpretation, by Jewish historians, is still caught between hasty ideological closure (such as the "catastrophe and redemption" theme) and a paralysis of attempts at global interpretation. For almost fifty years now, notwithstanding so much additional factual knowledge, we have faced surplus meaning or blankness, with little interpretive or representational advance. This evaluation applies also to my own work.

On Working Through

In *Beyond the Pleasure Principle*, Freud defines as traumatic "any excitations from outside which are powerful enough to break through the protective shield (*Reizschutz*)." He continues: "It seems to me that the concept of trauma necessarily implies a connection of this kind with a breach in an otherwise efficacious barrier against stimuli. Such an event as an external trauma is bound to provoke a disturbance on a large scale in the functioning of the organism's energy and to set in motion every possible defense measure."[17]

Aside from being aware and trying to overcome the defenses already mentioned, the major difficulty of historians of the Shoah, when confronted with echoes of the traumatic past, is to keep some measure of balance between the emotion recurrently breaking through "the protective shield" and a numbness that protects this very shield. In fact, the numbing or distancing effect of intellectual work on the Shoah is unavoidable and necessary; the recurrence of strong emotional impact is also often unforeseeable and necessary.

"Working through" means, first, being aware of both tendencies, allowing for a measure of balance between the two whenever possible. But neither the protective numbing nor the disruptive emotion is entirely accessible to consciousness. A telling example is Raul Hilberg's magisterial work.[18] More than most of us, he has succeeded in balancing the necessary distancing or "numbness" with elements of intense emotion. But the full impact of this emotion has on occasion been deflected toward overcritical comments on the behavior of the victims.

A main aspect of working through, however, lies elsewhere: it entails, for the historian, the imperative of rendering as truthful an account as documents and testimonials will allow, *without giving in to the temptation of closure*. Closure in this case would represent an obvious avoidance of what remains indeterminate, elusive and opaque. Put differently, working through means facing the dilemma which, according to Jean-François Lyotard, we try to escape in the face of "Auschwitz": "The silence," writes Lyotard, "that surrounds the phrase 'Auschwitz was the extermination camp,' is not a state of mind (*état d'âme*), it is a sign that something remains to be phrased which is not, which is not determined."[19]

The Presence of Commentary

The self-awareness of the historian of the Nazi epoch or the Shoah is essential. Such self-awareness should itself be accessible to critical reading. It seems therefore that this difficult historical quest imposes the sporadic but forceful presence of commentary. Whether this commentary is built into the narrative structure of a history or developed as a separate, superimposed text is a matter of choice, but the voice of the commentator must be clearly heard. The commentary should disrupt the facile linear progression of the narration, introduce alternative interpretations, question any partial conclusion, withstand the need for closure. Because of the necessity of some form of narrative sequence in the writing of history, such commentary may introduce splintered or constantly recurring refractions of a traumatic past by using any number of different vantage points.

The dimension added by commentary may allow for an integration of the so-called "mythic memory" of the victims within the overall representation of this past, without it becoming an "obstacle" for "rational historiography." For instance, whereas the historical narrative may have to stress the ordinary aspects of everyday life during most of the twelve years of the Nazi epoch, the "voice-over" of the victims' memories may puncture such normality, at least at the level of commentary.

The reintroduction of individual memory into the overall representation of the epoch also implies the use of direct or indirect expressions of contemporary individual experience. *Working through means confronting the individual voice* in a field dominated by political decisions and administrative decrees which neutralize the concreteness of despair and death. The *Alltagsgeschichte* of German society has its necessary shadow: the *Alltagsgeschichte* of its victims. In a letter of June 1939, Walter Benjamin mentioned the following item: the Viennese gas company had stopped supplying its Jewish clients, as precisely the most important consumers were using the gas to commit suicide and consequently left their bills unpaid.[20]

Commentary does not lead in any way to "the use of fact and fiction, document and imaginative reconstruction, to ponder how history is made."[21] But working through does mean a confrontation with the starkest factual information which loses its historical weight when merely taken as data. Raul Hilberg mentions the report sent by the commander of a German unit which entered the Russian city of Mariopol in 1941. Without a single additional word it stated that "The 8,000 Jews of Mariopol had been shot."[22] Working through means testing the limits of necessary and ever-defeated imagination.

Tentative Summation

Whether one considers the Shoah as an exceptional event or as belonging to a wider historical category does not affect the possibility of drawing from it a universally valid significance. The difficulty appears when this statement is reversed. No universal lesson seems to require reference to the Shoah to be fully comprehended. The Shoah carries an *excess*, and this excess is the "something which remains to be phrased which is not, which is not determined."

At the individual level a redemptive closure (comforting or healing in effect), desirable as it would be, seems largely impossible. On the collective level, however, regardless of the present salience of these events, there can hardly be any doubt that the passage of time will erase the "excess." Such erasure will, most probably, characterize the work of the majority of historians as well, perhaps because of what has been aptly called the "desublimization" of the discipline.[23] Thus, if we make allowance for some sort of ritualized form of commemoration, already in place, we may foresee, in the public domain, a tendency towards closure without resolution, but closure nonetheless.

There are two potential exceptions to this bleak forecast: notwithstanding present patterns of historiography, an extension of historical awareness may be attempted, possibly along some of the lines previously suggested. There is also a growing sensitivity to literature and art. The voices of the second generation are as powerful as the best work produced by contemporaries of the Nazi epoch. This sensitivity is not limited to the community of the victims. Sometimes it appears in unexpected cultural contexts, as in the case of an Indian novelist who at this very time is addressing himself to the Shoah. It may well be that for some the trauma, the insuperable moral outrage, the riddle whose decoding never seems to surrender a fully comprehensible text, may present an ongoing emotional and intellectual challenge. However, I would venture to suggest that even if new forms of historical narrative were to develop, or new modes of representation, and even if literature and art were to probe the past from unexpected vantage points, the opaqueness of "deep memory" would not be entirely dispelled. "Working through" may ultimately signify, in Maurice Blanchot's words, "to keep watch over absent meaning."[24]

Liberation

Abraham Sutzkever

How and with what will you fill
Your goblet on the day of Liberation?
In your joy, are you ready to feel
The dark scream of your past
Where skulls of days congeal
In a bottomless pit?

You will look for a key to fit
Your jammed locks.
Like bread you will bite the streets
And think: better the past.
And time will drill you quietly
Like a cricket caught in a fist.

And your memory will be like
An old buried city.
Your eternal gaze will crawl
Like a mole, like a mole —

Vilna Ghetto, February 14, 1943

Notes

Chapter 1   Introduction: Darkness Visible

1 Although the term "posthistoire" is recent (and far less common than its competitor "post-modern"), Lutz Niethammer has already assembled traces of its own history in *Posthistoire: Ist die Geschichte zur Ende?* (Rohwohlt, Hamburg, 1989). His concluding remarks have been translated as "Afterthoughts on posthistoire," *History and Memory*, 1 (1989), pp. 27–55.

2 Giovanni Leoni, see below, p. 211; James E. Young, "The counter-monument: memory against itself in Germany today," *Critical Inquiry*, 18, 2 (1992), p. 273. Dwork and Van Pelt, in their essay here, describe an architectural project of 1954 that aimed to defeat the inert and aggrandized space of monumental sites by turning Auschwitz into a monument to oblivion – one that would have, in effect, cursed those grounds and left them to become more of a ruin. Another paradoxical solution is proposed in Leoni's essay. "[O]ne seeks to restore to the victims not so much a voice as an image, to 'embody' them in the midst of an architecture that expresses the oppressor's will." Young, in his essay on the counter-monument cited above, describes actual attempts to build a self-destructing memorial. George Mosse's *Fallen Soldiers: reshaping the memory of the world war* (Oxford University Press, New York, 1990) includes a superb account of the relation of monuments to memory as the cult of the war dead – shared by all European nations – reaches its apogee in Nazi Germany and then fades after the Second World War. The issue of monumentalism converges on that of architecture in general: for a non-Holocaust related discussion, see Denis Hollier, *Against Architecture: the writings of Georges Bataille* (MIT Press, Cambridge, MA, 1989).

3 "Don't take your daughter to the extermination camp", *Tikkun*, January–February (1987).

4 For Friedlander's earlier analysis of the inadequacy (perhaps intrinsic) of historical language in the face of extreme events and above all of "Ausch-

witz," as well as the different though related inadequacy of literature and film, see *Reflections of Nazism: an essay on kitsch and death* (French publication 1982, English translation, Harper & Row, New York, 1984). Also Friedlander, ed., *Probing the Limits of Representation: Nazism and the "Final Solution"* (Harvard University Press, Cambridge, MA, 1992). The historian's "transferential relation" to his subject and the way it is worked through are a major concern of Dominick LaCapra: see, inter alia, his essay on the Historians' Debate in the Friedlander volume on the *Limits of Representation*.

5 Wieviorka suggests that this commonplace notion simply shifted responsibility for the silence of the *historians* onto the deportees.

6 Saul Friedlander, *When Memory Comes* (Farrar Strauss Giroux, New York, 1979), pp. 155–6.

7 *Le Juif Imaginaire* (Seuil, Paris, 1980). Jonathan Boyarin's *Polish Jews in Paris: the ethnography of memory* (Indiana University Press, Bloomington and Indianapolis, 1991) complements Finkielkraut's understanding of cultural discontinuity. Basing himself on the elderly rather than, as Finkielkraut does, the maturing generation (on the Paris *landsmannschaftn*), Boyarin not only records their way of life but provisionally substitutes for the missing generational link who has to "assume" – take upon himself or herself – the status of participant-observer. "Commemoration requires filiation" (p. 151). A tension remains, of course, between his role as ethnopersona and as American Jew. For why is this American in Paris if not because he needs the *landsmannschaftn*: in his own country these elders are not as cohesive or "hypercommunalized." For a sensitive inside view and portrait of the children of survivors, see Helen Epstein, *Children of the Holocaust: conversations with sons and daughters of survivors* (Putnam, New York, 1979).

8 See Saul Friedlander, "Shoah: between memory and history," *The Jerusalem Quarterly*, 53 (1990), and Tom Segev, *The Seventh Million: The Israelis and the Holocaust* (New York: Hill and Wang, 1993).
   For memorial politics, see also my article on Bitburg in the 1985 *Yearbook* of the *Jewish Encyclopedia* and the Introduction to *Bitburg in Moral and Political Perspective* (Indiana University Press, Bloomington, Ind., 1986).

9 The most thorough account of negationism, Pierre Vidal-Naquet's *Les assassins de la mémoire* (La Découverte, Paris, 1987), has now been translated (and with an excellent foreword) by J. Mehlman. See *Assassins of Memory: essays on the denial of the holocaust* (Columbia University Press, New York, 1992).

10 A balanced review of the issue is given by Michael R. Marrus, "The use and misuse of the Holocaust," in *Lessons and Legacies: the meaning of the Holocaust in a changing world*, ed. Peter Hayes (Northwestern University Press, Evanston, 1991).

11 David Tracy's call for Christian theology to continue its "return to history" after the Shoah goes in the same direction; and he describes this as a

"postmodern" development. I see it rather as a strong reaction to the post-modern and its "ether of discourse" (Charles Maier). The meaning of the term post-modern may differ according to different disciplines; it has not fully crystallized.

12 *La transparence du mal: essai sur les phénomènes extrêmes* (Gallimard, Paris, 1990). The basic argument is already found in his earlier *Simulacres et simulation* (Gallilée, Paris, 1981). Its section on "Holocaust" begins: "Forgetting the extermination is part of the extermination, for that also bears on memory, history, the social, etc.".

13 Erich Auerbach's *Mimesis*, a distinctly European book written in exile and published in 1946, may also derive some of its appeal from still being on the far side of that rift: it foresees something that has already happened.

14 I develop this point in "The Book of the Destruction," in *Probing the Limits of Representation: Nazism and the "Final Solution"*, ed. Saul Friedlander (Harvard University Press, Cambridge, MA, 1992), pp. 330–1.

15 See Alain Finkielkraut, *La mémoire vaine: du crime contre l'humanité* (Gallimard, Paris, 1989). Gouri's essay in this volume also understands the necessity of the Eichmann trial in this light.

16 Yosef Hayim Yerushalmi, *Zakhor: Jewish history and Jewish memory* (University of Washington Press, Seattle and London, 1982), chapter 4. For a more sanguine view of the rupture between history and "collective" memory, see Michael Kammen's massive and magisterial *Mystic Chords of Memory: the transformation of tradition in American culture* (Knopf, New York, 1991). A thoughtful overview of "Can there be too much memory?" is offered by Charles Maier's "Epilogue" to *The Unmasterable Past: history, Holocaust, and German national identity* (Harvard University Press, Cambridge, MA, 1988). Further scholarly considerations of the issue can be found in *Kultur und Gedächtnis*, eds J. Assmann and T. Hölscher (Suhrkamp, Frankfurt a/M, 1988), *Mnemosyne: Formen und Funktionen der kulturellen Erinnerung*, eds A. Assmann and D. Harth (Fischer, Frankfurt a/M, 1991), esp. pp. 342–9, *Usages de l'oubli* (Seuil, Paris, 1988), with contributions by Yerushalmi and others; also Amos Funkenstein, "Collective memory and historical consciousness," *History and Memory*, 1, 1 (1989). The notion of a collective memory is indebted, of course, to Maurice Halbwach's *La mémoire collective*, published posthumously in 1950. Halbwach already anticipates the history/memory split. "General history starts only when tradition ends and the social memory is fading or breaking up."

17 *Cosmos and History: the myth of the eternal return* (1949), tr. Willard R. Trask (Pantheon, New York, 1954). What Saturnalia remain can be described as feasts of memorization, and embrace one's entire life, as in Talmudic scholarship. The contemporary quiz show, with its in-built recognition of contingency or "Wheel of Fortune," is a trivia feast and a conspicuous consumption of memory compared to such scholarship.

18 Cf. *Usages de l'oubli*, cited in note 16. Recent sociology has done significant

work on institutional or systematic forgetting and generally on "the rhetorical organization of remembering and forgetting." See *Collective Remembering*, eds David Middleton and Derek Edwards (Newbury Park, London;
Sage Publications, New Delhi, 1990). British and American sociology often
combine Halbwachs with F. C. Bartlett's *Remembering* (Cambridge University Press, Cambridge, 1932), because, though the latter continues to
emphasize the individual, he studies "remembering as a form of constructive
activity, emphasizing that memory is not the retrieval of stored information,
but the putting together of a claim about past states of affairs by means
of a framework of shared cultural understanding." See Alan Radley's essay
in *Collective Remembering*.

19 See Pierre Nora, "Between memory and history: *Les lieux de mémoire*,"
Representations, 26, spring (1989).

20 For the literary critic, see, e.g., James Young, *The Texture of Memory:
Holocaust memorials and meaning in Europe, Israel and America* (Yale
University Press, New Haven, 1993). Young seeks to break down any
monolithic notion of collective memory in favor of a "collected memory,"
that is, a socially constructed process that enables us, through shared
forms and spaces, to attribute collective meaning to memories that remain,
nevertheless, personal and disparate. For the historian, see Pierre Vidal-
Naquet, in *Les assassins de la mémoire* [Essays on Revisionism] (La Découverte, Paris, 1987), partly translated in *Democracy*, April (1987); and
Hayden White, *The Content of the Form: narrative discourse and historical
representation* (Johns Hopkins University Press, Baltimore, 1987), chapter
3.

21 See Martin Broszat/Saul Friedlander, "A controversy about the historicization of National Socialism," *New German Critique*, 44, spring–summer
(1988).

22 An attempt has begun to analyze cultural discourse itself, in its over two-
century-old vacillation between forms of nationalism and universalism. But
this attempt, revealing that no group which aspired to autonomy and a
place (homeland) of its own was free of a discriminatory and if not Nazi-
like then violent and self-exalting rhetoric, seems to compromise our quest
for an absolute post-Holocaust fixing of blame. In the difficult closing
pages of his article on "The force of law," Jacques Derrida suggests (in
the name of Benjamin, but perhaps also in the name of deconstruction),
that our judgmental, historiographical and interpretive terms are still
"homogenous with the space in which Nazism developed up to and including the final solution." Is there a "complicity" between the discourses we
honor, or tolerate, and the worst of these, the murderous discourse of
Nazism? See "Deconstruction and the Possibility of Justice," *Cardozo Law
Review*, 11 (1990), pp. 1,042–5.

23 Alain Finkielkraut speaks of a "scenario of the lost illusion," which is the
myth into which the demystifiers lapse, or the object of their automatic
respect as they vow never to be deceived again. See his "La mémoire et

l'histoire" in *L'avenir d'une négation: Réflexion sur la question du génocide* (Seuil, Paris, 1982), p. 97. Oliver Stone could be said to create just such a scenario in his movie *JFK* though he calls it an "outlaw history" or "counter-myth." Historical films like *JFK* are complex symptoms expressing the fact, as Anton Kaes has observed, that certain photographic images are everywhere, "impossible to topple and destroy." These images take on a life of their own in the collective memory until the originating historical event is displaced into a movie myth, or what Baudrillard (in his earlier book on simulacra) defines as "models of a real without origin or reality: a hyperreal." See Kaes, "History and film: public memory in the age of electronic dissemination," *History and Memory*, 2, 1, (1990), and his epilogue "History, memory and film" in *From "Hitler" to "Heimat": the return of history as film* (Harvard University Press, Cambridge, MA, 1989).

24 Cf. Ellen S. Fine, "The absent memory" in *Writing and the Holocaust*, ed. Berel Lang (Holmes & Meier, New York, 1988). Raymond Federman writes in his novel *To Whom It May Concern* (Fiction Collective Two, Norman, Ill., 1990), which explores that absence in two children who survived the war but lost their families in the Holocaust: "the void of their lives can only find its fulfilment in the circumstances of that void . . . [Their] remembrance is of an absence, and they have made a lifetime occasion of it." Federman, at the same time, generalizes the "circumstances of that void" to challenge, in the name of (postmodernist) fiction, what he calls "the paralyzing holiness of realism." Norma Rosen's novel *Touching Evil* extends what she names "witnesses-through-the-imagination" to non-Jews. See also her "The second life of Holocaust imagery" in *Accidents of Influence: Writing as Woman and a Jew in America* (State University of New York Press, Albany, NY, 1992).

25 Comparing Pagis and Amir Gilboa suggests that there is no absolute divide between the representational modes of the first and second generation. One of the finest second-generation poems, dating from the early 1950s, is Gilboa's "Isaac." Its ellipses express the "absent memory" of the son who went to Israel before the Holocaust and, many years later, recalls the father(s) who stayed and perished. Rarely has a short poem succeeded more in conveying, through a powerful modification of the Akedah story, but without any explicit historical reference to the Shoah, a youngster's terror in having to face that event, and the accompanying fear that it may have amputated his generation.

26 "Writing after Auschwitz," in *Two States – One Nation?* (Harcourt Brace Jovanovich, New York, 1990). Moshe Kupferman's painterly minimalism also seems to explore those "shades of gray": here the art of a survivor has chosen a non-figurative mode, works on paper that create a different kind of "newspaper," that evoke the fragility of paper as it bears its always "new" constructions without the full palette of painting. Where Adorno can talk of "damaged life" and Grass of "damaged language", it is harder to conceive of "damaged color," which is one reason Grass celebrates grey.

Kitaj's "Varschreibt!," reproduced in this volume, faces in addition the absence of a strong imaging tradition in Judaism.

27 Cf. Friedlander, in this volume, p. 261: "Whether this commentary is built into the narrative structure or developed as a separate, superimposed text, is a matter of choice, but the voice of the commentator must be clearly heard."

28 Charlotte Salomon's operetta in pictures, although bravely concentrating on the *normal* joys and pains that link her exile to her previous life – "a little bit of love / a few rules / a young girl / a large bed / after so much dying / is this a life" also recovers something "barbaric" from a popular genre and transfers it quite starkly to painting.

29 Dan Pagis, *Points of Departure*, tr. Stephen Mitchell, (Jewish Publication Society of America, Philadelphia, 1981). Quoted by permission. The allusion to Maimonides's *Yigdal* is noted by Robert Alter in his introduction to the volume.

Chapter 2   On Testimony

1 Claude Lanzmann, *Shoah* (Random House, New York, 1985), p. 3. This work contains the complete text, both spoken words and subtitles, of the film.

2 Rudolf Vrba and Alan Bestic, *I Cannot Forgive* (Sidgwick and Jackson and Anthony Gibbs and Phillips, London, 1963).

3 Gitta Sereny, *Into That Darkness: from mercy killing to mass murder* (André Deutsch Ltd, London, 1974).

4 We are using here the terminology of Raul Hilberg. Chelmno Sobibor, Belzec and Treblinka were not KZ, concentration camps (where, although held in abominable conditions, the prisoners were not intended to be exterminated). They had no facilities for keeping the prisoners alive and working, if only to exterminate them (except for the small number of Jews who were forced to participate in the extermination process). Very few survived to give testimony. For example, there are no survivors from Belzec.

5 The only category of deportee that did not testify, to my knowledge, was the common criminal. There is no testimony in the post-war years by the many people deported for participation in the black market or prostitution.

6 In the United States, "the literature of the Holocaust" includes the works of all victims of the Second World War, judging only by those authors translated from the French: David Rousset and Anna Langfus, Robert Antelme and Piotr Rawicz or Charlotte Delbo. If Charlotte Delbo was confronted at Auschwitz with the extermination of the Jews, this was not the case for David Rousset or Robert Antelme, who deal with the concentration camp system but not the genocide.

7 Abraham Lewin, *A Cup of Tears: a diary of the Warsaw ghetto* (Basil Blackwell in association with the Institute for Polish–Jewish Studies, Oxford, 1988), p. 97.

8   Emanuel Ringelblum, *Chronique du ghetto de Varsovie (Chronicle of the Warsaw Ghetto)* (Robert Laffont, Paris, 1978), p. 21.

9   In Michel Borwicz, *L'insurrection du ghetto de Varsovie* (Gallimard/Julliard, Paris, 1966), p. 10.

10 Charlotte Wardi, *Le génocide dans la fiction romanesque (Genocide in the Novel)* (PUF, Paris, 1986), p. 34.

11 There was no "return of the deportees" but rather individual returns, via multiple itineraries, spread out between March and June, 1945, with some arriving even much later. Primo Levi, in *The Reawakening: long march home*, recounts his own return: a year passed between the Red Army's liberation of the several thousand prisoners at Auschwitz who had not been evacuated and his return to Italy.

12 Robert Antelme, "Témoignage du camp et poésie," *Le Patriote Résistant*, 53 (May 15, 1948), p. 5.

13 Jean Norton Cru, *Témoins: essai d'analyse et de critique des souvenirs de combattants édités en Français de 1915 à 1928* [*Witnesses: an analysis and critique of soldiers' testimonies published in French between 1915 and 1928*] (Paris: les Etincelles, 1929). See also an abridged version by the author, *Du Témoignage (On Testimony)* (NRF, Paris, 1930).

14 Maurice Rieuneau, *Guerre et révolution dans le roman français, 1919–1939* (*War and Revolution in the French Novel, 1919–1939*) (Klincksieck, Paris, 1974), p. 20.

15 Primo Levi, *If This is a Man* (Orion Press, New York, 1959), p. 64.

16 Milan Kundera, *The Book of Laughter and Forgetting*, tr. Michael Henry Heim (Knopf, New York, 1980), p. 91.

17 Pierre Francès-Rousseau, *Intact aux yeux du monde* (Hachette, Paris, 1987), p. 53.

18 Three transports of non-Jews were deported to Auschwitz. The deportees did not undergo selection and were transferred to Buchenwald or Ravensbrück. See especially Charlotte Delbo, *Le transport du 24 janvier* (*The Transport of January 24*) (Minuit, Paris, 1965).

19 Jean Puissant, *La colline sans oiseaux. Quatorze mois à Buchenwald* (Editions du Rond-Point, Paris, 1945). On Ravensbrück, the following were written in part or entirely at the camp: Dr Paulette Don Zimmet, *Les conditions d'existence et l'état sanitaire dans les camps de concentration de femmes déportées en Allemagne* (*Living Conditions and Sanitation in the Concentration Camps of Women Deported to Germany*) (Impr. Franco-Suisse, Thèse-Genève, Ambilly-Annemasse (Hte-Savoie), 1946); Germaine Tillion, *Ravensbrück* (Editions de la Baconnière, Neuchâtel, 1946); Simone Saint-Clair, *Ravensbrück, l'enfer des femmes* (*Ravensbrück: Women's Hell*) (Tallandier, Paris, 1945).

20 Marcel Conversy, *Quinze mois à Buchenwald* (*Fifteen Months at Buchenwald*) (Editions du milieu du monde, Geneva, 1945) and l'*Enclos des hommes perdus* (Sté d'Edit, Savoyarde, Thonon-les-Bains, 1946).

21 Interview with Simone Weil, June 1990.

22 The "Nacht und Nebel" or "Night and Fog" decree designates simultaneously a judicial procedure and a mode of imprisonment: detention in view of a judgment or in application of a judgment that falls initially under military law and later under civil law. The conditions of prisoners classified NN were not like those of other inmates, particularly as regards the secrecy surrounding their fates. In no case, as writers have often claimed, were they immediately destined to extermination. See in particular Joseph de la Martinière, *Les NN: Le Décret et la procédure Nacht und Nebel* (*NN: The Nacht und Nebel Decree and Procedure*) (FNDIRP, Paris, 1989).

23 Jean Puissant, *La Colline sans oiseaux*, p. 89.

24 Primo Levi, *The Drowned and the Saved* (Summit Books, New York, 1986), p. 104.

25 On this subject see Annette Wieviorka, "Indicible ou inaudible? La déportation: premiers récits" ("Inexpressible or Inaudible? First Accounts of the Deportation") *Pardès*, 9–10 (1989), pp. 23–59.

26 Annette Wieviorka and Itzhok Niborski, *Les Livres du souvenir: Mémoriaux juifs de Pologne* (*Memory Books: Jewish Memorials from Poland*) (Gallimard, Paris, 1983).

27 David Roskies, *Against the Apocalypse: responses to catastrophe in modern Jewish culture* (Harvard University Press, Cambridge, MA, 1984) and "La Bibliothèque de la catastrophe juive" ("The Library of the Jewish catastrophe") *Pardès*, 9–10 (1989), pp. 199–211.

28 Jacqueline Risset, introduction to *L'Enfer de Dante* (*Dante's Inferno*) (Flammarion, Paris, 1987), p. 7.

Chapter 3 The Library of Jewish Catastrophe

A version of this essay appeared as "La Bibliothèque de la catastrophe juive," *Pardès*, 9, 10 (1989), pp. 199–210.

1 H. J. Zimmels shows how the European rabbis applied this legal term to the unfolding Nazi terror. See "How far can the Nazi Holocaust be termed 'shaath ha-shemad' (religious persecution)?" in *The Echo of the Holocaust in Rabbinic Literature* (Marla, London, 1976), chapter 7. *Bish'at hahashmada* is my own coinage.

2 All subsequent quotations are drawn from *The Literature of Destruction: Jewish responses to catastrophe*, ed. David G. Roskies (Jewish Publication Society, Philadelphia, 1989).

3 For more on this epoch-making poem, see Alan Mintz, *Hurban: responses to catastrophe in Hebrew literature* (Columbia University Press, New York, 1984), chapter 4; and David G. Roskies, *Against the Apocalypse: responses to catastrophe in modern Jewish culture* (Harvard University Press, Cambridge, MA, 1984), chapter 4.

4 Bialik's commanding presence in the Nazi ghettos and concentration camps deserves a separate study. For some preliminary evidence, see Roskies,

Against the Apocalypse, chapters 8–9 and two remarkable documents from the Lodz ghetto, Simcha Bunem Shayevitsh's "Spring 1942," and Jozef Zelkowicz's "In these nightmarish days," *Lodz Ghetto: inside a community under siege*, ed. Alan Adelson and Robert Lapides (Viking, New York, 1989), pp. 250–62, 320. Shayevitsh's poem is both a continuation and parody of Bialik's "In the City of Slaughter." Likewise, the intertext of Zelkowicz's "Son of Man, Go Out into the Streets" is Bialik's poem.

5 Abraham Lewin, *A Cup of Tears: a diary of the Warsaw ghetto*, ed. Antony Polonsky (Basil Blackwell, Oxford, 1988), entry for July 26, 1942. Jewish literary and biblical references in Lewin's diary, including this one, are not identified in Polonsky's otherwise scrupulous edition.

6 For excerpts in English, see *The Literature of Destruction*, sect. 53 and my *The Dybbuk and Other Writings by S. Ansky* (Schocken Books, New York, 1992).

7 The Akedah or Binding of Isaac on Mt Moriah became the archetype of individual sacrifice. Hurban signifies the Destructions of the Temple in Jerusalem in 587 BCE and 70 CE and became the archetype of national catastrophe. *Kiddush Hashem*, the Sanctification of God's Name, is the Hebrew term for martyrdom, eventually defined as an act carried out in public during times of religious persecution. For a fuller discussion, see Roskies, *Against the Apocalypse*, chapter 2.

8 See *Against the Apocalypse*, chapter 10.

9 Cited by Zosa Szajkowski in his epilogue to Elias Tcherikower, *Di ukrainer pogromen in yor 1919* (YIVO, New York, 1965), p. 333. Szajkowski is my source on the Ukrainian pogroms.

10 See Max Weinreich, *Der veg tsu undzer yugnt: yesoydes, metodn, problemen fun yidisher yugnt-forshung* (YIVO, Vilna, 1935); Moses Kligsberg, *Child and Adolescent Behavior Under Stress: an analytic topical guide to a collection of autobiographies of Jewish young men and women in Poland (1932–1939) in the Possession of the YIVO Institute for Jewish Research* (YIVO, New York, 1965). On the revolutionary import of the autobiography contest in the history of the genre, see Marcus Mosley, "Jewish autobiography in Eastern Europe: the prehistory of a literary genre" (unpublished Ph.D. dissertation, Oxford University, 1990), chapter 7.

11 See Ringelblum's history and evaluation of the archive written in December 1943 in *The Literature of Destruction*, ed. David G. Roskies, sect. 71 – incorrectly dated January 1943.

12 For sample questionnaires, monograph outlines and other research projects of the Oyneg Shabes archive, see *To Live With Honor and Die With Honor! . . .: selected documents from the Warsaw ghetto underground archives*, ed. Joseph Kermish, Yad Vashem, Jerusalem, 1986.

13 Two memory lapses: Hannah's prayer is recorded in 1 Sam. 1, not in Judges. Eli did not drive Hannah from the Temple.

14 In 1988, Yad Vashem published *To Live with Honor and Die with Honor! . . .: selected documents from the Warsaw ghetto underground*

archives, ed. Joseph Kermish. The uneven quality of its translations and annotations as well as the idiosyncratic selection of materials render this 790-page volume almost unusable. In 1988, the YIVO Institute in New York published *The Documents of the Lodz Ghetto: an inventory of the Nachman Zonabend Collection*, compiled by Marek Web. The YIVO has also announced the publication in English of Herman Kruk's *Diary of the Vilna Ghetto*, tr. Barbara Hashav (Yale University Press, New Haven, 1993). Ber Mark's *The Scrolls of Auschwitz*, tr. from the Hebrew by Sharon Neemani and adapted from the Yiddish original (Am Oved, Tel Aviv, 1985) may be read in conjunction with Zalmen Gradowski's "The Czech transport," in Roskies, *The Literature of Destruction*, sect. 93.

Chapter 4   Voices from the Killing Ground

Bibliography

Auerbach, Rachel, "Yizkor, 1943," tr. Leonard Wolf, reprinted in *The Literature of Destruction*, ed. David G. Roskies, (Jewish Publication Society, Philadelphia, 1988), pp. 459–64.

Czerniakow, Adam, *The Warsaw Diary of Adam Czerniakow*, ed. Raul Hilberg, Stanislaw Staron, and Josef Kermisz, tr. Stanislaw Staron and the staff of Yad Vashem, (Stein & Day, New York, 1979).

Delbo, Charlotte, *Auschwitz et Après*, (Editions de minuit, Paris, 1970).

Dobroszycki, Lucjan (ed.), *The Chronicle of the Lodz Ghetto*, tr. Richard Lourie, Joachim Neugroschel and others, (Yale University Press, New Haven, 1984).

Fink, Ida, *A Scrap of Time: stories*, tr. Madeline Levine and Francine Prose, (Pantheon, New York, 1987).

Goldin, Leyb, "Chronicle of a single day," tr. Elinor Robinson, reprinted in *The Literature of Destruction*, ed. David G. Roskies, (Jewish Publication Society, Philadelphia, 1988), pp. 424–34.

Huberband, Shimon, *Kiddush Hashem: Jewish religious and cultural life in Poland during the Holocaust*, ed. Jeffrey S. Gurock and Robert S. Hirt, tr. David E. Fishman, (Yeshiva University Press, New York, 1987).

Kaplan, Chaim A., *The Warsaw Diary of Chaim A. Kaplan*, ed. Abraham I. Katsch, (Collier Books, New York, 1965).

Korczak, Janusz, *The Warsaw Ghetto Memoirs of Janusz Korczak*, tr. E. P. Kulawiec, (University Press of America, Washington, DC, 1978).

Levi, Primo, *The Drowned and the Saved*, tr. Raymond Rosenthal, (Summit, New York, 1986).

Ringelblum, Emmanuel, *Notes from the Warsaw Ghetto*, tr. Jacob Sloan, (McGraw Hill, New York, 1958).

— *Oneg Shabbes*, tr. Elinor Robinson, reprinted in *The Literature of Destruction*, ed. David G. Roskies, (Jewish Publication Society, Philadelphia, 1988), pp. 387–98.

Semprun, Jorge, *The Long Voyage*, tr. Richard Seaver, (Grove Press, New York, 1963).

Chapter 5   Jean Améry as Witness

1   Abraham I. Katsch, ed., *The Warsaw Diary of Chaim A. Kaplan* (Collier Books, New York, 1973), p. 30.
2   The words are Himmler's, addressed to a group of SS officers on October 4, 1943; quoted in Lucy Dawidowicz, *A Holocaust Reader* (Behrman House, New York, 1976), p. 133.
3   Translated by Sidney Rosenfeld and Stella P. Rosenfeld (Schocken Books, New York, 1990). All references to this book are to this edition and are cited by page number. The original German title is *Jenseits von Schuld und Sühne.*
4   As Sidney Rosenfeld, one of his American translators, described his situation: "Especially toward the end, he was downcast by increasing manifestations of a right-wing authoritarian restoration in German public life, along with the resurgence of antisemitism; his estrangement from the New Left, in whom his hopes had rested for a democratic Germany, had grown still more acute; the absorption of the Nazi past in its singularity and irreducibility into a universal theory of Fascism and totalitarianism, something he had foreseen in *At the Mind's Limits*, but in a still somewhat removed future, was becoming reality before his eyes. The grotesqueness of the Maidanek trial in Düsseldorf, where the witnesses, survivors of the Nazi death camp, were subjected to derision by reactionary defense lawyers, filled him with bitterness. His response to the debate on the Statute of Limitations was a terse, poignant request not to the parliamentarians but to German society not to condemn the last remaining *victims* by morally exonerating their former torturers and thereby vindicating the atrocities. He was beset by a feeling that he was speaking into the wind, and this led to a despondent anger, growing resignation, and finally indifference." (*At the Mind's Limits*, p. 110).
5   In addition to *At the Mind's Limits*, only one other of Améry's books is available in English translation: *Radical Humanism: Selected Essays*, tr. Sidney Rosenfeld and Stella P. Rosenfeld (Indiana University Press, Bloomington, 1984). Among the untranslated works are *Über das Altern* (1969), a book on aging; *Unmeisterliche Wanderjahre* (1973), a work of autobiographical reflection that is largely a self-study of the growth of an intellectual; *Widersprüche*, a collection of essays; and *Hand an sich legen. Diskurs über den Freitod* (1976), on suicide. Améry also wrote two novels, *Lefeu oder der Abbruch* (1974) and *Charles Bovary, Landarzt* (1978). Three volumes of essays appeared posthumously: *Örtlichkeiten* (1980), *Bücher aus der Jugend unseres Jahrhunderts* (1981), and *Weiterleben – aber wie?* (1982).

6 Améry, *Radical Humanism*, p. 65.
7 Ibid., pp. 64–5.

Chapter 6   Remembering Survival

1 Joseph Brodsky, "The condition of exile," *The New York Review of Books* (January 21, 1988), p. 20.
2 Primo Levi, *The Drowned and the Saved* (Summit, New York, 1988), pp. 70–1.
3 Ibid., p. 100.
4 Testimony of Michael R., tape T-22. Fortunoff Video Archives for Holocaust Testimonies at Yale, quoted by permission.
5 Testimony of Peter C., tape T-838.
6 Testimony of Eva K., tape T-845.
7 Ibid.
8 Testimony of Abraham P., tape T-738.
9 Jorge Semprun, *What a Beautiful Sunday!*, tr. Alan Sheridan (Harcourt Brace Jovanovich, New York, 1982), pp. 61, 105.
10 Ibid., pp. 107, 130.
11 Testimony of Leon W., tape T-2.
12 Testimony of Martin R., tape T-166.
13 Ibid.
14 Testimony of George S., tape T-938.
15 Ibid.

Chapter 7   Christian Witness and the Shoah

1 I have developed these genre issues of narrative, confession and gospel, with the citation of the appropriate biblical scholarship, in "On reading the Scriptures theologically," in *Theology and Dialogue: essays in conversation with George Lindbeck*, ed. Bruce D. Marshall (University of Notre Dame Press, Notre Dame, Ind., 1990), pp. 35–69. Throughout this essay, in keeping with its "thought-experiment" genre, I will keep the endnotes minimal. For further bibliographical information (e.g., on hermeneutics), see David Tracy, *The Analogical Imagination: Christian theology and the context of pluralism* (Crossroad, New York, 1981); David Tracy, *Plurality and Ambiguity: hermeneutics, religion and hope* (Harper & Row, San Francisco, 1985).
2 The "re-Judaizing" of some Christian political theologies in Germany is largely due to the influence of Walter Benjamin (and his reflections on "dangerous memory"). See, for example, Johann Baptist Metz, *Faith in History and Society* (Crossroad, New York, 1980). For Benjamin, see Walter Benjamin, *Illuminations* (Schocken, New York, 1969).
3 Some of the consequences of this for Christian theology, are discussed in

David Tracy, "Religious values after the Holocaust: a Catholic view," in *Jews and Christians after the Holocaust*, ed. A. J. Peck (Fortress Press, Philadelphia, 1982), 82ff; David Tracy, "Foreword," in Arthur A. Cohen, *The Tremendum* (Crossroad, New York, 1981).

4 It is not insignificant that the major philosopher who has recovered a genuine notion of "otherness" as central ethically and, therefore, philosophically is the Jewish thinker Emmanuel Levinas.

5 For philosophical studies of the category "witness," see Jean Nabert, *Le Désir de Dieu* (Aubèc, Paris, 1966), esp. Book III, "Metaphysique du témoinage et hermeneutique de l'absolu"; and Paul Ricoeur, "The hermeneutics of testimony," *Anglican Theological Review*, 56 (October 1979), pp. 435–61. These rigorous and suggestive studies of "witness" signal a philosophical need to engage with a hermeneutics of testimony as the central biblical genre for post-Shoah Christian theology once it "returns to history." The latter phrase is Emil Fackenheim's, in his well-known reflections on a post-Shoah and post-Rosenzweig Jewish theology. Inter alia, see his *God's Presence in History* (Harper, New York, 1972), and his magisterial *To Mend the World* (Schocken, New York, 1982).

6 Hans-Georg Gadamer, *Truth and Method* (Seabury, New York, 1975); Paul Ricoeur, *Hermeneutics and the Human Sciences* (Cambridge University Press, Cambridge, 1985).

7 For one development of this critique of Gadamer's hermeneutics, see David Tracy, *Plurality and Ambiguity*, esp. pp. 66–82.

8 See Norman Perrin, *The New Testament: an introduction* (Harcourt, Brace, Jovanovich, New York, 1974); Norman Perrin, *Jesus and the Language of the Kingdom* (Fortress Press, Philadelphia, 1978).

9 Note the similar structure of post-Shoah Jewish theology in Emil Fackenheim's reflections on root-experiences (Exodus, Sinai and the hope of Messianic redemption), and epoch-making events (such as the destruction of the Second Temple and, above all, the Holocaust). Note, also, Fackenheim's re-reading of the Jewish Bible, most recently in *The Jewish Bible after the Holocaust: a re-reading* (Indiana University Press, Bloomington, Ind., 1990). The Jewish theological continuation of the Midrashic tradition (as Fackenheim and Geoffrey Hartman have emphasized in their studies of midrash in contemporary Jewish thought) gives Jewish thought a flexibility often lacking in more conceptually oriented Christian theology.

10 For one study, see Robert Grant with David Tracy, *A Short History of the Interpretation of the Bible* (Fortress Press, Philadelphia, 1984).

11 Contrast, for example, the anti-semitism of even so courageous an anti-Nazi Christian as Martin Niemoeller with Dietrich Bonhoeffer's acknowledgment of the issue. On the latter, see Eberhard Bethge, *Ethical Responsibility: Dietrich Bonhoeffer's legacy to the churches* (Edwin Mellen Press, Lewiston, New York, 1981). For a careful study of both Catholic and Protestant theological responses (or lack thereof) to Judaism in Germany, consult Werner Jeanrond's enlightening article (forthcoming in a book on

the Resistance in Germany, edited by Michael Geyer and John Boyer, University of Chicago).

12 For the category, see Cohen, *The Tremendum*, and a forthcoming book on Jewish responses to the Holocaust by Susan Shapiro.

13 See Johann Baptist Metz, "Oekümene Nach Auschwitz: Zum Verhältnis von Christen und Juden in Deutschland," in *Gott nach Auschwitz: Dimensionen des Massenmords am Juedischen Volk* (Herder, Freiburg, 1979).

Chapter 8   Film as Witness: Claude Lanzmann's *Shoah*

1 "The loneliness of God," *Dvar Hashavu'a* (magazine of the newspaper *Davar*), Tel Aviv (1984). My translation from the Hebrew.

2 "To tell the truth, the whole truth, and nothing but the truth"; an oath, however, which is always, by its very nature, susceptible to perjury.

3 *The Record*, October 25, 1985; an interview with Deborah Jerome ("Resurrecting horror: the man behind *Shoah*").

4 *Shoah*, the complete text of the film by Claude Lanzmann (Pantheon Books, New York, 1985). Quotations from the text of the film will refer to this edition, and will be indicated henceforth only by page number (in the parenthesis following the citation).

5 John Kaplan, "Foreword" to Elizabeth F. Loftus, *Eyewitness Testimony* (Harvard University Press, Cambridge, MA, and London, 1979), p. vii.

6 Categories which Lanzmann borrows from Hilberg's historical analysis, but which the film strikingly *embodies* and rethinks. Cf. Raul Hilberg, *The Destruction of the European Jews* (Holmes and Meier, New York, 1985).

7 Interview given by Lanzmann on the occasion of his visit to Yale University, and filmed at the Fortunoff Video Archive for Holocaust Testimonies at Yale (interviewers: Dr Dori Laub and Laurel Vlock), May 5, 1986. Transcript, pp. 24–5. Hereafter, citations from this videotape will be referred to by the abbreviation "interview," followed by an indication of the page number of its (unpublished) manuscript.

8 Cf. Walter Benjamin, "The task of the translator," in *Illuminations*, tr. Harry Zohn, ed. Hannah Arendt (Schocken Books, New York, 1969), pp. 69–82.

9 "An evening with Claude Lanzmann," May 4, 1986, first part of Lanzmann's visit to Yale, videotaped and copyrighted by Yale University. Transcript of the first videotape, p. 2.

10 Cf., for instance, Robert Faurisson: "I have analyzed thousands of documents. I have tirelessly pursued specialists and historians with my questions. I have tried in vain to find a single former deportee capable of proving to me that he had really seen, with his own eyes, a gas chamber" (*Le Monde*, January 16, 1972). We have "a selective view of history," comments Bill Moyers. "We live within a mythology of benign and benevolent experience. . . . It is hard to believe that there exist about a hundred books all devoted to teaching the idea that the Holocaust was a fiction, that it did not

happen, that it had been made up by Jews for a lot of diverse reasons." Interview with Margot Strom, in *Facing History and Ourselves*, fall (1986), pp. 6 and 7.

11 Statement made in a private conversation that took place in Paris, January 18, 1987: "J'ai pris un historien pour qu'il incarne un mort, alors que j'avais un vivant qui était directeur du ghetto."

12 In this respect, the filmmaker shares the approach of the historian Hilberg: "In all my work," says Hilberg, "I have never begun by asking the big questions, because I was always afraid that I would come up with small answers; and I have preferred to address these things which are minutiae or details in order that I might then be able to put together in a gestalt a picture which, if not an explanation, is at least a description, a more full description, of what transpired" (p. 70).

13 The present essay is a modified version of part of a more extensive study of the film *Shoah*, published in a volume co-authored by Shoshana Felman and Dori Laub, MD, *Testimony: crises of witnessing in literature, psychoanalysis and history* (Routledge, New York and London, 1992).

Chapter 9 Charlotte Salomon's Inward-turning Testimony

For the use of reproductions and of the Charlotte Salomon Collection, I would like to thank the Charlotte Salomon Foundation and the Jewish Historical Museum in Amsterdam, as well as Paula Salomon-Lindberg of Amsterdam; for French materials I am grateful to the Centre de Documentation Juive Contemporaine of Paris; for travel funds I am indebted to the American Philosophical Association; for generous readings and suggestions, to John Felstiner and Geoffrey Hartman. An earlier version of this essay, entitled "Artwork as evidence," appeared in *Remembering for the Future: the impact of the Holocaust on the contemporary world* (Pergamon Press, Oxford, 1988).

1 On pictorial witness to the Holocaust, see the following: Ziva Amishai-Maisels, "The complexities of witnessing," *Holocaust and Genocide Studies*, 2, 1 (1987), pp. 123–47; Janet Blatter and Sybil Milton, *Art of the Holocaust* (Routledge, New York, 1981); Mary Costanza, *The Living Witness: art in the concentration camps* (Museum of American Jewish History, Philadelphia, 1978); Gerald Green, *The Artists of Terezin* (Hawthorn, New York, 1978); Kibbutz Lochamei HaGhettaot, *Spiritual Resistance: art from concentration camps, 1940–1945* (Union of American Hebrew Congregations, New York, 1978); Lawrence Langer, "The art of the concentration camps," *Sh'ma: A Journal of Jewish Responsibility* (September 29, 1978), pp. 177–8; Nelly Toll, *Without Surrender: art of the Holocaust* (Running Press, Philadelphia, 1978); *Testimony: art of the Holocaust*, eds Irit Salmon-Livne, Ilana Guri and Yitzchak Mais (Yad Vashem, Jerusalem, 1986). None of these works deals with Charlotte Salomon. On reading Holocaust testimony in general, see James E. Young,

Writing and Rewriting the Holocaust: narrative and the consequences of interpretation (Indiana University Press, Bloomington, 1988).

2　Anne Frank, *Anne Frank: the diary of a young girl*, tr. B. M. Mooyaart (Pocket Books, New York, 1972); Etty Hillesum, *An Interrupted Life: the diaries of Etty Hillesum*, tr. Arno Pomerans (Pantheon, New York, 1983). The work of Charlotte Salomon was found by her father and stepmother after the war in Villefranche-sur-Mer, hidden with a friend of the artist's. The paintings are now archived and exhibited in Amsterdam's Jewish Historical Museum. Reproductions can be seen in Charlotte Salomon, *Leben oder Theater? Ein autobiographisches Singspiel in 769 Bildern* (Kiepenheuer & Witsch, Cologne, 1981). The English translation is *Charlotte: Life or Theater? An autobiographical play by Charlotte Salomon*, tr. Leila Vennewitz (Viking Press in association with Gary Schwartz, New York, 1981). The page numbers in my notes refer to either the English or German editions, which are identically paginated. Translations from Charlotte Salomon's texts are my own. An earlier selection of eighty reproductions was published as Charlotte Salomon, *Ein Tagebuch in Bildern, 1917–1943* (Rowohlt, Hamburg, 1963), and in English as *Charlotte: a diary in pictures*, tr. Ralph Manheim (Harcourt, New York, 1963). Biographical information about Charlotte Salomon has appeared in the prefaces to *Charlotte: Life or Theater?* by Judith Herzberg, Judith Belinfante, and Gary Schwartz; in the introduction to *Charlotte: a diary in pictures* by Emil Strauss; in the film *Charlotte* by Judith Herzberg and Frans Weisz (1981); in the exhibition catalogue compiled by Christine Fischer-Defoy, published as *Charlotte Salomon – Leben oder Theater?* (Das Arsenal, Berlin, 1986); and in Mary Felstiner, "Taking her life/history: the autobiography of Charlotte Salomon,' in *Life/Lines: theorizing women's autobiography*, ed. Bella Brodzki and Celeste Schenk (Cornell University Press, Ithaca, 1988), pp. 320–37; and "Engendering an autobiography: Charlotte Salomon's 'Life or Theater?'" in *Revealing Lives: autobiography, biography and gender*, ed. Marilyn Yalom and Susan Bell (State University of New York Press, New York, 1990), pp. 183–92.

3　*Charlotte: a diary in pictures*, preface by Paul Tillich.

4　Judith E. Doneson, "The American history of Anne Frank's diary," *Holocaust and Genocide Studies*, 2, 1 (1987), p. 152.

5　Ann Birstein and Alfred Kazin, eds, introduction, *The Works of Anne Frank* (Greenwood, Westport, CT, 1974), p. 22.

6　Unnumbered text, Jewish Historical Museum, 81: N7. (Unnumbered texts are those Charlotte Salomon decided not to number for inclusion in *Leben oder Theater?*).

7　Peter Gay, *Art and Act: on causes in history – Manet, Gropius, Mondrian* (Harper & Row, New York, 1976), pp. 5, 3.

8　On historical events revealed primarily through surviving artistic evidence, see Sybil Milton, "The legacy of Holocaust art" in *Art of the Holocaust*, eds, Blatter and Milton, pp. 39–40.

9 Salomon, *Leben oder Theater?*, p. 654.
10 Salomon, *Leben oder Theater?*, p. 738.
11 Salomon, *Leben oder Theater?*, p. 762.
12 *L'Eclaireur du Soir* (Nice), May 27, 1940, p. 3 (Bibliothèque Nationale, Annexe des périodiques, Versailles).
13 Franz Schoenberner, *The Inside Story of an Outsider* (Macmillan, New York, 1949), p. 112.
14 Decree of 13 January 1940, in Hanna Schramm [and Barbara Vormeier], *Menschen in Gurs* (Heintz, Worms, 1977), p. 310.
15 Lion Feuchtwanger, *Exil* [1940] published in English as *Paris Gazette*, tr. Willa and Edwin Muir (Viking Press, New York, 1940); Alfred Kantorowicz, *Exil in Frankreich: Merkwürdigkeiten und Denkwürdigkeiten* (Schunemann, Bremen, 1971); Anna Seghers, *Transit*, tr. James A. Galston (Little Brown, Boston, 1944); Franz Schoenberner, *Inside Story of an Outsider* (Macmillan, New York, 1949).
16 Feuchtwanger, *Paris Gazette*, pp. 127–8.
17 Unnumbered text, Jewish Historical Museum, 81: N7.
18 Speech at Paris PEN Conference, 1939, quoted in "Postscript" to Ernst Weiss, *The Eyewitness*, tr. Ella R. W. McKee (Houghton Mifflin, Boston, 1977), p. 204.
19 Zweig, *The World of Yesterday: an autobiography* (Viking, New York, 1943; reprinted University of Nebraska, 1964), p. 431.
20 Unnumbered text, Jewish Historical Museum, 81: N7.
21 Salomon, *Leben oder Theater?*, p. 773.
22 Salomon, *Leben oder Theater?*, pp. 688, 761, 775, unnumbered text, Jewish Historical Museum, 81: N4.
23 Paula Salomon-Lindberg, interview with the author, Amsterdam, April 15, 1984.
24 Salomon, *Leben oder Theater?*, p. 3.
25 Schoenberner, *Inside Story of an Outsider*, p. 161.
26 *Alma Mahler-Werfel* journal, September 1938, quoted in Gilbert Badia, Françoise Joly, Jean-Baptiste Joly, Claude Laharie, Ingrid Lederer, Jean-Philippe Mathieu, Hélène Roussel, Joseph Rovan, and Barbara Vormeier, *Les Barbelés de l'exil: Études sur l'émigration allemande et autrichienne (1938–1940)* (Presses Universitaires, Grenoble, 1979), p. 74; Franz Werfel, *Jacobowsky and the Colonel: comedy of a tragedy in three acts*, tr. Gustave O. Arlt (Viking, New York, 1944).
27 Anna Seghers, *Transit*, p. 50.
28 Kantorowicz, *Exil in Frankreich*, p. 48 [my italics].
29 Schoenberner, *Inside Story of an Outsider*, p. 120.
30 Arthur Koestler, *Scum of the Earth* (Macmillan, New York, 1941), p. 278; Schoenberner, *Inside Story of an Outsider*, pp. 45–6.
31 Unnumbered text, Jewish Historical Museum, 81: N3.
32 Unnumbered text, 81: N4.
33 Salomon, *Leben oder Theater?*, p. 4.

34   Salomon, *Leben oder Theater?*, p. 682.
35   C. L. Flavian, *De la nuit vers la lumière* (J. Peyronnet, Paris, 1946), p. 62.
36   Rapport du président du Consistoire E. Montel, Centre de Documentation Juive Contemporaine, Paris, dossier CCXX-12; Jean-Louis Panicacci, "Les Juifs et la question juive dans les Alpes-Maritimes de 1939 à 1945," *Recherches Régionales: Côte d'Azur et contrées limitrophes*, 4 (1983), pp. 254–6.
37   Reproduced in Emily D. Bilski, *Art and Exile: Felix Nussbaum, 1904–1944* (The Jewish Museum, New York, 1985), p. 18.
38   On the scarcity of artistic materials, see Janet Blatter, "Art from the Whirlwind" in *Art of the Holocaust*, eds Blatter and Milton, pp. 25–6. Charlotte Salomon painted both sides of her sheets to save paper, then for the final version had to choose which side counted most.
39   Salomon, *Leben oder Theater?*, pp. 3, 4, 6.

Chapter 11   Conversation in the Cemetery: Dan Pagis and the Prosaics of Memory

I wish especially to thank David Shulman for his close reading and insightful comments on this manuscript.

1   *Variable Directions: the selected poetry of Dan Pagis*, tr. Stephen Mitchell (North Point Press, San Francisco, 1989), p. 9. Originally published as "Hamazkeret" in *Milim nirdafot* (Hakibbutz hameuhad, Tel Aviv, 1982).
2   *Dan Pagis: Kol hashirim* (Dan Pagis: Collected Poems), ed. Hanan Hever, T. Carmi (Hakibbutz hameuhad, and Mossad Bialik, Jerusalem, 1991). All English translations from the as yet untranslated passages in this volume are mine.
3   For a more comprehensive discussion of Pagis's poetry, see my "Dan Pagis – out of line: a poetics of decomposition," *Prooftexts* 10 (1990), pp. 335–63.
4   For a recent discussion of the discovery of the Laocoön, see Leonard Barkan, "Rome's Other Population," *Raritan*, fall, 1991. Archaeological metaphors have enriched the psychoanalytic and poetic exploration of memory in the twentieth century.
5   See, for example, "Akevot," ("Footprints"), and "Hamisdar" ("The Roll-call"), both published in *Gilgul* (Masada, Tel Aviv, 1970).
6   "Beka behomat hashikheha" is the way he phrased it in Hebrew in an interview with Yaira Genossar, "Dan Pagis – calling it by its name, taking a stand," *Iton 77*, 38 (February 1983), p. 33.
7   From an interview printed in *Hadoar*, November 14, 1986, p. 15, based on an interview in English held on December 24, 1984. Quoted in my "Dan Pagis – out of line," p. 339. "Il y a des lieux de mémoire parce qu'il n'y a plus de milieux de mémoire," writes Pierre Nora in his introduction

to the multi-volume study of "Les Lieux de Mémoire"; ". . . la mémoire s'enracine dans le concret, dans l'espace, le geste, l'image et l'objet," ("Entre Mémoire et Histoire," *Les lieux de mémoire* [Gallimard, Paris, 1984], pp. xvii, xix).

8   "Point of departure," in *Dan Pagis: points of departure*, tr. Stephen Mitchell, introduction by Robert Alter (Jewish Publication Society, Philadelphia, 1981), p. 40. Published originally as "Nekudat hamotzah" in *Moah* (Hakibbutz hameuhad, Tel Aviv, 1975).

9   "Honi," originally published in *Shehut meuheret* (Sifriat poalim, Merhavia, 1964).

10   *Pagis: Points of Departure*, pp. 35, 37.

11   Ibid., pp. 30–1. In addition to functioning as sinister historical referent, the train should be contextualized as setting for the perennial Jewish joke and as portable *shtetl* in the Yiddish fiction of such writers as S. Y. Abramovitsh and Sholem Aleichem.

12   *Iton 77* (February, 1983), p. 33.

13   Ibid.

14   Roland Barthes, *Camera Lucida: reflections on photography* (Hill and Wang, New York, 1981), p. 76.

15   Susan Sontag, *On Photography* (Farrar, Straus and Giroux, New York, 1977), p. 154. Footprints, as we have seen, and death masks are two of the primary trace elements in Pagis's universe.

16   Barthes, *Camera Lucida*, p. 6.

17   Paul John Eakin introduces his book on "reference in autobiography" by acknowledging that while Barthes goes "out of his way to undercut the notion that the discourse of autobiography is supported by a structure of reference [. . . 'Do I not know that, *in the field of the subject, there is no referent?*'], . . . when the austere tenets of poststructuralist theory about the subject came into conflict with the urgent demands of private experience, Barthes turned for solace . . . to photography, which he regarded as the supremely referential art." Intending, as he reported to his students, to write a "novel of memory," Barthes presents in his last work, *Camera Lucida*, what Eakin calls "an aesthetic of photography . . . founded . . . on this bearing of witness [to the existence of the beloved]." *Touching the World: reference in autobiography* (Princeton University Press, Princeton, 1992), pp. 4, 18. See also J. Gerald Kennedy, "Roland Barthes, autobiography, and the end of writing," *Georgia Review*, 35 (1981), pp. 381–98.

18   See, on this, my "The grave in the air: unbound metaphors in post-Holocaust poetry," in *Probing the limits of representation: Nazism and the "Final Solution"* ed. Saul Friedlander (Harvard University Press, Cambridge, MA, 1992).

19   Paul Ricoeur, *Time and Narrative*, tr. Kathleen McLaughlin and David Pellauer (University of Chicago Press, Chicago, 1984), Vol. 1, p. 3.

20   *Pagis: Points of Departure*, p. 3.

21 See, for example, the fiction of Aharon Appelfeld.
22 See the poem by that name ("Koah meshikhah' in Hebrew) in *Dan Pagis: Kol hashirim*, p. 257.
23 See the poem by that name ("Mihutz lashura" in Hebrew) in ibid., p. 256.
24 See "Misped leva'al signon" ("Eulogy for a stylist") in ibid., p. 259.
25 "L'mish'al sifruti," in ibid., p. 308; tr. as "For a literary survey," in Pagis, *Variable Directions*, p. 85.
26 This both on the evidence of the text itself, the marginalia which clearly indicate work in progress, and the personal testimony of Hanan Hever and T. Carmi, who worked closely with Pagis during his lifetime and co-edited the posthumous volume of his collected works.
27 "Abba" in *Pagis: Kol hashirim*, p. 364.
28 See, for example, Pagis's marginalia on the passage in which a bottle of Cherry Herring breaks in the airport just after the narrator receives word that his father has died: "Take out? If not, it can be less symbolic, even if the whole thing is *true*." *Pagis: Kol hashirim*, p. 380.
29 John Freccero, "Autobiography and Narrative," p. 17, in *Reconstructing Individualism: autonomy, individuality and the self in Western thought*, ed. Thomas C. Heller (Stanford University Press, Stanford, 1986). I am grateful to Lauren Fishman for bringing this reference to my attention.
30 "Abba," *Pagis: Kol hashirim*, p. 341.
31 "Parvot" – one of the prose-poems found in Pagis's papers. *Pagis: Kol hashirim*, p. 333.
32 "She'ela matzhikah," *Pagis: Kol hashirim*, p. 290.
33 Shuli Barzilai, "Borders of language: Kristeva's critique of Lacan," in *Publications of the Modern Language Association*, 106, 2 (March 1991), pp. 295–6.
34 "Hashem shelkha" (in "Abba") *Pagis: Kol hashirim*, p. 366. The play on the Hebrew idiom, "he who changes his place changes his luck," once again substitutes *self* for *place* as the major existential principle.
35 "Ready for parting," in *Pagis: Points of Departure*, p. 97. "Mukhan lif-reda" in the original in *Shehut Meuheret* (Sifriat poalim, Merhavia, 1964).
36 "Abba," *Pagis: Kol hashirim*, p. 347.
37 The poem concludes: "On the inside / I'm the one looking at her, four years old almost, / holding back my ball, quietly / going out of the photo and growing old, / growing old carefully, quietly, / so as not to frighten her." *Variable Directions*, p. 10. Originally published in *Shirim ahronim* (Hakibbutz hameuhad, Tel Aviv, 1987). I have argued elsewhere that in "Ein Leben" (one of Pagis's last poems, published posthumously), the artist, "unable to capture himself in any fixed temporal or spatial frame, unable to inhibit the march of time through the normal license of poetic control, ... is deprived of his own object (the discrete self in arrested moments) as a protected, frozen target of scrutiny." ("Dan Pagis – out of line," p. 341). But one can reasonably speculate that, recontextualized as part of the documentary apparatus, fixed in time and place in the dialogue

with the father, that very photograph might have furnished an autobiographical occasion from which the son would not have had to steal away.

38 *Camera Lucida*, p. 73.

39 Ricoeur, *Time and Narrative*, p. 175.

40 In an article on "Abba," Hanan Hever argues that this autobiographical text stands diametrically opposed to the standard Zionist story for it is the *father* who abandons the son to go to Palestine leaving the son to die, so to speak, and reversing the oedipal pattern. ("Sheharei kvar hega'anu, nakhon?" [*Devar*, February 21, 1992, p. 27]). Yet even as a parody or rewrite of the Zionist story, the text still engages the epic terms of the story.

41 In his most famous poem, "Written in Pencil in a Sealed Railway-Car," there is a direct, unfinished appeal to an extratextual audience:

> here in this carload
> i am eve
> with abel my son
> if you see my other son
> cain son of man
> tell him that i

> Pagis: *Points of Departure*, p. 23. In the original Hebrew published as "Katuv b'iparon bakaron hehatum" (*Gilgul*).

Chapter 12 Chinese History and Jewish Memory

1 This translation of Meng Jiao's poems appears in Stephen Owen's book: *Remembrances: the experience of the past in classical Chinese literature* (Harvard University Press, Cambridge, 1986), p. 18. This work with its insightful overview of the relationship between Chinese history and Chinese memory, has been critical to my reading of Jewish memoir literature.

2 The record of my initial, prolonged contact with intellectual-survivors of the Cultural Revolution appears in Vera Schwarcz, *Long Road Home* (Yale University Press, New Haven, 1984).

3 The preliminary results of that decade of part of my work on Chinese and Jewish historical memory has now appeared in Chinese, Vera Schwarcz, "Liuli de jiyi nushen" ("Mnemosyne abroad: reflections on Chinese and Jewish memory"), *Ershi yi shiji* (*Twenty-First Century*) (March 1991), pp. 105–21.

4 Owen, *Remembrances*, pp. 19–20.

5 My translation of Confucius, *Analects* VII.19. For a slightly different version see the bilingual edition of the *Analects* in James Legge, *The Chinese Classics*, Vol. 1 (Trubner & Co., London, 1861), p. 14.

6 Personal correspondence from my father, March, 1983. This phrase was also used by Lim in a draft preface he wrote for his memoir.

7 I am summarizing here an often told story, which also appears in Elmer
   Bubi Savin's "Encounters dictated by fate" (manuscript submitted to Yad
   Vashem), pp. 97–104.
8 Personal correspondence, September, 1983.
9 Ibid.
10 See especially author's "Afterword" in Carole Malkin, *The Journeys of
   David Toback* (Schocken Books, New York, 1981), pp. 214–16.
11 Nadine Fresco, "La diaspora des cendres," *Nouvelle Revue de Psycho-
   analyse*, 24 (1981), pp. 206–20.
12 Vera Schwarcz, *Rebellious Revolutionary: dialogues with Zhang Shenfu,
   philosopher and founder of the Chinese communist party* (Yale University
   Press, New Haven, 1992).
13 Zhang Shenfu, oral interview, March 10, 1980; June 3, 1981; and May
   23, 1983.
14 For a discussion of the origins of the *zizan* tradition, see Pei-yi Wu,
   "Varieties of the Chinese self," in *Designs of Selfhood*, ed. Vyntantis
   Kavolis (Associated University Press, Cranbury, NJ, 1987).
15 Vera Schwarcz, "You mean there was no sex in Auschwitz?", *Jewish
   Currents* (November, 1989), pp. 12–15.
16 Ibid., p. 12.
17 My reflections, on the meanings of "historicity," and its relationship to
   memory, have benefited greatly from conversations with Dr Dori Laub, as
   well as from his paper, co-authored with Nannette C. Auerhahn, "Annihilation and restoration: post-traumatic memory as a pathway and obstacle to
   recovery," *International Review of Psychoanalysis*, II (1984), pp. 327–43.
18 For a discussion of how the biblical commandment to "remember" has
   affected the Jewish relationship to history see, Yosef Hayim Yerushalmi,
   Zachor: Jewish history and Jewish memory (University of Washington
   Press, Seattle, 1983), and Amos Funkenstein's critique of Yerushalmi in
   "Collective memory and historical consciousness," *History and Memory*,
   1, 1 (1990), pp. 10–13.
19 I am indebted to Professor Yu Yingshi of Princeton University for extended
   conversations about the sources of personal and public memory in traditional China. It was Professor Yu who first drew my attention to the
   late third-century Daoist classic *Jin Shu* in which appears a most concise
   warning against indulgence in memory. The passage "Qing you yi sheng.
   Bu yi ze wu qing" may be translated as follows: "Feelings arise out of
   memory. If there is no memory, feelings will dissolve as well." This Daoist
   injunction against memory as the locus of disturbing emotion is also echoed
   in Confucian admonitions on filial piety that require one to maintain
   mental well-being – if not for one's own sake, at least for one's parents'.
   In the view of these Confucians, as well as Daoists, to dwell on the painful
   past is to arouse distressing, dangerous – and, in the long run, unfilial –
   emotions.

20 Saul Friedlander, *When Memory Comes* (Avon Books, New York, 1980), p. 135.

Chapter 14   Facing the Glass Booth

1 The underground military organization in Erez Israel (Palestine) from 1920 to 1948.
2 The subtitle and major theme of Hannah Arendt's famous book *Eichmann in Jerusalem* (Viking Press, New York, 1963).

Chapter 15   Andean Waltz

1 For early Jewish settlement in Bolivia see Jacob Beller, *Jews in Latin America* (Jonathan David, New York, 1969), pp. 211–12; Judith Laikin Elkin and Gilbert W. Merkx, eds., *The Jewish Presence in Latin America* (Allen & Unwin, Boston, 1987); Marc J. Osterweil, "The meaning of elitehood: Germans, Jews and Arabs in La Paz, Bolivia" (unpublished Ph.D. dissertation in Anthropology, New York University, 1978), pp. 55–8; Jacob Shatzky, *Comunidades Judias en Latinoamerica* (American Jewish Committee, Buenos Aires, 1952), pp. 100–1.
2 See the detailed account by Herbert A. Strauss, "Jewish emigration from Germany, Nazi policies and Jewish responses," (I and II) in *Leo Baeck Institute, Yearbook* 25 (1980), pp. 313–61 and 26 (1981), pp. 343–409. Although a large number of refugees were admitted to Bolivia conditionally, as *agricultores* – with visas stipulating that the immigrants settle in rural areas and engage in agriculture or related occupations – the majority, coming from urban backgrounds, managed to settle in the country's urban centers.
3 Dr Heinrich Stern, "Indianer-landschaft," (Cochabamba, Bolivia, July 1941). Unpublished typescript. My translation.
4 Egon Schwarz, *Keine Zeit für Eichendorff: Chronik unfreiwilliger Wanderjahre* (Athenäum, Königstein, 1979), p. 58; Videotaped interview with Andres J. Simon, La Paz, Bolivia, July 22, 1991; Videotaped interview with Renate Schwarz, Teaneck, NJ, May 2, 1991.
5 Videotaped interview with Werner Guttentag, Cochabamba, Bolivia, July 31, 1991. For Karl May see Christian Heermann, *Der Mann, der Old Shatterhand war: Eine Karl-May-Biographie* (Verlag der Nation, Berlin, 1988) and Martin Lowsky, *Karl May* (J. B. Matzlersche Verlagsbuchhandlung, Stuttgart, 1987).
6 Videotaped interview with Heinz Pinshower, Chicago, Ill., April 10, 1991.
7 Ibid.
8 Videotaped interview with Renate Schwarz, Teaneck, NJ, May 2, 1991.

9   Ibid.
10 Videotaped interview with Werner Guttentag, Cochabamba, Bolivia, July 31, 1991.
11 Egon Schwarz, *Keine Zeit für Eichendorff*, p. 66.
12 Schwarz, *Keine Zeit für Eichendorff*, pp. 65–6.
13 For an articulation of this feeling in a refugee memoir, see Schwarz, *Keine Zeit für Eichendorff*, pp. 72–3. For a discussion of climatic adjustment problems see von zur Mühlen, pp. 54–5.
14 In the course of my interviews with persons who were refugees or connected to the refugee experience in Bolivia, I always ask to be shown photographs and family albums of the early immigrant years.
15 For a stimulating discussion of representation in family albums, see Patricia Holland, "History, memory and the family album" in *Family Snaps: the meaning of domestic photography*, eds Jo Spence and Patricia Holland (Virago, London, 1991).
16 For a discussion of the *Rundschau vom Illimani* and Ernst Schumacher see Patrik von zur Mühlen, *Fluchtziel Lateinamerika: Die deutsche Emigration 1933–1945: politische Aktivitäten und soziokulturelle Integration* (Neue Gesellschaft, Bonn, 1988), pp. 217–19, 221–6. The importance of the *Aufbau* as a vehicle for refugee communication and as an instrument fostering a refugee community during the war, see Schwarz, *Keine Zeit für Eichendorff*, p. 79. The Wiener Library in London has a complete run of the *Jüdische Wochenschau* on microfilm.
17 The *Circulo Israelita*, founded in 1935 by Polish and Romanian Jews, was the first Jewish community organization in Bolivia. Although it would continue to exist as a separate entity throughout the war years and, in the 1950s, would absorb the, by then, much diminished Comunidad, it was the Comunidad with its (at the time) larger central European membership and its affiliated institutions, which dominated Jewish-immigrant community life. For a history of the Circulo Israelita see Circulo Israelita, *Medio Siglo de Vida Judia en La Paz* (Circulo Israelita, La Paz, 1987). Also see Schwarz, *Keine Zeit für Eichendorff*, p. 81.
18 *Jüdische Wochenschau* (monthly "Bolivia" sections of the Buenos Aires newspaper), and *Rundschau vom Illimani* (passim, 1939–42).
19 Circulo Israelita, *Medio Siglo*, pp. 171–5.
20 Schwarz, *Keine Zeit für Eichendorff*, p. 73.
21 Videotaped interview with Julius Wolfinger, Queens, New York, July 2, 1991.
22 Videotaped interview with Heinz Pinshower, Chicago, Ill., April 10, 1991.
23 Leo Spitzer, in a videotaped discussion with Heini and Liesl Lipczenko, August 12, 1990.
24 Videotaped interview with Julio Meier, La Paz, Bolivia, August 5, 1991.
25 A second wave of Jewish immigration to Bolivia, consisting largely of persons of Eastern European origin, many of whom were concentration camp survivors, occurred after the end of the war. Ironically, ex-Nazis like

the notorious Klaus Barbie, also found refuge in Bolivia in the late 1940s. See Marcel Ophuls' award-winning documentary film, *Hotel Terminus: the life and times of Klaus Barbie*.

26 Circulo Israelita, *Medio Siglo*, pp. 30–42; interview with Max Gans, New York City, June 26, 1991; videotaped interview with Heini and Liesl Lipczenko, August 12, 1990.

27 See, for example, Schwarz, *Keine Zeit für Eichendorff*, and interviews with Hanni and Heinz Pinshower, Heini and Liesl Lipczenko, Werner Guttentag, Julius Wolfinger, Renate Schwarz, Trude Hassberg (Queens, New York, May 4, 1991).

28 Many of the persons I interviewed have referred to these. For example: Julius Wolfinger, Heini and Liesl Lipczenko, Heinz and Hanni Pinshower, Werner Guttentag, Walter Guevarra (La Paz, July 14, 1991), Willi Becker (Los Angeles, Calif., March 16, 1991). Also see Schwarz, *Keine Zeit für Eichendorff*, pp. 82–3; Arthur Propp memoires, at the Leo Baeck Institute, New York.

29 Jerry W. Knudson, "The Bolivian Immigration Bill of 1942: a case study in Latin American anti-semitism," *American Jewish Archives*, 20, 1 (April 1968), pp. 138–59.

30 Ibid.

31 Ilse Herz, videotaped interview in Arsdale, NY, February 26, 1991.

32 David Lowenthal, *The Past is a Foreign Country* (Cambridge University Press, New York, 1985), p. 210.

33 The formulation is Alfred Adler's. See Leo Spitzer, *Lives in Between: Assimilation and Marginality in Austria, Brazil, West Africa, 1780–1945* (Cambridge University Press, New York, 1990), p. 132.

Chapter 16 German–Jewish Memory and National Consciousness

1 Jean-François Lyotard, *The Differend: phrases in dispute* (University of Minnesota Press, Minneapolis, 1988), pp. 57–9, 151–81.

2 John Tagliabue, "In Berlin, project for Jewish display is in doubt," *New York Times*, Wednesday August 7, 1991, B3.

3 Alexander and Margarete Mitscherlich, *The Inability to Mourn: principles of collective behavior* (Grove Press, New York, 1975).

4 Anson Rabinbach, "The Jewish question in the German question," *New German Critique*, 44, spring–summer (1988), pp. 159–92; Frank Stern, "The 'Jewish question' in the 'German question'," *New German Critique*, 52 winter (1991), pp. 155–72; Sander Gilman, "German reunification and the Jews," *New German Critique*, 52 winter (1991), pp. 173–91; Dan Diner, "Deutschland, die Juden und Europa: Vom fortschreitenden Sieg der Zukunft ueber die Vergangenheit," *Babylon*, 7 September (1990), pp. 96–104; Diner, "Zwischen Bundesrepublik und Deutschland," in *Von der Gnade der geschenkten Nation. Zur politischen Moral der Bonner Republik*, ed. Hajo Funke (Rotbuch Verlag, Berlin, 1990), pp. 188–99.

5 Theodor W. Adorno, "What does coming to terms with the past mean" (1961), in *Bitburg in Moral and Political Perspective*, ed. Geoffrey Hartman (Indiana University Press, Bloomington, 1986).

6 Hans Juergen Syberberg, *Vom Unglueck und Glueck der Kunst in Deutschland nach dem letzten Kriege* (Matthes & Seitz, Munich, 1990).

7 Edith Wyschogrod, *Spirit in Ashes: Hegel, Heidegger, and man-made mass death* (Yale University Press, New Haven and London, 1985), defines man-made mass death as "a form of life, a region of being, whose manner of being is to exist as the obliteration of cultures and as the possible extinction of human life" (p. XI). Wyschogrod's analysis has yet to find its way into the Holocaust literature.

8 On the question of guilt Anton Leist, "Deutsche Geschichte und historische Verantwortung," *Babylon*, 7 (September 1990), pp. 41–60, and Martin Loew-Beer, "Die Verpflichtungen der unschuldigen Nachgeborenen. Zu Anton Leists Verantwortungsethik," ibid., pp. 61–9. On the general debate see *Zerstoerung des moralischen Selbstbewusstseins: Chance oder Gefaehrdung. Praktische Philosophie in Deutschland nach dem Nationalsozialismus*, ed. by Forum fuer Philosophie Bad Homburg (Suhrkamp, Frankfurt, 1988), and Zygmunt Bauman, *Modernity and the Holocaust* (Cornell University Press, Ithaca and New York, 1989). This issue will be the subject of a separate essay.

9 Henryk Broder, "Ihr bleibt die Kinder Eurer Eltern," *Die Zeit*, February 27, 1981.

10 Anton Kaes, *From Hitler to Heimat. The return of history as film* (Harvard University Press, Cambridge, MA, and London, 1989), and Thomas Elsaesser, *New German Cinema: a history* (Rutgers University Press, New Brunswick, NJ, 1989), pp. 239–78.

11 The "classic" statement on the "integral personality" can be found in Gyorgy Lukacs, *The Theory of the Novel: a historico-philosophical essay on the forms of great epic literature* (MIT Press, Cambridge, MA, 1971).

12 Benjamin Buchloh, "Figures of authority, ciphers of regression," *October*, 16, spring (1981), pp. 39–68, has been the most persistent critic of historicizing narratives. Painting, rather than history, has been the main site for this debate.

13 Syberberg, *Vom Unglueck und Glueck der Kunst*, p. 190, expects "inner authenticity" and "liberation" "coming from the people itself, the seared people, glowing from within."

14 Wolfgang J. Mommsen, "The Germans and their Past: history and political consciousness in the Federal Republic of Germany," in *Coping with the Past: Germany and Austria after 1945*, eds Kathy Harms, Lutz Reuter, and Volker Dürr (University of Wisconsin Press, Madison, 1990), pp. 252–69; Eric Santner, *Stranded Objects: mourning, memory, and film in postwar Germany* (Cornell University Press, Ithaca and London, 1990).

15 Michael Schneider, "Fathers and sons retrospectively: the damaged relationship between two generations," *New German Critique*, 31, Winter (1984), pp. 3–52; Helmut Peitsch, "Autobiographical writing as *Vergangenheitsbewaeltigung*," *German History*, 7 (1989), pp. 47–70; Jack Zipes, "The return of the repressed," *New German Critique*, 31, winter (1984), pp. 201–10 is one of the first to use this term.

16 Christa Wolf, *A Model Childhood* (Farrar, Straus and Giroux, New York, 1980). On the uses of the present in Claude Lanzmann's *Shoah* see Gertrud Koch, "The aesthetic transformation of the image of the unimaginable," *October*, 48, spring (1989), pp. 15–24.

17 On this central theme of the historians' debate see Charles Maier, *The Unmasterable Past: history, Holocaust, and German national identity* (Harvard University Press, Cambridge, MA, and London, 1988), and Richard J. Evans, *In Hitler's Shadow: West German historians and the attempt to escape from the Nazi past* (Pantheon, New York, 1989).

18 This is the beginning of a development that led to the abdication of intellectuals in the face of national unity – the collapse of the discourse on the nation in the face of a national and "popular" discourse. This phenomenon is discussed in some detail by Andreas Huyssen, "After the Wall: the failure of German intellectuals," *New German Critique*, 52, winter (1991), pp. 109–43.

19 Guy Debord, *Society of the Spectacle* (Black & Red, Detroit, 1983).

20 Hanns-Josef Ortheil, *Koeder, Beute und Schatten – Suchbewegungen* (Fischer, Frankfurt, 1985); Michael Rutschky, *Erfahrungshunger. Ein Essay ueber die siebziger Jahre* (Fischer, Frankfurt, 1982).

21 Jean Baudrillard, "Simulacra and simulations," in his *Selected Writings*, ed. Mark Poster (Stanford University Press, Stanford, 1988).

22 Quoted in Detlev Claussen, "In the house of the hangman," *Germans and Jews since the Holocaust: the changing situation in West Germany*, eds Anson Rabinach and Jack Zipes (Holmes & Meier, New York, 1986), p. 63.

23 In this sense, the spectacular conversion of the Germans was potentially nothing less than the completion of the Nazi deed. See the tantalizing remarks about Nazi monuments of annihilation by James E. Young, "Memory and monument," in *Bitburg in Moral and Political Perspective*, pp. 103–13. The fact that *absence* needs presence is worth re-emphasizing, not least because the American debate points exactly in the opposite direction – the celebration of survival. Beyond this disjuncture of what is appropriate for Germany and the United States respectively, the whole issue points to the profound difficulties of history to narrativize the Holocaust; for history is meant to overcome death, whereas the recollection of mass death is at the center of Holocaust history. We will approach the problem of absence and (historical) representation in a separate essay.

24 Alexander Kluge and Oskar Negt, *Geschichte und Eigensinn* (Zweitausendeins, Frankfurt, 1981), p. 771.

Chapter 17   Negating the Dead

1 It is necessary to specify that this text was written in 1988, and only slightly revised for publication.

2 But I will refer to this group as "negationists," a more exact description – and the one now used by historians.

3 *Nürnberg or the Promised Land* and *Nürnberg or the Counterfeiters* (Les Sept Couleurs, Paris, 1948 and 1950).

4 *Le Monde*, December 28, 1978.

5 R. Aron, *De Gaulle, Israel et les Juifs* (Plon, Paris, 1968), p. 18, quoted by H. Rousso, *Le syndrome de Vichy, 1944–198. . .* (Le Seuil, Paris, 1987), p. 152.

6 The title of the main American "revisionist" work, (*The Hoax of the Twentieth Century*) by A. Butz (Historical Review Press, Southam, 1976).

7 "Auschwitz ou le grand alibi," *Programme communiste*, 11 (avril–juin 1960), pp. 49–53.

8 "Auschwitz ou le grand alibi," 2nd edn, supplement to no. 5 of *Mouvement communiste*, (La Vieille Taupe, Paris, 1970).

9 It was in Maurice Bardèche's extreme-right review, *Défense de l'Occident*, that Robert Faurisson, in June 1978, first published his interpretation, under the title "Le problème des chambres à gaz." On September 14, 1979, he gave a lecture on this theme in Washington DC, at the headquarters of the National Alliance, the American neo-Nazi party.

10 S. Thion, *Vérité historique ou vérité politique?* (La Vieille Taupe, Paris, 1980), p. 165.

11 S. Thion, "Histoire européenne et monde arabe," *Annales d'Histoire Révisionniste*, 1 spring (1987), p. 126. The delicacy of the phrase "what happened between the Nazis and the Jewish communities of Europe" is worth pointing out. The *Annales d'Histoire Révisionniste*, published between 1987 and 1990, was edited by P. Guillaume, the founder and head of La Vieille Taupe.

12 Ibid., p. 120.

13 Ibid., p. 135.

14 Quoted by P. L. Assoun, "De l'allégorie à la tautégorie: le mythe de l'Un," *Corps écrit*, 18 (1986), pp. 105–13.

15 W. Stäglich, *Le Mythe d'Auschwitz*, (La Vieille Taupe, Paris, 1986), p. 28. This book is described as "translated and adapted from the German," with no mention of a translator's name.

16 *Passage de la ligne*, and *Le Mensonge d'Ulysse*, published for the first time in 1948 and 1950 respectively, by the Editions Bressanes, were republished in 1979, in one volume, by La Vieille Taupe, Paris, under the title *Le Mensonge d'Ulysse*. (The page numbers in the text refer to the 1979 edition.)

17 *Ulysse trahi par les siens* (Librairie française, Paris, 1961; 2nd edn (La Vieille Taupe, Paris, 1980), pp. 64–5.

18　Les Sept Couleurs, Paris, 1962.
19　Les Sept Couleurs, Paris, 1964.
20　Nouvelles Editions Latines, Paris, 1967.
21　P. Rassinier, *Ulysse trahi par les siens*, p. 197, "Biographie de Paul Rassinier."
22　Thion, *Vérité historique ou vérité politique*, p. 165.
23　In 1986 Henri Roques' thesis was published in Paris under the title *Faut-il brûler Henri Roques?* by Ogmios, a confessedly extreme-right publishing house, specializing in National Socialist literature, which also distributes the *Annales d'Histoire Révisionniste* and all the revisionist works sponsored by La Vieille Taupe.

Chapter 18　"The First Blow": Projects for the Camp at Fossoli

The author wishes to thank Guido Fink for the kind interest he has shown.

1　For more detailed information on the subject of the Fossoli Camp and its role in the European Concentration camp system see the introduction by Enzo Collotti in *Trentacinque progetti per Fossoli*, ed. Giovanni Leoni (Electa, Milan, 1990), pp. 11–22. See also the following two essays in the same volume: Biondi E., Liotti, C., and Romagnoli, P., "Il Campo di Fossoli: evoluzione d'uso e transformazioni," pp. 35–49; Biondi, E., "Una città quasi realizzata," pp. 64–72. The most reliable reconstruction of the transit of Jewish prisoners through Fossoli can now be found in Picciotto Fargion L., *Il libro della memoria. Gli ebrei deportati dall'Italia (1943–1945)* (Mursia, Milan, 1991).
2　*Lettere di condannati a morte della Resistenza Europea*, eds P. Malvezzi and G. Pirelli, preface by Thomas Mann (Einaudi, Turin, 1960).
3　From a conversation with architect Belgiojoso (to whom thanks are due) held at Milan on December 12, 1988.
4　Primo Levi, *Se questo è un uomo* (1958), now in *Se questo e' un uomo. La tregua* (Einaudi, Torino, 1989), pp. 12–14. For the standard English translation see *Survival in Auschwitz and the Reawakening*, tr. Stuart Woolf (Summit Books, New York, 1985).
5　Jean Améry, *Jenseits von Schuld und Sühne. Bewältigungsversuche eines Überwältigten* (1977), Italian trans., *Intellettuale al Auschwitz*, introduced by C. Magris (Bollati Boringhieri, Turin, 1987), p. 69.
6　Levi, *La tregua* (1963), now in *Se questo è un uomo. La tregua*, p. 191.
7　Levi, *Se questo è un uomo. La tregua*, p. 23.
8　Ibid., pp. 95–6.
9　Ibid., p. 104.
10　Ibid., p. 119.
11　Levi, *I sommersi e i salvati* (*The Drowned and the Saved*) (Einaudi, Turin, 1986), pp. 64–5.
12　Améry, *Intellettuale al Auschwitz*, p. 73.

13   Levi, *Se questo è un uomo. La tregua*, p. 33.
14   Speaking of the victims of the Third Reich Améry says: "I do not intend
to erect a monument to them, for to be a victim is not itself an honor.
My intention has been only to describe their condition, which can never
be changed" (Améry, *Intellettuale al Auschwitz*, p. 18). Less pessimistically,
Levi writes in *The Drowned and the Saved* (p. 10): "Ceremonies and
commemorations, monuments and banners are not necessarily to be
deplored. Maybe a certain amount of rhetoric is indispensable in order
that the remembrance may endure." But plainly he shows no faith in the
commemoration itself as a means of penetrating the silence that enshrouds
the victims of the concentration camps.
15   Acknowledging the complexity of the problems posed by the theme of the
competition, the jury, in lieu of decreeing a single winner, awarded three
prizes *ex aequo*. In effect, this meant the acknowledgment of three possible
solutions, with their own logic and validity but incompatible among themselves. At this point, the definitive choice that will soon be made among
the projects (imminent at the moment of writing) is no longer a question
of merit but rather of method, and all the more difficult for that reason.

Chapter 19   Jewish Memory in Poland

This essay is adapted from the author's full length study, *The Texture of
Memory* (Yale University, New Haven, 1993).

1   The above lines open Jerzy Ficowski's "Script of a dead cemetery," in *A
Reading of Ashes*, tr. Keith Bosley with Krystyna Wandycz (Menard Press,
London, 1981), p. 21.
2   According to the office for Religious Denominations in Warsaw, of 434
major Jewish cemeteries in Poland, 22 were regarded as still in good condition
in 1979. Of the remaining 412 cemeteries, 68 were half destroyed during
the German occupation; 78 more were 90 percent devastated; and 136
revealed only traces of burial grounds. The other 129 cemeteries were
obliterated without a trace. (Cited in *Everlasting Memory: struggle and
extermination of Polish Jews* [Polish Interpress Agency, Warsaw, 1988],
pp. 22–3.)
3   See Malgorzata Niezabitowska, *Remnants: the last Jews of Poland*, tr.
William Brand and Hanna Dobosiewicz (Friendly Press, New York, 1986),
p. 67.
4   See Carol Herselle Krinsky, *Synagogues of Europe: architecture, history,
meaning* (MIT Press, Cambridge, MA and London, 1985), p. 431, for a
more complete list of extant Polish synagogues.
5   I am very grateful to Monika Krajewska for sharing her essay, "Na Cmen-
tarzu Cmentarza – Kazimierzu nad Visła" ("Cemetery of a cemetery –
Kazimierz on the Vistula"), *Nowiny-Kurier*, May 3, 1985, with me, and to
Tamara Ślusarska for her fine English translation of the essay.

6 "Transfer place" – where Jews were forcibly assembled before deportation.
7 For a more comprehensive discussion of the ways the Warsaw ghetto uprising is remembered by the state, see James E. Young, "The biography of a memorial icon: Nathan Rapoport's Warsaw Ghetto Monument," *Representations*, spring (1989), pp. 69–106.
8 For more on this tendency, see James E. Young, *Writing and Rewriting the Holocaust: narrative and the consequences of interpretation* (Indiana University Press, Bloomington and Indianapolis, 1988), pp. 175–8.

Chapter 20 Reclaiming Auschwitz

1 James E. Young, *Writing and Rewriting the Holocaust: narrative and the consequences of interpretation* (Indiana University Press, Bloomington and Indianapolis, 1988), pp. 174ff.
2 The present memorial camp is the 1940–1 *Schutzhaftlager* (protective custody camp); thus the prisoners' living space is presented with reasonable accuracy. By 1940–1, however, the *Konzentrationslager* (concentration camp) was already significantly larger. Surrounded by a barbed wire fence, it included a few dozen wooden barracks north and west of the *Schutzhaftlager* which were used as workshops. Most of these barracks were demolished; some were pulled down during the war to prepare the site for the extension of the camp, others were removed after the war to clear the site. The few still standing are not included in the memorial camp.
3 The designation is that given by the Central Architect's Office in Auschwitz. Kl points at *Konzentrationslager*, that is Auschwitz I. The number 160 designates the building project number. Buildings in Auschwitz II (Birkenau) were given the letters KGL which derives from *Kriegsgefangenlager* Auschwitz, the official status of Auschwitz–Birkenau.
4 Originally, Crematory I was a powder magazine. In July 1940 the powder magazine was transformed into a crematory to burn the bodies of prisoners who had died from disease or who had been murdered by means other than suffocation in a gas chamber. By the end of 1941, Crematory I had three, two-muffled furnaces, with a 340-corpse per 24-hour capacity. The morgue attached to the crematory was transformed into a homicidal gas chamber in the late fall of 1941. A year later this gas chamber was returned to its original use as a morgue. Probably 10,000 people were killed here, or less than 1 percent of those gassed in the crematories in Birkenau. See Jean-Claude Pressac, *Auschwitz: technique and operation of the gas chambers*, tr. Peter Moss (Beate Klarsfeld Foundation, New York, 1979), pp. 129ff.
5 See Pressac, Auschwitz, pp. 123ff.
6 Iwona Irwin-Zarecka, "Poland, after the Holocaust," in *Remembering For the Future: working papers and addenda* (3 vols, Pergamon Press, Oxford, 1989), vol. 1, p. 147.

7 Debórah Dwork, *Children With A Star: Jewish youth in Nazi Europe* (Yale University Press, New Haven and London, 1991), p. 210.

8 As quoted in S. I. Minerbi, "Pope John Paul II and the Shoah," in *Remembering for the Future*, vol. 3, p. 2976.

9 Irwin-Zarecka, "Poland, after the Holocaust," p. 147.

10 Wladyslaw T. Bartoszewski, *The Convent at Auschwitz* (George Braziller, New York, 1991), p. 7.

11 Minerbi, "Pope John Paul II", p. 2977.

12 Ibid., p. 2984.

13 Ibid., p. 2983.

14 The reposing figures that crown Etruscan and medieval tombs are exceptions. These sculptures have a private character, however, while those that show the dead in a martial pose claim a place in the public realm.

15 Nathan Rapaport's "Monument to the Heroes of the Ghetto," located in what was once the heart of the Warsaw ghetto, does not point to defeat, but to the horizon of victory. The figures depicted on the monument are larger than life; they have become immortal. "We may all perish in this fight, but we will not surrender," reads the inscription on the monument. "We are fighting for your freedom and for your human and national pride – and ours." The Christian ideology of the cross is similar.

16 This applies, of course, only to visitors who do not accept the Christian belief that pronounces these dead to be truly alive because their graves are gathered around the Cross – a sign that marks the church in particular and the space of the living in general with the explicit message that "His sacrifice was not in vain." By suppressing the third dimension of the tombs, the church authorities suppressed the ideology that people live on in, for example, the civic memory of a community, stressing instead the ideology that declares the Cross as the only gate to eternal life.

17 Konnilyn G. Feig, *Hitler's Death Camps: the sanity of madness* (Holmes & Meier, New York and London, 1981), p. 295.

18 The competition jury was chaired by the English sculptor, Henry Moore. After an initial selection, seven teams were invited to submit designs in a second round. Of these revised proposals, three won awards yet none was judged "entirely adequate." The best was the project submitted by Oskar and Zofia Hansen, Jerzy Jarnuszkiewicz, Julian Palka, Lechoslaw Rosinski, Edmund Kupiecki, and Tadeusz Plasota. This team's approach was considered "exceptionally brilliant," although the objections of the former inmates were recognized to be serious, and the lack of a plastic element to provide an emotional focus was seen as problematic.

   The jury proposed that the three award-winning teams work together on a final project. After years of haggling, a group was formed that included members of all three. The Hansens did not participate. This collaborative group's design was completed in 1967. See Henry Moore's comments in *Auschwitz Monument* (Panstwowe Muzeum, Oswiecim, 1959) and *Katalog*

Wystawy Projektow Nadeslanych Na Miedzynarodowy Konkurs Budowy W Oswiecimiu (Panstwowe Muzeum, Oswiecim, 1959).

19 Wolfgang Borchert, *The Man Outside*, tr. David Porter (New Directions, New York, 1971), p. 61.

Chapter 21   Trauma, Memory, and Transference

1 Aharon Appelfeld, "The Awakening," in this collection.

2 Lawrence L. Langer, *Holocaust Testimony: the ruins of memory* (Yale University Press, New Haven, 1991).

3 Lawrence L. Langer, "Remembering Survival" in this collection.

4 Saul Friedlander, "The *Shoah* between Memory and History," *The Jerusalem Quarterly*, 53, 1990.

5 Yosef H. Yerushalmi, *Zakhor, Jewish History and Jewish Memory* (University of Washington Press, Seattle, 1982); Alan Mintz, *Hurban: responses to catastrophe in Hebrew literature* (Columbia University Press, New York, 1984); David G. Roskies, *Against the Apocalypse: responses to catastrophe in modern Jewish culture* (Harvard University Press, Cambridge, 1984).

6 Yosef H. Yerushalmi, *Zakhor*, p. 99.

7 Dominick LaCapra, "Representing the Holocaust: reflections on the historians' debate," in Saul Friedlander, ed., *Probing the Limits of Representation: National-Socialism and the "Final Solution"* (Harvard University Press, Cambridge, 1992).

8 Andreas Hillgruber, *Zweierlei Untergang: Die Zerschlagung des deutschen Reiches und das Ende des Europäischen Judentums* (Siedler, Berlin, 1986).

9 See, for instance, Alexander and Margarethe Mitscherlich, *The Inability to Mourn: principles of collective behavior* (Grove Press, New York, 1975); Eric L. Santer, *Stranded Objects: mourning, memory, and film in postwar Germany* (Cornell University Press, Ithaca, 1990).

10 Cf. Raul Hilberg, in *Bitburg in Moral and Political Perspective*, ed. Geoffrey Hartman (Indiana University Press, Bloomington, 1986).

11 See Omer Bartov, *Hitler's Army: soldiers, Nazis, and the war in the Third Reich* (Oxford University Press, New York, 1991), p. 185.

12 For an English translation of Martin Broszat's "Plea" and for the subsequent exchange of letters between Broszat and myself, see Peter Baldwin (ed.), *Reworking the Past: Hitler, Holocaust and the historians' debate* (Beacon Press, Boston, 1990).

13 Jean Améry has spoken of a growing "entropy" in the writing of this history as of all history. See his *Radical Humanism: selected essays* (Indiana University Press, Bloomington, 1984), p. 65.

14 Cf. for instance Rainer Zitelmann and Michael Prinz (eds) *National Sozialismus und Modernisierung* (Wissenschaftliche Buchgesellschaft, Darmstadt, 1991).

15 This is not always the case. But, sometimes the framework is no less problematic than the lack of it. See for instance Goetz Aly and Suzanne Heim, *Vordenker der Vernichtung: Auschwitz und die deutschen Pläne für eine neue europäische Ordnung* (Hoffmann u. Campe, Hamburg, 1991).

16 On this particular incident see the interview with Raul Hilberg in Dan Diner (ed.), *Zivilisationsbruch: Denken nach Auschwitz* (Fischer, Frankfurt am Main, 1988).

17 Sigmund Freud, "Beyond the pleasure principle," *Standard Edition* (Hogarth Press, London) vol. 18, p. 29.

18 Raul Hilberg, *The Destruction of the European Jews* (Holmes & Meier, Chicago, 1961).

19 Jean-François Lyotard, *The Differend: phrases in dispute* (University of Minnesota Press, Minneapolis, 1988), pp. 56–7.

20 The full text of this part of Benjamin's letter [the post scriptum] runs as follows: "P.S. Karl Kraus ist denn doch zu früh gestorben. Hören Sie: die Wiener Gasanstalt hat die Belieferung der Juden mit Gas eingestelt. Der Gasverbrauch der jüdischen Bevölkerung brachte für die Gasgesellschaft Verluste mit sich, da gerade die grössten Konsummenten ihre Rechnungen nicht beglichen. Die Juden benutzten das Gas vorzugsweise zum Zweck des Selbstmords." Walter Benjamin, *Briefe 2* (Suhrkamp, Frankfurt am Main, 1978), p. 820.

21 This quote is taken from the dust jacket of Simon Schama's *Dead Certainties (Unwarranted Speculations)* (Knopf, New York, 1991).

22 Raul Hilberg in Berel Lang (ed.), *Writing and the Holocaust* (Holmes & Meier, New York, 1988).

23 Hayden White, "The politics of historical interpretation" in *The Content of the Form: Narrative Discourse and Historical Representation* (Johns Hopkins University Press, Baltimore, 1987).

24 Maurice Blanchot, *The Writing of the Disaster* (University of Nebraska Press, Lincoln, Nebraska, 1986), p. 42.

Liberation

Index

suicide, 65, 100, 106
survivors, 7, 19, 20, 34–46 *passim*,
51–2, 70–80 *passim*, 181,
216–18, 251
in Bolivia, 161–74
in Israel, 153–60
moment of liberation, 26, 31,
56–7, 208–9
"privileged" status of, 126
recognition of loss, 70, 75
silence of, 9, 10, 24, 25, 45, 63,
65, 102–3, 142, 150–2, 197,
209, 210–11, 259, 266n5
see also testimony
Sutzkeveir, Abraham, 3
Syberberg, Hans Juergen, 11, 176

Talmud, 41
Tcherikower, Elias, 36, 40
testimony, 23–32 *passim*, 33–41
passim, 42–58 *passim*, 91,
102–3, 104–16 *passim*, 156–7,
158–9
archives, 25, 36–41, 42, 48
autobiography, 37, 38, 104–16,
124, 126–7, 144, 273n10,
283n17, 285n40
changing role of, 6
and Christianity, 81
and chronology, 72–3, 116
by deportees, 26–32
diaries, 35, 43, 44, 48–9, 59
by former Nazis, 93–4, 95, 98–9
in French, 4, 6, 28–32
function of, 32, 68–9, 90–103
passim
ghetto writing, 42–58 *passim*
and imagined audience, 51, 52
and literature, 8, 18, 33–41
passim, 53–4, 59–69 *passim*,
71, 72–3
Lodz Ghetto Chronicle, 41,
42–58, 60
as moral witness, 9
multiple perspectives of, 38, 93,
96

Oneg Shabbes, 31, 37–9, 40, 41,
42–58, 273n12
in Polish
reception and transmission of, 23,
43, 44, 51, 52, 68, 77, 116
as religious imperative, 33, 38
The Scrolls of Auschwitz, 41
as *sheymes*, 33, 36, 40
by survivors, 43–6, 48, 51, 56, 58,
60–9, 70–80 *passim*, 90–103,
127, 156, 238, 253, 258–9
video tape, 23, 70–6, 253
in Yiddish, 6, 30–2, 39
yizker-biher, 31
Tillich, Paul, 87–8, 104
torture, 62, 207
Tracy, David, 9
Transnistria, 122
trauma, 6, 18, 74, 91, 105, 135,
214, 244, 252, 256, 257, 260,
261, 262
Treblinka, 30, 38, 39, 40, 94, 95,
98, 225, 227, 270n4
memorial at, 216, 248

van Pelt, Robert, 4
Vbra, Rudolph, *I Cannot Forgive*, 23
Veil, Simone, 29
Vilna, 34, 36, 41, 44
voice
of commentator, 270n27
of victims, 6

Wagner, Richard, 13
Warsaw, 34, 37–41, 42–58 *passim*,
99, 159, 218–19, 224–7, 256
Weinreich, Max, 37
Weiss, Ernst, 111
Werfel, Franz, "Lacobowsky and the
Colonel", 113
Wiesel, Elie, 3, 10, 25, 90, 117
Wieviorka, Annette, 4, 6
Wolf, Christa, 183–4
World War I, 2, 17, 25, 26, 31, 33,
35, 87
Wyschogrod, Edith, 176